Corpora and Intercultural Studies

Volume 9

This book series publishes original monographs and edited volumes in the investigations of different types of corpora (including text, speech and video) with a particular focus on intercultural studies. The differences in language use expressed in comparable corpora can be analyzed from an intercultural perspective. The emphasis is on excellence and originality in scholarship as well as synergetic interdisciplinary approaches and multicultural perspectives. Books exploring the role of the intercultural studies in the research fields of translation, linguistics, and culture, with a corpus-based approach will be especially welcome. The series publishes books that deal with emerging issues as well as those that offer an in-depth examination of underlying issues.

The target audiences of this series include both scholars and professionals who are interested in issues related to intercultural communication across different cultures and social groups, which are reflected by the investigation in comparable corpora.

Corpora and Intercultural Studies book series is published in conjunction with Springer under the auspices of School of Foreign Languages (SFL), Shanghai Jiao Tong University (SJTU). The first series editor is the Dean of SFL at SJTU, and the book series editorial board consists of leading scholars in the research field of corpora and intercultural studies in the world.

Kanglong Liu · Andrew K. F. Cheung
Editors

Translation and Interpreting in the Age of COVID-19

Springer

Editors
Kanglong Liu
Department of Chinese and Bilingual Studies
The Hong Kong Polytechnic University
Hong Kong, China

Andrew K. F. Cheung
Department of Chinese and Bilingual Studies
The Hong Kong Polytechnic University
Hong Kong, China

ISSN 2510-4802 ISSN 2510-4810 (electronic)
Corpora and Intercultural Studies
ISBN 978-981-19-6679-8 ISBN 978-981-19-6680-4 (eBook)
https://doi.org/10.1007/978-981-19-6680-4

This Springer imprint is published by the registered company Springer Nature Singapore Pte Ltd.
The registered company address is: 152 Beach Road, #21-01/04 Gateway East, Singapore 189721, Singapore

Preface

We lectured in the classroom. We met with students in our offices. We attended academic conferences and interacted with colleagues and peers. We told jokes at the dinner table. This is what normal life was like before COVID-19.

Two years have passed. Now, we teach classes on the Zoom platform. We meet with students online through Zoom or other web conferencing applications. We attend conferences and workshops online, deliver our presentations, and then close Zoom. We stay in our own home or office most of the time.

It's completely unthinkable that we haven't been able to live a "normal life" for more than 2 years. This shows how much our lives and work have been affected by this unprecedented pandemic. In fact, in the context of globalization, COVID-19 may be a "pandemic" in the true sense of the word. In an increasingly interconnected world like ours today, no one can possibly stay immune from its effects. When the COVID-19 epidemic broke out in Wuhan City in China, there was a lot of hope that it would soon pass. When we were told that face-to-face instruction would be suspended and replaced with online teaching, most of us were completely unprepared. Besides, we also had no idea how effective online instruction would be, especially for interpreting courses, which are usually taught in classroom interpreting booths equipped with headphones, microphones, monitors, and tape recorders. As the COVID situation improved, we switched to hybrid instruction, which is a combination of face-to-face and online modes of instruction, and students can choose to participate in either one depending on their particular situation related to COVID. Later, when Omicron ravaged Hong Kong and caused a large number of infections, we were forced to switch back to online teaching. To a large extent, we were forced to cope with various uncertainties and unknowns about COVID-19 and its impacts. When we shared our story with colleagues and friends around the world, many of them resonated and expressed the same thoughts and feelings. Given the magnitude of the impact of this pandemic, we believe that COVID-19 is a topic of interest to people from all industries and disciplines. That's how we first conceived the book project in the summer of 2020.

Based on our own experience as translation and interpreting (T&I) teachers and researchers, we thought it would be meaningful to put together an edited volume describing how COVID-19 affects the daily work and lives of T&I practitioners, teachers, and researchers around the world, and to allow them to share their unique experiences. It is likely that the social and emotional disruption caused by COVID will not disappear anytime soon. As more variants of COVID emerge, there is no doubt that our world will continue to remain vulnerable. In this sense, this book will continue to be of relevance in the COVID and post-COVID era. We sincerely hope that it will contribute to the ongoing research efforts to address the impact of COVID-19 on T&I as an industrial practice and teaching and research field.

Finally, we would like to thank Prof. Kaibao Hu and Prof. Hongwei Ding, who have been very supportive of our book project. We are also grateful to our colleague, Dr. Dechao Li, for his encouragement and support when we discussed with him this project on T&I and COVID. Finally, we would also like to thank the many authors who contribute to this book despite their busy schedules which have been constantly impacted by COVID. This book would not have been possible without their dedicated and inspiring efforts.

Hong Kong, China

Kanglong Liu
Andrew K. F. Cheung

Contents

Editors and Contributors

About the Editors

Kanglong Liu is an Assistant Professor at The Hong Kong Polytechnic University. His research interests include corpus-based translation studies, language and translation pedagogy, and *Hongloumeng* translation research. He is currently the Associate Editor of Translation Quarterly, the official publication of the Hong Kong Translation Society. He has published widely in scholarly journals and authored the monograph *Corpus-Assisted Translation Teaching: Issues and Challenges* (Springer, 2020).

Andrew K. F. Cheung is an Associate Professor at The Hong Kong Polytechnic University. He holds a Ph.D. from the University of East Anglia. He is a member of the editorial boards of Babel and the Translation Quarterly. He is a member of the *Association internationale des interprètes de conférence* (AIIC). His research interests include quality perception of interpreting and corpus-based interpreting studies.

Contributors

Marta Buján WTO, Genève, Switzerland

Andrew K. F. Cheung The Hong Kong Polytechnic University, Hong Kong, China

Yu Kit Cheung University of Manchester, Manchester, UK

Camille Collard ESIT, Paris, France

Marie Diur United Nations Office at Geneva (UNOG), Genève, Switzerland

Damien Fan National Taiwan Normal University, Taipei, Taiwan

Deborah Giustini KU Leuven, Leuven, Belgium

Chonglong Gu The Hong Kong Polytechnic University, Hong Kong, China

Chen-En Ho Queen's University Belfast, Belfast, UK

Soňa Hodáková Department of Translation Studies, Constantine the Philosopher University, Nitra, Slovakia

Ho Ling Kwok The Hong Kong Polytechnic University, Hong Kong, China

Dechao Li The Hong Kong Polytechnic University, Hong Kong, China

Wenjing Li The Hong Kong Polytechnic University, Hong Kong, China

Kanglong Liu The Hong Kong Polytechnic University, Hong Kong, China

Yufeng Liu The Hong Kong Polytechnic University, Hong Kong, China

Petra Lea Láncos Faculty of Law and Political Sciences, Pázmány Péter Catholic University (PPKE), Budapest, Hungary

Emília Perez Department of Translation Studies, Constantine the Philosopher University, Nitra, Slovakia

Maura Radicioni Faculty of Translation and Interpreting, University of Geneva, Geneva, Switzerland

Lucía Ruiz Rosendo Faculty of Translation and Interpreting, University of Geneva, Geneva, Switzerland

David B. Sawyer The University of Maryland, College Park, Maryland, USA

Márta Seresi Department of Translation and Interpreting, Eötvös Loránd University (ELTE), Budapest, Hungary

Sai Cheong Siu School of Translation and Foreign Languages, The Hang Seng University of Hong Kong, Hong Kong, China

Nancy Tsai National Taiwan Normal University, Taipei, Taiwan

Nan Zhao Department of Translation, Interpreting and Intercultural Studies, Tong Hong Kong Baptist University, Hong Kong, China

Yuan Zou Queen's University Belfast, Belfast, UK

Chapter 1
Translation and Interpreting in the Age of COVID-19: Challenges and Opportunities

Kanglong Liu and Andrew K. F. Cheung

Abstract This introductory chapter provides a detailed overview of how COVID-19 has impacted on translation and interpreting (T&I) practice, teaching and research. While recognizing the challenges and threats imposed by COVID-19, this chapter also highlights the opportunities brought on by this unprecedented pandemic. Specifically, COVID-19 has served as a catalyst for accelerating the adoption of technology in both T&I practice and teaching. Following the overview of the key issues facing T&I in the context of COVID-19, we have given a brief summary of the contributions selected for this edited volume. It is hoped that by providing first hand accounts of T&I research and practice across different nations in the age of COVID-19, we are able to paint a more complete and clearer picture of the impact the pandemic is having on T&I.

Keywords Translation · Interpreting · COVID-19 · Pandemic · Challenges and opportunities · Translation teaching · Technology

1.1 Introduction

The novel coronavirus disease 2019 (COVID-19) which began as a health crisis has quickly turned into a social and economic crisis (Liu et al. 2020). COVID-19 has fundamentally changed the way people work, socialize, interact and notably communicate with other people (Sikali 2020). With the lockdowns and quarantine measures imposed to contain the spread of the virus, globalization faces perhaps the toughest test in decades (Gössling, Scott, and Hall 2020; Shrestha et al. 2020). The COVID-19 pandemic is a major public health emergency that has had a great impact on people's health, but it is also a political, social, economic, and humanitarian

K. Liu (✉) · A. K. F. Cheung
The Hong Kong Polytechnic University, Hong Kong, China
e-mail: kl.liu@polyu.edu.hk

A. K. F. Cheung
e-mail: andrew.cheung@polyu.edu.hk

K. Liu and A. K. F. Cheung (eds.), *Translation and Interpreting in the Age of COVID-19*, Corpora and Intercultural Studies 9,
https://doi.org/10.1007/978-981-19-6680-4_1

crisis that has brought fundamental change. Undoubtedly, this crisis is limiting many aspects of our lives, including how we form and maintain relationships, how we learn and work with one another, and the context in which we live and make choices. People have to find ways to adapt to the "new normal" where virtual interaction has replaced face-to-face interaction to become the chief mode of communication in both social and professional settings. While the changes are challenging, they have also brought new opportunities, compelling people to engage in technological innovation and embrace transformation.

COVID-19 is a global pandemic that poses a serious public health threat to the human world in this globalization age. In this sense, communication, particularly multilingual communication, plays an increasingly crucial role in addressing the various issues associated with the COVID-19 pandemic.

Since the outbreak of COVID-19 in late 2019, substantial health and medical research has been conducted to study the symptoms and treatment of COVID-19, whereas relatively little has been done to examine issues from the perspective of language and communication (Declercq and Federici 2020). As an important means of facilitating interpersonal and intercultural communication, the role of translation and interpreting (T&I) in coping with this global pandemic remains underexplored. It should be noted that when facing such a severe global-scale health crisis, social and economic inequalities between countries and communities have been greatly exacerbated by a lack of information, and outright misinformation and disinformation rampant on social media platforms. Communication, especially multilingual communication facilitated by T&I, is essential. Thus, to address the many challenges brought by the global pandemic, it is important to investigate and understand the role of T&I in this process, which cover issues such as assisting medical professionals to learn from their peers, providing the public, especially minorities and marginalized communities with the proper information to combat the virus, and even the use of translation technology for obtaining COVID-related information. It is no exaggeration to claim that T&I has been at the forefront in facing these new challenges brought by the global pandemic.

1.2 Impact of COVID-19 on Translation and Interpreting

Under the impact of COVID-19, T&I as an industrial practice and also a teaching and research field has also faced great changes and serious difficulties. Translation activities lessened as a result of the reduction of industrial and commercial activities and limitation of movement. Remote interpreting has replaced on-site interpreting as most meetings are conducted by remote communication and forbid in-person attendance. Translation and interpreting classes are held virtually through ZOOM video conferencing or other online tools. These are just some of the impacts faced by T&I. As more contagious COVID-19 variants emerge, the world remains vulnerable—particularly in a highly connected society such as we live in today, implying that it is highly unlikely for human society to return to pre-COVID days. To a large extent, the practical and emotional challenges that people are facing will continue to have a significant impact on T&I practitioners, researchers, teachers and students.

The COVID-19 epidemic has impacted most occupations. Many businesses have switched to online or remote operations in order to adapt to the changing business environment. The translation profession is no exception. According to a survey conducted by the French professional association SFT (*Société française des traducteurs*) from mid-June to mid-July 2020 (Chaillou and Van Der Kallen 2020), 57% agreed that the pandemic would have a negative influence on their work. Of this group of people, 48% believed they would take on an extra job, 23% were thinking of retraining, 15% were considering suspending their work for a temporary period of time and 7% were thinking of leaving the translation profession permanently. This shows that the translation profession has clearly been affected by the pandemic as business activities slowed with the impact of control measures to curb COVID-19.

As pandemic-related information is not evenly distributed across languages of the world (Lee and Wang 2022: 2), the role of translation has become even more crucial and complicated in this age of information explosion, where people may be exposed to both true and false information about the epidemic. The values and conflicts reflected in the different approaches and control measures adopted by different countries to deal with the virus inevitably manifest themselves in translation. The lack of COVID-related information provided to minority groups has also become an issue in a time when communities have become multicultural and multiethnic due to globalization (see the paper by Yu Kit Cheung of this volume for a detailed discussion). This situation may be greatly exacerbated by a lack of information on epidemic prevention in their own language for immigrants who continue to receive information from their home countries that advocate different measures to prevent and control the epidemic. Many Asian countries have imposed mask-wearing mandates since the beginning of COVID-19 while mask-wearing has remained a controversial issue in the west. As COVID has evolved, social distancing and mask-wearing guidelines for example may change in some jurisdictions. Confusion due to different coronavirus prevention practices and measures is expected to continue into the future while the virus remains active. An example of such confusion is that of Chinese immigrants or students who are still wearing white protective suits at many airports which sets them apart from others around them. Translation clearly has a larger role to play in such settings.

This pandemic has not only had an impact on professional translation practice and services, but the disruption is also felt in the translation classroom as well. The world was forced to switch to remote working and learning in response to the pandemic. Such a transition has caught many teachers and students unprepared, both emotionally and logistically. With increased use of an online teaching mode, interaction in the translation classroom has been largely reduced. When faced with a screen, the teacher has little control over student participation or responses. This is also the case with interpreting teaching. Interpreting classes have traditionally been interactive in nature, with different practice sessions simulating actual interpreting settings. Some interpreter-trainers and trainees have found it difficult to adjust to the sudden shift from in-person teaching to remote teaching. Additionally, some trainers might find it challenging to engage students during classes, while some students also face difficulties in focus.

Interpreting has been disproportionately affected by the pandemic, chiefly because of lockdowns and travel restrictions. The United Nations (UN) General Assembly recognizes multilingualism as a core value, which is manifested in its provision of simultaneous interpreting in six official languages at most of its open meetings, among others (Song and Cheung 2019; Ma and Cheung 2020; Wu et al. 2021). However, SI services were suspended because of technical constraints during COVID-19 induced lockdowns in New York, where the UN headquarters is located. Consequently, the UN Security Council conducted its daily meetings remotely and only in English for as long as a month or so before implementing remote interpreting (Cheung 2022). That the UN could conduct its daily meetings relying solely on English without the involvement of interpreters is a wakeup call for interpreters and interpreter-trainees. Remote interpreting, especially remote simultaneous interpreting (RSI), has revolutionized the way interpreters work. Remote conferences have democratized conference attendance as speakers and attendants are no longer limited by expensive travel costs. Furthermore, differences in geographical locations and time zones are no longer a concern for conference attendance. Similarly, interpreters could work for events taking place in different countries without having to travel. However, when working from home, the reliability of internet connection and unwanted noise could be among the top concerns. Besides, unless interpreters work from a hub, those working from home would no longer experience continuous interaction with colleagues throughout the working day. Gone are the days when interpreters could gesture to seek help or a turn taking.

An interpreter's role may no longer be limited to only serving the purpose of immediate communication. For remote interpreting and hybrid events with some remote speakers and some attending in person, the *modus operandi* may also be challenging. Speakers located in time zones far away from that of the conference may choose to provide pre-recorded presentations. After receiving these recordings, interpreters may use different tools to extract their audio tracks and automatically produce the transcripts to be translated into the target language. The interpreters would then read the translated scripts during the SI process, in a manner similar to dubbing. One of the motivating factors behind implementing this could be that some conference organizers choose to archive their renditions to be later accessed by attendants who could not attend the event live. The interpreters' output, therefore, would no longer be just transient audio signals, but records that could be scrutinized openly.

The pandemic, which has wreaked havoc on people in many ways, has also been a catalyst for technological innovation and adoption. Although the use of translation technology such as corpora and machine translation has been extensively discussed and applied in translation and interpreting teaching (Liu 2015, 2020; Liu et al. 2022), the use of other types of technology such as online platforms and computer-assisted technology was less touched upon in the pre-COVID era. Notwithstanding the various impacts the epidemic has brought, it has accelerated the digitization and adoption of technology in human society. The need to navigate change and continuity is the key to the future of translation and interpreting. English will continue to dominate the global linguistic landscape, while remote teaching is anticipated to persist even after COVID-19. However, our desires to understand and be understood remains unchanged. The relevance of translators and interpreters as well as T&I trainers and trainees will be determined by how they adapt to the post-COVID-19 new normal. The changes and turbulence brought on by the COVID-19 pandemic will no doubt continue to impact on translation and interpreting in the post-COVID era.

1.3 The Current Volume

Against such a background, it is necessary as well as urgent to re-examine the role of T&I in this unstable, uncertain and highly polarized era. This current volume aims to bring together the views and voices of how T&I has responded and adapted to the constraints imposed by the COVID-19 pandemic. The book presents the insights and observations of T&I researchers, practitioners, teachers and students, as well as the trends and issues shaping and shaped by the changing practice and new conceptualizations of T&I against the backdrop of COVID-19. In the studies brought together in this edited volume, T&I scholars from varied backgrounds have examined in their empirical studies a plethora of issues such as translation of vaccine metaphors, use of machine translation to evaluate COVID-related health information, remote simultaneous interpreting and humanitarian interpreting during the COVID period and also the adoption of new technology and tools to aid T&I teaching in the wake of the outbreak of the pandemic. These contributions not only show researchers' understanding of the importance of T&I to cope with COVID, but also their concern and awareness regarding how teaching methods and learning environment have changed as a result of the pandemic. The volume is divided into three sections, each covering a research area, namely, (1) Reconceptualising Translation in the Age of COVID-19; (2) Reconceptualising Interpreting in the Age of COVID-19; and (3) Translation and Interpreting Teaching in the Age of COVID-19. The studies included in this volume, which covers current key issues emerging from COVID-19, will make a valuable contribution to T&I studies, but also the expanding scholarly discourse of COVID-19 and the impact it brings to the humanities.

The first section is devoted to "Reconceptualising Translation in the Age of COVID-19". As a major form of communication enabling people from different linguistic and socio-cultural backgrounds to effectively share knowledge and information, translation clearly plays a crucial role to mitigate the spread of the pandemic. This involves the transfer of correct information, promote understanding between different countries and communities, and also help underprivileged groups and minorities find the right information to make decisions regards COVID. In this volume, the section devoted to the investigation of the connection between translation and COVID-19 opens with a paper by **Yufeng Liu** and **Dechao Li.** The authors investigate the metaphor transfer in Chinese/English news headlines to show the different stance mediation adopted by a Chinese and a British news outlet in re(framing) COVID-19 discourse. Drawing on an analytical model that integrates framing, corpus linguistics and appraisal theories, the authors reveal that the two news outlets differ significantly in the use of conceptual metaphors, framing strategies and also attitudinal graduation. While *The Global Times Editorial* takes a pro-China and anti-US stance, *The Economist Global Business Review* (EGBR) adopts an anti-China and pro-US perspective. The study has highlighted the different narratives regards China and the United States that emerged from the different preventive and control measures implemented by respective countries to cope with COVID. It can be seen from their study that some tensions and conflicts between the two countries in relation to COVID control practices are reflected in the translation of the COVID-related metaphors of the respective media organizations. **Chonglong Gu**'s paper examines how translation and multilingual communication have been mobilized to facilitate communication in Hong Kong during the COVID-19 public health crisis. To this end, the author analyses in depth both the top-down (official and government-led) and bottom-up (e.g. by individuals and small businesses) translation materials collected from various platforms and formats. The author has highlighted the crucial role of translation and multilingual text production in disseminating information and promoting awareness in ethnically and culturally diverse multilingual communities. By examining Chinese translations of the UK Government's guidance and regulations for the public, **Yu Kit Cheung** problematises the notion of Chinese translation in the context of the United Kingdom. The author found that these texts deviated from the defining features of "Chinese" in one way or another, thereby affecting the efficiency of communication. In general, the majority of Chinese translations only exist in simplified Chinese script subsumed under the generic term, whereas traditional Chinese versions were not available until early 2022. Considering that a Cantonese-speaking population makes up a measurable portion of the UK population, the lack of translation into traditional Chinese necessarily affects access to reliable anti-epidemic information for this cohort. The study has underscored the importance of quality translation in a proper language script to aid minorities in a multicultural country in the midst of an unprecedented pandemic. The section ends with a paper by **Sai Cheong Siu** in which he investigates the performance of COVID-19 MT Evaluator, a platform for the evaluation of machine translation of public health information related to the pandemic. COVID-19 is a global-scale pandemic, thus the information related to COVID is naturally presented in different languages. To keep the public informed of the latest pandemic situation and enable people of different linguistic communities to work together to combat the pandemic requires timely and accurate translation. The availability of machine translation (MT) can clearly play a role in this process. It is with this in mind that the author systematically compared two English/Chinese MT products provided by Google Translate to illustrate the use of the evaluation platform. His study has shown that the evaluation platform can help medical translators, healthcare professionals, researchers and developers for quick assessment of MT performance given its performance. This study has demonstrated that MT can play a helpful role in the context of the COVID-19 crisis and public health emergencies.

The second section titled "Reconceptualising Interpreting in the Age of COVID-19" contains six papers that examine the role and status of interpreting in the context of the pandemic. The section begins with **Andrew K. F. Cheung**'s paper in which he examines the use of remote simultaneous interpreting (RSI) from a hub or home. By conducting an empirical experiment, he compared the RSI quality of English into Mandarin Chinese by interpreters working from a hub compared to that of interpreters working from home. He found that the performance of the hub group had better performance in interpreting numbers by using more approximation strategy than the home group. The results also show that the hub group experienced a lower perceived cognitive load than the home group, suggesting that the interpreting setting is of vital importance for interpreters' performance. In a similar vein, **Marta Buján** and **Camille Collard** discuss how conference interpreters perceive remote simultaneous interpreting in the context of COVID-19. To this end, they conducted a survey between March and April 2021, one year into the pandemic, gathering data from 849 respondents from 19 countries. It was found that conference interpreters have adapted to the new working environment by developing new working habits, such as shorter shifts and flexible ways to handle handover. Their study reveal that the interpreters are largely consistent in their assessment and perception of the various challenges and constraints of RSI. Besides, interpreters working in the private market are generally more optimistic about the benefits of RSI than those working in professional organizations who seem to have a more conservative view. Notwithstanding the challenges and opportunities brought by RSI, many interpreters believe that RSI as a necessary evil it's here to stay. Their study has demonstrated that interpreting as a profession, like other business areas, has embraced technological innovation to sustain against the onslaught of the pandemic. The paper by **Marie Diur** and **Lucía Ruiz Rosendo** addresses how COVID-19 has greatly changed the working and testing procedures of conference interpreting at the United Nations. Based on archival analysis and their own experience, they have shown that the outbreak of the COVID-19 pandemic has accelerated the adoption of remote interpreting. In line with this new arrangement, the UN has also adopted online testing procedures to recruit new interpreters. By analyzing and elaborating on the changes and challenges taking place in conference interpreting at the UN, the authors have provided a contextual and nuanced description of the challenges facing interpreters and interpreter trainers working in international organizations in the context of COVID-19. In the fourth paper in this section, **Lucía Ruiz Rosendo** and **Maura Radicioni** focus on the issue of humanitarian interpreting, which is a new and emerging discipline within Translation and Interpreting Studies. The authors provide some background information on this area and address some important issues and challenges that interpreters working in humanitarian organizations face in this COVID health crisis. Still within the field of remote interpreting, **Márta Seresi** and **Petra Láncos** conducted semi-structured interviews with trained conference interpreters to investigate how cooperation and communication between simultaneous interpreters change when interpreters work using RSI platforms. Their results show that most interpreters have decided not to cooperate because of difficulties such as unsmooth handover or ineffectiveness to help the active partner. Despite the difficulties, they come up with alternative strategies to handle many of the problems. Finally, **Deborah Giustini** explores the role of technology in remote interpreting in the context of COVID-19 using a sociological perspective rooted in practice theory. Based on data collected from language industry sources and surveys, the author examines how technology has reshaped and problematized interpreting. Her study sheds light on some of the emerging issues in the field and makes us rethink communication that is mediated as well as constrained by technology.

The third section titled "Translation and Interpreting Teaching in the Age of COVID-19" is concerned with T&I teaching which has been significantly impacted by COVID-19. **Kanglong Liu, Ho Ling Kwok** and **Wenjing Li**'s paper focuses on how students perceive the hybrid teaching mode in the translation classroom, which allows face-to-face and online teaching modes that students can choose between to attend in view of their particular situation related to COVID. By analyzing data collected from surveys and semi-structured interviews, they have shown that most students see more benefit in the implementation of the hybrid teaching mode than weaknesses for teaching translation courses, despite some technological challenges and limitations. **Nancy Tsai** and **Damien Fan** present a study that address the advantages of online T&I teaching which they sum up as the 4Cs: immediacy, privacy, intimacy, and democracy. The authors argue online classrooms provide Chinese T&I teachers and students a chance to break free from cultural confinements imposed by Confucian values. They introduce the concept of "social presence" into T&I teaching, offering an alternative perspective to understand benefits brought by online teaching that transcends the "face-to-face" versus "online" dichotomy. **Soňa Hodáková** and **Emília Perez**'s contribution provides an empirical study that examines how T&I teachers and students at Slovak universities perceive remote training mode for translators and interpreters in the early and later stages of the COVID-19 pandemic. By conducting surveys and semi-structured interviews, they reveal that students' and teachers' perspectives regards remote teaching and training have changed as COVID evolves. Their study sheds light on the strengths and limitations of remote T&I teaching from a diachronic perspective. Similarly, **David B. Sawyer** conducted focus groups with students and instructors at the program of Graduate Studies in Interpreting and Translation (GSIT) in the University of Maryland's Department of Communication to examine their attitudes towards in-person and remote teaching. His study has found that both students and instructors have become more positive about online teaching through their own experience. Interestingly, both groups recommend maintaining an online component to increase flexibility and convenience after the pandemic despite the challenges. In light of the findings, the author also suggests that T&I programs can consider integrating online instruction into the curriculum in a principled way. Also within the field of T&I teaching, **Chen-En Ho** and **Yuan Zou** explores how some challenges in remote interpreter teaching can be mitigated using the proximity-based platform "Gather". They introduced two mock events using online CI and SI teaching followed by a survey to gauge students' perceptions and experience with the platform. Their study found that most participants are positive about the platform which comes with a proximity-sensitive feature that can largely overcome the limitations of mainstream video-conferencing platforms such as Zoom and MS Teams. In the closing chapter of this section, **Nan Zhao** examines how computer-assisted interpreting (CAI) technologies including remote interpreting (RI), computer-assisted interpreting training (CAIT), pre-task tools, and in-task tools, can be harnessed to aid interpreting in the age of COVID-19. By providing a detailed review of the state-of-the-art and development of CAI technologies, the author also addresses the use of these CAI technologies in real-life scenarios.

1.4 Concluding Remarks

This edited volume, which includes contributions from T&I researchers and scholars around the world, presents an assortment of original studies of social and academic relevance. It focuses on how T&I as a field of study has been affected by and adapted to the disruptions and challenges caused by the COVID-19 pandemic. Despite the difficulties, T&I researchers, teachers and students have come up with innovative solutions to cope with the changes imposed by COVID-19. To a certain extent, COVID-19 has served as an unexpected catalyst for T&I institutions, practitioners and researchers to accelerate the adoption of new technologies in their operation and working practices. This edited volume has provided a balanced perspective on the challenges as well as opportunities brought about by COVID-19. By providing first hand accounts of T&I research and practice across different nations in the age of COVID-19, we are able to paint a more complete and clearer picture of the impact the pandemic is having on T&I.

We hope that this edited volume, with contributions from scholars and teachers working in academic institutions and practitioners working at the coalface, will contribute towards a better understanding of the impact and implications of COVID-19 on translation and interpreting studies. We also hope that the articles will stimulate important conversations among T&I scholars and teachers and those who are working in related fields including linguistics, communication and education.

References

Chaillou, J., and A. Van Der Kallen. 2020. COVID-19: How has it affected the world of translation? https://blogs.ec.europa.eu/emt/covid-19-how-has-it-affectedthe-world-of-translation/.

Cheung, A.K.F. 2022. Listeners' perception of the quality of simultaneous interpreting and perceived dependence on simultaneous interpreting. *Interpreting* 24 (1): 38–58. https://doi.org/10.1075/intp.00070.che.

Declercq, C., and F.M. Federici. 2020. *Intercultural crisis communication: Translation, interpreting and languages in local crises*. London/New York: Bloomsbury Publishing.

Gössling, S., D. Scott, and C.M. Hall. 2020. Pandemics, tourism and global change: A rapid assessment of COVID-19. *Journal of Sustainable Tourism* 29 (1): 1–20. https://doi.org/10.1080/09669582.2020.1758708.

Lee, T.K., and D. Wang. 2022. Introduction: Translation in the time of #COVID-19. In *Translation and social media communication in the age of the pandemic*, ed. T.K. Lee and D. Wang, 1–11. New York: Routledge.

Liu, K. 2015. Investigating corpus-assisted translation teaching: A pilot study. In *Conducting research in translation technologies*, ed. P. Sánchez-Gijón, O. Torres-Hostench, and B. Mesa-Lao, 141–162. Oxford: Peter Lang Verlag.

Liu, K. 2020. *Corpus-assisted translation teaching: Issues and challenges*. Springer Singapore, Singapore.

Liu, K., H.L. Kwok, J. Liu, and A.K.F. Cheung. 2022. Sustainability and influence of machine translation: Perceptions and attitudes of translation instructors and learners in Hong Kong. *Sustainability* 14 (11): 6399. https://doi.org/10.3390/su14116399.

Liu, Y., L.-M. Yan, L. Wan, T.-X. Xiang, A. Le, J.-M. Liu, M. Peiris, L.L.M. Poon, and W. Zhang. 2020. Viral dynamics in mild and severe cases of COVID-19. *The Lancet Infectious Diseases* 20 (6): 656–657. https://doi.org/10.1016/S1473-3099(20)30232-2.

Ma, X., and A.K.F. Cheung. 2020. Language interference in English-Chinese simultaneous interpreting with and without text. *Babel* 66 (3): 434–456. https://doi.org/10.1075/babel.00168.che.

Shrestha, N., M.Y. Shad, O. Ulvi, M.H. Khan, A. Karamehic-Muratovic, U.-S.D.T. Nguyen, M. Baghbanzadeh, et al. 2020. The impact of COVID-19 on globalization. *One Health* 11: 100180. https://doi.org/10.1016/j.onehlt.2020.100180.

Sikali, K. 2020. The dangers of social distancing: How COVID-19 can reshape our social experience. *Journal of Community Psychology* 48 (8): 2435–2438. https://doi.org/10.1002/jcop.22430.

Song, S., and A.K.F. Cheung. 2019. Disfluency in relay and non-relay simultaneous interpreting: An initial exploration. *Forum* 17 (1): 1–19. https://doi.org/10.1075/forum.18016.che.

Wu, B., A.K.F. Cheung, and J. Xing. 2021. Learning Chinese political formulaic phraseology from a self-built bilingual United Nations Security Council corpus: A pilot study. *Babel* 67 (4): 500–521. https://doi.org/10.1075/babel.00233.wu.

Kanglong Liu is Assistant Professor of Department of Chinese and Bilingual Studies of The Hong Kong Polytechnic University. His research interests include corpus-based translation studies, language and translation pedagogy, *Hongloumeng* translation research. He is currently Associate Editor of Translation Quarterly, the official publication of the Hong Kong Translation Society. He has published widely in scholarly journals and authored the monograph "*Corpus-Assisted Translation Teaching: Issues and Challenges*" (Springer, 2020).

Andrew K. F. Cheung is Associate Professor of Department of Chinese and Bilingual Studies of The Hong Kong Polytechnic University. He holds a Ph.D. from the University of East Anglia. He is Member of the editorial boards of Babel and the Translation Quarterly. He is Member of the *Association internationale des interprètes de conférence* (AIIC). His research interests include quality perception of interpreting and corpus-based interpreting studies.

Part I
Reconceptualising Translation in the Age of COVID-19

Chapter 2
Metaphor Translation as Reframing: Chinese *Versus* Western Stance Mediation in COVID-19 News Reports

Yufeng Liu and Dechao Li

Abstract This study investigates the stance mediation of a Chinese and a British newspaper in (re)framing the COVID-19 pandemic in 2020 with a focus on metaphor transfer in news headlines. The database includes 97 pairs of Chinese/English news headlines from *The Global Times Editorial* (GTE) and 77 pairs from *The Economist Global Business Review* (EGBR). Drawing on an analytical model that combines framing, corpus and Appraisal Theory, the study found that the conceptual metaphors, framing strategies and attitudinal graduation in GTE and EGBR differ significantly. Whereas GTE generally takes a pro-China and anti-US/West stance, EGBR adopts an anti-China and pro-West perspective. The study highlights stance mediation in non-political reports within news agencies that resort to self-translation and metaphor as a frame in stance mediation, a finding that may foster interdisciplinary collaborations between framing studies and journalistic and metaphor translation studies.

Keywords News translation · Metaphor translation · (re)framing · Framing strategies · Stance mediation · Coronavirus

2.1 Introduction

Recent decades have witnessed an increasing growth of literature in news translation research from both home (e.g., Liu 2017; Pan and Liao 2020; Qin and Zhang 2018; Wu and Zhang 2015; Zhang 2013) and abroad (e.g., McLaughlin 2015; Spiessens and Van Poucke 2016; Valdeón 2015a, b, 2016, 2020). In this growing body of research, news translation has been scrutinized through such theoretical lens as power relations, politics, imagology, and ideology (Bielsa and Bassnett 2008; Valdeón 2016), among which the framing model borrowed from Baker (2006, 2007) and Appraisal Theory

Y. Liu (✉) · D. Li
The Hong Kong Polytechnic University, Hong Kong, China
e-mail: yufengkiki.liu@connect.polyu.hk

D. Li
e-mail: dechao.li@polyu.edu.hk

K. Liu and A. K. F. Cheung (eds.), *Translation and Interpreting in the Age of COVID-19*, Corpora and Intercultural Studies 9,
https://doi.org/10.1007/978-981-19-6680-4_2

(AT) established by Martin and White (2005) are the two most frequently applied frameworks of analysis.

In contradistinction to the multiple theoretical vantage points from which news translation has been conducted, most existing metaphor translation research was conducted within Lakoff and Johnson's (2008) framework of Conceptual Metaphor Theory (CMT) (Schäffner and Shuttleworth 2013; Sun 2017). In CMT, metaphors can be understood with the formula *A IS B*, where the target domain (*A*) is compared to a source domain (*B*). Hence, metaphor involves conceptual mapping (Kövecses 2020; Lakoff and Johnson 2008; Mannoni 2021), ideology (Boulanger 2016; O'Halloran 2010) and politics (Bazzi 2014). To date, there has been only a small amount of research that coalesces metaphor and journalistic translation (Bazzi 2014; Van Poucke and Belikova 2016), focusing on metaphor types (e.g., cultural *versus* ideological metaphors, Bazzi 2014), corresponding transfer methods (e.g., literal *versus* free translation, Van Poucke and Belikova 2016), etc. Given that metaphor is a frequently-used device for expressing attitudes, it is argued here that by investigating the translation of metaphors, the mediation of stance including attitudes can also be analysed. Metaphor translation in journalistic discourse has been analysed in our related study (see Liu and Li 2022a), albeit with a slightly different focus on the conflict between Chinese and American newspapers for the use of metaphors about the COVID-19 pandemic. The current study can provide further evidence of the reframing power of metaphor translation in news discourse by including new materials and drawing on Appraisal Theory in the analysis.

With its varied definitions, stance is "by no means a monolithic concept" (Englebretson 2007: 1). It usually includes basic components such as value judgments, assessments and attitudes. Englebretson (2007) advocated an inclusive definition of stance by developing a model "which recognizes the heterogeneous and multifaceted nature of stancetaking" (2). According to Zhang (2013), mediation is correlated with "manipulation" and "rewriting". Thus, she defined the concept as "the ways the translator intervenes, rewrites or manipulates in the [news] transediting process, with an effort to accommodate in the target text stances dissenting from those in the original text" (398). Zhang's definition is adopted in the current study since the study also uses news discourse where news transediting is common. The study also follows Entman (1991) who argued that metaphor is an important frame (7), and attempts to provide more evidence for the framing power of metaphor by investigating how news agencies in China and the West use metaphor transfer in news headlines to mediate their stance when reporting the COVID-19 pandemic.

In what follows, this study first introduces the general and political background of the COVID-19 pandemic before highlighting the significance of making this global challenge the object of analysis. The theoretical framework, analytical model, and data compilation are then elaborated in detail, followed by a discussion of the analysis results and their scholarly significance.

2.2 News Reports of COVID-19 in 2020

Coronavirus disease 2019 (COVID-19) is a contagious disease caused by a newly discovered coronavirus that has evolved into an ongoing pandemic with a wide-ranging impact. Indeed, the COVID-19 pandemic is an issue associated with politics and power relations, as different news media may take a different stance in their narratives (Dionne and Turkmen 2020). For instance, this global pandemic has been called the "China virus," "Wuhan virus," or "Kung flu" in numerous American mass media (Budhwani and Sun 2020). To counter Western media's misinterpretations of China in the pandemic, *Global Times Editorial* (GTE) began to release COVID-19-related English news reports in March 2020. *Global Times* is a daily tabloid newspaper owned by *People's Daily*, which is an official newspaper of the Chinese Communist Party. It is regarded as China's foreign propaganda machine (Brady 2015) and even a "foreign mission" (Ruwitch and Kelemen 2020). It is also claimed that *Global Times* spreads conspiracy theories and misinformation during the COVID-19 pandemic (Molter and DiResta 2020).

The Economist, on the other hand, is an international newspaper covering political, economic, technological, cultural, and social topics, which has been censored and blocked in China since 2016 (Horwitz 2016). With a claim to equip the Chinese reader with an international perspective, *The Economist* released its English-Chinese bilingual digital version, *The Economist Global Business Review* (EGBR). In 2020, EGBR had a series of special reports on the COVID-19 pandemic, with the hashtag "*新冠报道*" (literally "COVID-19 Report") in the Chinese version.

Indeed, the pandemic has produced rich metaphorical narratives, in which non-WAR metaphors on COVID-19 are especially discussed in the #reframecovid initiative (Olza, Pérez-Sobrino, and Koller 2020). Hence, it is vital to analyse how GTE and EGBR (re)frame the pandemic with metaphors, which may unveil their attitudes towards the pandemic and parties involved in it.

2.3 Analytical Framework

2.3.1 The Framing Model and Appraisal Theory in News Translation Research

Baker (2007) has introduced the framing model into Translation Studies from narrative theory, sociology and the study of social movements. A summary of this model can be found in Liu (2017), Pan and Liao (2020), Qin and Zhang (2018) and Valdeón (2008). In Baker's (2007, 160) view, the manipulation of titles is "an important site of framing", which is also the focus of the current study. According to Baker (2006), there are four types of framing strategies, namely, temporal and spatial framing, selective appropriation of textual material, labelling and repositioning participants.

Temporal and spatial framing and repositioning participants are non-textual strategies, involving the temporal and spatial context and the paratextual commentaries. Selective appropriation and labelling are more relevant to the present study because they highlight the shifts of narrative elements at the textual level. Selective appropriation is to "suppress, accentuate or elaborate particular aspects of a narrative encoded in the source text or utterance, or aspects of the larger narrative(s) in which it is embedded" by omitting or adding textual materials (114). Labelling refers to "any discursive process that involves using a lexical item, term or phrase to identify a person, place, group, event or any other key element in a narrative" (122). The relation between metaphor and framing has also been investigated in a multimodal context (see Liu and Li 2022b) where framing is understood as selection and salience. The current study provides more insights in news discourse.

Martin and White's (2005) Appraisal Theory (AT) analyses positive or negative textual assessments and the intensity or directness of attitudinal utterances. Pan and Liao (2020), White (2015) and Zhang (2013) have reviewed AT in news translation research. There are three sub-systems in AT, namely attitude, graduation, and engagement. Among them, attitude and graduation are more relevant to the present study. Attitude refers to positive and negative assessments, whereas graduation refers to the speaker/writer/translator's "personal investment in the propositions being advanced in the text" (White 2015: 4). Graduation can be analysed at two levels, i.e., *force* (to strengthen or mitigate the propositions) and *focus* (to blur or sharpen the boundaries of semantic categories).

2.3.2 The Corpus Model in Metaphor Translation Research

Compared with news translation research, metaphor studies applied less diverse models as most of these studies only aim at drawing up a relatively exhaustive list of metaphors in large corpora and exploring replicable procedures for identifying metaphors, during which processes corpora are often utilized to locate particular semantic prosody features or to search for concordance (Charteris-Black 2004; Deignan 1999, 2005; Mannoni 2021; Shuttleworth 2017; Stefanowitsch and Gries 2007). For instance, to identify the metaphoricity of the linguistic expressions, Pragglejaz Group's (2007) MIP (Metaphor Identification Procedure) and Steen et al.'s (2010) MIPVU (Metaphor Identification Procedure Vrije Universiteit) use corpus-based dictionaries, such as Macmillian Dictionary (www.macmillandictionary.com). To verify the source domain of each metaphorical expression, Ahrens and Jiang (2020) developed the corpus-based Source Domain Verification Procedure (SDVP) that uses sources such as Suggested Upper Merged Ontology (SUMO, www.ontologyportal.org), WordNet (wordnetweb.princeton.edu/perl/webwn) and Sketch Engine (www.sketchengine.eu).

2.3.3 An Analytical Model for the Current Research

The current study combines the framing model in news translation research, the AT model and the corpus model in metaphor translation research to analyse how metaphor is translated in news discourse and how stance is mediated based on such metaphor translation.

To ensure the replicability of the study, MIPVU (Steen et al. 2010) is adopted to identify metaphors before using Ahrens and Jiang's (2020) SDVP to identify their corresponding source domains. Example (1) below is a detailed elaboration of how to identify a conceptual metaphor in a source text (ST) and a target text (TT).

(1).[1]

ST: 美国 和 中国, 究竟 谁 在 胁迫[2] 世界
měiguó hé zhōngguó, jiūjìng shuí zài xiépò shìjiè
US and China, exactly who be coerce world

TT: Who is **coercing** the world, China or US? (GTE, June 10, 2020)

The first step is to scrutinize both ST and TT on a word-by-word basis to establish a general understanding of the meaning. In this case, the Chinese writer is questioning the US for coercing the world.

The second step is to determine the lexical units. ICTCLAS-NLPIR system (Zhang 2014) is used here to segment Chinese lexical units, which are later manually checked for their accuracy. For the English texts, lexical units are the words that have a separate tag in the British National Corpus.

The third step is to establish the meaning of each lexical unit in context. For each lexical unit, we need to determine whether it has a more basic meaning than the one in the given context. In this case, the lexical units "*美国*" (US), "*和*" (and), "*中国*" (China), "*究竟*" (exactly), "*谁*" (who), "*在*" (is), "*胁迫*" (coerce) and "*世界*" (world) in ST and "who," "be," "coerce," "the" and "world" in TT have been analysed by referring to the *Handian* online Chinese Dictionary (https://www.zdic.net/) and Macmillan Dictionary (https://www.macmillandictionary.com/).

The fourth is to decide whether there is distinct contrast between the contextual meaning and the basic meaning but the two meanings are related. If so, mark the lexical unit as metaphorical. If the contextual meaning and the basic meaning are the same, then we check whether the lexical unit is human-oriented, but used in a non-human context. If so, we also mark it as metaphorical since it is a possible personification. In this case, the contextual meaning and the basic meaning of "*胁迫*" in the ST and "coerce" in the TT are the same: "to make someone do something by using force or threats". However, both "胁迫" and "coerce" are human-oriented words but are used to describe the countries in the example. Thus, both words are metaphorical.

---

[1] Examples listed in the current paper are glossed in accordance with the Leipzig Glossing Rules.

[2] Metaphorical lexical units in the examples are bolded throughout the paper.

After all metaphorical lexical units have been marked, the next step is to identify the source domains with SDVP (Ahrens and Jiang 2020), a process which Suggested Upper Merged Ontology (SUMO, https://www.ontologyportal.org/), WordNet http://wordnetweb.princeton.edu/perl/webwn), *Handian* Dictionary (https://www.zdic.net/), and the Word Sketch function in Sketch Engine (https://www.sketchengine.eu/) are used. A final decision is made after going through all these four language resources. In this case, *Handian* Dictionary clarifies the origin of "*胁迫*" as "to compel a political power to step down with armed forces". "*胁迫*" is described in Sketch Engine (via Chinese Web 2017 corpus) as an action usually conducted by an illegal political body. Thus, the source domain of "TERRORIST" can be summarized. The corresponding target domain can be determined based on the context: "THE US". We can also work out a formula for the conceptual metaphor of this example: "THE US IS TERRORIST".

The proposed metaphor translation strategies vary among scholars (e.g., Newmark 1988; Pedersen 2017; Sjørup 2013; Shuttleworth 2017; Toury 2012; van den Broeck 1981). Toury's (2012) six-fold classification of metaphor transfer methods is more comprehensive than others, as it exhausts the following possibilities in metaphor translation, including retaining (M-M), substituting (M1-M2), paraphrasing (M-P), omitting (M-O), creating (O-M) and from non-metaphor to metaphor (P-M). Since the strategies of paraphrasing and translating non-metaphorical language to metaphorical language are seldom used in news headline translations, only four categorizations, i.e., M-M, M1-M2, M-O, O-M, are taken into consideration in this study. Metaphor is a special labelling in most cases as metaphorical expressions conceptualize abstract ideologies with concrete images. Moreover, selective appropriation corresponds to M-O, O-M, and M1-M2 strategies, depending on the situation. Thus, in the present study, the fourfold metaphor transfer strategies are more suitable than the twofold framing strategies.

Moreover, attitudinal transfer via metaphor is labelled in accordance with the AT model, which classifies attitude as positive, negative, or neutral. The propositions can be strengthened, weakened, or kept unchanged. See Fig. 2.1 for a flowchart of the analytical model.

2.4 Data Compilation

The current study compares the stance mediation of a Chinese and a British newspaper on COVID-19-related issues based on an in-depth analysis of metaphor transfer in news headlines between GTE and EGBR. All bilingual news reports on the pandemic on GTE and EGBR in 2020 are collected for analysis. Altogether 325 news reports on the topic were found on GTE's official English website (https://www.globaltimes.cn/opinion/editorial/) in 2020. Among them, only 133 contain the keywords "COVID-19", "COVID", "pandemic," "epidemic", or "pneumonia" in either their titles or

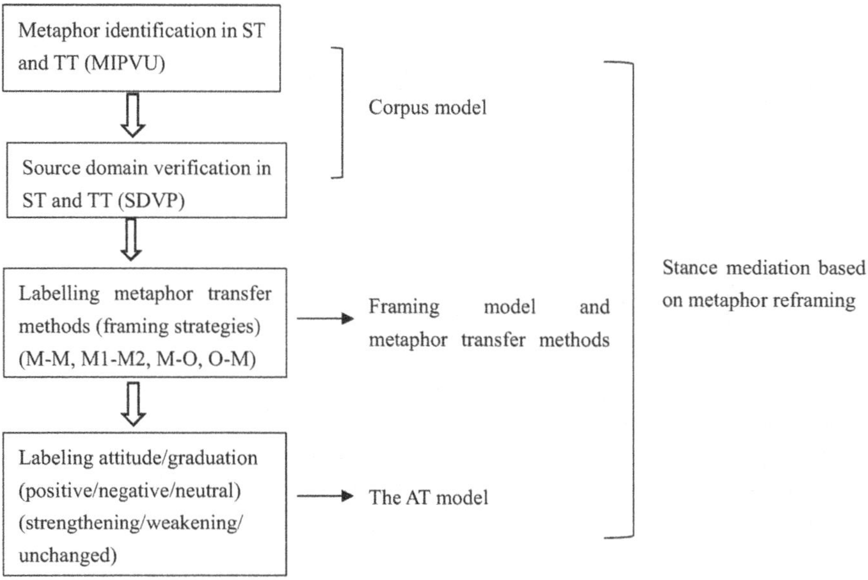

Fig. 2.1 Flowchart of the analytical model

content. Only 97 of them have corresponding Chinese versions on GTE's official Chinese website (https://opinion.huanqiu.com/editorial/). On EGBR's official mobile app, there are in total 437 Chinese-English bilingual news reports in 2020. Among them, only 77 have the keywords "COVID-19", "COVID", "pandemic", "epidemic", or "pneumonia" in either the titles or the content. GTE started to report the pandemic in both Chinese and English in March, whereas EGBR began to report COVID-19 in February. To balance the datasets, two EGBR reports in February are eliminated. Table 2.1 describes the size of the dataset.

The number of bilingual reports is relatively comparable between GTE and EGBR, but the number of tokens in headlines differs significantly. This is because GTE releases opinion articles written in more colloquial language, whereas EGBR is well-known for its concise style. Moreover, one Chinese word actually accounts for two tokens, making the Chinese texts longer than the English texts in tokens. The incomparability of tokens will not influence the current analysis as the focus is on metaphor transfer. More importantly, the datasets are comparable in the reported topic (i.e., the COVID-19 pandemic), ideological affinity (Valdeón and Calafat 2020)

Table 2.1 Research data from GTE and EGBR's bilingual reports in 2020

	The number of bilingual reports	Total word count of English headlines	Total word count of Chinese headlines
GTE	97	775	1,622
EGBR	75	242	381

to the government, and metaphorical richness. By metaphorical richness, we mean the significant number of metaphors used in the two newspapers' news headlines and the manipulation of the metaphors in translation, such as creating new metaphors in the TT.

2.5 Results

2.5.1 *Conceptual Metaphors in GTE and EGBR*

Based on the analytical model sketched above, two linguists were trained to identify all metaphors in GTE and EGBR datasets based on MIPVU and to utilize SDVP to verify their source domains. One linguist was responsible for coding the complete datasets, whereas another cross-checked the codes. A final agreement was reached after discussions. Table 2.2 summarizes the top ten source domains for the target domain "COVID-19" in ST and TT of the datasets. Rank is calculated by means of source domain frequency in ST. Table 2.3 displays the χ^2 test of independence with $\alpha = 0.05$ as the criterion for significance.

The χ^2 test of independence ($\chi^2 = 38.823$, $df = 16$, $\alpha < 0.005$) illustrates that there is a significant difference between GTE and EGBR in terms of the source domains for "COVID-19" with a strong effect size[3] ($V = 0.750$, $\alpha < 0.005$). Aside from the shared source domains, i.e., "WAR", "SEA WAVE" and "BAD WEATHER" which

Table 2.2 Top ten source domains for COVID-19 based on frequency in GTE and EGBR

Rank	(GTE) COVID-19 IS__	ST (Chinese)	TT (English)	Rank	(EGBR) COVID-19 IS__	ST (English)	TT (Chinese)
1	War	20	19	1	War	10	8
2	Crime	3	2	2	Criminal	5	4
3	Marathon	2	0	3	Sea wave	4	4
4	Shock wave	1	1	4	Killer	3	6
5	Sea wave	1	0	5	Bad weather	3	3
6	Bomb explosion	1	0	6	Math problem	3	3
7	Flood	1	0	7	Danger	3	2
8	Test	1	0	8	Short break	3	2
9	Competition	1	0	9	Opportunity	2	2
10	Bad weather	0	1	10	War weapon	2	2

[3] Cramér's V is an effect size measurement for the chi-square test of independence. The effect size can be weak, moderate or strong when the value is smaller than 0.2, between 0.2 and 0.6 or larger than 0.6.

Table 2.3 Chi-Square test of independence between source domain for "COVID-19" and new outlets

	Value	*df*	Asymptotic significance (2-sided)
Pearson Chi-Square	38.823[a]	16	0.001
Likelihood Ratio	51.748	16	0.000
Cramér's V	0.750		0.001
N of Valid Cases	69		

[a]32 cells (94.1%) have expected count less than 5. The minimum expected count is 0.45
The significance level is set at 0.05 ($\alpha = 0.05$), which means that the study allows at most 5% chance of making the wrong decision when the null hypothesis is true. Hence, the results are significant when $\alpha < 0.05$

compare the pandemic to natural disasters, GTE depicts COVID-19 as a "CRIME", indicating the existence of a suspicious culprit, whereas EGBR regards the pandemic per se as the "CRIMINAL". Moreover, COVID-19 in GTE is also a "COMPETITION", a "TEST", and a "MARATHON" in which China takes the lead. All these images are omitted in TT. On the contrary, EGBR depicts the pandemic as a "MATH PROBLEM", a "SHORT BREAK", and an "OPPORTUNITY". For instance, in Example (2), "*调查*" in ST and "probe" in TT indicate that the US is a "SUSPECT" who commits the COVID-19 "CRIME", whereas in Example (3), COVID-19 is the "CRIMINAL" who robs people's saving box.

(2) (CM formula: COVID-19 IS CRIME / US IS SUSPECT)

ST: 中国 不 怕 科学 公正 的 调查, 美国 怕
zhōngguó bú pà kēxué gōngzhèng de diàochá, měiguó pà
China no fear science justice AUX investigation, US fear
TT: It's US that fears **probe** on virus origin (GTE, May 18, 2020)

(3) (CM formula: COVID-19 IS CRIMINAL)

ST: **Raid** on the piggy banks (EGBR, June, 2020)
TT: 抢 砸 储蓄罐
qiǎng zá chǔxùguàn
rob break saving box

News headlines in GTE also contain various direct comments on different parties involved in the pandemic, especially China, the US, and the West. Table 2.4 summarizes their most oft-used metaphors. In GTE, China is a "HERO", "CHAMPION", "WINNER", "SHARPSHOOTER", "STEPPINGSTONE" for American politics and "EXCUSE" for the American government's incompetence. In stark contrast, the US is a "TERRORIST", "ACTOR", "SINNER", "LIAR", "MANIAC", "CRIMINAL", "WAR MAKER" and "BURDEN". Likewise, the West is a "WAR MAKER", "HYPOCRITE", "FACELESS MAN", "IMMORAL MAN" or "WITCH". However, TT

Table 2.4 Top 10 source domains for "China", "US" and "the West" based on frequency in GTE

Rank	China is__	ST	TT	Rank	US IS__	ST	TT	Rank	The west is__	ST	TT
1	Hero	2	2	1	Terrorist	5	4	1	War maker	1	0
2	Champion	1	0	2	Actor	4	1	2	Faceless man	1	0
3	Excuse for the US	1	0	3	Sinner	3	2	3	Immoral man	1	0
4	Stepping stone for the US	1	0	4	Burden	2	2	4	Witch	0	1
5	Humble man	1	0	5	Militant	2	1	5	Hypocrite	0	1
6	Sharpshooter	1	0	6	Liar	2	1	6	——	——	——
7	Suspect	1	0	7	Maniac	2	1	7	——	——	——
8	Tool for the US	0	1	8	Tricker	0	3	8	——	——	——
9	Winner	0	1	9	Criminal	1	1	9	——	——	——
10	——	——	——	10	War maker	2	0	10	——	——	——

sees less usage of these metaphors. On the contrary, EGBR seldom directly comments on any parties involved in the pandemic.

(4) (CM formula: CHINA IS STEPPINGSTONE / US IS TRCIKER)

ST: 想 踩着 中国 爬 上 连任, 白宫 想 错 了

xiǎng cǎizhe zhōngguó pá shàng liánrèn, báigōng xiǎng cuò le

think tread China climb up reappointment, White House think wrong AUX

TT: Smearing China a lame **trick** to aid reelection for White House (GTE, April 19, 2020)

(5) (CM formula: US IS WAR MAKER / US IS HOOLIGAN)

ST: 华盛顿 被迫 改 口, 但 对 华 攻击 不会 松

Huáshèngdùn bèipò gǎi kǒu, dàn duì huá gōngjī búhuì song

Washington force-PASS change remarks, but towards China attack not loose

TT: US system fuels Trump team's political **hooliganism** (GTE, May 7, 2020)

2.5.2 Framing Strategies of Metaphorical Expressions in GTE and EGBR

The GTE and EGBR datasets were coded based on the fourfold framing strategies of M-M, M1-M2, M–O, and O-M. Analyses show that the two news agencies manipulate ST and TT metaphors in different measures (see Fig. 2.2). GTE uses the four framing strategies interchangeably, maintaining, replacing, omitting original metaphors or creating new ones to serve different purposes. However, EGBR usually keeps the original images (M-M) and seldom omits (M–O) or creates metaphors (O-M) in TT. The corresponding χ^2 test of independence demonstrates that the two news outlets differ moderately in this regard ($\chi^2 = 31.505$, $df = 3$, $\alpha < 0.001$; $V = 0.374$, $\alpha < 0.005$) (see Table 2.5).

(6) (M-M; M1-M2)

ST: 抗 疫, 蓬佩奥 们 至少 留 下 三 大 历史 罪名

kàng yì, péngpèiào men zhìshǎo liú xià sān dà lìshǐ zuìmíng

fight virus, Pompeo PL at least leave AUX three big historical crimes

TT: Pompeo's three **sins** in global virus **fight** (GTE, March 26, 2020)

(7) (M-M)

ST: Covid **carnage** (EGBR, March 2020)

TT: 病毒 大屠杀

bìngdú dàtúshā

virus massacre

Both Example (6) and (7) have used the M-M strategy ("抗疫"—"virus fight"; "carnage"— "大屠杀") to depict COVID-19 as a "WAR". In Example (6), GTE also transfers the CM "AMERICAN POLITICIANS ARE CRIMINALS" into "AMERICAN POLITICIANS ARE SINNERS". Thus, GTE judges American politicians legally in ST but morally in TT.

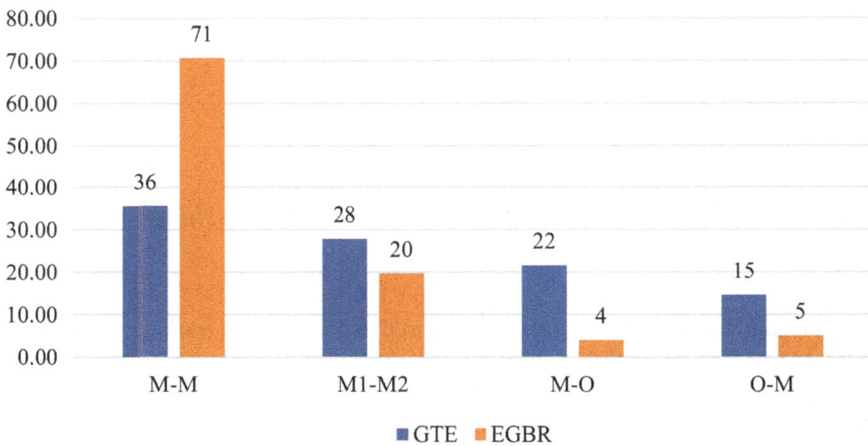

Fig. 2.2 Frequency count of framing strategies in GTE and EGBR (Unit: %)

Table 2.5 Chi-Square test of independence between framing strategies and news outlets

	Value	*df*	Asymptotic significance (2-sided)
Pearson Chi-Square	31.505[a]	3	0.000
Likelihood Ratio	33.712	3	0.000
Cramér's V	0.374		0.001
N of Valid Cases	225		

[a]0 cells (0.0%) have expected count less than 5. The minimum expected count is 10.24

The significance level is set at 0.05 ($\alpha = 0.05$), which means that the study allows at most 5% chance of making the wrong decision when the null hypothesis is true. Hence, the results are significant when $\alpha < 0.05$

(8) (M-O; M1-M2; O-M)

ST: 全球抗疫马拉松, 中国跑得好瞒不住
quánqiú kàng yì mǎlāsōng, zhōngguó pǎo dé hǎo mán bú zhù
Globe fight virus marathon, China run AUX well hide no COMP

TT: China's achievement of COVID-19 **fight** obvious (GTE, May 10, 2020)

In Example (8), "*甩锅*" (literally "to throw a pot") is a Chinese internet slang that means to shirk one's responsibilities by finding a scapegoat. The conceptual metaphor "CHINA IS SCAPEGOAT" in ST is omitted in TT (M–O). In the same example, the original metaphor "US IS MANIAC" is replaced with "US IS LIAR" (M1-M2). In TT, a new metaphor is created (O-M) with the word "weather", i.e., "COVID-19 IS BAD WEATHER".

2.5.3 Evaluation of Attitude and Graduation in GTE and EGBR

As illustrated in the analytical model above, attitude in metaphorical expressions can be positive, neutral or negative; whereas propositions can be strengthened, weakened or unchanged. Table 2.6 presents the study's analytical codes applied to analyse the evaluative attitude and graduation.

Figure 2.3 illustrates the evaluative attitudinal transfer in GTE and EGBR. In effect, most metaphors (70% and 55% for GTE and EGBR, respectively) in the news headlines are negative, which implies that overall, the two newspapers acknowledge the pandemic's destructive influence. Besides, EGBR has a stronger tendency to remain a neutral stance than GTE (28% *versus* 15%). The two newspapers differ in positivity towards COVID-19-related issues. The datasets show that GTE is primarily optimistic about China's achievements during the pandemic such as Example (9), while EGBR is more confident about the pandemic's future trajectory such as Example (10). Nevertheless, the results of Chi-Square test of independence

Table 2.6 Analytical codes for evaluative attitude and graduation

Attitude	–	Negative (Ng)	Neutral (Nt)	Positive (P)
		Ng-Nt	Nt-Ng	P-Ng
		Ng-P	Nt-P	P-Nt
	–	Ng-Ng	Nt-Nt	P-P
Graduation	Strengthening (St)	Ng-St	Nt-St	P-St
	Weakening (Wk)	Ng-Wk	Nt-Wk	P-Wk
	Unchanged (Un)	Ng-Un	Nt-Un	P-Un

in Table 2.7 show that the two newspapers' differences in attitudinal transfer are not statistically significant ($\chi^2 = 10.146$, $df = 6$, $V = 0.246$, $\alpha > 0.05$).

(9) (P-P towards China)

ST: 全球抗疫马拉松, 中国跑得好瞒不住
quánqiú kàng yì mălāsōng, zhōngguó pǎo dé hǎo mán bú zhù
Globe fight virus marathon, China run AUX well hide no COMP

TT: China's achievement of COVID-19 **fight** obvious (GTE, May 10, 2020)

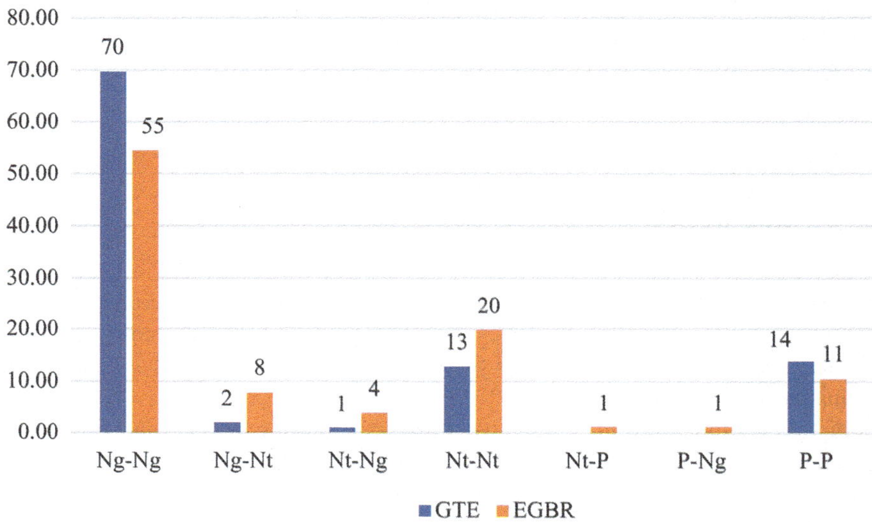

Fig. 2.3 Frequency count of attitudinal transfer in GTE and EGBR (Unit: %)

Table 2.7 Chi-Square test of independence between attitudinal transfer and new outlets

	Value	*df*	Asymptotic Significance (2-sided)
Pearson Chi-Square	10.146[a]	6	0.119
Likelihood Ratio	10.997	6	0.088
Cramé's V	0.246		0.119
N of Valid Cases	168		

[a]8 cells (57.1%) have expected count less than 5. The minimum expected count is 0.45
The significance level is set at 0.05 ($\alpha = 0.05$), which means that the study allows at most 5% chance of making the wrong decision when the null hypothesis is true. Hence, the results are significant when $\alpha < 0.05$

(10) (P-P towards the pandemic)

ST: Getting better (EGBR, November 2020)
TT: 渐入佳境

jiàn rù jiā jìng

gradually enter good situation

Figure 2.4 shows the percentages of evaluative graduation in GTE and EGBR. In general, GTE displays a more mixed pattern regarding negative propositions, while EGBR attempts to keep its negativity unchanged. Moreover, EGBR strengthens or retains its neutral stance more often than GTE (25% *versus* 6%). These differences are statistically significant ($\chi^2 = 28.729$, $df = 8$, $\alpha < 0.01$) with a moderate effect size ($V = 0.414$, $\alpha < 0.01$) as shown in Table 2.8.

Most news headlines in the EGBR dataset are comments on the COVID-19 pandemic except Example (11) which mentions China. Nevertheless, GTE has direct comments on China and the US, and the corresponding frequency of evaluative graduation is plotted in Fig. 2.5. Overall, GTE holds a pro-China (18%) and anti-US stance (82%), and both stances have a strong propensity to be weakened in the TT (9% of P-Wk towards China and 33% of Ng-Wk towards the US). GTE's evaluative graduation towards China and the US is diametrically opposite as shown in Table 2.9 ($\chi^2 = 66.000$, $df = 5$, $\alpha < 0.01$) with a strong effect size ($V = 1.000$, $\alpha < 0.01$). Example (12), (13) and (14) illustrate GTE's anti-US stance.

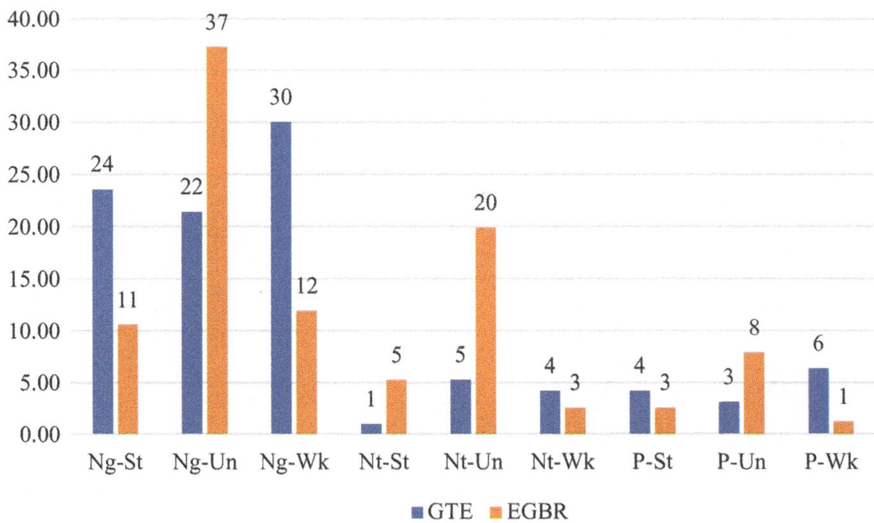

Fig. 2.4 Frequency count of graduation in GTE and EGBR (Unit: %)

Table 2.8 Chi-Square test of independence between evaluative graduation and new outlets

	Value	*df*	Asymptotic Significance (2-sided)
Pearson Chi-Square	28.729[a]	8	0.000
Likelihood Ratio	29.941	8	0.000
Cramé's V	0.414		0.000
N of Valid Cases	168		

[a]10 cells (55.6%) have expected count less than 5. The minimum expected count is 2.23
The significance level is set at 0.05 ($\alpha = 0.05$), which means that the study allows at most 5% chance of making the wrong decision when the null hypothesis is true. Hence, the results are significant when $\alpha < 0.05$

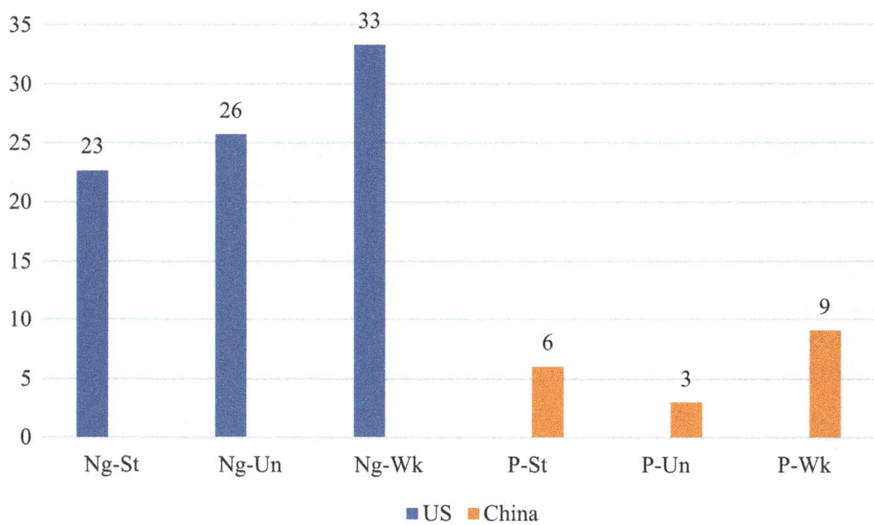

Fig. 2.5 Frequency count of evaluative graduation towards China and the US in GTE (Unit: %)

Table 2.9 Chi-Square test of independence between evaluative graduation and countries in GTE

	Value	*df*	Asymptotic Significance (2-sided)
Pearson Chi-Square	66.000[a]	5	0.000
Likelihood Ratio	62.586	5	0.000
Cramér's V	1.000		0.000
N of Valid Cases	66		

[a]9 cells (75.0%) have expected count less than 5. The minimum expected count is 0.36
The significance level is set at 0.05 ($\alpha = 0.05$), which means that the study allows at most 5% chance of making the wrong decision when the null hypothesis is true. Hence, the results are significant when $\alpha < 0.05$

(11) (Ng-Un towards China)

ST: Still **made** in China (EGBR, April 2020)
TT: 仍 是 中国 制造

réng shì zhōngguó zhìzào

still is China manufacture

(12) (Ng-Wk towards the US)

ST: 甩 锅 第二 集: 华盛顿 撕咬 世卫

shuǎi guō dìèr jí: huáshèngdùn sīyǎo shìwèi

throw pot second episode: Washington worry WHO

TT: Washington makes WHO a **scapegoat** (GTE, April 8, 2020)

(13) (Ng-St towards the US)

ST: 新 发现 越来越多, 看 华盛顿 如何 演 下去

xīn fāxiàn yuèláiyuèduō, kàn huáshèngdùn rúhé yǎn xiàqù

new discovery more and more, look Washington how act down

TT: Washington's **plot** hard to sustain with new virus discoveries (GTE, May 7, 2020)

(14) (Ng-Un towards the US)

ST: 和平 的 中国 和 好斗 的 美国, 谁 才 像 纳粹

hépíng de zhōngguó hé hǎodòu de měiguó, shuí cái xiàng nàcuì

peace AUX China and belligerence AUX US, who just like Nazi

TT: Who's like **Nazi** Germany: peace-loving China or **belligerent** US? (GTE, June 7, 2020)

2.6 Discussion

The previous analyses show that GTE and EGBR differ significantly in terms of the adopted source domains for the target domain "COVID-19", framing strategies and the evaluative graduation towards the pandemic and the parties at stake. By and large, GTE reframes its pro-China and anti-US/West stance in a more considerable measure than EGBR's reframing of its anti-China stance. According to Wu (2018), factors in reframing may include institutional protocols, sociocultural values and beliefs, and linguistic differences. GTE and EGBR as institutions with competing ideologies need to reframe their stance in the target culture to cater for the readers' needs or to conform to the target norms. Nevertheless, it is not the factors of reframing that the current study aims to highlight but the non-political context of stance mediation in news reports and the significance of metaphor as a frame for stance mediation investigation.

2.6.1 Stance Mediation in News Translation Beyond Political Reports

Stance mediation in political reports has been well documented in the contexts of South China Sea disputes (Wu and Zhang 2015), China-Japan disputes (Wu 2018), Tibet riots (Pan and Liao 2020), etc. These topics, which involve political and economic conflicts, usually provide a fertile ground for stance research, as such political and economic events take news outlets' contrasting ideologies to extremes. Nonetheless, such stance mediations can also find evidence in reports of non-political events as in this case.

To date, the ideological mediation in reports on healthcare matters has not received due attention, a situation which needs to be rectified. In the first place, the ongoing COVID-19 pandemic is a universal challenge that affects people's daily life on the globe. However, news media or agencies all over the world join the battle of blaming, giving new names to the virus, e.g., "China virus", "Wuhan virus" or "Kung flu" in the West (Budhwani and Sun 2020) and "American poisoning", or "United States biological weapon" in China ("COVID-19 misinformation" 2020). In the second place, translation plays a vital role in reframing the COVID-19-related narratives and the corresponding stance mediation. Invisible as it is, translation, *ipso facto*, is the major actor in the making of international politics, not only in translating political discourse (Zanettin 2016), but in translating news matters (Bielsa and Bassnett 2008). Such a reframing practice happens within the news outlets as GTE and EGBR practice self-translation for target readers, which corroborates Qin and Zhang's (2018) claim for more studies on the stance mediation of news agencies sharing the same ideology.

2.6.2 Metaphor as a Frame in Stance Mediation

The current study illustrates that metaphor can act as a frame in stancetaking and translation of such frames affects the way of understanding world events. In other words, the study associates news translation with framing. Admittedly, Liu (2015) proposed a *transframing* model to represent the close-knit relationship between framing and news translation studies. Although she analyses story tones, types, sensitivity and the corresponding transframing devices and strategies, metaphor is not a focus of her study. In Pan and Huang's (2021) study on (re)framing and stance mediation in the translation, their findings are limited in terms of the text type (i.e., political speeches), methodology (i.e., case study), theoretical framework (i.e., Appraisal Theory) and metaphor types (i.e., linguistic metaphors). The current study can further enrich their research findings by including conceptual metaphors and non-political texts into the analysis.

2.7 Conclusion

This study has drawn upon the corpus model, framing model and the AT model to investigate how GTE and EGBR use metaphors to (re)frame the era of the COVID-19 pandemic for their Chinese and English readers. The source domains used to describe the target domain "COVID-19", framing strategies and evaluative graduation in GTE and EGBR are significantly different with a moderate to high effect size. Both news agencies have acknowledged the pandemic's destructive influence. Nevertheless, GTE portrays the US as a culprit, while EGBR presents China as a reprobate. Overall, GTE takes a pro-China and anti-US/West stance which is prone to be weakened in the target English text, whereas EGBR retains its anti-China stance in the target Chinese text. The current study highlights the existence of stance mediation in non-political reports within news agencies that practice self-translation of news reports. Most importantly, by exemplifying how metaphor can serve as a frame in stance establishment and mediation with a systematic analytical model, the current study contributes to framing studies, journalistic translation studies and metaphor translation studies.

References

Ahrens, K., and M. Jiang. 2020. Source domain verification using corpus-based tools. *Metaphor and Symbol* 35 (1): 43–55. https://doi.org/10.1080/10926488.2020.1712783.

Baker, M. 2006. *Translation and conflict: A narrative account*. London and New York: Routledge.

Baker, M. 2007. Reframing conflict in translation. *Social Semiotics* 17 (2): 151–169. https://doi.org/10.1080/10350330701311454.

Bazzi, S. 2014. Foreign metaphors and Arabic translation: An empirical study in journalistic translation practice. *Journal of Language and Politics* 13 (1): 120–151. https://doi.org/10.1075/jlp.13.1.06baz.

Bielsa, E., and S. Bassnett. 2008. *Translation in global news*. London and New York: Routledge.

Boulanger, P.P. 2016. When the media translate the crisis: The metaphor used by the mainstream press during the subprimes crisis. *Meta* 61: 144–162.

Brady, A.M. 2015. Authoritarianism goes global (II): China's foreign propaganda machine. *Journal of Democracy* 26 (4): 51–59. https://doi.org/10.1353/jod.2015.0056.

Budhwani, H., and R. Sun. 2020. Creating COVID-19 stigma by referencing the Novel Coronavirus as the "Chinese virus" on Twitter: Quantitative analysis of social media data. *Journal of Medical Internet Research* 22 (5): e19301. https://doi.org/10.2196/19301.

Charteris-Black, J. 2004. *Corpus approaches to critical metaphor analysis*. New York: Springer.
COVID-19 misinformation. 2020. *Wikipedia*. Last modified 23 May 2020. https://en.wikipedia.org/wiki/COVID-19_misinformation.
Deignan, A. 1999. Linguistic metaphors and collocation in nonliterary corpus data. *Metaphor and Symbol* 14 (1): 19–36. https://doi.org/10.1207/s15327868ms1401_3.
Deignan, A. 2005. *Metaphor and corpus linguistics*. Amsterdam: John Benjamins Publishing.
Dionne, K., and F.F. Turkmen. 2020. The politics of pandemic othering: Putting COVID-19 in global and historical context. *International Organization* 74 (S1): E213–E230. https://doi.org/10.1017/S0020818320000405.
Englebretson, R. 2007. Stancetaking in discourse: An introduction. In *Stancetaking in discourse: Subjectivity, evaluation, interaction*, ed. R. Englebretson, 1–26. Amsterdam: John Benjamins Publishing.
Entman, R. 1991. Framing US coverage of international news: Contrasts in narratives of the KAL and Iran Air incidents. *Journal of Communication* 41 (4): 6–27. https://doi.org/10.1111/j.1460-2466.1991.tb02328.x.
Horwitz, J. 2016. The Economist's website is now censored in China—and all it took was one satirical cover. *Quartz*, April 7. https://qz.com/655995/the-economists-website-is-now-censored-in-china-and-all-it-took-was-one-satirical-cover/. Accessed 12 Mar 2021.
Kövecses, Z. 2020. *Extended conceptual metaphor theory*. Cambridge: Cambridge University Press.
Lakoff, G., and M. Johnson. 2008. *Metaphors we live by*. Chicago: University of Chicago Press.
Liu, N.X. 2015. *Transframing: A new paradigm of news framing through translation*. PhD diss.: University of Nottingham.
Liu, N.X. 2017. Same perspective, different effect: Framing the economy through financial news translation. *Perspectives* 25 (3): 452–463. https://doi.org/10.1080/0907676X.2017.1287203.
Liu, Y., and D. Li. 2022a. The US-China battle over Coronavirus in the news media: Metaphor transfer as a representation of stance mediation. *Discourse & Society* 33 (4): 456–477. https://doi.org/10.1177/09579265221088122.
Liu, Y., and D. Li. 2022b. Multimodal metaphor (re)framing: A critical analysis of the promotional image of China's Hubei Province in the post-pandemic era on new media. *Social Semiotics*. https://doi.org/10.1080/10350330.2022.2094233.
Mannoni, M. 2021. A corpus-based approach to the translation of conceptual metaphors in legal language: Chinese Yuān (冤) and English 'Injustice', 'Wrong' and 'Tort.' *Perspectives* 29 (2): 199–216. https://doi.org/10.1080/0907676X.2020.1797132.
Martin, J.R., and P.R. White. 2005. *The language of evaluation*. London: Palgrave Macmillan.
McLaughlin, M.L. 2015. News translation past and present: Silent witness and invisible intruder. *Perspectives* 23 (4): 552–569. https://doi.org/10.1080/0907676X.2015.1015578.
Molter, V., and R. DiResta. 2020. Pandemics and propaganda: How Chinese state media creates and propagates CCP coronavirus narratives. *Harvard Kennedy School Misinformation Review* 1 (3). https://doi.org/10.37016/mr-2020-025.
Newmark, P. 1988. *A textbook of translation*. Harlow: Longman.
O'Halloran, K. 2010. Investigating metaphor and ideology in hard news stories. In *Introducing applied linguistics: Concepts and skills*, ed. S. Hunston and D. Oakey, 97–107. London and New York: Routledge.
Olza, I., P. Pérez-Sobrino, and V. Koller. 2020. *#ReframeCovid*. https://sites.google.com/view/reframecovid/initiative?authuser=0.
Pan, L., and C. Huang. 2021. Stance mediation in media translation of political speeches: An analytical model of appraisal and framing in news discourse. In *Advances in discourse analysis of translation and interpreting*, ed. B. Wang and J. Munday, 131–149. London and New York: Routledge.
Pan, L., and S. Liao. 2020. News translation of reported conflicts: A corpus-based account of positioning. *Perspectives* 29 (5): 722–739. https://doi.org/10.1080/0907676X.2020.1792519.
Pedersen, J. 2017. How metaphors are rendered in subtitles. *Target* 29 (3): 416–439.

Pragglejaz Group. 2007. MIP: A method for identifying metaphorically used words in discourse. *Metaphor and Symbol* 22 (1): 1–39.

Qin, B., and M. Zhang. 2018. Reframing translated news for target readers: A narrative account of news translation in Snowden's discourses. *Perspectives* 26 (2): 261–276. https://doi.org/10.1080/0907676X.2017.1377265.

Ruwitch, J., and M. Kelemen. 2020. Trump administration labels 4 more Chinese news outlets 'foreign missions'. *NPR*, 22 June. https://www.npr.org/2020/06/22/881755421/trump-administration-labels-4-more-chinese-news-outlets-foreign-missions. Accessed 12 Mar 2021.

Schäffner, C., and M. Shuttleworth. 2013. Metaphor in translation: Possibilities for process research. *Target* 25 (1): 93–106. https://doi.org/10.1075/target.25.1.08shu.

Shuttleworth, M. 2017. *Studying scientific metaphor in translation*. Oxford: Taylor and Francis.

Sjørup, A. C. 2013. Cognitive effort in metaphor translation: An eye-tracking and key-logging study. PhD dissertation, LIMAC PhD School.

Spiessens, A., and P. Van Poucke. 2016. Translating news discourse on the Crimean crisis: Patterns of reframing on the Russian website InoSMI. *The Translator* 22 (3): 319–339. https://doi.org/10.1080/13556509.2016.1180570.

Steen, G., A.G. Dorst, B. Herrmann, A.A. Kaal, T. Krennmayr, and T. Pasma. 2010. *A method for linguistic metaphor identification: From MIP to MIPVU*. Amsterdam: John Benjamins Publishing.

Stefanowitsch, A., and S.T. Gries. 2007. *Corpus-based approaches to metaphor and metonymy*. Berlin: Walter de Gruyter.

Sun, Y. 2017. A tracing into metaphor translation studies abroad during the past four decades (1976–2015). *Foreign Language Learning Theory and Practice* 3: 80–90.

Toury, G. 2012. *Descriptive translation studies and beyond*. Revised. Amsterdam: John Benjamins Publishing.

Valdeón, R.A. 2008. Anomalous news translation: Selective appropriation of themes and texts in the internet. *Babel* 54 (4): 299–326. https://doi.org/10.1075/babel.54.4.01val.

Valdeón, R.A. 2015a. Fifteen years of journalistic translation research and more. *Perspectives* 23 (4): 634–662. https://doi.org/10.1080/0907676X.2015.1057187.

Valdeón, R.A. 2015b. (Un)stable sources, translation and news production. *Target* 27 (3): 440–453. https://doi.org/10.1075/target.27.3.07val.

Valdeón, R.A. 2016. The construction of national images through news translation. In *Interconnecting translation studies and imagology*, ed. L. van Doorslaer, P. Flynn, and J. Leerssen, 219–237. Amsterdam: John Benjamins Publishing.

Valdeón, R.A. 2020. Journalistic translation research goes global: Theoretical and methodological considerations five years on. *Perspectives* 28 (3): 325–338. https://doi.org/10.1080/0907676X.2020.1723273.

Valdeón, R. A, and C. Calafat. 2020. Introduction: The politics of translation and the translation of politics. *Translation and Interpreting* 12 (2): 1–6. https://doi.org/10.12807/ti.11222.2020.a01.

van den Broeck, R. 1981. The limits of translatability exemplified by metaphor translation. *Poetics Today* 2 (4): 73–87.

Van Poucke, P., and A. Belikova. 2016. Foreignization in news translation: Metaphors in Russian translation on the news translation website InoSMI. *Meta* 61 (2): 346–368. https://doi.org/10.7202/1037763ar.

White, P.R. 2015. Appraisal theory. In *The international encyclopedia of language and social interaction*, ed. K. Tracy, 1–7. New Jersey: Wiley Blackwell.

Wu, G., and H. Zhang. 2015. Translating political ideology: A case study of the Chinese translations of the English news headlines concerning South China Sea disputes on the website of www.ftchinese.com. *Babel* 61 (3): 394–410. https://doi.org/10.1075/babel.61.3.05gua.

Wu, X. 2018. Framing, reframing and the transformation of stance in news translation: A case study of the translation of news on the China-Japan dispute. *Language and Intercultural Communication* 18 (2): 257–274. https://doi.org/10.1080/14708477.2017.1304951.

Zanettin, F. 2016. 'The deadliest error': Translation, international relations and the news media. *The Translator* 22 (3): 303–318. https://doi.org/10.1080/13556509.2016.1149754.
Zhang, H. 2014. ICTCLAS-NLPIR. V. 2.1. http://ictclas.nlpir.org.
Zhang, M. 2013. Stance and mediation in transediting news headlines as paratexts. *Perspectives* 21 (3): 396–411. https://doi.org/10.1080/0907676X.2012.691101.

Yufeng Liu is a Ph.D. Candidate at the Department of Chinese and Bilingual Studies, The Hong Kong Polytechnic University. Her research interests include metaphor translation studies, news translation studies and corpus based translation studies.

Dechao Li is an Associate Professor at the Department of Chinese and Bilingual Studies, The Hong Kong Polytechnic University. His main research areas include corpus-based translation studies, empirical approaches to translation process research, history of translation in the late Qing and early Republican periods and problem-based learning and translator/interpreter training. He has published over 50 articles in journals such as Perspectives: Studies in Translatology, The Translator and Interpreter Trainer, Interpreting, Discourse & Society, Target, Frontiers in Psychology as well as some book chapters published by Routledge, Springer and Wayne State University Press.

Chapter 3
COVID-19 Translated: An Account of the Translation and Multilingual Practices Enacted in Hong Kong's Linguistic Landscape During the Pandemic Crisis Communication

Chonglong Gu

Abstract The COVID-19 pandemic has given rise to a dramatic upsurge in medical and scientific research. However, despite the importance of language in communicating medical and scientific knowledge to people from different sociocultural, religious and linguistic backgrounds, the role of translation and multilingual communication remains significantly underexplored. Against a backdrop of globalization, our world is increasingly diverse and multilingual, where people might not be able to understand adequately the message delivered only in the official language(s). Arguably, how well public health information (e.g. on mask wearing, social distancing, and vaccination) is communicated multilingually can make or break a place's anti-COVID efforts. This highlights the crucial need of translation and multilingual communication at times of public health crises as a matter of great urgency. As a former British colony and now a special administrative region of China, Hong Kong is a major global financial centre in East Asia. Whilst ethnic Chinese Hongkongers make up the majority of Hong Kong's population, for historical and socioeconomic reasons, immigrants and workers from around the world (e.g. India, Pakistan, Nepal, Bangladesh, Indonesia, the Philippines, Vietnam, and Thailand) can be found in the SAR. Hong Kong, therefore, represents an exhilarating case of micro-cosmopolitanism and a society of superdiversity (Piller 2018; Vertovec 2007). Undoubtedly, as a major global city, Hong Kong serves as a site *par excellence* for studying how various multilingual resources notably including translation have been mobilized to facilitate communication during the COVID-19 public health crisis. Through examining various multilingual resources enacted in Hong Kong's multilingual landscape, this study takes a general descriptive account of the top-down and bottom-up translation and multilingual communication practices in the SAR on various platforms (e.g. the traditional physical linguistic landscape and also the virtual and even audio-scape).

C. Gu (✉)
The Hong Kong Polytechnic University, Hong Kong, China
e-mail: Chonglong.Gu@polyu.edu.hk

K. Liu and A. K. F. Cheung (eds.), *Translation and Interpreting in the Age of COVID-19*, Corpora and Intercultural Studies 9,
https://doi.org/10.1007/978-981-19-6680-4_3

Keywords Covid-19 · Multilingual crisis communication · Translation · Linguistic landscape · Hong Kong

3.1 Introduction

COVID-19 understandably has so far mostly been investigated as first and foremost a medical and public health issue as evidenced in an explosion of recent publications, for example, on nonpharmaceutical interventions such as mask wearing (Wang, Pan, and Cheng 2020), airborne aerosol transmission (Greenhalgh et al. 2021), symptoms of COVID-19 (Chan and Brownstein 2020), and immunity (Goldberg et al. 2022). More recently, there has been more scholarly attention, *inter alia*, on policy-making (cf. Cairney and Wellstead 2021). However, the role of language and communication remains largely under-explored at a time of global health crisis (cf. Declercq and Federici 2020). This is despite the fact that the COVID-19 pandemic has brought to the fore the importance of effective communication in getting the intended scientific and medical knowledge and anti-COVID measures across in different languages.

As a unique form of communication, COVID-related crisis communication has a few main characteristics and features. Firstly, COVID-related communication represents a typical case of experts-to-laypeople communication. No doubt, the pandemic has notably witnessed a proliferation of relatively new scientific, medical and epidemiological notions and concepts such as 'social distancing', 'universal masking', 'aerosol transmission', 'R0', 'herd immunity', 'flattening the curve', 'immune escape', 'asymptomatic infection', 'viral load', 'super-spreading events', 'dynamic zero policy', and 'self-quarantine' that were previously unfamiliar to the ordinary people. Secondly, most of these medical and scientific concepts, knowledge and know-how have tended to be created and coined in the technologically more advanced developed countries. This, as such, highlights the crucial need of communication between countries with different socioeconomic situations and varying levels of economic and public health developments. Also, given the severity and urgency of the pandemic and our recent technological advancements, communication is never a one-way process. In lieu of the traditional type of vertical top-down communication, various social actors and agents are involved in a more dynamic, multi-directional and multi-thread communication process at various levels and utilizing numerous modalities and platforms (e.g. both top-down communication and communication between friends and family members via social media and other digital platforms) in an interactive manner. Most importantly, a major hallmark of the COVID-19 crisis communication is its essentially multilingual nature beyond the borders of individual nations. That is, a global pandemic is by definition global in scale, thus necessitating effective and targeted communication multilingually.

Indeed, from this perspective, multilingual communication can be considered pivotal, given the fact that how the pandemic might be contained or managed is largely dependent upon the diffusion and dissemination of crucial preventive information and medical insights (Ahmad and Hillman 2020) to all sections of our increasingly multilingual and multicultural societies at a time of crisis communication (Declercq and Federici 2020; Piller et al. 2020). For Haddow and Haddow (2014), recognizing language and cultural differences, using clear language, identifying and relying on trustworthy community leaders, and utilizing appropriate media platforms have been established as some of the key communication strategies in order to reach out to people effectively and efficiently. By doing so, various public messages can be successfully produced in order to create specific responses from the general public (cf. Reynolds and Seeger 2005). In addition, successful multilingual communication is also vital from the perspective of preventing misinformation and 'fake news'.

So far, only a handful of studies have explored the linguistic and communication aspects of the COVID-19 pandemic in extant research. Piller (2020a) and Piller et al. (2020) discussed the language challenges brought about by the pandemic, highlighting the crucial need for linguistic diversity as part of multilingual crisis communication. Notably, Piller (2020a) eloquently argued that the COVID-19 crisis has forced us to "take linguistic diversity seriously", considering the imperative to get 8 billion people speaking different languages to follow various social distancing and anti-COVID rules. Focusing on the specific Qatar context, Ahmad and Hillman (2020) examined the use of migrant languages in the process of COVID-19 awareness campaign. Also, Marshall (2021) has explored COVID-related linguistic landscape in Vancouver's North Shore in Canada.

In addition, Rudwick, Sijadu, and Turner (2021) explored the politics of language in COVID-19, taking a multilingual perspective from the context of South Africa. Also, Wang, Bahry, and An (2022) have examined non-dominant languages and focused on minority communities' creation and dissemination of multilingual anti-COVID materials in China's Yunnan and Gansu provinces. Employing a comparative case study approach across 11 minority language settings in Europe, Bober and Willis (2021) examined the pandemic and minority language media in Europe relating to the spring 2020 lockdowns. Interestingly, Chen (2020) looked into the unexpected role of classical Chinese poetry in the fight against COVID-19 in East Asia. Abdulla (2020) examined visual language communication relating to the pandemic available on print-based signage.

In comparison, the role of translation and multilingual communication during the COVID pandemic remains seldom explored in the context of Hong Kong, despite the intimate involvement of translation in various forms and modalities in multilingual crisis communication. A former UK colony, Hong Kong is now a Special Administrative Region (SAR) of China and a global city attracting people from around the world. While Cantonese-speaking Chinese Hongkongers represent the majority, visible ethnic minorities from such countries as India, Pakistan, Nepal, Bangladesh, Indonesia, Thailand, the Philippines, the US, and the UK can be found in Hong Kong. As such, considering its unique status as a former British colony and an international financial centre, Hong Kong represents an exhilarating case of micro-cosmopolitanism and a society of superdiversity (Piller 2018; Vertovec 2007). As a major global city, Hong Kong, without doubt, serves as a site *par excellence* for studying how various multilingual resources including translation have been mobilized to facilitate communication during the COVID-19 public health crisis, which represents a hitherto un(der)explored topic in Hong Kong's pandemic prevention and control efforts.

To bridge the aforementioned research gap, this study draws on a corpus of real-world data taken from Hong Kong's LL (Linguistic Landscape) relating to COVID-19. Essentially interdisciplinary in nature, this study aims to shed light on the following socially oriented questions: What minority languages are usually included and represented in Hong Kong's COVID-related multilingual landscape in addition to Chinese and English? What are some of the common avenues and modalities of Hong Kong's multilingual crisis communication? What features can be observed in the multilingual communication?

Rather than taking a prescriptivist approach to prescribe how COVID-related information should or must be communicated and commenting on translation quality (e.g. how accurate and faithful the various multilingual versions are), this much-needed study takes a non-judgmental and descriptivist approach to language. That is, this study aims to describe and unpack the translation and multilingual practices in Hong Kong relating to the pandemic at a general level, drawing on real-world data. This interdisciplinary study promises to contribute to scholarship in translation studies, multilingual communication, public crisis communication, linguistic landscape and urban studies. This study also is poised to share much-needed translation and multilingual communication experiences with other multilingual and multicultural societies such as New York, Paris, London, Manchester, Birmingham, Toronto, Dubai, Qatar, and Singapore.

3.2 Setting the Scene: Minority Languages and Multilingual Crisis Communication

For some time, information has mostly been available in a few major dominant languages in the world. To reach this conclusion, one needs to look no further than the fact that websites on the Internet these days are mostly available in a few powerful languages such as English, French and Chinese. This lopsidedness and imbalance can also be seen in translation, where translation and multilingual and intercultural communication in general are frequently conducted between major languages (e.g. between Chinese and English or between French and Arabic). In comparison, information is rarely translated from less influential and peripheral languages into major ones (e.g. English) and also there is often relatively scant information translated into lesser known and neglected languages, for example, spoken by ethnic minorities and marginalized groups.

However, at a time of a global health crisis, this lopsidedness and imbalance (cf. Piller et al. 2020) can prove problematic at best and fatal and even disastrous at worst. That is, faced with a once-in-a-century global pandemic like COVID-19, whilst arguably everyone may be more or less affected, ethnic minorities, temporary workers and other disadvantaged and marginalized groups tend to be disproportionately affected for various social and economic reasons. In addition to these sociopolitical and economic factors, communication issues notably due to linguistic barriers and a lack of relevant information have been established as a major reason that explains why ethnic and linguistic minorities and/or other marginalized groups might be hit particularly hard in various crises and disasters (cf. Piller et al. 2020; Tan and Said 2015; Uekusa 2019). This is for the simple reason that being 'out of the loop' on vital information means that linguistic minorities and other marginalized groups are ill-prepared and ill-equipped to face the challenges brought about by crises and disasters.

As illustrated convincingly in Lha (2020), not all groups within a society can adequately understand the messages in the official language of the locale during disasters and crises. For example, Lha's (2020) study points to the reality that in the Tibetan regions of China's Sichuan Province, a considerable number of people including senior citizens cannot understand China's official language Mandarin Chinese adequately. As such, relying solely on official languages at the expense of smaller community or minority languages can be counterproductive and even risky as far as the promotion of public health awareness is concerned.

Unfortunately, in the current structure, global mass communication still tends to be dominated by major languages such as English and Chinese often at the expense of other smaller and marginalized minority languages (Piller et al. 2020). This sorry situation highlights the importance of multilingual communication in ensuring that important public health information is readily accessible to all groups in our increasingly diverse society. The successful dissemination of important information multilingually can be instrumental in promoting awareness, building trust and as a result enhancing conformity to relevant anti-COVID rules and measures. It is only when all groups in our society are united as one, make concerted efforts, and sing from the same hymn sheet that we can eventually defeat or at least arrive at an acceptable *modus operandi* in living with the virus. To this end, the provision of translation and other multilingual resources has a big part to play in the crisis communication process.

3.3 Translation, Linguistic Landscape (LL), and Multilingual Crisis Communication

Our cities are becoming increasingly multilingual against a backdrop of globalization. It is fair to say that no city is completely monolingual in the twenty-first century. Without doubt, translation is intimately involved in the very making of our increasingly multilingual world. For Cronin (2017), without translation, there will be no connectivity or globalization whatsoever. Indeed, our multilingual urban landscape is first and foremost a translation space, which represents a locus of micro-cosmopolitan analysis (Cronin 2006). Such major contributions as Lee (2013, 2021) have explored in-depth the intimate relationships between translation and our urban spaces.

For Mcculloch (2020), COVID-19 constitutes the biggest translation challenge in human history. As such, it is of great relevance to explore relatively systematically the translation and multilingual communication practices enacted in Hong Kong's multilingual urban space during the pandemic. In this socially oriented study focusing on crisis communication, translation and multilingual communication are deemed as almost interchangeable. This is because, given the nature of the public health communication, translation permeates and is intimately involved in the entire multilingual communication process and the successful deployment of a place's multilingual resources and 'multilingual repertoires' (cf. Piller et al. 2020) is itself largely reliant upon translation carried out at different levels and on various themes/topics. Here, translation is understood and conceptualized both as a micro process where individual texts are translated from one language into the other and also in a macro way as the practice of multilingual communication. As such, multilingual communication or translation at a macro level is made up of numerous instances of smaller micro translation processes and various translated texts in different languages. Similarly, in this study, 'translators' can mean professionals and non-professionals who translate the actual texts from one language into another language in a strict sense. At the same time, 'translators' in this study can also be taken in a broad sense to refer to multilingual communicators, that is, individuals or organizations that are equipped with knowledge in another language and are able to convey and communicate COVID-related information either in full or partially in another language at a time of a global health crisis (e.g. a radio or TV host who 'translates', broadcasts, reads out loud, or simply summarizes and paraphrases the key government anti-COVID policies and/or information about vaccination in a language that can be understood by certain ethnic and linguistic groups).

Having discussed translation and multilingual communication, attention is now focused on linguistic landscape (LL). Concerned mainly with the sociolinguistic aspects of language use in a real-world setting, linguistic landscape (LL) is a relatively recent yet rapidly developing area within linguistics. LL, for Landry and Bourhis (1997: 23), traditionally has explored the 'visibility and salience of languages on public and commercial signs' in a particular locale. Road signs, official notices, shop and restaurant signs, advertisements and public billboards, and graffiti etc. represent some of the commonly studied subjects in this burgeoning area. According to Ben-Rafael et al. (2006), there are top-down signs (e.g. officially enacted by governments and other organizations and agencies) and bottom-up signs (e.g. produced by individuals, non-official groups, and small business owners) in a place's LL.

Essentially interdisciplinary in nature, LL can be seen as being located at the junction of sociolinguistics, geography, demographic research, sociology, social psychology, and media and communication studies. In sociolinguistics in general, language use is often seen as both reflective of the broader sociopolitical and cultural realities and at the same time also as a shaping force of the broader society with potentially far-reaching ramifications (cf. Gu 2018, 2019, 2022). From this perspective, the LL of a particular place constitutes a socially shaped and socially shaping 'discourse', offering fascinating insights into the sociopolitical, cultural, economic, religious, demographic, and even ideological aspects of that place.

Traditionally, research into the linguistic landscape (LL) of a place tends to focus on static written information (e.g. public signs and shop fronts). LL in this study is expanded to include both traditional written content outdoors and also information available on the digital and virtual space (e.g. various dedicated and purpose-made websites and audio-visual materials aimed at promoting awareness) and sound-space (e.g. public announcements). The inclusion of the latter two components is particularly relevant, given the recent technological advancements and also the fact that people need to access vital COVID-related information and guidelines through different platforms. It is believed that these (both physical public space, the virtual and digital space and the sound-space) holistically make up Hong Kong's multilingual Covidscape for the purpose of this study.

3.4 History, Demographics and Linguistic Profile of Hong Kong

For more meaningful discussion, it is important to elaborate on Hong Kong's history and demographic and linguistic profile. Hong Kong had largely been a fishing village and a far-flung outpost of China's Qing dynasty with a small population before the industrialized and militarily superior British took control of the territory and made it a UK colony in the 1840s. During the UK colonial rule, Hong Kong became a global financial centre and major port, partly because of Hong Kong's strategic location next to mainland China. Hong Kong was returned to China in 1997 and became a special administrative region (SAR) of the country under the 'one country two systems' policy.

In Hong Kong, the vast majority of the local population have been ethnic Chinese from different backgrounds. Over the years during the UK colonial rule, there were waves of immigration, where Chinese people mostly from the mainland (largely Chinese people from the adjacent Guangdong province) migrated and settled in Hong Kong to escape war, poverty and political turmoil. This explains why Cantonese over time became the predominant variety of Chinese spoken in Hong Kong by the majority of Chinese Hongkongers.

After the handover in 1997, the official language policy of 'biliteracy and trilingualism' is implemented in recognition of Hong Kong's complicated colonial history, demographic profile, current status as a global financial centre and reality as China's special administrative region. The aim of the official language policy, for Wang and Kirkpatrick (2015), is to train Hong Kong people to be biliterate (in written English and written Chinese) and trilingual (in the dominant local Cantonese variety of Chinese, Putonghua or standard Mandarin Chinese, and spoken English).

Whilst ethnic Chinese Hongkongers form the decided majority, for historical and economic reasons, ethnic minorities, temporary workers and refugees from other countries are highly visible in Hong Kong. For example, there has notably been a sizeable south Asian community in Hong Kong. Traditionally, Hong Kong has enjoyed strong links with the Indian subcontinent. During the British colonial period, Hindus, Muslims and Sikhs from the Indian subcontinent (including current-day India, Pakistan, Nepal, and Bangladesh etc.) moved to Hong Kong to act as prison guards, police officers, soldiers, sailors, and traders. In addition to those South Asians who chose to remain in Hong Kong after the 1997 handover, many Indians, Pakistanis, Bangladeshis and Nepalese people from the Indian subcontinent have decided to live in Hong Kong for economic reasons in recent years. They tend to work in a wide range of sectors, acting as bankers and financial specialists, security guards, delivery men, tailors, labours, construction workers, restaurant waiters, and small-business owners. Also, asylum seekers and refugees from countries like India and Pakistan can be found in Hong Kong. South Asian communities are visible across Hong Kong and such languages as Hindi, Urdu, Punjabi, Nepali, Bengali are spoken. In particular, the Yau-Tsim-Mong district is known for a high concentration of people of South Asian origins. Notably, the Chungking Mansions and neighbouring buildings along Nathan Road are known for the sheer number of South Asian restaurants, stores and shops, representing a kind of 'low-end globalization' (Mathews and Yang 2012) between China and the developing world.

Also, amongst those from ethnic minority groups in Hong Kong are a sizeable number of foreign domestic helpers, who are employed to conduct various household duties such as purchasing everyday items, preparing, cooking and serving food, cleaning and dishwashing, babysitting, and taking care of children and pets. Often well trained, these domestic helpers are mostly from the Philippines and Indonesia and there is also a small percentage of domestic helpers from Thailand and other countries. These domestic helpers are usually speakers of Tagalog, Indonesian (Bahasa Indonesia), and Thai etc. Domestic helpers are normally not allowed to become permanent residents and citizens in the Hong Kong SAR according to the law.

To sum up, for historical, sociopolitical and economic reasons, Hong Kong has been a meeting point of different languages and cultures and a magnet attracting immigrants and workers from around the world. From this perspective, Hong Kong represents an exhilarating case of micro-cosmopolitanism and a society of superdiversity (Piller 2018; Vertovec 2007). As a global financial centre and major entrepôt strategically located in Asia, Hong Kong is a site *par excellence* for LL study relating to the pandemic. This highlights the significance of the current study that explores how various multilingual resources and repertoires may be mobilized, using real-world examples from Hong Kong's multilingual LL.

3.5 Methodology and Data Collection

Methodologically, a multi-stage process was followed. To collect multilingual data regarding Hong Kong's physical linguistic landscape and sound-scape, a wayfaring approach was taken in what is described as 'walking ethnography' (cf. Lee and Ingold 2006; Marshall 2021) methodologically, where the researcher walked around the streets of Hong Kong to document data. Relevant data were photographed and/or recorded using a mobile phone with high-quality camera. In terms of digital and virtual data, keywords were searched on Google and other major video-sharing websites to establish relevant videos and webpages for further analysis.

3.6 Analysis and Discussions

Instead of a micro-level linguistic analysis per se on whether certain concepts/message are translated from one language into the other accurately or not, this article focuses on an under-explored topic relating to multilingual crisis communication in Hong Kong's multilingual landscape. That is, attention is focused on the macro-level deployment and provision of translation and multilingual resources in the Hong Kong SAR during the pandemic.

While multilingual signs are by no means a completely new phenomenon in Hong Kong, oftentimes, the expected norm is that official signs are made available bilingually in Chinese and English in the SAR. However, the COVID-19 pandemic has certainly served as a catalyst that has given rise to the more widespread use of multilingual communication. As some of the general observations, it is established that translated multilingual texts are part and parcel of Hong Kong's Covidscape during the pandemic. In addition to important languages Chinese and English that are central to Hong Kong's official linguistic policy, other minority languages such as Hindi, Urdu, Punjabi, Bengali, Nepali, Tagalog, Indonesia, Vietnamese and Thai can also be found to varying degrees in Hong Kong's multilingual landscape evidenced in both top-down and bottom-up signs (Ben-Rafael et al. 2006). In comparison, other 'major' languages such as Arabic, Russian, Spanish, and French are rarely used in Hong Kong's multilingual crisis communication, despite the wide-spread nature and/or importance of these languages internationally. This arguably is because there are not sufficient speakers who speak these languages in Hong Kong.

This is broadly reflective of the SAR's demographic and linguistic profiles. In sociolinguistics, language use is seen as both reflective of the broader sociopolitical, demographic, and cultural contexts and at the same time also as a shaping force of the broader society with potentially far-reaching ramifications. From this perspective, what languages are selected and used as part of Hong Kong's multilingual communication practices can reflect Hong Kong's demographics and suggest what languages are of importance in the SAR in addition to Chinese and English. In turn, once used, these multilingual signs can effect change on a societal level (in this case in helping promote public awareness, regulating people's behaviours, and urging people to follow relevant COVID rules). The employment of multilingual signs (e.g. directives, instructions and warnings) in otherwise relatively rarely used minority languages in Hong Kong can be seen as a case of what is termed as 'multilingual commanding urgency' (Chesnut et al. 2022) at times of crisis and emergency.

In addition, notably, in the overall provision and deployment of translation and multilingual resources, a general yet differentiated approach is taken. That is, while multilingual information regarding COVID rules and vaccination etc. can be found in general in high-profile and frequently visited locations and major official websites to cover as many people as possible, translated and/or multilingual information is also made available to certain ethnic and linguistic groups in ethnically diverse areas in a targeted manner.

The detailed findings are discussed in the form of examples covering different scenarios, dimensions, and modalities. The observations are discussed around translation and multilingual communication on Hong Kong's (1) traditional physical linguistic landscape, (2) digital and virtual space and (3) audio-landscape or sound-space.

3.6.1 Translation and Multilingual Communication on Hong Kong's Traditional Physical Linguistic Landscape

Top-down translated and multilingual COVID-related information made available on Hong Kong's physical LL constitutes a most common sight in the SAR's multilingual crisis communication. These top-down multilingual signs usually appear in high-profile locations with high traffic to cover as many people as possible from diverse backgrounds (e.g. in popular commercial and business areas, Inland Revenue Department building, government-approved quarantine hotels, and other quarantine facilities). These include a multilingual warning sign asking people to wear a mask and not to gather and engage in illegal hawking activities in the Causeway Bay area (Fig. 3.1), a multilingual sign about language-specific hotlines for those under quarantine (Fig. 3.2), and a multilingual text on how to access multilingual translation and interpreting services (Fig. 3.3). Usually, such languages as Chinese, English, Hindi, Nepali, Urdu, Tagalog, and Indonesian are available. Information in other languages such as Panjabi, Thai, Vietnamese, Bengali, and Sinhala might also be provided.

Also, in addition to this multilingual communication in a general manner to cover as many people as possible, a more differentiated approach can be found in certain areas of Hong Kong. As illustrated below (Fig. 3.4), COVID-19 testing service was provided to domestic helpers in Central, where domestic helpers mostly from the Philippines and Indonesia tend to gather and relax during the weekend. As such, multilingual texts featuring versions in Chinese, English, Tagalog and Indonesian can be found in the photograph to convey the information in a targeted manner.

Fig. 3.1 Multilingual warning sign asking people to wear a mask and not to gather and engage in illegal hawking activities

Similarly, in addition to Central, the Victoria Park and adjacent areas in Causeway Bay in general are also the location of choice for domestic helpers from Indonesia and the Philippines to gather during their day off. Mirroring the targeted approach mentioned above, in the green sign below (Fig. 3.5), a police notice (featuring Indonesian and Tagalog versions) is highly visible. The presence of this multilingual warning sign serves as a constant reminder of the need to follow relevant rules (e.g. wear a mask) to avoid a penalty and other consequences.

Furthermore, the world-famous Chungking Mansions in Tsim Sha Tsui is an iconic building in Hong Kong, which symbolizes multilingualism and multiculturalism in the Hong Kong SAR. Particularly, the Chungking mansions is known for the sheer number of South Asian shops, stores, restaurants, and hotels. Given that the business owners, shopkeepers, customers, and residents here are largely of South Asian backgrounds (e.g. from Pakistan, India, and Bangladesh), COVID-related information available multilingually in South Asian languages such as Nepali, Hindi and Urdu is played on a big screen at the entrance of the Chungking Mansions to help

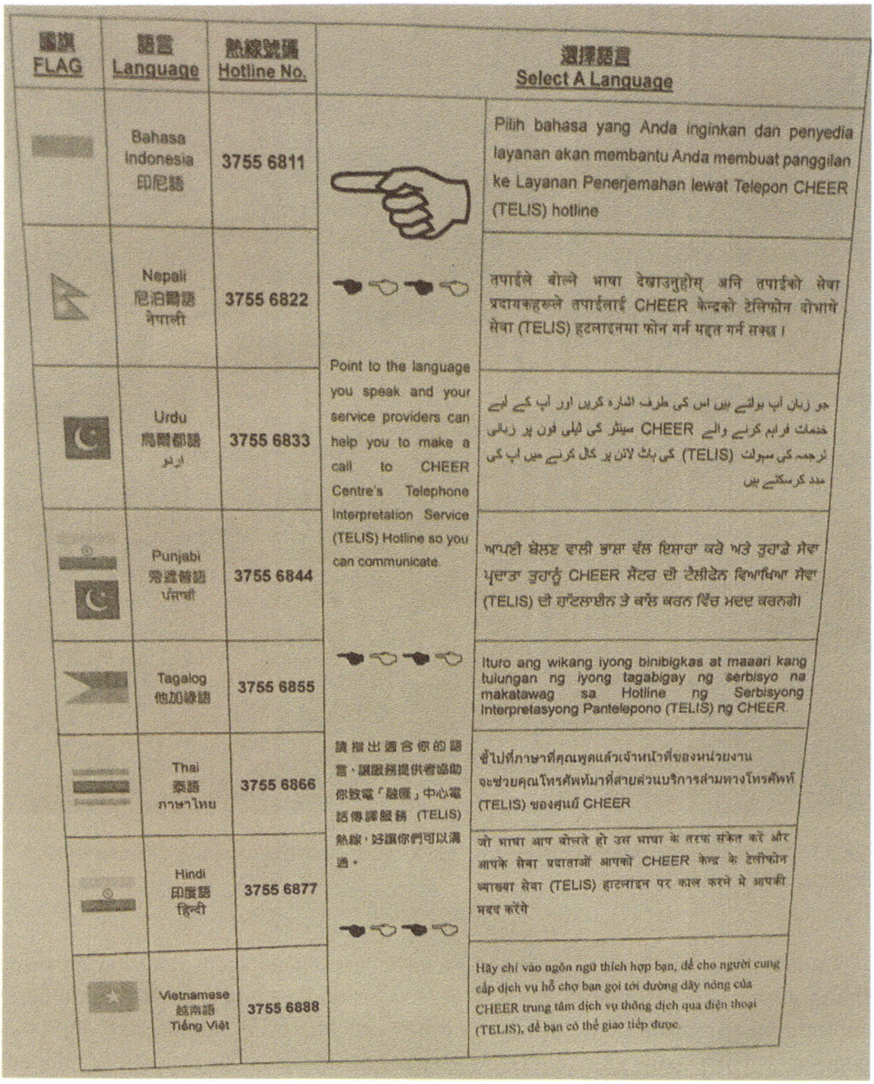

Fig. 3.2 Multilingual sign about a hotline for those under quarantine

promote awareness. As seen in Fig. 3.6, the multilingual information is provided as a top-down sign in a targeted manner by the Home Affairs Bureau in Hong Kong.

Another example of this targeted and differentiated approach can be found below. During a local outbreak of coronavirus in Hong Kong's Jordan and Yau Ma Tei areas, testing was made compulsory in these communities. Given that this is an ethnically diverse area with a relatively high concentration of residents of South Asian backgrounds (e.g. notably from India, Nepal, and Pakistan), Hindi is featured

Fig. 3.3 Multilingual text on how to access multilingual translation and interpreting services

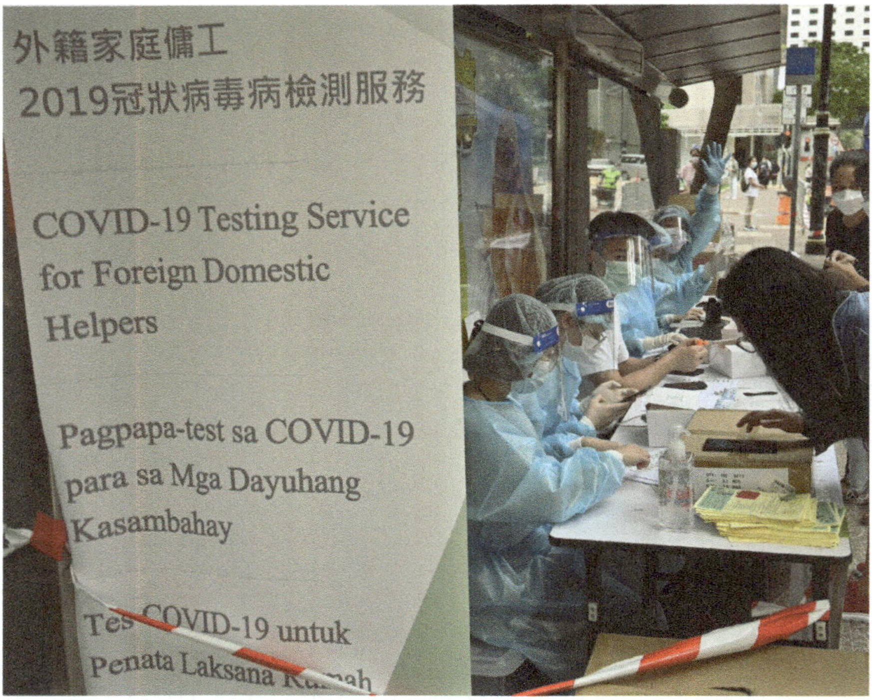

Fig. 3.4 The prominent use of Tagalog and Indonesian in Central

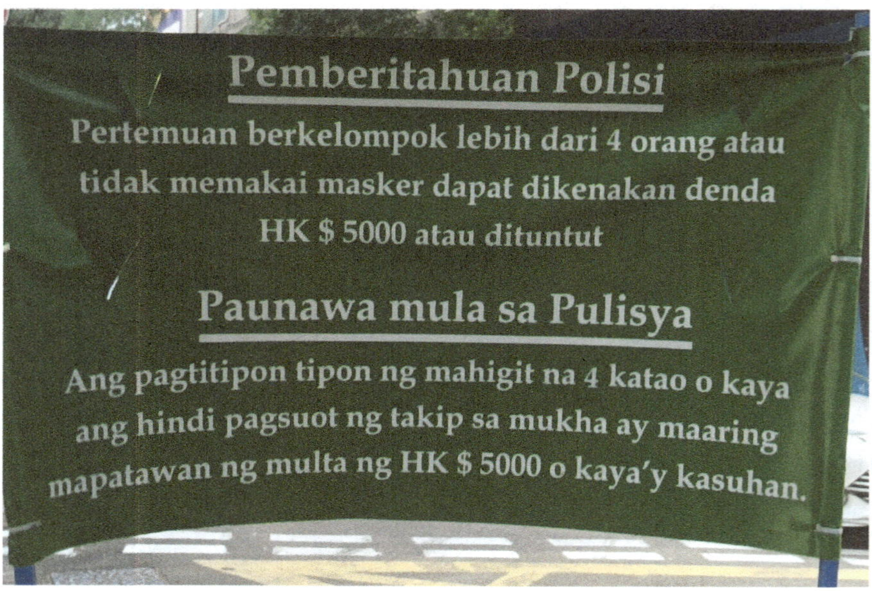

Fig. 3.5 Multilingual police notice near the Victoria Park in Indonesian and Tagalog

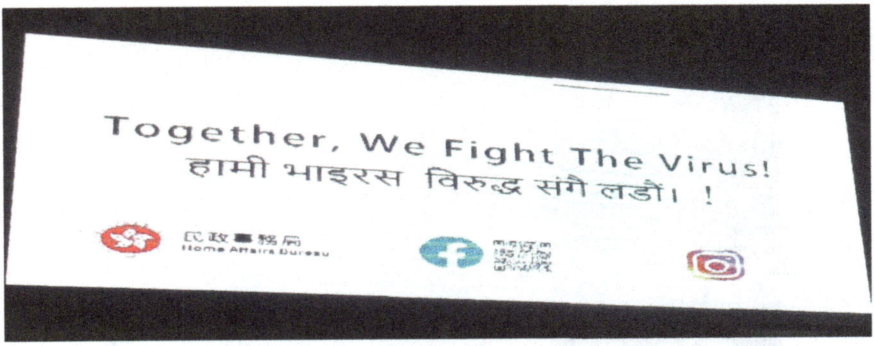

Fig. 3.6 Multilingual sign involving South Asian languages at the entrance of the Chungking Mansions

prominently along with Chinese and English on this particular ad hoc top-down multilingual sign, asking local residents to get registered for testing (Fig. 3.7).

In addition to these top-down translated multilingual signs, bottom-up signs can also be found in different physical spaces at a grassroots level (e.g. in small businesses and ethnically diverse neighbourhoods) to raise awareness and urge people to be united. Given that the text producers are often non-professional individuals without sufficient training in translation, these translated multilingual signs may be handwritten or printed out in a casual way and on an ad hoc basis. These multilingual signs may sometimes even contain grammatical and spelling mistakes. For example, the bottom-up bilingual sign (Fig. 3.8) in Chinese and English is found on Queen's Road Central. While the bilingual text posted by the business owner is clear in meaning, it is grammatically iffy, to say the least.

Also, as mentioned previously, Jordan, Yau Ma Tei and other adjacent areas in Hong Kong's Yau Tsim Mong District feature a concentration of ethnic minority groups, for example, from Nepalese, Indian and Pakistani origins. As seen in Fig. 3.9, multilingual writings in English and a south Asian language Hindi using the Devanagari script can be found in an ethnically and linguistically diverse neighbourhood on Saigon Street in Jordan, Kowloon, which highlights the importance of hygiene in fighting against the virus. Given the largely identical script used, it is also partially understandable to Nepali speakers.

3.6.2 Translation and Multilingual Communication on Hong Kong's Digital and Virtual Space

Given our increasingly mediatized and digital world and the highly transmissible nature of the coronavirus thriving on close human-to-human contact, a range of COVID-related multilingual information can be found in Hong Kong's digital and virtual spaces that are government-run or run by private commercial companies.

Fig. 3.7 Ad hoc multilingual sign in Hindi along with Chinese and English

To illustrate, the high-traffic official website contains information available in various languages (Fig. 3.10), providing crucial and authoritative information (e.g. on COVID measures, travel restrictions and vaccination) to the public. In addition to traditional Chinese, simplified Chinese and English, multilingual information is available in Hindi, Nepali, Urdu, Thai, Indonesian, Tagalog, Sinhala, Bengali and Vietnamese. Users can choose their preferred language(s) from the homepage by clicking.

Fig. 3.8 Bottom-up bilingual sign posted by business owner in Central

Fig. 3.9 Bottom-up multilingual sign involving Hindi in a local community

Fig. 3.10 Official COVID-related website in Hong Kong including information in different languages

Once users choose a language, they will be directed to a dedicated website containing information in the language. Users will be able to access various (translated) documents available in the language. Figure 3.11 below shows a typical page containing COVID-related information in Urdu, an important South Asian language widely used by Muslims in Pakistan and in India.

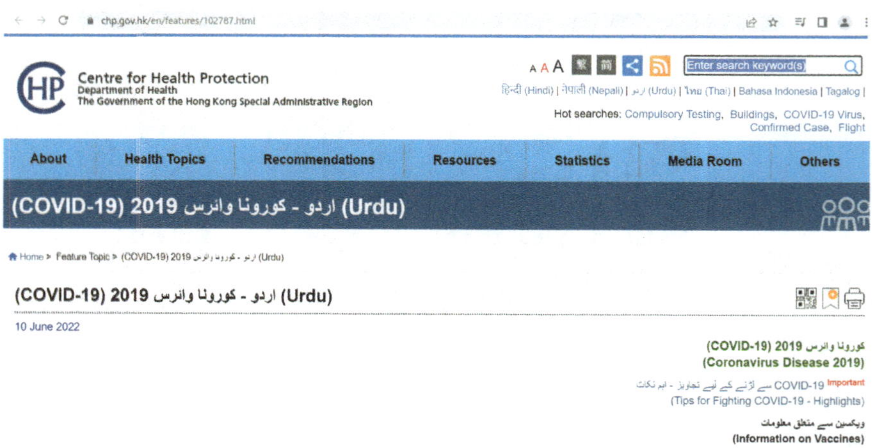

Fig. 3.11 Official COVID-related website featuring information in Urdu

In addition to written texts on official websites, in Hong Kong's multilingual crisis communication, the conveyance of relevant information can also be heard in the form of radio programs, dedicated videos and other audiovisual materials on different websites and/or digital platforms. The Urdu language radio program 'Hong Kong Ki Shaam' on offer by RTHK (Radio Television Hong Kong) is a good case in point (Fig. 3.12). Under the Commerce and Economic Development Bureau of the Hong Kong Government, the radio program 'Hong Kong Ki Shaam' is broadcast in Urdu. The program is hosted by Abid Ali Baig, a poet and writer with decades of experience in broadcasting. In his program, in addition to the common components such as news, entertainment, interviews, religious content, and South Asian music, the host routinely communicates important COVID-related information (e.g. preventive measures and vaccination) to the target audience in Urdu in his program since the pandemic began. While his pandemic-related announcements in Urdu are not exactly word-for-word translations of entire documents in Chinese or English in the strict sense, he nevertheless has served as a vital 'translator' and multilingual communicator to convey and signpost important messages to Pakistanis and the South Asian communities in general in Hong Kong.

The inclusion of multilingual information can also be found on digital platforms run by commercial corporations in Hong Kong. Under Metro Broadcast Corporation, the DESI TADKA program (Fig. 3.13) is sponsored by the Hong Kong SAR government's Home Affairs Department. The presenter is Bitto Singh and the radio program is delivered in Hindi (and sometimes in Punjabi). Mostly targeting the South Asian communities or the Desi diaspora in Hong Kong, South Asian music of different genres and styles is played on the show.

In recent months during the pandemic, at the beginning of the program, the presenter routinely makes an announcement in Hindi, updating the audience of Hong Kong's COVID situation and summarizing the latest rules and other useful

Fig. 3.12 Urdu language radio program 'Hong Kong ki Shaam' webpage

Fig. 3.13 Hindi language radio program 'Desi Tadka' webpage

information (e.g. wearing masks, social distancing, quarantine requirements, and vaccination). The verbally delivered Hindi announcement itself can be seen as a (partial) translation of the government's official policies and positions originally made available in the SAR's official languages. Interestingly, in the Hindi announcement, rather than resorting to 'shudh Hindi' (शुद्ध हिन्दीor 'pure Hindi' featuring sophisticated, formal, archaic, and difficult-to-understand Sanskrit-derived words), there is a liberal use of English words and expressions (e.g. 'social distance', 'serious', 'COVID cases', 'situation', 'surgical mask', 'vaccination', 'reservation', 'free of charge', 'work from home', 'designated clinics', 'community', 'alcohol-based hand rub', 'social gathering', 'dynamic zero', 'you know', 'Hong Kong government'). For illustrative purposes, the following is a partial transcript of an episode of this Hindi program broadcast in March 2022 at the height of Hong Kong's fifth wave.

Hindi utterances in Latin script: Kyonki COVID cases zyada bahut badh rahe hain…toh abhi situation yaha pe kafi serious hai…toh abhi yeh situation hai…work from home karen…aap apne reservations online booking system se le sakte hain..jald se jald appointment le lijiye!...aapne aap protect karna zaruri hai..please apne personal aur environmental hygiene maintain rakhen.

Rough meaning in English: Because COVID cases are very much rising…so right now the situation over here is very serious…so this is the situation right now…please do work from home…you can make reservations yourselves from the online booking system…make an appointment as soon as possible…protecting yourselves is essential…please maintain your personal and environmental hygiene.

The host's language use is interesting. This is partly because some of the novel technical and medical concepts (e.g. nouns like 'social distance') might not necessarily have readily available equivalents in Hindi. Also, this more relaxed and informal style of announcement is reflective of the latest trends in India and South Asia as a whole in recent decades, where English words and expressions are extensively used in local languages. Furthermore, from a communicative perspective, this style of announcement is more friendly and accessible to many local Indians and South Asians in Hong Kong who have lived in a multilingual and multicultural environment for generations (where code-switching for example between a South Asian language and English is commonplace). This illustrates the flexibility and even creativity enjoyed by relevant agent(s) during the crisis communication process. As a 'translation' of the government's official COVID policies, rules, and advice to the South Asian communities in Hong Kong, this relaxed and approachable style of delivery is arguably more effective during crisis communication, compared with a more rigid style of 'translation' using language in the pure, formal and 'correct' form.

3.6.3 Translation and Multilingual Communication on Hong Kong's Audio-Landscape

Having discussed translation/multilingual communication evidenced on Hong Kong's physical linguistic landscape and digital/virtual space, attention now is focused on Hong Kong's audio-landscape or sound-space. While physical and visible linguistic landscape traditionally is almost the 'go-to' area for researchers, this article argues that audio-landscape or sound-scape also constitutes an integral part of a place's linguistic repertoires during its multilingual crisis communication. For example, in various high-profile and popular locations (e.g. Central and Tsim Sha Tsui) with a high footfall, COVID-related public announcements can be heard. Compared with one particular multilingual written text, audio messages communicated via a loudspeaker arguably cover a significantly wider area and may thus be more effective in conveying a sense of urgency and drawing people's attention to the COVID rules.

Notably, multilingual public announcements in Cantonese, Mandarin and English are routinely made in sections of the Tsim Sha Tsui promenade along the waterfront of the world-famous Victoria Harbour. Since this is a popular area where families and friends tend to gather to relax and admire Hong Kong's skyline, it makes sense that multilingual announcements are made here via the loudspeaker to constantly remind people to wear masks and socially distance. Given that the waterfront area of the Victoria Harbour is visited by people from different backgrounds (rather than one homogeneous group), the Mandarin, Cantonese and English versions available can arguably reach out to and cover maximum number of people possible.

In comparison, a targeted approach is, for example, taken in Admiralty on Hong Kong island. Surrounded by the Central Government Offices of Hong Kong Government, the office of the chief executive and the Legislative Council Complex, the Tamar Park in Admiralty is a particularly popular area amongst domestic helpers from Indonesia and the Philippines during the weekend when they have their day off. During the weekends, these domestic helpers tend to relax, rest, have meals, and even party, play music and sing in and around Tamar park. Given the high concentration of these domestic helpers, non-stop multilingual announcements in Tagalog and Indonesian are constantly played from a few loudspeakers in a targeted manner in addition to Cantonese and English. As such, the announcements work to urge them to socially distance, wear a mask, and follow relevant COVID rules and regulations. This without doubt constitutes a case of 'multilingual commanding urgency' (Chesnut, Curran, and Kim 2022) in an audio form.

3.7 Conclusions

This interdisciplinary study has bridged a research gap by studying the macro-level translation and multilingual communication practices in the Hong Kong SAR in a general way against a backdrop of crisis communication relating to the COVID-19 pandemic. Going beyond the traditional focus only on static written content, LL in this study was innovatively expanded to include both traditional written content outdoors and also information available on the digital space (e.g. various dedicated and purpose-made websites and audio-visual materials) and sound-space (e.g. public announcements) aimed at promoting the awareness of the public and certain targeted groups. In addition, this study has taken account of both the top-down (official and government-led) and bottom-up (e.g. by individuals and small businesses) translation and multilingual communication practices in the SAR at various levels and using various platforms and formats.

In particular, in the SAR's top-down multilingual crisis communication, a general but differentiated approach has been established in the provision of translation and multilingual resources. That is, while relevant information regarding COVID rules and vaccination etc. is generally provided multilingually (e.g. major official websites, quarantine facilities and high-profile locales), multilingual materials are usually available and accessible in ethnically diverse areas in a more targeted manner. This makes sense, given that ethnic minority groups tend to be concentrated in certain areas. In addition, bottom-up multilingual content devised by the general public can be found at a grass-roots level, which complements the official top-down multilingual resources. The top-down and bottom-up resources together make up Hong Kong's multilingual Covidscape.

Notably, multilingual crisis communication in Hong Kong is very much an ongoing process as COVID-19 is here to stay. Given the inherent complexity of this topic containing multifarious aspects and elements and the pervasive nature of COVID-19 related signs, it is outwith the scope of this article to conduct a systematic quantitative study (nor is it realistic to address and cover all the issues in this article). The current study is but one humble attempt at unpacking the translation and multilingual communication practices in Hong Kong overall during COVID-19. Beyond the current macro-level analysis, more detailed, fine-tuned and in-depth analysis can be carried out going forward to, for example, focus on specific language(s) and ethnic group(s). Methodologically, it also would be useful to get more first-hand information from the actual translators, text producers, and policy-makers for example via interviews, if at all possible.

Nevertheless, this empirical study has shed light on the various translation and multilingual communication practices in Hong Kong, highlighting the primacy of translation and multilingualism in disseminating information and promoting awareness in a global city. Interdisciplinary in nature, this study contributes to scholarship in translation studies, linguistic landscape, multilingual communication, urban studies, crisis and disaster communication, and also the underexplored area of 'crisis sociolinguistics' (cf. Piller 2020b). Without doubt, through sharing the translation and multilingual communication experiences in Hong Kong, it is hoped that this study will help open up meaningful dialogues with other ethnically and culturally diverse multilingual societies like Dubai, Doha, Riyadh, Singapore, Bangkok, London, Manchester, Birmingham, Leicester, Bradford, Toronto, and New York.

References

Abdulla, D. 2020. Keep your distance, wear a mask and stay safe: The visual language of Covid-19 print-based signage. *Visual Resources* 36 (3): 218–246.

Ahmad, R., and S. Hillman. 2020. Laboring to communicate: Use of migrant languages in COVID-19 awareness campaign in Qatar. *Multilingua* 40 (3): 303–337.

Ben-Rafael, E., E. Shohamy, M. Hasan Amara, and N. Trumper-Hecht. 2006. Linguistic landscape as symbolic construction of the public space: The case of Israel. *International Journal of Multilingualism* 3 (1): 7–30.

Bober, S., and C. Willis. 2021. The Covid-19 pandemic and minority language media in Europe: The effects of spring 2020 lockdowns. *Journal of Multilingual and Multicultural Development.*

Cairney, P., and A. Wellstead. 2021. COVID-19: Effective policymaking depends on trust in experts, politicians, and the public. *Policy Design and Practice* 4 (1): 1–14.

Chan, A.T., and J.S. Brownstein. 2020. Putting the public back in public health - Surveying symptoms of COVID-19. *The New England Journal of Medicine* 383: e45.

Chen, X. 2020. Fighting COVID-19 in East Asia: The role of classical Chinese poetry. *Multilingua* 39 (5): 565–576.

Chesnut, M., N. M. Curran, and S. Kim. 2022. From garbage to COVID-19: Theorizing 'Multilingual Commanding Urgency' in the linguistic landscape. *Multilingua*.

Cronin, M. 2006. *Translation and identity*. London: Routledge.

Cronin, M. 2017. *Eco-translation: Translation and ecology in the age of the Anthropocene*. London: Routledge.

Declercq, C., and F.M. Federici. 2020. *Intercultural crisis communication: Translation, interpreting and languages in local crises*. London/New York: Bloomsbury Publishing.

Goldberg, Y., M. Mandel, Y.M. Bar-On, O. Bodenheimer, L.S. Freedman, N. Ash, S. Alroy-Preis, A. Huppert, and R. Milo. 2022. Protection and waning of natural and hybrid immunity to SARS-CoV-2. *New England Journal of Medicine* 386: 2201–2212.

Greenhalgh, T., J.L. Jimenez, K.A. Prather, Z. Tufekci, D. Fisman, and R. Schooley. 2021. Ten scientific reasons in support of airborne transmission of SARS-CoV-2. *The Lancet* 397 (10285): 1603–1605.

Gu, C. 2018. Forging a glorious past via the 'present perfect': A corpus-based CDA analysis of China's past Accomplishments discourse mediat(is)ed at China's interpreted political press conferences. *Discourse, Context and Media* 24: 137–149.

Gu, C. 2019. (Re)manufacturing consent in English: A corpus-based critical discourse analysis of government interpreters' mediation of China's discourse on PEOPLE at televised political press conferences. *Target* 31 (3): 465–499.

Gu, C. 2022. Interpreters as vital (re)tellers of China's reform and opening-up meta-narrative: A digital humanities (DH) approach to institutional interpreters' mediation. *Frontiers in Psychology* 13: 892791.

Haddow, G.D., and K. Haddow. 2014. *Disaster communications in a changing media world*. Amsterdam: Butterworth-Heinemann.

Landry, R., and R.Y. Bourhis. 1997. Linguistic landscape and ethnolinguistic vitality: An empirical study. *Journal of Language and Social Psychology* 6: 23–49.

Lee, J., and T. Ingold. 2006. Fieldwork on foot: Perceiving, routing, socializing. In *Locating the field: Space, place and context in anthropology*, ed. S. Coleman and P. Collins, 67–85. London: Routledge.

Lee, T.K. 2013. *Translating the multilingual city: Cross-lingual practices and language ideology*. Oxford: Peter Lang.

Lee, T.K. 2021. *The Routledge handbook of translation and the city*. London: Routledge.

Lha, Y. 2020. Fighting the coronavirus in local languages. *Language on the Move*. https://www.languageonthemove.com/fighting-the-coronavirus-in-local-languages/. Accessed 7 July 2020.

Marshall, S. 2021. Navigating COVID-19 linguistic landscapes in Vancouver's North Shore: Official signs, grassroots literacy artefacts, monolingualism, and discursive convergence. *International Journal of Multilingualism*.

Mathews, G., and Y. Yang. 2012. How Africans pursue low-end globalization in Hong Kong and Mainland China. *Journal of Current Chinese Affairs* 41 (2): 95–120.

Mcculloch, G. 2020. Covid-19 is history's biggest translation challenge. *Wired*. https://www.wired.com/story/covid-language-translation-problem/. Accessed 14 July 2020.

Piller, I. 2018. Dubai: Language in the ethnocratic, corporate and mobile city. In *Urban sociolinguistics: The city as a linguistic process and experience*, ed. D. Smakman and P. Heinrich, 77–94. Abingdon, Oxon: Routledge.

Piller, I. 2020a. Covid-19 forces us to take linguistic diversity seriously. In *12 perspectives on the pandemic*, ed. G. Boomgaarden, 12–17. Berlin: De Gruyter.

Piller, I. 2020b. Language challenges of Covid-19 are a pressing issue. *Language on the Move*. https://www.languageonthemove.com/language-challenges-of-covid-19-are-a-pressing-issue/.

Piller, I., J. Zhang, and J. Li. 2020. Linguistic diversity in a time of crisis: Language challenges of the COVID-19 pandemic. *Multilingua* 39 (5): 503–515.

Reynolds, B., and M. Seeger. 2005. Crisis and emergency risk communication as an integrative model. *Journal of Health Communication* 10 (1): 43–55.
Rudwick, S., Z. Sijadu, and I. Turner. 2021. Politics of language in COVID-19: Multilingual perspectives from South Africa. *Politikon* 48 (2): 242–259.
Tan, M.S., and S.B. Said. 2015. Linguistic landscape and exclusion: An examination of language representation in disaster signage in Japan. In *Conflict, exclusion and dissent in the linguistic landscape*, ed. R. Rubdy and S.B. Said, 145–169. London: Palgrave Macmillan UK.
Uekusa, S. 2019. Disaster linguicism: Linguistic minorities in disasters. *Language in Society* 48 (3): 353–375.
Vertovec, S. 2007. Super-diversity and its implications. *Ethnic and Racial Studies* 29 (6): 1024–1054.
Wang, G., S. A. Bahry, and W. An. 2022. Minority language revitalization and social media through the lens of Covid-19 in Yunnan and Gansu, western China. *Journal of Multilingual and Multicultural Development*.
Wang, L., and A. Kirkpatrick. 2015. Trilingual education in Hong Kong primary schools: An overview. *Multilingual Education* 5: 3.
Wang, X., Z. Pan, and Z. Cheng. 2020. Association between 2019-nCoV transmission and N95 respirator use. *Journal of Hospital Infection* 105 (1): 104–105.

Chonglong Gu is currently Assistant Professor in translation and interpreting at The Hong Kong Polytechnic University. Taking an interdisciplinary and socially engaged perspective to language, his research interests lie in translation and interpreting studies, discourse analysis, corpus linguistics, media and communication studies, multilingualism, linguistic landscape, and Chinese studies. His miscellaneous writings have appeared in several SSCI-indexed journals including Target, The Translator, Perspectives, Translation and Interpreting Studies, Discourse, Context and Media, Critical Discourse Studies, Language and Intercultural Communication, Frontiers in Psychology, and various book chapters (Routledge, Springer, Peter Lang etc.). He previously taught at different universities in mainland China, Hong Kong and the UK.

Chapter 4
What is Chinese? A Case Study of the Chinese Translations of Government Guidance and Regulations in Relation to COVID-19 in the UK

Yu Kit Cheung

> *This disease is beyond my practice.*
> *—William Shakespeare, Macbeth 5.1.60*
> (See Proudfoot et al. 2011)

Abstract This paper is a report of my mixed-methods study of the government guidance and regulations in relation to COVID-19 published by the UK Health Security Agency. The aims are to address a series of questions regarding Chinese translations in the medical context of the United Kingdom and to assess the quality of the Chinese translated materials. There were three major findings. First, Chinese translations of the guiding materials for the public were provided only on a selective basis. Second, Traditional Chinese as a writing script has been misinterpreted as the written form of Cantonese. Third, quantitative analysis showed that the translators of the documents in question were likely to be aware of the meaning-based feature of the Chinese language, suggesting their attempt to keep sentences concise. Nevertheless, a textual study of the translation of 'you' and 'your' in the excerpts demonstrated that more of them should be taken out in the target text so as to better conform to the norm of the Chinese language. In addition to the above discoveries, it has also been pointed out that results from Chinese corpora may not be indicative of how Chinese translation should be done. Cheung's (2021) seven defining characteristics of the Chinese language may offer an outline of the norms of Chinese. Finally, much as a fit-for-purpose translation may be acceptable for one reason or another, it is argued that a translation demonstrating a high quality of writing in the target language does not only ensure effective communication but also shows respect for the ethnic minorities in a multicultural country in this unprecedented pandemic!

Y. K. Cheung (✉)
University of Manchester, Manchester, UK
e-mail: yukit.cheung@manchester.ac.uk

K. Liu and A. K. F. Cheung (eds.), *Translation and Interpreting in the Age of COVID-19*, Corpora and Intercultural Studies 9,
https://doi.org/10.1007/978-981-19-6680-4_4

Keywords Chinese translation · Quality assessment · Traditional Chinese · Simplified Chinese · COVID-19

4.1 Introduction

The role of translation in a pandemic such as COVID-19 requires no elucidation. It is not only necessary to facilitate effective communication between medical personnel and the patient in a medical setting but also to ensure that guidance for the general public is understood by those who may struggle with the official language(s) in a multicultural society such as the United Kingdom.

In this country, there is not an official translation policy laid down by the government. In the medical context, every hospital trust or even surgery makes its own policy and provides translations and interpreting services as per their needs. These services of up to 30 languages are provided in response to the *Human Rights Act* (1998) and *Equality Act* (2010). Article 14 of the Human Rights Act 1998 prohibits discrimination of human rights on grounds of language:

> The enjoyment of the rights and freedoms set forth in this Convention shall be secured without discrimination on any ground such as sex, race, colour, *language*, religion, political or other opinion, national or social origin, association with a national minority, property, birth or other status (*Human Rights Act* 1998: Schedule 1; emphasis added).

Moreover, an authority is obliged to 'reduce the inequalities of outcome which result from socio-economic disadvantage' (*Equality Act* 2010: Part 1, Sect. 1)—race is one of the nine characteristics under protection by this Act (ibid.: Part 2, Cp. 1, Sect. 4).

Information about COVID-19 is released by a variety of departments of the UK Government. One of them which plays a central role is the UK Health Security Agency (hereinafter 'UKHSA'), a successor of Public Health England—the former has replaced the latter after April 2021 as the executive agency of the Department of Health and Social Care. Since the start of the pandemic, 117 documents under the category of 'Guidance and Regulations' with respect to COVID-19 have been published by UKHSA, and Chinese translation is available in nearly 30 of them to date (UK Government n.d.).

A quick survey of them gives rise to some interesting observations. For example, a distinction between Traditional Chinese and Simplified Chinese is made in some documents but not in others. Instead, the generic term 'Chinese' is adopted, which refers only to the latter. The word 'Cantonese' is sometimes added after 'Traditional', which is perplexing as the former refers to a dialect whereas the latter one of the two Chinese writing scripts.[1] This paper seeks to address three sets of questions:

[1] Whilst Cantonese is generally subsumed under Chinese as a dialect, its differences in grammar and pronunciation from Mandarin, the official variety of Chinese, are so vast that they are somewhat mutually unintelligible, defying our conventional understanding of 'dialect' in Linguistics (Crystal 2008: 142).

i. It is obvious that translation is provided only on a selective basis. What documents are translated? What are the selection criteria, if any?
ii. Chinese as a language is a pluralistic concept, for there are two written scripts: Traditional Chinese and Simplified Chinese. Does 'Chinese' necessarily refer to the latter in the context of the UK? Whilst Traditional Chinese is officially adopted in Hong Kong, Macau, and Taiwan, Simplified Chinese is the official variety in Mainland China, Singapore, and Malaysia. If translation is available in both scripts, do the two versions differ only in the script?
iii. What is the quality of the Chinese translated texts? Is there translation-ese? If so, does it impede the effective conveyance of message to the target text readers?

4.2 Research Methods

This study is as quantitative as it is qualitative, intending to problematise the notion of Chinese translation in the medical context of the United Kingdom through a case study of the government guidance and regulations concerning COVID-19 published by UKHSA. Questions i and ii are answered in Sects. 3 and 4. Documents with Chinese translations on the pandemic from UKHSA, including those inherited from Public Health England, together with four relevant documents available in English only, are collected from the Government portal for information and services (UK Government n.d.). They are presented in Table 4.1, arranged in accordance with the date of the last update. In addition to the title of the document, there are four more columns (*d*–*g*) in the table to indicate the version of the document in English, whether there is just a Chinese translation in general (column *e*), or a distinction has been made between Simplified Chinese (column *f*) or Traditional Chinese (column *g*).

Question iii will be addressed in Sect. 5, which is a statistical and textual study of the Chinese versions. Light will first be cast upon the complexity of the notion of natural translation in Chinese. Attention will then be paid to *nin* 您 as a translation of 'you' or 'your'. Whilst it will be pointed out statistically that there is usually a smaller number of *nin* in the Chinese texts than the second-person pronoun 'you' or determiner 'your' in the English counterpart, showing the translator's awareness of the meaning-based nature (*yihe* 意合) of Chinese as a language, it will be argued from a qualitative perspective that a great many *nin* in the Chinese translations can actually be taken out without compromising the meaning of the translated text. As a matter of fact, preserving the only necessary *nin* in the Chinese text can make it an even more concise read, enhancing the fluency and hence the effectiveness of the Chinese versions.

This study is significant in pushing the frontiers of the Chinese translation of medical texts in the UK, arguing that a translation demonstrating a high quality of writing in the target language does not only enhance communication but also shows respect for the ethnic minorities in a multicultural country such as the United Kingdom.

4.3 Data

The data collected for this study are presented in Table 4.1.

4.4 Data Analysis

Several observations emerged from Table 4.1. The texts of guidance are presented in various forms. In addition to articles, they are sometimes in the form of posters, for example, Document 7 which encourages pregnant women to be inoculated. In fact, along with the poster is provided a set of social media banners for use on social media 'including Facebook, Twitter, WhatsApp' (UK Health Security Agency 2021).

Chinese translation is offered for most of the documents. In the 28 documents collected, only Documents 10, 19, 21 and 27 are not provided with translations. These documents seem to be those with a smaller readership in their original language. Document 10 is for parents of children between 5 and 11 years old at high risk; Document 19 is a poster informing patients of the termination of the 15-min observation policy after vaccination. Document 21 provides guidance for schools rather than the general public. That means, translation is not required as readers are presumably proficient in English. Document 27 is an easy guide to the vaccination of the COVID-19 booster jab. Considering the small number of ethnic Chinese in the UK—393,141 according to Census of England and Wales 2011 (UK Government 2020), it makes sense that the Chinese version is not provided for these four documents as the need for them, if any, amongst Chinese readers will proportionately be reduced.

There could be a time lag between the Chinese translated version and the latest version of the source text. Whilst Version 3 of the guidance for parents of young people and children regarding the COVID-19 vaccination was available to the English readers, available in Chinese is, in fact, the first version (UK Government 2021), according to the webpage 'COVID-19 vaccination: resources for schools and parents' (ibid.). Nevertheless, it was found that the Chinese version available for download is already the third version (UK Health Security Agency and NHS 2021).

It seems that no distinction was made between Traditional Chinese and Simplified Chinese before the year 2022. All Chinese translations were in Simplified Chinese given under the all-encompassing term 'Chinese'. The choice between Traditional Chinese and Simplified Chinese is rather a recent phenomenon, beginning only in 2022.

The provision of the Simplified Chinese version only by the UK Government sounds well-grounded because this is the variety of Chinese writing script adopted in Mainland China, the largest Chinese-speaking community in the world. Nevertheless, this could stand in contrast to the real picture in the UK, at least in some of the largest cities such as London and Manchester (UK Government 2020). The Traditional Chinese script, in fact, seems to be in popular use among Chinese people in the UK because a great number of migrants in the twentieth century were Cantonese

Table 4.1 Guidance for the Public respecting COVID-19

a	b	c	d	e	f	g
No.	Title of Document	Last updated	Version (if any)	Chinese	Simplified Chinese	Traditional Chinese
1	Living Safely with Respiratory Infections, including COVID-19 (Apr 2022)	16 June 2022	N/A		✓	✓
2	People with Symptoms of a Respiratory Infection including COVID-19 (Apr 2022)	10 June 2022	N/A		✓	✓
3	Reducing the Spread of Respiratory Infections, including COVID-19, in the Workplace (Apr 2022)	10 June 2022	N/A		✓	✓
4	Patient Information for Molnupiravir (Feb 2022)	4 May 2022	N/A		✓	✓ (Cantonese)
5	Patient Information for Paxlovid (Feb 2022)	4 May 2022	N/A		✓	✓ (Cantonese)
6	Pregnant? Have your COVID-19 vaccinations (Aug 2020)	11 April 2022	N/A	✓		
7	Pregnant? Have your COVID-19 vaccinations [Poster] (2020)	11 April 2022	N/A	✓		

(continued)

Table 4.1 (continued)

a	b	c	d	e	f	g
8	COVID-19 Vaccination: A guide for parents of children aged 5 to 11 (Mar 2022)	28 March 2022	V1		✓	✓ (Cantonese)
9	What to Expect after your Child's COVID-19 Vaccination? (Jan 2022)	28 March 2022	V1		✓	✓ (Cantonese)
10	COVID-19 Vaccinations: A guide for parents of children aged 5 to 11 years of age at high risk (Jan 2022)	28 March 2022	V1	N/A	N/A	N/A
11	COVID-19 Vaccine: A guide to the spring booster for those aged 75 years and older residents in care homes (Feb 2022)	24 March 2022	V2		✓	✓ (Cantonese)
12	COVID-19 Vaccine for People with a Weakened Immune System (2021/ March 2022s)	24 March 2022	V3		✓	✓ (Cantonese)
13	COVID-19 Vaccine: Your guide to booster vaccination [for people aged 18 years & over, and those aged 16 years & who are at risk] (Dec 2021)	2 February 2022	V1	✓		

(continued)

Table 4.1 (continued)

a	b	c	d	e	f	g
14	COVID-19 Vaccine: Your guide to booster Vaccination [for people aged 16 years & over, and those aged 12 years & over who are at risk] (Dec 2021)	2 February 2022	V1	✓		
15	COVID-19 Vaccination: A guide for children and young people [aged 12 to 17] (Nov 2021)	1 February 2022	V3	✓		
16	Your Guide to a Second Dose of COVID-19 Vaccine: Are you 16 or 17? (Nov 2021)	1 February 2022	V1	✓		
17	COVID-19 Vaccination: A guide for children and young people [aged 12 to 17 & booster for aged 16 to 17 and children at risk aged 12 to 15] (Jan 2022)	1 February 2022	V3	✓		
18	What to Expect after your COVID-19 Vaccination: Advice for children and young people (Nov 2021)	1 February 2022	V2	✓		

(continued)

Table 4.1 (continued)

a	b	c	d	e	f	g
19	End to 15 min Observation after your COVID-19 Vaccination! (2021) [poster]	1 February 2022	N/A	N/A	N/A	N/A
20	COVID-19 Vaccine: Waiting after your COVID-19 vaccination (Dec 2021)	1 February 2022	V1	✓		
21	Coronavirus (COVID-19) Vaccination programme for children and young people: Guidance for schools (2021)	19 January 2022	V3	N/A	N/A	N/A
22	Coronavirus (COVID-19) Vaccination programme for Children and Young People: Guidance for parents (Nov 2021)	19 January 2022	V3	✓		
23	COVID-19 Vaccination for Adults: A guide to the programme (Nov 2021)	19 January 2022	N/A	✓		
24	A Guide to your COVID-19 Vaccination (easy read) (Oct 2021)	2 December 2021	N/A	✓		
25	What to Expect after Vaccination (easy read) (Feb 2021)	2 December 2021	N/A	✓		

(continued)

Table 4.1 (continued)

a	b	c	d	e	f	g
26	A Guide for Women who might Get Pregnant, who are Pregnant or are Breastfeeding their Baby (easy read) (Aug 2021)	2 December 2021	N/A	✓		
27	Easy Read Guide to the COVID-19 Booster Vaccination (Nov 2021)	2 December 2021	N/A	N/A	N/A	N/A
28	What to Expect after your Vaccination (Sep 2021)	9 November 2021	V6	✓		

speakers (Minority Rights Group International 2018). It is widely seen in the arches of Chinatowns, road signs, Chinese newspapers such as *Sing Tao Daily*, Chinese dim-sum restaurant menus, Chinese supermarkets and beyond.

Nevertheless, Chinese translation as a concept and option could be ambiguous and used loosely. Whilst there are two options—Chinese (Simplified) and Chinese (traditional, Cantonese)—provided on the website (UK Government 2022), such a distinction is not consistently made in the printed copy of Document 9 (UK Health Security Agency and NHS 2022f).

It is interesting to note that 'Cantonese' is placed in brackets after 'Traditional Chinese' in six documents such as Documents 5 and 8 (UK Health Security Agency and NHS 2022c, g). In these guidance materials, written Chinese has obviously been conflated with the spoken language. It is important to note that the dichotomy between Traditional Chinese and Simplified Chinese refers to the script only. In spite of a great number of dialects across China, there is just one written language comprised of characters. It is worthy to mention that 'Cantonese' has been discarded after 'Traditional' in the latest documents (e.g. Documents 1 and 3) (UK Health Security Agency n.d. a; UK Health Security Agency n.d. c) where Chinese versions in both scripts are available. Nonetheless, it is not clear whether this is out of an awareness of the inappropriate mapping of a writing script onto a dialect until there are further documents providing translations into both Traditional Chinese and Simplified Chinese are available.

The confusion is highly likely the result of the association of Traditional Chinese with Cantonese, a dialect spoken by nearly 90% of the population in Hong Kong

(2021 Population Census Office, Census and Statistics Department, HKSAR 2022). It is noted that the inclusion of 'Cantonese' after 'traditional' did not start until early 2022 (see e.g. Document 5) (UK Health Security Agency and NHS 2022g). This could be ascribed to the increasing number of Hong Kongers residing in the UK owing to a new settlement scheme offered to holders of the British National (Overseas) passport in Hong Kong from 31st January 2021 by the UK Government (Home Office 2022), although further evidence is required to establish this link.

Nevertheless, such misinterpretation does not seem to be an individual problem of the UK Government; the inaccurate understanding of the relationship between Cantonese and Traditional Chinese is also seen in the newspaper. The following is a recent example from *The Telegraph*, a reputable newspaper in the UK:

> The estate agent has placed signs in Cantonese in its windows and set up a special Asia Pacific helpdesk to deal with the huge increase in demand (Warrington 2022).

The Cantonese referred to is likely to be the Traditional Chinese script.

This misconception is even seen in professional bodies. In a list of 'Certification Languages Tested' offered by The National Accreditation Authority for Translators and Interpreters Ltd (NAATI) of Australia, Cantonese is one of the languages offered for the 'Certified Translator' test, which is a written test (NAATI 2022: 1). This misapprehension is further confirmed when Mandarin is not offered for this written test (ibid.: 2). On the 'about' page introducing NAATI, Cantonese is one of the written languages (NAATI 2021a). Nonetheless, when one clicks on the link 'Cantonese', the Chinese equivalent is, somewhat surprisingly, 'Traditional Chinese' (NAATI 2021b).

The stereotypical connection between Cantonese and Hong Kong is evident from NAATI's self-introduction on its English website. Before each language (including dialect) is given the flag for the territory where that language is spoken. In front of Cantonese is the regional flag of the Hong Kong Special Administrative Region (NAATI 2021a). Nonetheless, this is a reductive understanding because Cantonese is also spoken in Guangzhou and Macau. Likewise, the national flag of the People's Republic of China is provided before Mandarin (ibid.). This, too, seems to be an overgeneralisation, for Mandarin is also one of the official languages of Singapore and Malaysia, to name but two.

Where both the Simplified Chinese translation and Traditional Chinese translation are provided, the two versions are sometimes quite different, for example, Documents 1 and 2. It is reasonable to establish that they were translated separately. In some documents such as Documents 4, 5, 11, and 12, however, the Traditional Chinese version and Simplified Chinese version are generally identical in every way, except for a few terms which reflect the difference in usage between Mainland China and Hong Kong. For example, whilst 'information' is normally rendered as *xinxi* 信息 in Mainland China, *zixun* 資訊 is more commonly seen as a Chinese equivalent in Hong Kong. Such a difference is duly displayed in the two Chinese versions of Document 3 (UK Health Security Agency n.d. b: 1; UK Health Security Agency n.d. c: 1). Nevertheless, this is not always the case. Much as HIV is correctly rendered as *aizibing du* 艾兹病毒 in the Simplified Chinese version of Document 12 (UK Health Security Agency and NHS 2022d: 1), the more common translation *aizibing du* 愛

滋病毒 in Hong Kong has not been adopted in the Traditional Chinese version.[2] Instead, the translation is the same as the Simplified Chinese version (UK Health Security Agency and NHS 2022e: 1).

These discoveries generate a series of questions for further research: the provision of the Traditional Chinese version suggests that the commissioner is aware of the evolving Chinese population and needs. As will be seen, the Chinese translations unveil deviation from the defining characteristics of the Chinese language in one way or another. Is there a gatekeeper in the UK Government of the (Chinese) translations? If so, what is their background? What is the process of quality assurance and quality control of the LSP(s) (language services providers) concerned?

4.5 Quality

This section addresses our third question: what is the quality of the translation? In particular, is the quality of Chinese writing high? Is the communication function of the translation impeded by any translation-ese? I argue, as mentioned, that a high quality of Chinese writing in the translation of these materials can enhance not only communication, not least the publication outlets such as posters and social media cards necessitate concise Chinese, but also the level of respect for the Chinese community in a multicultural country.

Quality is a multifaceted concept that can be looked into from different perspectives. From the translation industry's point of view, quality can be conceptualised in three ways according to Mossop, Hong, and Teixeira's seminal work on translation revision and editing (2001/2020: 6–12). The first is how far the translation can satisfy the client's specifications (ibid.: 7). For example, in their guide to potential users of translation services, the American Translators Association has made it clear that '[t]he quality of a translation is the degree to which it follows the agreed-upon specifications' (Durban and Melby 2008: 4).

The second type of quality refers to how well is the translation so as to 'protect and promote the target language' (Mossop, Hong, and Teixeira 2001/2020: 8). With reference to ISO 17100 'Translation Services –Requirements for Translation Services', Mossop refers to the third type of quality as 'suitability' for the translation purpose (ibid.).

Lauscher (2000) has also provided an overview of the three approaches to exploring 'quality'. Pointing out the inadequacy of the existing Translation Quality Assessment (TQA) models such as the well-known one designed by Juliane House, Lauscher (2000) argues that in addition to the 'equivalence-based approaches' (ibid.: 151–156), 'functional approaches' (ibid.: 156–158), the quality of translation is also 'a matter of agreement' (ibid.: 162–163).

[2] Notwithstanding identical transliteration of the two translations, the first character in the two Chinese renditions is not the same. The pronunciation of 愛 and 艾 is different in Cantonese.

There is a plethora of TQA models and critical ideas on translation quality, which have been comprehensively covered in Chapters two and four of Drugan (2013: 35–80; 125–181). It is notable, however, that the importance of the quality of writing in the target language has not usually been given considerable attention until Toury's norms. In his hierarchy norms, one of them that might be relevant to the issue in question is textual-linguistic norms, which 'govern the selection of linguistic material for the formulation of the target text' (Toury 1995/2012: 83), although they 'may be more or less general' (ibid.). Chesterman has put forward another set of norms, and the one pertinent to our discussion is the expectancy norms, which refer to the 'expectations of readers of a translation (of a given type) concerning what a translation (of this type) should be like' (Chesterman 1997/2016: 62).

There might be two reasons why the writing quality of the target language has not assumed a more prominent position. The first is that this has generally not been the major object of scrutiny. In the long line of translation theories, the critical debate has revolved around the very issue of equivalence (Pym 2010/2014: 3). From the industry's perspective, the translation product is only part of the multi-stage process, much less the writing quality of the target language. For various reasons, a good enough quality of writing in the target language could be more cost-efficient and preferable.

The quality of writing in the target language seems to play a greater role in the translation tests administered by professional bodies, though. According to the assessment rubrics of the Certified Translator Test of NAATI, one of the assessment criteria is the ability to apply 'textual norms and conventions'—to obtain the highest band, a translation is expected to demonstrate 'accomplished use of register, style and text structure appropriate to the genre and consistent with the *norms and conventions of the target language*' (NAATI 2020: 2; emphasis added). In terms of language competence of the target language, the translator is expected to use the 'written language competently and idiomatically, in accordance with the norms of the target language' in a consistent manner (ibid.).

The importance of the norms in the evaluation of the translation is further seen when the language competence requirement for Band 1 is compared with that of the lower bands (Band 2—Band 5). The measurement of the translator's target language competence is the degree to which the use of language of the translated text conforms to the norms of the target language: 'mostly' (Band 2), 'some' (Band 3), 'limited' (Band 4), or 'no demonstrated ability' (Band 5) (NAATI 2020: 2).

In addition to the norms of the target language, some assessment rubrics may go even further to make it clear that a translation of the highest quality should be able to pass as a piece of original writing in the target language. The Chartered Institute of Linguists (CIOL) of the UK has recently launched a new translation test for Certificate in Translation (CertTrans). To obtain the highest band of score in the unit for 'Government and Public Service Translation Skills', it is expected that.

> [t]he target language reads like a piece originally written in the target language with one or two minor errors (CIOL 2022: 14).

CIOL is not alone in the expectation of the target language quality. In the Tripos of the Faculty of Modern and Medieval Languages and Linguistics, translations into English are also expected to 'read fluently like an authentic piece of English' in Papers A2, B2, and C in order to obtain a mark of 70 or above, a 'very good' or 'excellent' mark (Faculty of Modern and Medieval Languages and Linguistics 2020b: 1; Faculty of Modern and Medieval Languages and Linguistics 2020c: 1), although there does not seem to be an equivalent requirement in the translation into a foreign language (Faculty of Modern and Medieval Languages and Linguistics 2020a).

The notion of norm goes hand in hand with corpora as it was because of the development of corpus linguistics which led to Baker's (1993) paper of formative influence on identifying translation universals from corporal findings. Nevertheless, corporal results may not be indicative of how a linguistic item should be translated. This is because the norms of Chinese are inevitably, as one can imagine, different in various Chinese-speaking communities, considering the wide divergence in social developments and ways of life between Mainland China, Hong Kong, and Taiwan, not to mention Malaysia and Singapore. An expression or a sentence structure common in one region could be considered unacceptable in another. The choice of the measure word (*liangci* 量詞) when translating the noun phrase 'an apple' is a case in point: although it is common to say *yili pingguo*一粒蘋果 instead of *yige pingguo*一個蘋果 in Malaysia, *li* 粒 is generally not considered to be a correct measure word by speakers of Chinese in Mainland China, Hong Kong, and Taiwan.

A high frequency of a linguistic item in the corpus does not necessarily ensure translation quality due to common errors in the usage of Chinese. For instance, '*quanqiu fanwei nei* 全球範圍內', repeatedly seen in commercial texts, is often taken to be an equivalent of 'globally', appearing 2446 times in the corpus of the BLCU Corpus Centre (Dashuju yu yuyan jiaoyu yanjiusuo n.d.) and 1213 times in the corpus of the Center for Chinese Linguistics of Peking University (Center for Chinese Linguistics PKU n.d. a). Nonetheless, *fanwei nei* (in the area) renders the whole phrase verbose insomuch as *quan* (whole) in *quanqiu* (the whole word) already encapsulates the meaning of 'in the area'. A frequency of 1213 or 2446 is not high when compared with *fazhan* 發展, for example, which appears 518,710 times according to the CCL corpus (Center for Chinese Linguistics PKU n.d. b), but it unquestionably answers the purpose to illustrate that it is recurrently used.

4.5.1 Translation Quality and the Defining Characteristics of Chinese

It has been shown the tension between the importance of 'norms' as a measurement of the success of a translation and the challenge to specify them. To this end, the defining characteristics of the Chinese language discussed in Cheung (2021) may serve a good purpose in measuring the effectiveness of Chinese writing of the texts in question.

Arguing that translation as a linguistic activity is resistance against under-representation of the linguistic features of the target language, Cheung (2021) proposes the inclusion of the defining characteristics of the Chinese language in textbooks or course syllabi on English-Chinese translation for more effective teaching. There are seven:

(a) *yihe* (meaning-based)
(b) linearity
(c) dynamism
(d) concreteness
(e) emphasis on humans and human relationship
(f) emphasis on a sense of balance
(g) emphasis on holism.

These features are defining because they reflect the Chinese cultural characteristics and worldview.

The meaning-based feature of the Chinese language is more commonly known as parataxis in academic discourse. Nevertheless, this concept mainly refers to a syntactic phenomenon where 'constructions of equal status (co-ordination)…are linked solely through juxtaposition and punctuation/intonation' (Crystal 2008: 350). However, the idea of *yihe*, literally meaning 'meaning connection', is much broader than 'parataxis'. According to Lee and Tse, the reader makes sense of the grammatical relationship of a sentence from the context (1994: 11), unlike the English language where the relationship between constituents in a sentence is generally more clearly spelt out, although it must be pointed out that Chinese does have its grammar (see, for example, Ross and Ma 2014). Light has been cast on such confusion between 'parataxis' and the 'meaning-based' feature of Chinese in Li (2011). As the context has a greater part to play in Chinese sentences, what is required in English may sometimes be legitimately excluded in the Chinese translation.

One of the constituents that can be left out is connectives on condition that the relationship between sentences is unambiguous from the context. Sentence subjects, once mentioned, may not be required in subsequent sentences as well. Moreover, pronouns, which might be required as a subject or object in English, may sometimes be removed in Chinese.

Since Chinese has relatively fewer connecting devices and any component in a sentence can be—in theory—excised due to the meaning-based feature of the language, it is common to see that the word order of a sentence is arranged in accordance with the causal relationship or time sequence of events.

Cheung (2021: 447) argues that there is a close relationship between the world view of Chinese culture and the Chinese language. That Chinese people see the world as a 'dynamic system where constant alternation between the *yin* energy and *yang* energy tak[ing] place' has contributed to the strong preference for verbal constructions in Chinese. Moreover, concreteness is preferred to abstraction. It may be noted that an inanimate subject in an English sentence would often have become an animate one, or even human, in a Chinese sentence.

In addition to the fondness for concreteness and human subjects, it is often found that speakers of Chinese have a penchant for structures displaying a sense of balance such as repetition of monosyllabic words or the frequent use of bi-syllabic words and four-character expressions. Moreover, these linguistic items showing a balanced structure present a holistic picture simultaneously through a juxtaposition of both positivity and negativity.

Amongst these seven characteristics, the most relevant one to our textual analysis is the meaning-based feature because several types of texts are involved in our data. According to the text-type taxonomy proposed by Reiss (1971; in Venuti 2000: 163–164), the collected texts are informative, although they are, to a certain extent, operative, for they are meant to persuade the readers (general public) to follow the guidelines. Nonetheless, the fact that they have different intended readers and therefore are published in different outlets has implications on the sentence lengths. Included in our data, as mentioned, are web pages, leaflets, posters or even social media cards. Given the limited space allowed in a poster or social media card, sentences are usually shorter. Therefore, this study will focus only on the conformity to the meaning-based feature of Chinese in the target text. In particular, attention will be paid to the translation of the second-person pronoun 'you', based on the statistics in Table 4.2 as 'you' and 'your' have been employed extensively.

4.5.2 Translation of Pronouns

To examine if there is verbosity in the texts concerned, the use of 'you', 'your', 'yourself', '*ni*你', and '*ni* 您', '*nin de* 您的' in all the documents which provide both Traditional Chinese and Simplified Chinese versions has been documented in Table 4.2.

4.5.2.1 Statistical Analysis

'You' can be rendered as either *ni* 你 or *nin* 您, the former is the neutral form and the latter an honorific form. The determiner 'your' is literally translated as *ni de* 你的 or *nin de* 您的. The reflexive pronoun 'yourself' can be recast literally as *ni ziji* 你自己 or *nin ziji* 您自己. Table 4.2 shows that the honorific form of the second person pronoun has been consistently adopted in order to show respect for the readers, conforming to the Chinese politeness principle of holding the addressee in high regard. Therefore, there is no need for separate columns for *ni de* and *ni ziji* in the table.

It was discovered that there is usually a reduction in the number of *nin* (you) in the translation, except for Document 9, where the number of *nin* is higher than the total number of 'you', although the difference is just 1. Document 3 is an exception—the number of *nin* and that of 'you' are the same.

Table 4.2 Statistical data of the Chinese translation of 'you' and 'your'

Document no.	Title of document	English			Traditional Chinese			Simplified Chinese		
		You	Your	Your-self	*Ni* 你	*Nin* 您	*nin de* 您的	*Ni* 你	*Nin* 您	*nin de* 您的
1	Living Safely with Respiratory Infections, including COVID-19 (Apr 2022)	43	28	1	0	38	7	0	37	5
2	People with Symptoms of a Respiratory Infection including COVID-19 (Apr 2022)	124	54	4	0	98	18	0	97	17
3	Reducing the Spread of Respiratory Infections, including COVID-19, in the Workplace (Apr 2022)	5	4	0	0	5	1	0	5	1
4	Patient Information for Molnupiravir (Feb 2022)	15	6	0	0	14	7	0	14	7
5	Patient Information for Paxlovid (Feb 2022)	38	17	0	0	34	14	0	34	14
8	COVID-19 Vaccination: A guide for parents of children aged 5 to 11 (Mar 2022)	30	31	1	0	28	17	0	27	16
9	What to Expect after your Child's COVID-19 Vaccination? (Jan 2022)	16	33	2	0	17	19	0	17	22
11	COVID-19 Vaccine: A guide to the spring booster for those aged 75 years and older residents in care homes (Feb 2022)	41	20	0	0	35	8	0	35	8
12	COVID-19 Vaccine for People with a Weakened Immune System (2021/ March 2022)	31	24	0	0	29	13	0	29	13

The pattern of '*nin de*' seems to be more straightforward. Most of the time, there are fewer '*nin de*' than the corresponding 'your', save Document 4, where there is one more '*nin de*' than 'your'.

Judging from the identical number of *nin* and '*nin de*' in the Traditional Chinese version and Simplified Chinese version in Documents 3, 4, 5, 11, and 12, it is highly likely that the two versions were not translated separately. That said, as pointed out above, attempts have been made to ensure that the choice of words is familiar to the readers of a particular script, although such adjustment is not always correct. Nevertheless, it is not certain whether such changes were done by machine or manually.

Comparing both versions, one may find that the Simplified Chinese version tends to be more concise. Statistically, there are fewer *nin* and '*nin de*' in the Simplified Chinese Version when the number of *nin* and '*nin de*' in the two versions are different. The only case of inconsistency seems to be Document 9—there is no difference in the number of *nin* in both versions whilst the number of '*nin de*' is higher in the Simplified Chinese Version.

4.5.2.2 Textual Analysis

The usual decrease in the number of *nin* and '*nin de*' suggests that the translator is possibly aware of the meaning-based feature of the Chinese language. Nevertheless, textual analysis is still crucial to ascertain whether the translator has demonstrated *enough* awareness of this charactertisic, thereby keeping the use of pronouns to a minimum.

<u>Excerpt 1 (*from Document 5*)</u>

> 即使[1]<u>您的</u>症狀有所改善和/或感覺好轉，也請確保[2]<u>您</u>完成為期五天的療程，以減少病毒出現耐藥性版本的機會。(UK Health Security Agency and NHS 2022g: 1)
>
> *Jishi* ***<u>nin de</u>*** *zhengzhuang you suo gaishan he/huo ganjue haozhuan, ye qing quebao* ***<u>nin</u>*** *wancheng wei qi wutian de liaocheng, yi jianshao bingdu chuxian naiyaoxing banben de jihui.*
>
> Please make sure that [2]**<u>you</u>** complete a 5-day course of this medicine, even if [1]**<u>your</u>** symptoms improve and/or ***<u>you</u>** feel better, to reduce the chances of a treatment-resistant version of the virus developing. (UK Health Security Agency 2022b)

'You' appears twice and 'your' once in the source text. The corresponding positions in the target text have been indicated with a number in square brackets. One may find that the 'you' before 'feel better' in the English version has not been translated. Whilst the use of '*nin de*' and *nin* in the two marked positions is not an error according to the grammar of Standard Modern Chinese, they are, beyond any doubt, redundant, for it is an unspoken understanding in the target language that the guidance is applicable to the reader *and* anybody to whom the document may apply. That means, restricting the subject to the reader is unnecessary, if not rendering the Chinese version awkward to Chinese ears.

Excerpt 2 (*from Document 8*)

Traditional Chinese version:

如果**[1]**您擔心**[2]**您的孩子, 請撥打 NHS 111(或使用文本電話撥打 18001 111) 或訪問111 網站。確保告訴**[3]**他們 **[4]**您孩子接種的疫苗, 或向**[5]**他們出示**[6]**您孩子的記錄卡。(UK Health Security Agency and NHS 2022c: 5)

Simplified Chinese version:

如果**[1]**您担心**[2]** 您的孩子, 请拨打NHS 111 (或使用文本电话拨打 18001 111) , 或访问111网站。确保告诉**[3]** 他们 **[4]**您孩子所接种的疫苗, 或向**[5]**他们出示**[6]**您孩子的记录卡。(UK Health Security Agency and NHS 2022b: 5)

*Ruguo **nin** danxin **nin de** haizi, qing boda NHS111 (huo shiyong wenben dianhua boda 18001 111) huo fangwen 111 wangzhan. Quebao gaosu **tamen nin** haizi jiezhong de yimiao, huo xiang **tamen** chushi **nin** haizi de jiluka.*

English version:

If **[1] you** are worried about **[2] your** child call NHS 111 (or call 18001 111 on a textphone) or go to the NHS 111 website. Make sure ***you** tell **[3] them** about the vaccination **[4] your** child has received, or show **[5] them [6] your** child's record card. (UK Health Security Agency and NHS 2022a: 5)

In this selected text, all pronouns and their possessive forms have been translated, except for 'you' after 'make sure' in the second sentence. For clarity and to facilitate discussion, it has been marked with an asterisk above. Since both versions are identical as far as this excerpt is concerned, the transliteration is given once only.

The first pronoun [1]*nin* makes sense as this is the sentence subject. Nevertheless, the pronouns and their possessive forms [2], [4] and [6] are dispensable. Considering that 'you' has already been mentioned at the beginning, it is well understood that the 'children' in the sentence must be 'your children'. '[5] Them' in the last sentence is required; '[3] them' has to be replaced by 'a member of the staff' as the Chinese language shows a strong preference for concreteness. A pronoun is possible only when a concrete referent is already in place in Standard Modern Chinese.

Excerpt 3 (*from Document 1*)

Traditional Chinese version:

如果[1]您有如 COVID-19 等的呼吸道感染的病徵, 並且[2]您發燒或者覺得不舒服而無法去上班或進行正常活動, 則建議[3]您盡量留在家並避免與他人接觸。(UK Health Security Agency n.d. a: 2)

*Ruguo **nin** you ru COVID-19 deng de huxidao ganran de bingzheng, bingqie **nin** fashao huozhe juede bushufu er wufa qu shangban huo jinxing zhengchang huodong, ze jianyi **nin** jinliang liu zai jia bing bimian yu taren jiechu.*

Simplified Chinese version:

如果[1]您有呼吸道感染症状, 如COVID-19, 并且发高烧或感觉不适, 导致[*]您不能去工作或进行日常活动, 建议[3]您尽量留在家, 避免与他人接触。(UK Health Security Agency n.d. d: 2)

Ruguo **nin** *you huxidao ganran zhengzhuang, ru COVID-19, bingqie fa gaoshao huo ganjue bushi, daozhi* **nin** *buneng qu gongzuo huo jinxing richang huodong, jianyi* **nin** *jinliang liu zai jia, bimian yu taren jiechu.*

English version:

If [1] **you** have symptoms of a respiratory infection, such as COVID-19, and [2] **you** have a high temperature or do not feel well enough to go to work or carry out normal activities, [3] **you** are advised to try to stay at home and avoid contact with other people. (UK Health Security Agency 2022a)

In the Traditional Chinese version, the second-person pronoun 'you' in the three positions of the English version has been brought across correspondingly—all three have been translated. In the Simplified Chinese version, the 'you' before 'have a high temperature' has not been translated. However, the *nin* marked by an asterisk was added unnecessarily by the translator. In any case, both [*]*nin* and [2]*nin* are expendable because subsequent subjects, once mentioned, can be omitted in a Chinese sentence if the subject is unambiguous.

As a matter of fact, this excerpt reveals other problems which also fall within the ambit of the meaning-based feature of the Chinese language. In both versions, various connecting devices have been employed to shed light on the causal relationship. For example, *daozhi* and *er* have been deployed in the Simplified Chinese version and Traditional Chinese version respectively to reflect the causal relationship between feeling unwell and therefore being unable to go to work. However, a comma suffices in Chinese so as to avoid risking a cumbersome sentence. In a similar vein, the *bing* connecting *liu zai jia* and *bimian yu taren jiechu* should be replaced by a comma to prevent the sentence from running too long.

4.6 Concluding Remarks

To sum up, this study has answered a number of questions on the Chinese translations of the UK Government's guidance and regulations for the public. First, Chinese translation is not available for all texts of this genre. Those having a smaller number of readers may not be translated. Second, Chinese as a language is a complex concept employed sometimes in a confusing manner. For example, the Traditional Chinese writing script has been misconstrued by the UK Government and beyond as the written form of Cantonese, which is mainly referred to as a spoken concept. Third, at the start of the COVID-19 pandemic, only Chinese translation in the Simplified Chinese script under the generic term 'Chinese' came along. The Traditional Chinese version was not provided until early 2022. In Sect. 5 of this paper, a statistical analysis showed that the translators of these documents might probably be aware of the meaning-based feature of the Chinese language, suggesting their attempt to keep sentences concise. Nevertheless, a textual study of the translation of 'you' and 'your' in the excerpts demonstrated that more of them should be taken out in the target text so as to better conform to the meaning-based feature of the Chinese language.

This paper has not only thrown light on the Chinese translation of the guiding material for the public on the pandemic. It has also pointed out that conformity to the norm of the target language as a gauge of the success of a translation, which forms an important pillar in the assessment rubrics of the translation tests administered by professional bodies, may not be reliable as far as Chinese is concerned, for findings from Chinese corpora may be misleading. Cheung's (2021) seven defining characteristics of the Chinese language may offer an outline of the norms of Chinese. Finally, much as LSPs may find a fit-for-purpose translation acceptable for one reason or another, I argue that a translation demonstrating a high quality of writing in the target language does not only ensure effective communication but also, more importantly, shows respect for the ethnic minorities in a multicultural country in this unprecedented pandemic!

References

2021 Population Census Office, Census and Statistics Department, HKSAR. 2022. A111: Proportion of population aged 5 and over able to speak selected languages/dialects as the usual spoken languages/ dialects, Proportion of population aged 5 and over able to speak selected languages/dialects as another spoken languages/dialects, Proportion of population aged 5 and over able to speak selected languages/dialects by selected language/dialect and year. *2021 Population Census*. https://www.census2021.gov.hk/en/main_tables.html. Accessed 26 July 2022.

Baker, M. 1993. Corpus linguistics and translation studies: Implications and applications. In *Text and technology: In honour of John Sinclair*, ed. M. Baker, G. Francis, and E. Tognini-Bonelli, 233–250. Amsterdam and Philadelphia, PA: John Benjamins.

Center for Chinese Linguistics PKU. n.d. a. Center for Chinese Linguistics PKU Corpus. http://ccl.pku.edu.cn:8080/ccl_corpus/search?q=%E5%85%A8%E7%90%83%E8%8C%83%E5%9B%B4%E5%86%85&start=0&num=50&index=FullIndex&outputFormat=HTML&encoding=UTF-8&maxLeftLength=30&maxRightLength=30&orderStyle=score&LastQuery=&dir=xiandai&scopestr=. Accessed 25 July 2022.

Center for Chinese Linguistics PKU. n.d. b. Center for Chinese Linguistics PKU Corpus. http://ccl.pku.edu.cn:8080/ccl_corpus/search?q=%E5%8F%91%E5%B1%95&start=0&num=50&index=FullIndex&outputFormat=HTML&encoding=UTF-8&maxLeftLength=30&maxRightLength=30&orderStyle=score&LastQuery=&dir=xiandai&scopestr=. Accessed 25 July 2022.

Chesterman, A. 1997/2016. *Memes of translation: The spread of ideas in translation theory*. Revised ed. Amsterdam/Philadelphia: John Benjamins.

Cheung, Y. K. 2021. Blending language learning with translation teaching: A new perspective on the teachability of Chinese translation. In *Diverse voices in Chinese translation and interpreting: Theory and practice*, ed. R. Moratto and M. Woesler, 433-453. Singapore: Springer.

CIOL. 2022. Qualification specification: CIOL qualifications level 6 Certificate in Translation (CertTrans). https://www.ciol.org.uk/sites/default/files/30647%20Cert%20Trans%20Spec%20FNL.pdf. Accessed 10 July 2022.

Crystal, D. 2008. *A dictionary of linguistics and phonetics*, 6th ed. Oxford: Blackwell Publishing.

"Dashuju yu yuan jiaoyu yanjiusuo" 大數據與語言教育研究所. n.d. BCC. http://bcc.blcu.edu.cn/zh/search/0/%E5%85%A8%E7%90%83%E8%8C%83%E5%9B%B4%E5%86%85. Accessed 25 July 2022.

Drugan, J. 2013. *Quality in professional translation: Assessment and improvement*. London: Bloomsbury.

Durban, C. and A. Melby. 2008. Translation—Buying a non-commodity: How translation standards can help buyers & sellers. https://atanet.org/wp-content/uploads/2020/06/translation_buying_guide.pdf. Accessed 25 July 2022.

Equality Act. 2010. https://www.legislation.gov.uk/ukpga/2010/15/section/1. Accessed 26 June 2022.

Faculty of Modern and Medieval Languages and Linguistics. 2020a. Marking criteria: MML Part IB—Translation into the Foreign Language (Paper B3) (Prose Composition). https://www.mmll.cam.ac.uk/sites/www.mmll.cam.ac.uk/files/updated_b3_into_foreign_language_updated_for_tripos_2022.pdf. Accessed 11 July 2022.

Faculty of Modern and Medieval Languages and Linguistics. 2020b. Marking criteria: Translations into English (MML). https://www.mmll.cam.ac.uk/sites/www.mmll.cam.ac.uk/files/a2_into_english_updated_for_tripos_2022.pdf. Accessed 11 July 2022.

Faculty of Modern and Medieval Languages and Linguistics. 2020c. Marking criteria: Translations into English (MML). https://www.mmll.cam.ac.uk/sites/www.mmll.cam.ac.uk/files/updated_b2_and_c1_into_english.pdf. Accessed 11 July 2022.

Home Office. 2022. Policy paper: British National (Overseas). Updated 2 March 2022. https://www.gov.uk/government/publications/nationality-and-borders-bill-british-national-overseas-factsheet/british-national-overseas#:~:text=On%2031%20January%202021%2C%20the,and%20their%20immediate%20family%20members.

Human Rights Act. 1998. https://www.legislation.gov.uk/ukpga/1998/42/schedule/1. Accessed 26 June 2022.

Lauscher, S. 2000. Translation quality assessment. *The Translator* 6 (2): 149–168. https://doi.org/10.1080/13556509.2000.10799063.

Lee, K. S., and Y. K. Tse. 1994. "Hanyu texing yu Zhongwen chuanyi" 漢語特性與中文傳意 [Characteristics of the Chinese language and Chinese communication]. In *"Hanyu de texing yu yunyong" 漢語的特性與運用*, ed. K. S. Lee and Y. K. Tse, 5-22. Hong Kong: Hong Kong University Press.

Li, J. 2011. Xinghe vs. Yihe in English-Chinese translation—Analysis from the perspective of syntactic construction. *Perspectives* 19 (3): 189–203. https://doi.org/10.1080/0907676X.2010.514347.

Minority Rights Group International. 2018. World directory of minorities and indigenous peoples—United Kingdom: Chinese. https://www.refworld.org/docid/49749c907.html. Accessed 14 July 2022.

Mossop, B., J. Hong, and C. Teixeira. 2001/2020. *Revising and editing for translators.* 4th ed. London and New York: Routledge.

NAATI. 2020. Certified translator test assessment rubrics. https://www.naati.com.au/wp-content/uploads/2020/10/Certified-Translator-Assessment-Rubrics.pdf. Accessed 14 July 2022.

NAATI. 2021a. About NAATI. https://www.naati.com.au/about-us/about-naati/. Accessed 14 July 2022.

NAATI. 2021b. "Guanyu NAATI" 關於NAATI [About NAATI]. https://www.naati.com.au/%e9%97%9c%e6%96%bcnaati/?lang=zh-hant. Accessed 14 July 2022.

NAATI. 2022. Certification languages tested. https://www.naati.com.au/wp-content/uploads/2022/03/Certification-Testing-Languages_Mar22-.pdf. Accessed 14 July 2022.

Proudfoot, G.R., A. Thompson, and D.S. Kastan. 2011. *The Arden Shakespeare complete works.* Revised ed. London: Bloomsbury Publishing.

Pym, A. 2010/2014. *Exploring translation theories.* 2nd ed. London and New York: Routledge.

Reiss, K. 1971/2000. Type, kind and individuality of text: Decision making in translation. In *Translation studies reader*, ed. L. Venuti, 160–171. London and New York: Routledge.

Ross, C. and J.-h. S. Ma. 2014. *Modern Mandarin Chinese grammar: A practical guide.* 2nd ed. London and New York: Routledge.

Toury, G. 1995/2012. *Descriptive translation studies—and beyond.* Revised ed. Amsterdam/Philadelphia: John Benjamins.

UK Government. n.d. Search. https://www.gov.uk/search/all?content_purpose_supergroup%5B%5D=guidance_and_regulation&level_one_taxon=5b7b9532-a775-4bd2-a3aa-6ce380184b6c&order=updated-newest&organisations%5B%5D=uk-health-security-agency&page=1&parent=uk-health-security-agency. Accessed 14 July 2022.

UK Government. 2020. Chinese ethnic group: Facts and figures. https://www.ethnicity-facts-figures.service.gov.uk/summaries/chinese-ethnic-group. Accessed 23 June 2022.

UK Government. 2021. COVID-19 vaccination: Resources for schools and parents. https://www.gov.uk/government/publications/covid-19-vaccination-resources-for-schools. Accessed 14 July 2022.

UK Government. 2022. COVID-19 vaccination: Resources for children aged 5 to 11 years. 13 January. Updated 28 March. https://www.gov.uk/government/publications/covid-19-vaccination-resources-for-children-aged-5-to-11-years.

UK Health Security Agency. n.d. a. "Anquandi yu baokuo COVID-19 zai nei de huxidao ganran gongcun" 安全地與包括 COVID-19 在內的呼吸道感染共存 [Living safely with respiratory infections, including COVID-19]. https://assets.publishing.service.gov.uk/government/uploads/system/uploads/attachment_data/file/1068754/20220412-Living_safely_with_respiratory_-_Chinese_Traditional.pdf. Accessed 17 July 2022.

UK Health Security Agency. n.d. b. "Jianshao gongzuo changsuo huxidao ganran baokuo (COVID-19) chuanbo" 减少工作场所呼吸道感染包括(COVID-19)传播 [Reducing the spread of respiratory infections, including COVID-19, in the workplace]. https://assets.publishing.service.gov.uk/government/uploads/system/uploads/attachment_data/file/1077031/20220520-Reducing_spread_of_respiratory_infections_in_workplaces_-_Simplified_Chinese.pdf. Accessed 23 June 2022.

UK Health Security Agency. n.d. c. "Jianshao gongzuo changsuo huxidao ganran baokuo (COVID-19) chuanbo" 減少工作場所呼吸道感染包括 (COVID-19) 傳播 [Reducing the spread of respiratory infections, including COVID-19, in the workplace]. https://assets.publishing.service.gov.uk/government/uploads/system/uploads/attachment_data/file/1077032/20220520-Reducing_spread_of_respiratory_infections_in_workplaces_-_Traditional_Chinese.pdf. Accessed 23 June 2022.

UK Health Security Agency. n.d. d. "Yu huxidao ganran (baokuo COVID19) anquan gongcun" 与呼吸道感染(包括COVID19)安全共存 [Living safely with respiratory infections, including COVID-19]. https://assets.publishing.service.gov.uk/government/uploads/system/uploads/attachment_data/file/1068753/20220412-Living_safely_with_respiratory_-_Chinese_Simplified.pdf. Accessed 17 July 2022.

UK Health Security Agency. 2021. COV2021PGSCH Pregnant? Have your COVID-19 vaccines social media cards—Chinese. https://www.healthpublications.gov.uk/ViewArticle.html?sp=Spregnanthaveyourcovid19vaccinessocialmediacardschinese.

UK Health Security Agency. 2022a. Living safely with respiratory infections, including COVID-19. Updated 16 June 2022a. https://www.gov.uk/guidance/living-safely-with-respiratory-infections-including-covid-19.

UK Health Security Agency. 2022b. Patient information for Paxlovid. Updated 4 May 2022b. https://www.gov.uk/government/publications/covid-19-antiviral-treatment-paxlovid.

UK Health Security Agency and NHS. 2021. "Guanzhuang bingdu (COVID-19) ertong he qingshaonian yimiao jiezhong jihua: mianxiang fumu de zhinan" 冠狀病毒(COVID-19)兒童和青少年疫苗接種計劃: 面向父母的指南 [COVID-19 vaccination programme for children and young people: guidance for parents]. https://www.healthpublications.gov.uk/ViewArticle.html?sp=Scovid19vaccinationfactsheetforparentschinese. Accessed 14 July 2022.

UK Health Security Agency and NHS. 2022a. COVID-19 vaccination: A guide for parents of children aged 5 to 11. https://assets.publishing.service.gov.uk/government/uploads/system/uploads/attachment_data/file/1058694/COVID-19-guide-for-parents-of-children-aged-5-11-years.pdf.

UK Health Security Agency and NHS. 2022b. "COVID-19 Yimiao jiezhong gei 5 zhi 11 sui ertong jiazhang de zhinan" COVID-19疫苗接种给5至11岁儿童家长的指

南. https://www.healthpublications.gov.uk/ViewArticle.html?sp=Swhattoexpectafteryourcovid19vaccinationguideforparents5to11yearsofagechinese.

UK Health Security Agency and NHS. 2022c. "COVID-19 Yimiao jiezhong gei 5 zhi 11 sui ertong jiazhang de zhinan" COVID-19 疫苗接種給5至11歲兒童家長的指南. https://www.healthpublications.gov.uk/ViewArticle.html?sp=Swhattoexpectafteryourcovid19vaccinationguideforparents5to11yearsofagechinesetraditionalcantonese.

UK Health Security Agency and NHS. 2022d. "COVID-19 Yimiao yong yu mianyi xitong jiao ruo de ren COVID-19" 疫苗用于免疫系统较弱的人 [COVID-19 for people with a weakened immune system]. https://www.healthpublications.gov.uk/ViewArticle.html?sp=Scovid19vaccineforthosewithaweakenedimmunesystemchinesesimplified. Accessed 23 June 2022d.

UK Health Security Agency and NHS. 2022e. "COVID-19 Yimiao yong yu mianyi xitong jiao ruo de ren" COVID-19 疫苗用於免疫系統較弱的人 [COVID-19 for people with a weakened immune system]. https://www.healthpublications.gov.uk/ViewArticle.html?sp=Scovid19vaccineforthosewithaweakenedimmunesystemchinesetraditionalcantonese. Accessed 23 June 2022e.

UK Health Security Agency and NHS. 2022f. What to expect after your child's COVID-19 vaccination: A Guide for parents of children aged 5 to 11 years of age. https://assets.publishing.service.gov.uk/government/uploads/system/uploads/attachment_data/file/1045901/COVID-19-what-to-expect-5-11years.pdf. Accessed 14 July 2022f.

UK Health Security Agency and NHS. 2022g. "Zhongyao de COVID zixun—nin jieshou le yixia zhendui COVID-19 de zhiliao" Paxlovid重要的COVID-19 資訊—您接受了以下針對 COVID-19 的治療: Paxlovid. Updated 4 May 2022g. https://www.healthpublications.gov.uk/ViewArticle.html?sp=Spaxlovidleafletchinesetraditionalcantonese.

Warrington, J. 2022. The unlikely London suburb where fleeing Hongkongers are starting new lives. *The Telegraph*, 10 July. https://www.telegraph.co.uk/business/2022/07/10/unlikely-london-suburb-where-fleeing-hongkongers-starting-new/.

Yu Kit Cheung is Lecturer in Chinese Translation Studies at the University of Manchester, UK. He is also one of the steering committee members of the East Asian Translation Pedagogy Advance first founded in the UK. He has recently edited the Chinese translation of an academic volume on Translation Studies and published academic articles on Confucianism, literary translation, and translation pedagogy. In addition to academic works, he is keen to share his thoughts with his readers on language and translation on Fans of Translation, his personal website: www.fansoftranslation.com, where he publishes short articles on these two subjects on a regular basis.

Chapter 5
COVID-19 MT Evaluator: A Platform for the Evaluation of Machine Translation of Public Health Information Related to COVID-19

Sai Cheong Siu

Abstract In the wake of the COVID-19 outbreak, timely and accurate translation of public health information has become more critical than ever as it helps keep the public informed of the latest pandemic situation, personal hygiene advice and preventive measures, enabling speakers of different languages in the community to work together in the fight against the epidemic. While recent advances in machine translation (MT) featuring the use of deep artificial neural networks may enhance the cross-lingual dissemination of pandemic-related information, their overall performance in English/Chinese translation of COVID-19-related messages is largely understudied. It is against this background that in this article we present COVID-19 MT Evaluator, a platform for the evaluation of MT of public health information related to the pandemic. The system integrates major well-tested MT evaluation metrics and test datasets, with a view to facilitating the assessment of the quality of MT output and the detection and analysis of translation issues. We compare two English/Chinese MT products provided by Google Translate to illustrate the use of the evaluation platform.

Keywords COVID-19 · Machine translation · Public health information · Quality evaluation · Google translate · English-Chinese translation

5.1 Introduction

Since the outbreak of COVID-19, the publication and dissemination of cross-lingual public health information has become more important than ever because of its critical role in keeping citizens and healthcare professionals speaking different languages informed of the situation. Timely and accurate translation of public health information related to COVID-19 is crucial for not only bilingual cities like Hong Kong, but

S. C. Siu (✉)
School of Translation and Foreign Languages, The Hang Seng University of Hong Kong, Hong Kong, China
e-mail: scsiu@hsu.edu.hk

K. Liu and A. K. F. Cheung (eds.), *Translation and Interpreting in the Age of COVID-19*, Corpora and Intercultural Studies 9,
https://doi.org/10.1007/978-981-19-6680-4_5

also monolingual communities, given the need to alert ethnic minority residents and tourists to the development of the epidemic.

Translation technology may enhance public health communication across languages. For example, the use of machine translation (MT) engines could facilitate the translation of health-related documents by automatically generating draft translations for post-editing by professional translators. However, little is known about the performance of MT in the context of the translation of COVID-19 information although there has been much discussion of MT evaluation in general (e.g., Freitaget al. 2021a; Rivera-Trigueros 2021).

In this regard, we propose COVID-19 MT Evaluator, which features (1) the integration of domain-specific MT evaluation tools, such as public health test datasets; (2) the use of well-tested machine translation evaluation metrics that correlate with human judgment of translation quality; and (3) the generation of interactive MT reports for the visualization and analysis of the assessment results. The system aims to help MT users and researchers (1) assess and compare translation systems and (2) identify and analyse MT issues for continuous improvement of automatic translation applications. Given the ever-changing global health landscape, this evaluation platform could complement crowd-sourced human assessment tasks, which may take more time (Sellam et al. 2020), especially when we need rapid feedback on MT models for system design and enhancement.

The present work is structured as follows: For the purpose of discussing COVID-19 MT Evaluator, Sect. 5.2 introduces the features of COVID-19 public health information, and Sect. 5.3 gives an overview of recent developments in neural machine translation. Section 5.4 explores the design of the Evaluator, explaining (1) the development of domain-specific assessment tools (e.g., test datasets) by using online bilingual public health information, (2) the incorporation of a broad spectrum of MT evaluation metrics, namely BLEU, CHRF, BERTScore, BLEURT, and COMET, and (3) the generation of MT reports with interactive charts presenting the results of the analysis. Section 5.5 illustrates the use of the system by comparing the performance of two automatic translation services provided by Google. Section 5.6 suggests future research work.

5.2 Public Health Information Related to COVID-19

Public health information related to COVID-19 can be divided into several categories. In Hong Kong, for example, we have press releases reporting the latest infections (e.g., the number of confirmed cases), announcements about social distancing measures, testing notices, information on quarantine and isolation arrangements, tips and guidelines on personal hygiene, health information related to vaccination, travel advice, specialized information for healthcare professionals, and other pandemic-related multimedia content (e.g., posters and video clips). Table 5.1 gives some examples:

Table 5.1 Examples of COVID-19 Information in Hong Kong

Category	Examples
Infection situation	**Example 1**: "CHP investigates locally acquired SARS-CoV-2 virus cases with 1 035 cases tested positive by nucleic acid tests and 1 713 cases by RATs verified as well as 197 imported cases" (Centre for Health Protection 2022a) **Example 2**: "HK logs 2.8 k local infections" (news.gov.hk 2022)
Testing	**Example 1**: "Government gazettes compulsory testing notice" (HKSAR Government 2022g) **Example 2**: "Rapid Antigen Tests" (HKSAR Government 2022i)
Vaccination	**Example 1**: "Vaccine Pass" (HKSAR Government 2022j) **Example 2**: "Vaccination fact sheet for CoronaVac" (Department of Health 2022)
Public health measures	**Example 1**: "Frequently asked questions on new requirements to reduce gatherings" (HKSAR Government 2022e) **Example 2**: "Government extends existing social distancing measures" (HKSAR Government 2022f)
Health advice	**Example 1**: "Guidelines on prevention of Coronavirus Disease 2019 (COVID-19) for the general public" (Centre for Health Protection 2022b) **Example 2**: "Health advice on prevention of COVID-19 for returnees (Interim)" (Centre for Health Protection 2021)

COVID-19 health information is characterized by the use of a variety of technical terms, including not only medical terminology in different specialties, such as epidemiology, microbiology, biostatistics, and clinical research, but also terms from other fields, such as engineering (e.g., ventilation facilities to prevent virus transmission), law (especially information on public health measures that are legally binding) and government and public affairs (e.g., names of different departments and units that formulate and implement anti-epidemic initiatives; disease control and prevention plans and programs). Table 5.2 gives bilingual examples of technical expressions associated with COVID-19.

5.3 Neural Machine Translation

Neural machine translation featuring the use of multilayer artificial neural networks is one of the most popular approaches to automatic translation, as evidenced by its wide adoption by major MT service providers such as Google (Caswell and Bapna 2022) and a surging number of research papers on it (Stahlberg 2020). Neural machine translation engines have been shown to outperform their predecessors, such as statistical machine translation tools characterized by the use of language and translation models (see, for example, Bojar et al. 2016).

Table 5.2 Examples of Technical Terms in COVID-19-related Public Health Information

Technical Domain	Bilingual Examples (English Term; Chinese Term)
Medicine	**Example 1**: Reverse transcription polymerase chain reaction (RT-PCR); 反轉錄聚合酶連鎖反應 *Explanation:* This is a viral diagnostic test that amplifies and detects the ribonucleic acid sequences that constitute the genetic material of SARS-CoV-2, the virus that causes COVID-19. (Centers for Disease Control and Prevention 2021) **Example 2**: Remdesivir; 瑞德西韋 *Explanation:* Remdesivir is an antiviral drug approved by the U.S. Food and Drug Administration for the treatment of COVID-19. (National Institutes of Health 2022)
Law	**Example 1**: Cap. 599 J Prevention and Control of Disease (Compulsory Testing for Certain Persons) Regulation; 第599J章《預防及控制疾病(對若干人士強制檢測)規例》 *Explanation:* The Regulation provides a legal framework in Hong Kong that enables the Secretary for Health to issue compulsory testing notices or make restriction-testing declarations for the purpose of enhancing COVID-19 testing. (HKSAR Government 2022b) **Example 2**: scheduled premises; 表列處所 *Explanation:* The Secretary for Health may issue directions to scheduled premises (e.g., amusement game centers, beauty parlors, fitness centers, and shopping malls) for the prevention and control of COVID-19 under Cap. 599F Prevention and Control of Disease (Requirements and Directions) (Business and Premises) Regulation, Laws of Hong Kong. (Hong Kong e-Legislation 2022)
Government initiatives	**Example 1**: LeaveHomeSafe; 安心出行 *Explanation:* This is a mobile application designed by the HKSAR Government to record visits to places such as restaurants and government buildings and to store COVID-19 vaccination records and test results. (HKSAR Government 2022h) **Example 2**: Come2HK Scheme; 來港易 *Explanation:* This is a travel scheme for non-Hong Kong residents from Guangdong Province or Macau, allowing them to enter Hong Kong without being subject to compulsory quarantine. (HKSAR Government 2022a)

Neural machine translation models generally consist of two artificial neural networks: an encoder and a decoder. The encoder converts the source text into an intermediate representation, which is then used by the decoder to generate the target text. There are different types of neural networks for MT, such as Long Short-term Memory (e.g., Wu et al. 2016), convolutional neural networks (e.g., Gehring et al. 2017), and self-attention neural networks (e.g., Vaswani et al. 2017).

The training of neural machine translation models typically relies on parallel sentences and sometimes includes back translation of monolingual sentences in the target language to increase the size of the training set (e.g., Sennrich et al. 2016). To increase the quality of machine translation results, we may consider domain adoption methods for building specialized MT engines (e.g., Chu et al. 2017), as well as the use of different decoding strategies (e.g., dynamic beam allocation (Post and Vilar 2018) and re-ranking (Liu et al. 2018) or multiple models, such as model assembling (e.g., Sutskever et al. 2014; Cromieres et al. 2016; Ng et al. 2019).

5.4 Design of COVID-19 MT Evaluator

5.4.1 System Features

Our COVID-19 MT Evaluator is designed for the automatic evaluation of machine translation, with the following three main features:

First, we offer assessment tools tailored to the evaluation of specialized translation in the context of COVID-19. For example, the system offers coronavirus-related bilingual test datasets that could be used as a benchmark for evaluating the automatic translation of COVID-19 information. There is also a terminology module for the checking of the translation of public health terms related to the epidemic. These domain-specific tools differentiate our system from other evaluation platforms for general MT (e.g., Interactive BLEU score evaluator (Tilde 2021)), which tend to focus on the computation of translation scores, with less emphasis on features geared to the evaluation of the translation of specialized documents. See Sect. 5.4.2 for more information.

Second, we integrate a wide spectrum of MT evaluation metrics into the platform, from those based on string comparisons (e.g., BLEU) to those based on the computation of sentence embeddings using large pre-trained language models consisting of artificial neural networks. Refer to Sect. 5.4.3 for details.

Third, we provide interactive visualization tools to help users analyse translation scores, compare MT results with reference translations, and identify noteworthy issues for further investigation. See Sect. 5.4.4.

The user interface of the system is shown in Fig. 5.1. Users are first prompted to use one of the spreadsheets containing our test datasets (see Step 1 in Fig. 5.1). As shown in the sample spreadsheet in Fig. 5.2, the first and second columns are source and reference sentences, and the third and fourth columns allow users to provide their MT results for evaluation. Users can use their own source and reference texts by replacing the first two columns of the worksheet or using the "Blank Spreadsheet Template" with the column headings only. They upload the completed spreadsheet to the platform after MT (Step 2) and confirm the source and target languages (Step 3). The system then computes the scores and compiles an evaluation report, which is available in the download area (Step 4) when ready.

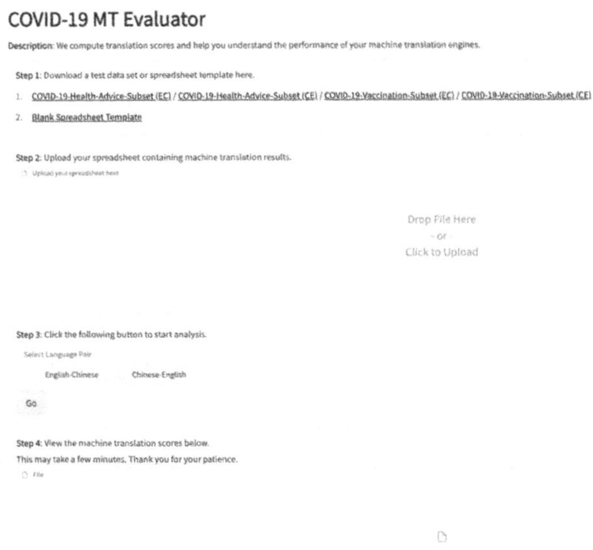

Fig. 5.1 User interface of COVID-19 MT Evaluator

	A	B	C	D	E
1	source	reference	MT1	MT2	
2	17. Are the existing COVID-19 vaccines effective against different variants?	17. 現有新冠疫苗能有效應對不同變異株嗎？			
3	Delivery of vaccines	疫苗遞送			
4	It is concluded that for most frail elderly, the benefit of reducing the risk of a severe COVID-19 disease course outweighs the risk of receiving the vaccine.	總括而言，對絕大部分體弱長者來說，接種疫苗以減低嚴重2019冠狀病毒病獲得的益處大於其所帶來的風險。			
5	143. Each kind of vaccine is suitable for everyone?	143. 每一種疫苗都適用於所有人士？			
6	If you are unable to get the correct vaccination record or you need to seek assistance, you can re-declare your non-local vaccination record at the 18 designated Hong Kong Post Offices and get the printed electronic vaccination record together with the local vaccination record with assistance from the staff free of charge. For the addresses and the opening hours for the designated post office, please refer to https://www.hongkongpost.hk/en/services/non_local_covid19_vr/index.html#list	如未能正確顯示有關紀錄又或者需要協助，你亦可到18間指定的香港郵政局重新申報非本地疫苗接種紀錄，並由職員協助列印一併顯示的電子疫苗接種紀錄，費用全免。有關指定郵政局的地址及相關營業時間等資料，請參閱 https://www.hongkongpost.hk/sc/services/non_local_covid19_vr/index.html#list。			
7	25. Glucose-6-phosphate dehydrogenase (G6PD) deficiency	25. 葡萄糖六磷酸去氫酵素缺乏症（G6PD缺乏症／蠶豆症）			
8	Healthcare workers may regularly have contact with severely ill patients who have higher viral load. Healthcare workers may also have contact with vulnerable patients who have weak immune systems.	醫護人員有機會與重病的患者經常接觸，這些患者的病毒水平往往較高。醫護人員亦有機會接觸到一些免疫力較弱因而容易受感染的病人。			
9	Please refer to question 17.	請參閱問題17。			

Fig. 5.2 Example of a spreadsheet containing a bilingual test dataset with source and reference sentences in the first two columns, followed by two columns storing translation candidates generated by MT systems (MT1 and MT2)

5.4.2 COVID-19 Test Datasets and Terminology Checker

Our bilingual test datasets could facilitate the evaluation of MT systems in terms of the translation of COVID-19 information, especially when users do not have their own test data. The details of the datasets are as follows:

- **COVID-19-Health-Advice**: This dataset is based on the English and Chinese articles in "Q&As on COVID-19 and related health topics" on the website of the World Health Organization, covering different issues such as "Staying at hotels and accommodation establishments," "Travel advice for the general public," and "Ventilation and air conditioning." See World Health Organization (2022a, b) for the English and Chinese articles.
- **COVID-19-Vaccination**: This is based on the bilingual content posted in the Frequently Asked Questions (FAQs) section of the official website of the HKSAR COVID-19 vaccination program. The FAQs section contains 145 questions about COVID-19 vaccines and covers nine areas, such as "Recommendations on the use of COVID-19 vaccines," "Vaccination records," and "Myths and facts about vaccines." Refer to HKSAR Government (2022c, d) for the English and Chinese versions.
- **COVID-19-Health-Advice-Subset**: This is a subset of the COVID-19-Health-Advice dataset, with approximately 10% of the sentences or paragraphs randomly selected from the original dataset for rapid evaluation purposes.
- **COVID-19-Vaccination-Subset**: This is a subset of the COVID-19-Vaccination dataset. Like COVID-19-Health-Advice-Subset, this subset consists of around 10% of the sentences or paragraphs randomly selected from the original dataset to allow for rapid assessment.

The test datasets are tokenized with NLTK (2022) (for English content) and Jieba (2020) (for Chinese content). Table 5.3 gives examples of the COVID-19-Health-Advice and COVID-19-Vaccination test sets. Table 5.4 summarizes the statistics of the datasets.

In addition to the test datasets, the system provides a terminology checker with bilingual terms extracted from COVID-19 information in English and Chinese. The checker can detect COVID-19-related terms for each segment in the source text and check the presence of corresponding translations in the MT output. The results are presented in the interactive assessment report generated by the Evaluator (see Sect. 5.4.4).

5.4.3 Evaluation Metrics

The evaluation metrics built into the system fall into two categories: (1) metrics based on string comparisons and (2) metrics based on sentence embeddings. The former compares a machine translation candidate with a reference translation by, for

Table 5.3 Samples of bilingual sentences in the test datasets

Test Dataset	Examples
COVID-19 Health-Advice	**Sample 1** **English**: Pregnant people and those who have recently given birth are at high risk for experiencing severe influenza and severe COVID-19. **Chinese**: 孕婦和最近分娩的婦女患嚴重流感和COVID-19重症的風險很高。 **Sample 2** **English**: Does WHO recommend hydroxychloroquine as a treatment for COVID-19? **Chinese**: 世衛組織是否建議使用g氯喹來治療COVID-19?
COVID-19-Vaccination	**Sample 1** **English**: According to the product information of CoronaVac vaccine, the clinical data of pregnant or breastfeeding women are not available at present but it is not a Contraindication. **Chinese**: 根據克爾來福疫苗的產品資料, 目前尚未獲得孕婦及哺乳期婦女使用「克爾來福」的臨床試驗數據. 然而, 此並非疫苗的禁忌症。 **Sample 2** **English**: As CoronaVac only contains killed virus, it will not give you COVID-19. **Chinese**: 由於克爾來福只含已被殺死的病毒, 故不會引致2019冠狀病毒病。

Table 5.4 Token statistics of the test datasets

Test Dataset	No. of tokens in English	No. of tokens in Chinese
COVID-19 Health-Advice	66,887	62,656
COVID-19-Vaccination	17,103	15,983
COVID-19 Health-Advice-Subset	6,835	6,460
COVID-19-Vaccination-Subset	1,244	1,163

example, considering the number of words (or n-grams) that appear in both versions of the text. The latter computes the sentence embeddings of the MT output and reference translation using a pre-trained language model (e.g., BERT (Devlin et al. 2018)) and compares the similarity.

We adopt five scoring metrics, namely BLEU, CHRF, BERTScore, BLEURT, and COMET, all of which were considered by the Sixth Conference on Machine Translation (WMT21) Metrics Shared Task (Freitag et al. 2021b). BLEU and CHRF are string comparison metrics, and the other three are embedding-based metrics. The details are as follows:

BLEU The Bilingual Evaluation Understudy (BLEU) metric, presented by Papineni et al. (2002), has been widely adopted by the MT research community, as evidenced by its use by major developers like Google (e.g., Caswell and Liang 2020) and MT conferences such as Conference on Machine Translation (WMT) (e.g., Akhbardeh et al. 2021). This metric calculates the weighted geometric mean of n-gram precision. More specifically, the metric computes (1) modified n-gram precision scores that consider n-grams up to a length of N and clip the total count of each candidate n-gram occurring in the reference translation by its maximum reference count, and (2) the geometric mean of the modified precision scores with a brevity penalty that reduces the final score when the candidate is shorter than the reference. Formally, if we consider the BLEU score at the corpus level and assume that there is only one reference translation, we have

$$BLEU = \exp\left(min\left(1 - \frac{r}{c}, 0\right) + \sum_{n=1}^{N} w_n log(P_n)\right)$$

where r is the total number of tokens of the reference sentences, c is the total number of tokens of the candidate sentences, P_n is the modified n-gram precision score, and w_n is the weight of P_n. The range of the BLEU score is between 0 and 1. The latter means that the candidate is identical to the reference translation.

Post (2018) proposed SacreBLEU, a Python library for improving the reporting and comparability of BLEU scores, as BLEU depends on preprocessing methods and parameters such as the number of reference translations, the maximum length of n-grams, the way in which the length penalty is computed, and the smoothing method for zero-counts of n-grams. The SacreBLEU library standardizes preprocessing and expects detokenized input sentences by providing internal preprocessing methods. We use the functions `corpus_bleu` and `sentence_bleu` with the default arguments to compute BLEU scores at the corpus and segment levels, respectively.

CHRF Popović (2015) proposed the CHRF score, which is the computation of the F-score based on n-grams at the character level (as opposed to n-grams at the word level) for MT scoring. Formally, we have

$$CHRF = (\beta^2 + 1) \times \frac{P_{CHR} \times R_{CHR}}{\beta^2 P_{CHR} + R_{CHR}}$$

where P_{CHR} and R_{CHR} refer to character n-gram precision (the percentage of character n-grams in the MT output that are present in the reference translation) and recall (the percentage of character n-grams in the reference translation that can also be found in the MT output), respectively, and β indicates the relevant importance between recall and precision. The standard CHRF score, where $\beta = 1$, is the F-measure with equal importance of recall and precision.

Our evaluator uses SacreBLEU to calculate CHRF scores, which, like BLEU scores, are precision values that compare n-grams of an MT candidate with a reference translation and may be affected by factors such as preprocessing methods and parameters as discussed in Post (2018). We use the functions `corpus_chrf` and `sentence_chrf` to calculate dataset-level and segment-level CHRF scores, respectively, using the default arguments with $\beta = 2$. Similar to BLEU, the CHRF scores range from 0 to 1.

BERTScore Proposed by Zhang et al. (2019), BERTScore features the adoption of the BERT model (Devlin et al. 2018) for the generation of contextual embeddings for each token in the reference sentence and MT output. The embedding for each token is generated using a Transformer (Vaswani et al. 2017) encoder, which is composed of multiple self-attention and non-linear layers and considers the contextual information provided by the other tokens in the sentence. The similarity between a token in the reference sentence and a token in the MT output can then be computed based on the cosine similarity of the two corresponding embeddings, as opposed to the matching of the two strings on the surface as in BLEU and CHRF. If we consider BERTScores without importance weighting, given the reference sentence t and MT output $\tilde{t}$, we have

$$F_{BERT} = 2 \times \frac{P_{BERT} \times R_{BERT}}{P_{BERT} + R_{BERT}}$$

with

$$P_{BERT} = \frac{1}{|t|} \sum_{i=1}^{|t|} \max_{j} \boldsymbol{t}_i^{\top} \tilde{\boldsymbol{t}}_j$$

and

$$R_{BERT} = \frac{1}{|\tilde{t}|} \sum_{j=1}^{|\tilde{t}|} \max_{i} \boldsymbol{t}_i^{\top} \tilde{\boldsymbol{t}}_j$$

where $\boldsymbol{t}_i$ is the embedding of the i-th token of t and $\tilde{\boldsymbol{t}}_j$ is the embedding of the j-th token of $\tilde{t}$, and $|t|$ and $|\tilde{t}|$ refer to the length of t and $\tilde{t}$, respectively. After re-scaling using monolingual datasets, P_{BERT}, R_{BERT} and F_{BERT} typically range from 0 to 1 (Zhang et al. 2019). In our system, we compute F_{BERT} scores using the base multilingual BERT model (Devlin et al. 2018) without importance weighting.

BLEURT Sellam et al. (2020) presented BLEURT, a regression model characterized by the fine-tuning of a pre-trained multilingual BERT model (Devlin et al. 2018) to learn the mapping between (1) the embeddings of sentence pairs consisting of reference sentences and MT results and (2) the corresponding translation scores assigned by human evaluators. In other words, the scoring task becomes a regression problem: the first step is to fine-tune a pre-trained BERT model on tuples each containing a reference sentence t, an MT candidate $\tilde{t}$, and the corresponding human score. To determine the MT score for a new input sentence pair of t and $\tilde{t}$, the fine-tuned model computes a fixed-length embedding of the sentence pair, which is followed by a linear transformation of the embedding as follows:

$$BLEURT = \boldsymbol{W} \cdot \text{mBERT}(t, \tilde{t}) + \boldsymbol{b}$$

where $\boldsymbol{W}$ and $\boldsymbol{b}$ refer to the weight matrix and bias, respectively. Our evaluator uses the BLEURT-20 model with support for 13 languages, the recommended checkpoint at the time of writing (Google Research 2021), and clips the scores to ensure that they fall between 0 (a random translation) and 1 (a perfect output). We adopt the D3 variant of the model for faster inference.

COMET The Crosslingual Optimized Metric for Evaluation of Translation (COMET) (Rei et al. 2020), which is based on XLM-RoBERTa (Conneau et al. 2020), is a large-scale pre-trained multilingual masked language model. This cross-lingual model, together with a pooling layer, encodes the source sentence s, the reference translation t, and the MT candidate $\tilde{t}$ and generates three sentence embeddings $\boldsymbol{s}$, $\boldsymbol{t}$, and $\tilde{\boldsymbol{t}}$, , respectively. Adopting the RUSE framework (Shinmanaka et al. 2018), COMET combines the three embeddings by concatenating the results of element-wise multiplication and absolute element-wise subtraction. The resulting embedding is fed into a feed-forward neural network for regression to compute the translation score. Formally, we have

$$COMET = \boldsymbol{W}_2\left(\tanh\left(\boldsymbol{W}_1\left[\tilde{\boldsymbol{t}}; \boldsymbol{t}; \tilde{\boldsymbol{t}} \odot \boldsymbol{s}; \tilde{\boldsymbol{t}} \odot \boldsymbol{t}; \left|\tilde{\boldsymbol{t}} \ominus \boldsymbol{s}\right|; \left|\tilde{\boldsymbol{t}} \ominus \boldsymbol{t}\right|\right] + \boldsymbol{b}_1\right)\right) + \boldsymbol{b}_2$$

where $\boldsymbol{W}_1$ and $\boldsymbol{W}_2$ are weight matrices, $\boldsymbol{b}_1$ and $\boldsymbol{b}_2$ are bias vectors, [;] denotes embedding concatenation, and $\odot$ and $\ominus$ are element-wise multiplication and absolute element-wise subtraction, respectively. According to Unbabel (2021), while COMET scores are theoretically unbounded, a segment with a higher COMET score suggests that it is of higher quality, and most of the scores generated by the COMET regression model wmt20-comet-da, which is designed to predict direct assessment scores in WMT20 (see Mathur et al. 2020), range between -1.5 and 1. To reduce the inference time, our system adopts the lightweight version of the COMET model called COMETinho, which is based on a distilled version of XLM-RoBERTa (Rei et al. 2021).

5.4.4 Interactive Report for Visualization and Analysis

After receiving the user's spreadsheet, the system calculates the MT scores based on the evaluation metrics discussed in Sect. 5.4.3 and generates an assessment report with interactive components that visualize the scores and help the user analyse the results and identify noteworthy issues.

The MT evaluation report (Fig. 5.3), which is in HTML format, consists of 6 sections with different types of interactive charts to visualize the assessment results. Each section is presented in a collapsible panel for easy access and navigation.

The first section of the report is "General Statistics" (Fig. 5.4), which includes a table and a bar chart summarizing the overall scores of the MT results based on the five metrics. Users can interact with the chart in two ways: (1) They can move

Fig. 5.3 Main page of the machine translation report generated by COVID-19 MT Evaluator

the mouse cursor over a bar, after which a hover label appears and provides more information about the data point. (2) Users have the option to view the score chart for a single MT system or the integrated chart for both engines for performance comparison. The two interactive features are also available for the other graphs in the report.

The second section "Overview of Scores" (Fig. 5.5) describes the characteristics of MT scores at the segment level to help better understand the calculation of the overall ratings. For each metric, the report includes (1) a table with the mean, standard deviation, and a five-number summary of the scores (the quartiles and minimum and maximum values), and (2) a box-and-whisker plot to visualize the quartiles and outliers, with the underlying data displayed next to it. An additional table is available

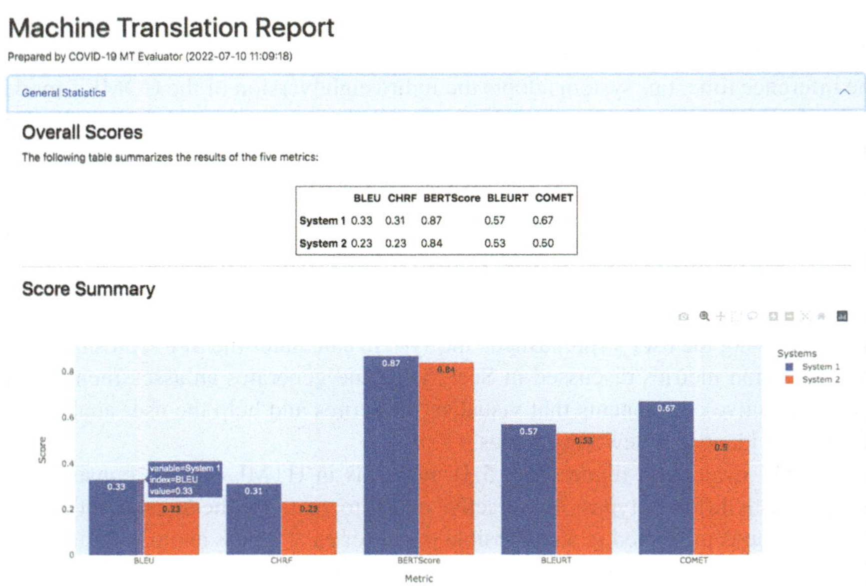

Fig. 5.4 The "General Statistics" section summarizes the overall scores of two machine translation engines (System 1 (blue bars) and System 2 (red bars)) with respect to the five metrics

for BLEU, showing the corresponding *n*-gram precision scores and other parameters such as the brevity penalty.

The third section "Score Distributions" (Fig. 5.6) shows the frequency distributions of MT scores using tables (in relative frequency) and histograms (in absolute frequency), with scores grouped into ranges. Marginal distribution plots are inserted above the main plot for the visualization of the score distributions.

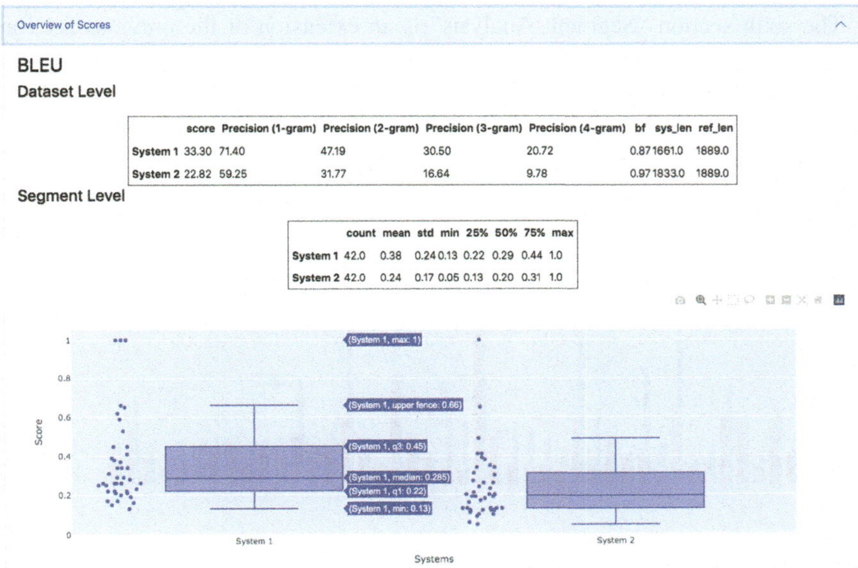
Overview of Scores

BLEU

Dataset Level

	score	Precision (1-gram)	Precision (2-gram)	Precision (3-gram)	Precision (4-gram)	bf	sys_len	ref_len
System 1	33.30	71.40	47.19	30.50	20.72	0.87	1661.0	1889.0
System 2	22.82	59.25	31.77	16.64	9.78	0.97	1833.0	1889.0

Segment Level

	count	mean	std	min	25%	50%	75%	max
System 1	42.0	0.38	0.24	0.13	0.22	0.29	0.44	1.0
System 2	42.0	0.24	0.17	0.05	0.13	0.20	0.31	1.0

Fig. 5.5 The "Overview of Scores" section summarizes the characteristics of MT scores at the segment level. BLEU is given as an example

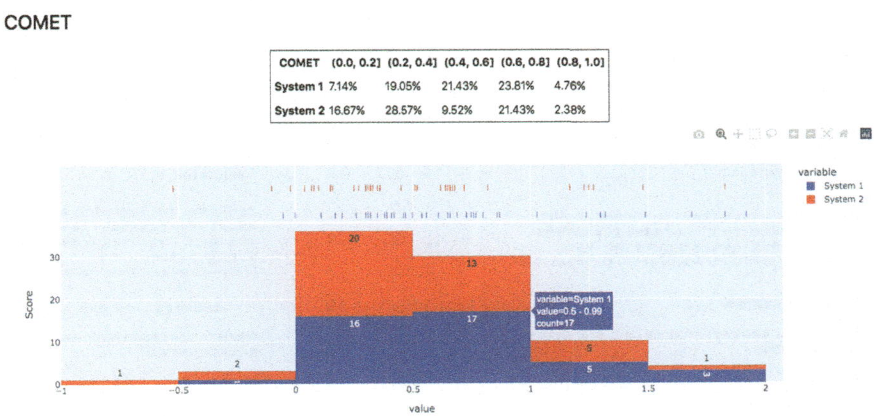
COMET

COMET	(0.0, 0.2]	(0.2, 0.4]	(0.4, 0.6]	(0.6, 0.8]	(0.8, 1.0]
System 1	7.14%	19.05%	21.43%	23.81%	4.76%
System 2	16.67%	28.57%	9.52%	21.43%	2.38%

Fig. 5.6 The "Score Distributions" section visualizes the frequency distributions of MT scores using histograms and marginal distribution plots. COMET is given as an example

The fourth section "Segment Statistics" (Fig. 5.7) visualizes the scores of each segment to help users identify segments with higher (or lower) scores or larger score differences between the engines, which could be useful for analysing and comparing MT systems.

The fifth section "Segment Summary" tabulates the evaluation scores (and other numerical attributes such as segment length) along with the corresponding source and reference sentences and MT outputs (see Fig. 5.8) to help users select segments for analysis.

The sixth section "Segment Analysis" is an extension of the previous section, providing the details of each segment for users to investigate translation issues at the segment level. As shown in Fig. 5.9, in addition to the source and reference sentences,

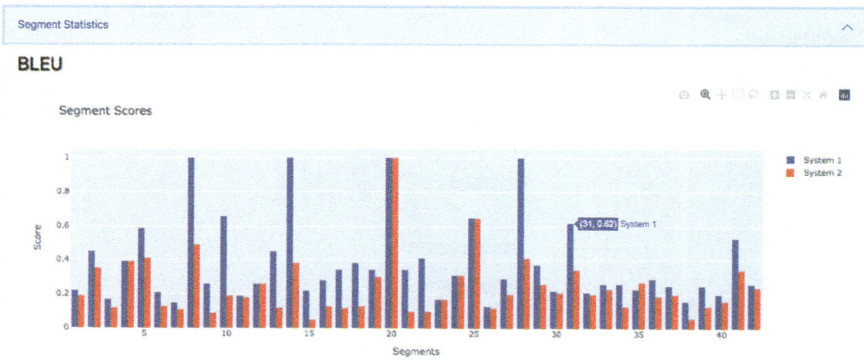

Fig. 5.7 The "Segment Statistics" section visualizes the scores of each segment to help users identify segments worthy of further exploration. BLEU is given as an example

Segment Summary

Automatic Translation (MT 1)	Length of ST (MT 1)	BLEU (MT 1)	CHRF (MT 1)	BERTScore (MT 1)	BLEURT (MT 1)	COMET (MT 1)	Automatic Translation (MT 2
17. 現有的 COVID-19 疫苗是否對不同的變種有效？	14	0.22	0.23	0.84	0.58	0.65	17.現有的COVID-19疫苗是否有效地針對不同的變種有
運送疫苗	3	0.45	0.42	0.92	0.96	1.49	輸送疫苗
得出的結論是，對於大多數體弱的老年人來說，降低嚴重 COVID-19 病程風險的好處超過了接種疫苗的風險。	31	0.17	0.16	0.80	0.48	0.50	可以得出結論，對於大多數脆弱的老年人來說，降低嚴重風險的好處超過接受疫苗的風險。
143. 每種疫苗都適合所有人嗎？	11	0.39	0.38	0.92	0.66	1.24	143.每種疫苗都適合所有人？
如未能取得正確的疫苗接種紀錄或需要尋求協助，可到18間指定的香港郵政局重新申報非本地接種紀錄，並連同打印的電子接種紀錄連同本地的接種紀錄一起領取工作人員免費協助。有關指定郵局的地址及營業時間，請參閱 https://www.hongkongpost.hk/sc/services/non_local_covid19_vr/index.html#list	101	0.59	0.67	0.91	0.53	0.80	如果您無法獲得正確的疫苗接種記錄或需要尋求幫助，港郵局重新銷售非本地疫苗接種記錄，並獲得印刷的電地疫苗接種記錄，並帶有本地疫苗接種記錄員工的協助地址和開放時間，請參閱 https://www.hongkongpost.hk/en/services/non_local_c
25. 葡萄糖-6-磷酸脫氫酶 (G6PD) 缺乏症	12	0.21	0.26	0.87	0.59	0.56	25. 6-磷酸葡萄糖脫氫酶 (G6PD) 缺乏症
醫護人員可能會定期接觸病毒載量較高的重症患者。醫護人員也可能與免疫系統較弱的弱勢患者接觸。	31	0.15	0.16	0.84	0.48	0.76	醫療保健工人可能會定期與病毒負荷較高的嚴重患者接免疫系統弱的弱勢患者接觸。
請參閱問題 17。	6	1.00	1.00	1.00	0.75	1.32	請參考問題17。

Fig. 5.8 The "Segment Summary" section lists the source, reference and MT segments, source text length, and evaluation scores

Sentence 24

Source:
66. What should we consider before administration of CoronaVac vaccine?
Reference:
66. 接種克爾來福疫苗前我們應該考慮甚麼？
System 1:
66. 接種克爾來福 CoronaVac 疫苗前我們應該考慮甚什麼？
System 2:
66.接種克爾來福在服用冠狀疫苗之前，我們應該考慮甚什麼？
Scores:

	Automatic Translation	Length of ST	BLEU	CHRF	BERTScore	BLEURT	COMET
System 1	66. 接種 CoronaVac 疫苗前應該考慮什麼？	12	0.31	0.28	0.89	0.72	0.86
System 2	66.在服用冠狀疫苗之前，我們應該考慮什麼？	12	0.31	0.28	0.89	0.55	0.82

Terminology Analysis:

		System 1	System 2
CoronaVac vaccine	克爾來福疫苗	Not Detected	Not Detected

Fig. 5.9 The "Segment Analysis" section provides the details of the assessment of each segment, including the source and reference sentences, the MT results (with automatic highlighting of the differences between the reference sentence and MT output in green, red and blue colours for easier comparison), the evaluation scores, and, if available, the results of terminology analysis (e.g., in the example, the Chinese translation of the term "CoronaVac vaccine" was "not detected" in the MT results)

the report provides the MT results and their corresponding evaluation scores based on the different metrics. For each MT output, the differences between the candidate and the reference translation are shown in three colours (green for additional characters/words in the MT output, red for deletions, and blue for substitutions), which could facilitate the comparison between MT and human translation. For segments with terms detected by the terminology checker, the report indicates in the "Terminology Analysis" section whether the corresponding target language terms can be identified in the MT output.

5.5 Use of the System: A Preliminary Analysis of Two MT Products

To illustrate the use of COVID-19 MT Evaluator, this section presents the results of a preliminary comparison of two Google Translate services by using the platform.

5.5.1 Google Translate Products

Google Translate (Google 2022b) is an online translation service with support for more than 100 languages. The translation service is made available through different channels, such as the official translation website, translation apps (e.g., Android and

Table 5.5 Different Google Translate Results

	Sentence in the source/target language
Source Text in English	Pregnant people and those who have recently given birth are at high risk for experiencing severe influenza and severe COVID-19.
Reference Translation	孕婦和最近分娩的婦女患嚴重流感和COVID-19重症的風險很高。
MT Output 1 (Google Translate Website)	孕婦和最近分娩的人患嚴重流感和嚴重 COVID-19 的風險很高。 (Back translation: Pregnant women and people who have recently given birth are at high risk of developing severe influenza and severe COVID-19.)
MT Output 2 (Google Sheets)	孕婦和最近出生的人患有嚴重流感和嚴重的Covid-19。(Back translation: Pregnant women and those recently born suffer from severe influenza and severe Covid-19.)

iOS apps), Cloud Translate (as an Application Programming Interface), and Google Sheets (in the form of the spreadsheet function GOOGLETRANSLATE). It is worth noting that at the time of writing, the output of the same source sentence may vary from one Google Translate product to another. Table 5.5 gives an example with MT results provided by the official Google Translate website and the GOOGLETRANSLATE function. The noun phrase "those who have recently given birth" in the source sentence was translated as "最近出生的人" ("those recently born") in the second MT output, and the expression "at high risk" was missing in the result; however, they were translated correctly in the first MT output.

In our analysis, we selected the following two products and compared their performance: (1) the official website of Google Translate and (2) the GOOGLETRANSLATE function of Google Sheets, with the following syntax:

```
=GOOGLETRANSLATE(src_text,src_language,tgt_language)
```

There are three arguments, which specify the text to be translated (`src_text`), the source language (`src_lang`), and the target language (`tgt_lang`) (see Google (2022a) for details). Here is a simple example:

```
=GOOGLETRANSLATE(A1,"en","zh")
```

The above expression translates the content of cell A1 from English into Chinese.

5.5.2 *Overall Performance of Google Translate and Its Spreadsheet Function*

The comparison of the two translation services was based on the COVID-19-Vaccination-Subset (see Sect. 5.4.2) Tables 5.6 and 5.7 show that for both English-Chinese and Chinese-English translation, Google Translate website outperformed the spreadsheet translation function in all metrics.

Table 5.6 Summary of English-Chinese MT Evaluation Results

	BLEU	CHRF	BERTScore	BLEURT	COMET
Google Translate Website	**0.33**	**0.31**	**0.87**	**0.57**	**0.67**
GOOGLETRANSLATE	0.23	0.23	0.84	0.53	0.50

Table 5.7 Summary of Chinese-English MT Evaluation Results

	BLEU	CHRF	BERTScore	BLEURT	COMET
Cloud Translate Website	**0.28**	**0.57**	**0.86**	**0.63**	**0.52**
GOOGLETRANSLATE	0.18	0.47	0.82	0.54	0.13

Google Translate Website scored 0.03–0.17 and 0.04–0.39 points higher than GOOGLETRANSLATE at the dataset level for English-Chinese and Chinese-English translation, respectively.

The box-and-whisker plots in Fig. 5.10 show that the dispersion of the BLEU scores for Google Translate was slightly higher than that of the scores for the spreadsheet function in the case of English-Chinese translation. The scores for Google Translate were mostly between 0.2 and 0.45, while the scores for GOOGLETRANSLATE were between 0.1 and 0.3.

Figure 5.11 gives an overview of the COMET ratings (English-Chinese translation) at the segment level. The blue and red bars represent System 1 (Google Translate Website) and System 2 (the spreadsheet function) respectively. For most segments, System 1 scored higher than System 2, which is consistent with the overall ratings based on the other metrics in Table 5.6 and indicates that System 1 tended to perform better than System 2 in English-Chinese translation.

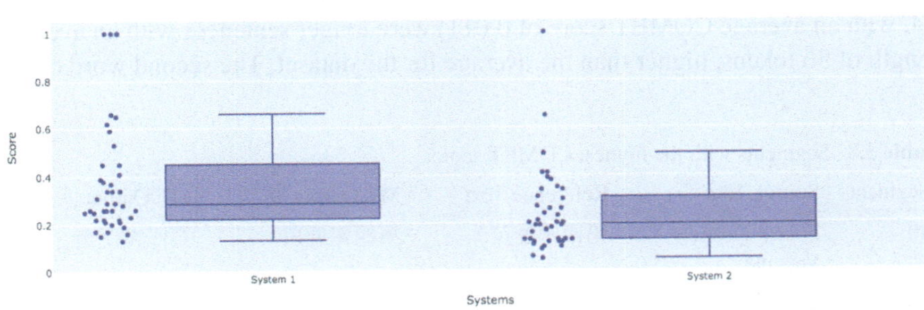

Fig. 5.10 Box-and-whisker plots showing the dispersion of BLEU scores for the two systems (English-Chinese translation)

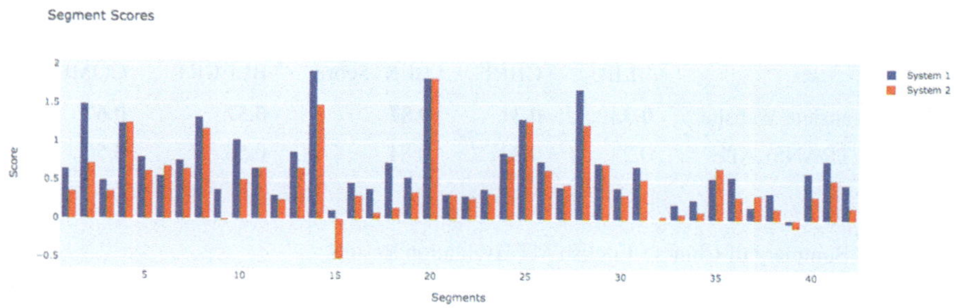

Fig. 5.11 COMET scores at the segment level (English-Chinese translation)

5.5.3 MT Performance Analysis

The interactive report not only describes the overall performance of the two systems as discussed above, but also provides insights into the segments that are worth further investigation. To illustrate this, we focus on the bar chart in Fig. 5.11, which shows the COMET scores for the two translation services at the segment level. We can first consider the segments with the best scores and their characteristics. The five highest-scoring segments were 20, 14, 28, 25, and 8, with an average COMET score of 1.50. They were short segments with an average length of 5.8 tokens, well below the average of all segments in the test dataset (31.5 tokens). In general, they were simple sentences or phrases with common expressions, and the machine translation results were similar, if not identical, to the reference sentences, as shown in Table 5.8.

Figure 5.12 (left) is a word cloud based on the words in the 10 highest-scoring segments (COMET), showing the use of a small number of common words (e.g., "vaccine," "dose," "days," "receive," and "time") in the source sentences.

In contrast, the segments with the lowest scores (Segments 15, 39, 32, 33, and 34, with an average COMET score of 0.011) were longer sentences with an average length of 36 tokens, higher than the average for the dataset. The second word cloud

Table 5.8 Segments with the highest COMET scores

Segment	Source Text	Reference Text	MT Output 1	MT Output 2
20	Fourth Dose Vaccine	第四劑疫苗	第四劑疫苗	第四劑疫苗
14	Third Dose Vaccine	第三劑疫苗	第三劑疫苗	第三劑量疫苗
28	19. A child or an adolescent	19. 兒童或青少年	19. 兒童或青少年	19.孩子或青少年
25	84. How does a Community Vaccination Centre operate?	84. 社區疫苗接種中心的運作為何?	84. 社區疫苗接種中心如何運作?	84.社區疫苗接種中心如何運作?
8	Please refer to question 17.	請參閱問題17。	請參閱問題 17。	請參考問題17。

Fig. 5.12 Word clouds based on top 10 segments with higher (left) and lower (right) COMET scores

in Fig. 5.12 (right), based on the 10 lowest-scoring segments, shows that a wider range of expressions, including technical terms and proper nouns, were used in these segments. For example, we can consider Segment 15, one of the lowest-scoring segments with a large difference in the COMET scores between the two MT engines, as we can see in Fig. 5.11. Table 5.9 shows the scores with respect to the five metrics (all lower than the overall scores in Table 5.6) and the score differences between the two services (between 0.06 and 0.82). Table 5.10 provides the source and reference sentences and the corresponding MT results.

Table 5.10 shows that Segment 15 is more complicated in content and structure than the high-scoring segments in Table 5.8. The two MT candidates had lower COMET scores mainly because the names of the two vaccines "Comirnaty" and "CoronaVac" were not translated, as automatically highlighted in the "Segment Analysis" section of the interactive report. The second MT candidate received a lower score because of the clarity of the message (e.g., the unclear meaning of the expression "接受兩次劑量的Comirnaty(Biontech)或Coronavac(Sinovac)疫苗接受第三次劑量" (literal translation: "receiving two doses of Comirnaty (Biontech) with the receipt of the third dose")), with the unnecessary repetition of "18歲以上" ("aged 18 or above") in the target text.

Table 5.9 MT Scores of Segment 15

	BLEU	CHRF	BERTScore	BLEURT	COMET
Google Translate Website [a]	**0.24**	**0.21**	**0.81**	**0.48**	**0.21**
GOOGLETRANSLATE [b]	0.05	0.1	0.75	0.38	−0.61
Difference [b-a]	−0.19	−0.11	−0.06	−0.1	−0.82

Table 5.10 Details of Segment 15

	Sentence in the source/target language
Source text in English	(i) Individuals aged 18 years or above who had received two doses of Comirnaty(BioNTech) or CoronaVac(Sinovac) vaccine are recommended to receive the third dose (CoronaVac or Comirnaty vaccine) as soon as 90 days after the second dose.
Reference translation	(i) 已接種兩劑克爾來福疫苗的或復必泰疫苗的18歲或以上人士, 第三劑疫苗(克爾來福或復必泰)建議於接種第二劑疫苗90日後盡快接種。
MT Output 1 (Google Translate Website)	(i) 18 歲或以上人士曾接種過兩劑 Comirnaty(BioNTech) 或 CoronaVac(Sinovac) 疫苗, 建議在第二劑接種後 90 天盡快接種第三劑(CoronaVac 或 Comirnaty 疫苗)。 (Back translation: Individuals aged 18 or above who have received two doses of Comirnaty (BioNTech) or CoronaVac (Sinovac) vaccine are recommended to receive a third dose (CoronaVac or Comirnaty vaccine) as soon as 90 days after the second dose.)
MT Output 2 (Google Sheets)	(i) 在第二劑劑量後90天, 建議接受18歲以上的年齡在18歲以上接受兩次劑量的Comirnaty(Biontech)或Coronavac(Sinovac)疫苗接受第三次劑量(Coronavac或comirnaty疫苗)。 (Back translation is not available here as the meaning of the MT candidate is unclear.)

Our preliminary analysis suggests that issues in MT of COVID-19 information can be attributed to the complexity of the source text and its terminology. Therefore, it may be beneficial for MT developers to explore ways to enhance the processing of long sentences and the accuracy of the translation of coronavirus-related terminology. One of the possibilities is domain adaptation (e.g., Luong and Manning 2015; Chu et al. 2017; Chu and Wang 2018), such as fine-tuning translation engines with public health articles.

The goal of our discussion here is to suggest some possible ways in which users can analyse and compare MT systems with the help of the platform, rather than to conduct a comprehensive study of the performance of the two services. There are many other possibilities for the assessment of the translation tools, such as examining scores other than COMET and analysing segments with large differences in MT scores with respect to the other metrics. In summary, the wealth of information provided by the report could enable users to conduct an in-depth analysis of MT scores and compare source, reference, and MT sentences, so as to find ways to improve the quality of automatic translation.

5.6 Concluding Remarks

In this article, we presented COVID-19 MT Evaluator, which is developed for the evaluation of automatic translation of public health information related to COVID-19. The system features the integration of multiple evaluation metrics; the design of domain-specific tools for the evaluation of MT of healthcare-related documents; the adoption of deep learning-driven evaluation metrics that go beyond string comparison between MT candidates and reference translations on the surface; and the incorporation of visualization tools for the detection and deeper analysis of translation issues, in addition to the computation of MT scores.

The system is useful for medical translators, healthcare professionals, researchers and developers for quick assessment of MT performance. For future research, it would be desirable to conduct larger-scale studies to evaluate common MT engines available on the market, compare the quality of translation results, and assess their performance when translating different types of COVID-19 information. By doing so, we could develop a better understanding of the quality of MT in the context of public health. The assessment results provided by the platform could enhance the selection and continuous development of MT systems and thus facilitate cross-lingual healthcare communication.

For further development of the evaluation platform, we could enhance its support for languages other than English and Chinese, expand its test datasets for the evaluation of MT of other types of public health information, incorporate more evaluation metrics, improve MT scoring algorithms and relevant pre-trained language models, and offer a wider range of tools for the analysis of MT performance (e.g., paired bootstrap resampling as discussed in Koehn (2004) and tools for quality estimation (Specia et al. 2021) or human MT evaluation with frameworks such as Multidimensional Quality Metrics (e.g., Freitag et al. 2021a).

Given the long-lasting and perhaps irreversible impact of COVID-19, coupled with other public health issues such as emerging infectious diseases and food safety, the need for automatic translation of public health information is expected to remain at a high level even after the pandemic subsides. We hope that the present work will provide a starting point for streamlining the evaluation of MT of COVID-19 information and other medical publications and contribute to the advancement of MT systems geared towards effective dissemination of health information across language barriers.

References

Akhbardeh, F., A. Arkhangorodsky, M. Biesialska, O. Bojar, R. Chatterjee, V. Chaudhary, and M. R. Costa-jussa et al. 2021. Findings of the 2021 conference on machine translation (WMT21). In *Proceedings of the Sixth Conference on Machine Translation*, 1–88. Association for Computational Linguistics.

Bojar, O., R. Chatterjee, C. Federmann, Y. Graham, B. Haddow, M. Huck, and A. Jimeno Yepes, et al. 2016. Findings of the 2016 conference on machine translation. In *Proceedings of the First Conference on Machine Translation: Volume 2, Shared Task Papers*, 131–198. Association for Computational Linguistics.

Caswell, I, and A. Bapna. 2022. Unlocking zero-resource machine translation to support new languages in Google Translate. https://ai.googleblog.com/2022/05/24-new-languages-google-translate.html. Accessed 15 July 2022.

Caswell, I., and B. Liang. 2020. Recent advances in Google Translate. https://ai.googleblog.com/2020/06/recent-advances-in-google-translate.html. Accessed 15 July 2022.

Centre for Health Protection. 2021. Health advice on prevention of COVID-19 for returnees (Interim). https://www.chp.gov.hk/files/pdf/nid_health_advice_for_returnees_eng.pdf. Accessed 15 July 2022.

Centre for Health Protection. 2022a. CHP investigates locally acquired SARS-CoV-2 virus cases with 1 035 cases tested positive by nucleic acid tests and 1 713 cases by RATs verified as well as 197 imported cases. https://www.info.gov.hk/gia/general/2022a07/08/P2022a070800679.htm. Accessed 15 July 2022a.

Centre for Health Protection. 2022b. Guidelines on prevention of Coronavirus Disease 2019 (COVID-19) for the general public. https://www.chp.gov.hk/files/pdf/nid_guideline_general_public_en.pdf. Accessed 15 July 2022b.

Centers for Disease Control and Prevention. 2021. Nucleic Acid Amplification Tests (NAATs) https://www.cdc.gov/coronavirus/2019-ncov/lab/naats.html. Accessed 15 July 2022.

Chu, C., R. Dabre, and S. Kurohashi. 2017. An empirical comparison of simple domain adaptation methods for neural machine translation. *arXiv preprint* arXiv:1701.03214.

Chu, C., and R. Wang. 2018. A survey of domain adaptation for neural machine translation. In *Proceedings of the 27th International Conference on Computational Linguistics*, 1304–1319. Association for Computational Linguistics.

Conneau, A., K. Khandelwal, N. Goyal, V. Chaudhary, G. Wenzek, F. Guzmán, E. Grave, M. Ott, L. Zettlemoyer, and V. Stoyanov. 2020. Unsupervised cross-lingual representation learning at scale. In *Proceedings of the 58th Annual Meeting of the Association for Computational Linguistics*, 8440–8451. Association for Computational Linguistics.

Cromieres, F., C. Chu, T. Nakazawa, and S. Kurohashi. 2016. Kyoto university participation to WAT 2016. In *Proceedings of the 3rd Workshop on Asian Translation (WAT2016)*, 166–174. The COLING 2016 Organizing Committee.

Department of Health. 2022. Vaccination fact sheet for CoronaVac. https://www.covidvaccine.gov.hk/pdf/COVID19VaccinationFactSheet_CoronaVac_ENG.pdf. Accessed 15 July 2022.

Devlin, J., M. W. Chang, K. Lee, and K. Toutanova. 2018. Bert: Pre-training of deep bidirectional transformers for language understanding. *arXiv preprint* arXiv:1810.04805.

Freitag, M., G. Foster, D. Grangier, V. Ratnakar, Q. Tan, and W. Macherey. 2021a. Experts, errors, and context: A large-scale study of human evaluation for machine translation. *Transactions of the Association for Computational Linguistics* 9: 1460–1474.

Freitag, M., R. Rei, N. Mathur, C.-k. Lo, C. Stewart, G. Foster, A. Lavie, and O. Bojar. 2021b. Results of the WMT21 metrics shared task: Evaluating metrics with expert-based human evaluations on TED and news domain. In *Proceedings of the Sixth Conference on Machine Translation*, 733–774. Association for Computational Linguistics.

Gehring, J., M. Auli, D. Grangier, D. Yarats, and Y. N. Dauphin. 2017. Convolutional sequence to sequence learning. In *Proceedings of the 34th International Conference on Machine Learning*, 1243–1252. PMLR.

Google. 2022a. Google Docs Editors help. *GOOGLETRANSLATE*. https://support.google.com/docs/answer/3093331?hl=en. Accessed 15 July 2022.

Google. 2022b. Google Translate. https://translate.google.com/about/. Accessed 15 July 2022.

Google Research. 2021. BLEURT: A transfer learning-based metric for natural language generation. https://github.com/google-research/bleurt. Accessed 15 July 2022.

HKSAR Government. 2022a. Come2hk—Travel scheme for non-Hong Kong residents coming from Guangdong Province or Macao to Hong Kong without being subject to quarantine under the Compulsory quarantine of certain persons arriving at Hong Kong regulation (Cap. 599C) (Come2hk Scheme). https://www.coronavirus.gov.hk/eng/come2hk-scheme.html. Accessed 15 July 2022a.

HKSAR Government. 2022b. Compulsory testing for certain persons. https://www.coronavirus.gov.hk/eng/compulsory-testing.html. Accessed 15 July 2022b.

HKSAR Government. 2022c. COVID-19 vaccination program FAQs. https://www.covidvaccine.gov.hk/en/faq. Accessed 15 July 2022c.

HKSAR Government. 2022d. COVID-19 vaccination program FAQs (Chinese version). https://www.covidvaccine.gov.hk/zh-HK/faq. Accessed 15 July 2022d.

HKSAR Government. 2022e. Frequently asked questions on new requirements to reduce gatherings. https://www.coronavirus.gov.hk/eng/social_distancing-faq.html. Accessed 15 July 2022e.

HKSAR Government. 2022f. Government extends existing social distancing measures. https://www.info.gov.hk/gia/general/2022f06/27/P2022f062600402.htm. Accessed 15 July 2022f.

HKSAR Government. 2022g. Government gazettes compulsory testing notice. https://www.info.gov.hk/gia/general/2022g07/07/P2022g070700732.htm. Accessed 15 July 2022g.

HKSAR Government. 2022h. LeaveHomeSafe. https://www.leavehomesafe.gov.hk/en/. Accessed 15 July 2022h.

HKSAR Government. 2022i. Rapid antigen tests. https://www.coronavirus.gov.hk/rat/eng/rat.html. Accessed 15 July 2022i.

HKSAR Government. 2022j. Vaccine pass. https://www.coronavirus.gov.hk/eng/vaccine-pass.html. Accessed 15 July 2022j.

Hong Kong e-Legislation. 2022. Cap. 599F Prevention and control of disease (requirements and directions) (business and premises) regulation. https://www.elegislation.gov.hk/hk/cap599F. Accessed 15 July 2022.

Jieba. 2020. "Jieba" (Chinese for "to stutter") Chinese text segmentation: Built to be the best Python Chinese word segmentation module. https://github.com/fxsjy/jieba. Accessed 15 July 2022.

Koehn, P. 2004. Statistical significance tests for machine translation evaluation. In *Proceedings of the 2004 Conference on Empirical Methods in Natural Language Processing*, 388–395. Association for Computational Linguistics.

Liu, Y., L. Zhou, Y. Wang, Y. Zhao, J. Zhang, and C. Zong. 2018. A comparable study on model averaging, ensembling and reranking in NMT. In *Natural Language Processing and Chinese Computing. NLPCC 2018*, ed. M. Zhang, V. Ng, D. Zhao, S. Li, and H. Zan, 299–308. Cham: Springer.

Luong, M. T., and C. D. Manning. 2015. Stanford neural machine translation systems for spoken language domains. In *Proceedings of the International Workshop on Spoken Language Translation*, 76–79.

Mathur, N., J. Wei, M. Freitag, Q. Ma, and O. Bojar. 2020. Results of the WMT20 metrics shared task. In *Proceedings of the Fifth Conference on Machine Translation*, 688–725. Association for Computational Linguistics.

National Institutes of Health. 2022. Antiviral drugs that are approved, authorized, or under evaluation for the treatment of COVID-19. https://www.covid19treatmentguidelines.nih.gov/therapies/antiviral-therapy/summary-recommendations/. Accessed 15 July 2022.

news.gov.hk. 2022. HK logs 2.8k local infections. https://www.news.gov.hk/eng/2022/07/20220707/20220707_170515_117.html. Accessed 15 July 2022.

Ng, N., K. Yee, A. Baevski, M. Ott, M. Auli, and S. Edunov. 2019. Facebook FAIR's WMT19 news translation task submission. In *Proceedings of the Fourth Conference on Machine Translation (Volume 2: Shared Task Papers, Day 1)*, 314–319. Association for Computational Linguistics.

NLTK. 2022. Natural language toolkit. https://www.nltk.org/. Accessed 15 July 2022.

Papineni, K., S. Roukos, T. Ward, T., and W.-J. Zhu. 2002. Bleu: A method for automatic evaluation of machine translation. In *Proceedings of the 40th annual meeting of the Association for Computational Linguistics*, 311–318.

Popović, M. 2015. chrF: Character n-gram F-score for automatic MT evaluation. In *Proceedings of the Tenth Workshop on Statistical Machine Translation*, 392–395. Association for Computational Linguistics.

Post, M. 2018. A call for clarity in reporting BLEU scores. In *Proceedings of the Third Conference on Machine Translation (WMT), Volume 1: Research Papers*, 186–191. Association for Computational Linguistics.

Post, M., and D. Vilar. 2018. Fast lexically constrained decoding with dynamic beam allocation for neural machine translation. In *Proceedings of the 2018 Conference of the North American Chapter of the Association for Computational Linguistics: Human Language Technologies, Volume 1 (Long Papers)*, 1314–1324. Association for Computational Linguistics.

Rei, R., A. C. Farinha, C. Zerva, D. van Stigt, C. Stewart, P. Ramos, T. Glushkova, A. F. T. Martins, and A. Lavie. 2021. Are references really needed? Unbabel-IST 2021 submission for the metrics shared task. In *Proceedings of the Sixth Conference on Machine Translation*, 1030–1040. Association for Computational Linguistics.

Rei, R., C. Stewart, A. C. Farinha, and A. Lavie. 2020. COMET: A neural framework for MT evaluation. In *Proceedings of the 2020 Conference on Empirical Methods in Natural Language Processing (EMNLP)*, 2685–2702. Association for Computational Linguistics.

Rivera-Trigueros, I. 2021. Machine translation systems and quality assessment: A systematic review. *Language Resources and Evaluation* 56: 593–619.

Sellam, T., D. Das, and A. Parikh. 2020. BLEURT: Learning robust metrics for text generation. In *Proceedings of the 58th Annual Meeting of the Association for Computational Linguistics*, 7881–7892. Association for Computational Linguistics.

Sennrich, R., B. Haddow, and A. Birch. 2016. Improving neural machine translation models with monolingual data. In *Proceedings of the 54th Annual Meeting of the Association for Computational Linguistics (Volume 1: Long Papers)*, 86–96. Association for Computational Linguistics.

Shimanaka, H., T. Kajiwara, and M. Komachi. 2018. Ruse: Regressor using sentence embeddings for automatic machine translation evaluation. In *Proceedings of the Third Conference on Machine Translation: Shared Task Papers*, 751–758. Association for Computational Linguistics.

Specia, L., F. Blain, F., M. Fomicheva, C. Zerva, Z. Li, V. Chaudhary, and A. F. T. Martins. 2021. Findings of the WMT 2021 shared task on quality estimation. In *Proceedings of the Sixth Conference on Machine Translation*, 684–725. Association for Computational Linguistics.

Stahlberg, F. 2020. Neural machine translation: A review. *Journal of Artificial Intelligence Research* 69: 343–418.

Sutskever, I., O. Vinyals, and Q.V. Le. 2014. Sequence to sequence learning with neural networks. *Advances in Neural Information Processing Systems* 27: 3104–3112.

Tilde. 2021. Interactive BLEU. https://www.tilde.com/products-and-services/machine-translation/features/interactive-bleu. Accessed 15 July 2022.

Unbabel. 2021. COMET: High-quality machine translation evaluation (frequently asked questions). https://unbabel.github.io/COMET/html/faqs.html. Accessed 15 July 2022.

Vaswani, A., N. Shazeer, N. Parmar, J. Uszkoreit, L. Jones, A. N. Gomez, Ł. Kaiser, and I. Polosukhin. 2017. Attention is all you need. In *Proceedings of the 31st International Conference on Neural Information Processing Systems*, 6000–6010.

World Health Organization. 2022a. Q&As on COVID-19 and related health topics. https://www.who.int/emergencies/diseases/novel-coronavirus-2019/question-and-answers-hub. Accessed 15 July 2022a.

World Health Organization. 2022b. Q&As on COVID-19 and related health topics (Chinese version). https://www.who.int/zh/emergencies/diseases/novel-coronavirus-2019/question-and-answers-hub. Accessed 15 July 2022b.

Wu, Y., M. Schuster, Z. Chen, Q. V. Le, M. Norouzi, W. Macherey, M. Krikun, et al. 2016. Google's neural machine translation system: Bridging the gap between human and machine translation. *arXiv preprint* arXiv:1609.08144.

Zhang, T., V. Kishore, F. Wu, K. Q. Weinberger, and Y. Artzi. 2019. BERTScore: Evaluating text generation with BERT. *arXiv preprint* arXiv:1904.09675.

Sai Cheong Siu is an Associate Professor in the School of Translation and Foreign Languages, The Hang Seng University of Hong Kong. He is the Programme Director of the Bachelor of Translation with Business and the Master of Arts in Translation (Computer-Aided Translation) and the former Director of Deep Learning Research and Application Center. His research focuses on technology for translation and language services. His publicly funded projects include "Machine Translation of IPO Documents" and "A Hybrid Approach to the Translation of Government Press Releases," supported by the Innovation and Technology Fund and the Research Grants Council respectively.

Part II
Reconceptualising Interpreting in the Age of COVID-19

Chapter 6
Remote Simultaneous Interpreting from Home or Hub: Accuracy of Numbers from English into Mandarin Chinese

Andrew K. F. Cheung

Abstract The use of remote simultaneous interpreting (RSI) would probably continue post COVID-19 pandemic, and RSI could take place either from a hub or home. Does RSI quality vary from setting to setting? In an experiment that focused on numbers, the RSI quality of English into Mandarin Chinese by interpreters working from a hub was compared to that of interpreters working from home. Specifically, we compared the renditions of numbers in two segments, segment 1 began slightly more than 3 min after the start of the source language, and segment 2 began after more than 20 min. Using the Paas scale, the participants also indicated their perceived cognitive load for their task. The performance of numbers in segment 1 between the two groups was almost identical. However, while both groups struggled with numbers that required mental conversion when interpreting into Chinese, the hub group adopted the approximation strategy more extensively than did the home group. The hub group also had a lower Paas scale than the home group. The results suggest that interpreters can be more strategic in the hub setting probably because of a lower perceived cognitive load.

Keywords Remote simultaneous interpreting · Numbers · Cognitive load · Experiment · Home or hub

6.1 Introduction

Just as many people view the Nuremberg trials as the beginning of the widespread use of simultaneous interpreting (SI), the ongoing COVID-19 pandemic may be viewed in the future as the beginning of the widespread use of internet-based remote SI (RSI). Pre-COVID-19, SI interpreters normally worked onsite, where they are present at the same time and at the same location as conference speakers and attendees. In the onsite setting, interpreters work in teams with other interpreters in soundproof booths with a

A. K. F. Cheung (✉)
The Hong Kong Polytechnic University, Hong Kong, China
e-mail: andrew.cheung@polyu.edu.hk

K. Liu and A. K. F. Cheung (eds.), *Translation and Interpreting in the Age of COVID-19*, Corpora and Intercultural Studies 9,
https://doi.org/10.1007/978-981-19-6680-4_6

physical console. When technical problems occur, interpreters could seek help from the onsite technicians. Although technology has "greatly diversified the interpreter's working environment" (Neagu and Georgescu 2020: 37), no extensive research has been conducted on the impact of RSI on interpreters' performance (Cheung 2022b).

RSI refers to SI services provided on cloud-based web conferencing platforms to meet the language needs of multilingual online conferences. Many conferences take place online because of sheltering in orders and travel restrictions imposed following the COVID-19 pandemic outbreaks (Cheung 2022a). One possible upside of online conferences is the democratization of attendance, as some individuals may be able to attend conferences they may otherwise not be able to attend if these were to be conducted onsite (Chew and Cheung 2022). With conferences taking place online, speakers and conference participants also attend conferences virtually. Owing to this shift of onsite to online, conference interpreters are also now providing RSI services.

RSI allows interpreters to work from a hub or home. When working from home, interpreters use their personal computers or notebook computers to login to a platform to deliver their interpretation via the Internet. Working from home minimizes travel time, travel costs, and time away from home. However, before COVID-19, not having to travel to work did not seem to be a strong advantage to interpreters if they had a choice between working from home and working from a hub. Seeber et al. (2019) found that interpreters preferred to work from a hub than their homes in a study that investigated the attitudes of interpreters working in the hub setting at the 2014 FIFA World Cup.

When RSI became the *modus operandi* following the COVID-19 outbreak, professional interpreters seemed to have a divided preference for working from a hub or from home. Other than not being in the same space with conference speakers and attendees in the onsite interpreting setting, working from a hub is quite similar to working onsite. In fact, one of the reasons for interpreters' preference for working from a hub to home may be the similarity of working conditions between working onsite and working from a hub (Ziegler and Gigliobianco 2018). In the wake of the COVID-19 pandemic, the International Association of Conference Interpreters, commonly known as AIIC, published a set of guidelines (AIIC 2020) recommending that interpreters work from a hub and only work from home in extreme circumstances, such as lockdowns. This recommendation is partly due to the benefits of working from a hub (Table 6.1).

How working from home or from a hub could affect interpreters' performances has not been extensively studied. Understandably, the SI performance of interpreters is subject to an array of source language problem triggers (Cheung 2001; Gile 2009), such as unfamiliar accents (Cheung 2003, 2015), numbers, and proper names; delivery rate (Rosendo and Galván 2019); information density (Hild 2015); intelligibility (Reithofer 2020); sentence complexity (Liu et al. 2004); and word order (Cheung 2012). These factors and more could lead to such issues as omission (Cheung 2011), disfluency (Song and Cheung 2019), and interference (Ma and Cheung 2020), among other problems. Some evidence also suggests that SI performance could be subject to the interpreter's visual access to the speakers, given that

Table 6.1 Major features of working from hub and working from home (modified from Chaves 2020)

Working from hub	Working from home
Interpreters are co-located therefore ease of handover and relay	Interpreters are not co-located making handover and relay difficult
Onsite technicians	Remote technical support
Permanent internet connection	Connectivity problems may arise
Confidentiality of communication	Connection may not be safe
Soundproof setting	Background noise interference
Physical interpreters' consoles	Soft consoles

multisensory input of the speakers' facial and bodily movement and auditory utterance brings optimal perceptual benefits to the interpreter (Simon and Wallace 2018). Visibility of lip movements, specifically, aids understanding particularly if the sound quality is limited (Massaro et al. 1993: 446). However, Moser-Mercer (2003) and Roziner and Shlesinger (2010) compared the SI performance of interpreters between hub and onsite settings and found no significant difference, even though interpreters working from a hub may have fewer multisensory input compared to those working onsite.

The physical working environments when working from a hub and working onsite are similar because interpreters are not distant from one another. Onsite technical support is normally available in the hub setting. However, interpreters seem to prefer onsite SI as they claim that working onsite is less cognitively taxing than working from a hub (Kurz 2002; Moser-Mercer 2005; Roziner and Shlesinger 2010). In an experiment that involved 12 participants, Moser-Mercer (2005) found that working from a hub could lead to an early onset of fatigue, as evidenced by a decline in performance that occurs faster than when working onsite. However, Moser-Mercer (2003) and Roziner and Shlesinger (2010) found no significant difference between interpreters' performance between hub and onsite settings. Specifically, Roziner and Shlesinger (2010) found no significant differences in the SI performance between onsite and hub conditions after analysing the SI renditions of 36 participants. As the working conditions between working from home and from a hub could be very different, interpreters' performance may also differ.

Interpreters working from home may experience challenges similar to students learning remotely, such as the sense of isolation and alienation and the constant worry about unstable Internet connection. It is not uncommon for students to complain about connection problems and noise when attending online classes during COVID-19 school closures (Sugino 2021). Peper et al. (2021) reported that more than 90% of 325 poll respondents, all students of an American university, had moderate to considerable difficulties with online learning during COVID-19 campus closure. The analysis of Bolatov et al. (2021), who carried out a survey study involving 619 undergraduate medical school students, showed that students engaged in online learning during campus closure are more prone to fatigue than they are in traditional face-to-face learning because of an increase in mental efforts associated with online learning.

Being on a task for too long may lead to more errors in numbers. The findings of Moser-Mercer et al. (1998) suggested that prolonged turns longer than 30 min could have a negative impact on interpreters' performance, although generalization is difficult with only five professional interpreters as participants. The cognitive taxing nature of SI requires that interpreters work in teams of two or three, each taking a 15- or 20-min turn. In the home setting, turns may be prolonged by interpreters on purpose. Handover may be less convenient compared to being in a booth with another colleague (Chaves 2020), as when working remotely, interpreters often have to use a second device to monitor and communicate with their colleague for turn-taking (Fedorenkova 2020). Given such cumbersome handover process, some interpreters may opt to hand over when a speaker finishes the entire speech, and so a turn is determined by the entirety of the speech instead of a pre-determined duration. This practice may minimize some of the risks posed by remote turn-taking; however, it also suggests that an interpreter may exceed the normal duration of a 20-min turn depending on the length of a speech. Whether errors of number increase as time on the task increases has not been extensively investigated.

6.2 Numbers in SI

Numbers are common problem triggers in SI (Cheung 2008, 2009; Gile 2009; Pinochi 2009) and "are particularly vulnerable to incompleteness and inaccuracy" (Mead 2015: 286). Some interpreters working between signed and spoken languages also find numbers to be challenging (Chew and Cheung 2022). Numbers in the source language pose challenges to the SI process because they have "low predictability, low redundancy and high informative content" (Mazza 2001: 90). Unlike lexical-semantic units in the source language, numbers cannot be paraphrased (Jones 2002) partly because they are symbols that are "devoid of semantic content" (Timarová et al. 2014) and can rarely "be inferred from the context" (Braun and Clarici 1996: 87). Findings in neuroscience indicate that the cognitive representation of numbers is different from the representation of lexical-semantic concepts (Cheung 2009). The cognitive pathway that processes numbers may be different from the one that processes lexical-semantic units. Therefore, numbers are challenging to interpreters who need to shift from one pathway to another when processing numbers in the source language (Cheung 2009). The high error rates of numbers could also be attributed partly to the increase in cognitive load.

The translation of numbers between languages is not always a straightforward transcoding from one language into another. Additional cognitive resources may be required for mental conversion when translating numbers from one language into another. In some North Asian languages, such as Chinese, Japanese, and Korean, large numbers are grouped in ten thousand instead of thousand, and in Chinese, two hundred thousand is twenty ten thousand. Therefore, when interpreting numbers between English and North Asian languages, interpreters need to convert numbers mentally, thus increasing their mental loads (Cheung 2008, 2009, 2014).

Cognitive load can be measured indirectly by inferring its effect on performance. Ample indirect evidence supports that numbers may lead to an abrupt increase of cognitive efforts during SI (Plevoets and Defrancq 2016). The results of an eye-tracking study (Korpal and Stachowiak-Szymczak 2018) show that the mean fixation duration on numbers is longer than on other linguistic elements, suggesting that processing numbers in SI may be cognitively taxing. This conclusion was based chiefly on the assertion that a longer fixation time is an indication of different cognitive processes (see Cahuliac et al. 2020). Defrancq and Fantinuoli (2021) surveyed experimental studies that involve trainee-interpreters and professional interpreters and found that "error rates [of numbers] typically range between 30 and 70%" (75). An analysis on the European Parliament corpus showed that around 70% of numbers in the source languages are accurately interpreted (Kajzer-Wietrzny et al. 2021). This finding is consistent with Plevoets and Defrancq (2016), who observed in their corpus that numbers in the source language tend to be accompanied by a higher frequency of disfluencies in the SI renditions, probably due to the higher cognitive load.

Having visual access may help interpreters cope with numbers in SI. Results in Seeber et al. (2020) suggest that visual access to oral utterance helps interpreters "offload short-term memory" during SI. Therefore, visual access may reduce the cognitive load of interpreters and potentially lead to improved accuracy rates in numbers. Desmet et al. (2018), Stachowiak-Szymczak and Korpal (2019), Chmiel et al. (2020), Defrancq and Fantinuoli (2021), and Pisani and Fantinuoli (2021) provided compelling evidence to suggest that having visual access to numbers used in oral speech could improve the accuracy rate of numbers in SI.

Managing cognitive resources could help circumvent the challenges of numbers in SI. Meuleman and Van Besien (2009), Stachowiak-Szymczak and Korpal (2019), and Chmiel et al. (2020) suggested that interpreters may be aware of the importance and difficulties of numbers and therefore allocate cognitive resource to try to interpret numbers correctly. Specifically, some interpreters may internalize the ways in which they cope with numbers, such as switching rapidly between meaning-based to form-based interpreting approaches to translate numbers (Riccardi 2005). Meaning-based interpreting assumes that "every part of the input is mediated through the conceptual stage" (Seeber 2011: 190), and form-based interpreting, or transcoding, suggests "where the interpreter's level of processing will be no deeper than needed" (Seeber 2011: 190). It is therefore crucial that interpreters develop coping techniques for numbers that require mental conversion. As Gile (2009) cautioned, "[T]ranslate [a number] fully or just indicate its general order of magnitude, any such local decision may have significant implications on cognitive load and determine success or failure" (70).

Whether the approximation strategy should be used is debatable. Studies such as Čeňková et al. (2014) and Lamberger-Felber (2001) used a binary approach to classify correctly and incorrectly translated numbers and categorized approximations as incorrect. However, both Pinochi (2009) and Korpal and Stachowiak-Szymczak

(2020) accepted approximation as a strategy to cope with number-induced difficulties in SI. In an English-into-Chinese SI experiment involving trainee-interpreters, Cheung (2008) reported three coping techniques of participants, namely, translating all digits, approximating by rounding off, and omitting all digits. The capability of approximation to circumvent difficulties is probably because fewer cognitive resources are required when interpreters attempt to round off a number, as they only have to remember a few digits. The approximation approach may be preferred specially when interpreters are running low on cognitive resources, which tend to deplete as fatigue resulting from performing the SI tasks could lead to errors. As Moser-Mercer et al. (1998) stated, there is "a continuous rise in meaning errors with increasing time on task" (54).

Numbers are problematic to SI interpreters of different languages, so much so that they are "interpreters' nemesis" (Altman 1994: 32). Interpreters' performance in numbers may serve as an informative dependent variable for studying factors that may threaten their SI performance. Korpal and Stachowiak-Szymczak (2020) showed that fast delivery speed of the source language could lead to a decline in number accuracy. Comparing number accuracy between interpreters working from home and working from a hub would reveal how the former differs in terms of accuracy of numbers from the latter.

Whether and how SI performance of numbers differs between the hub and home settings have not been investigated extensively. Empirical studies (Braun and Claric 1996; Cheung 2008, 2009, 2014; Lamberger-Felber 2001; Mazza 2001; Pinochi 2009; Timarová 2005; Desmet et al. 2018; Stachowiak-Szymczak and Korpal 2019; Chmiel et al. 2020; Defrancq and Fantinuoli 2021; Pisani and Fantinuoli 2021) that investigated how numbers are handled in SI were conducted in a lab setting with professional and trainee interpreters as participants before the COVID-19 pandemic. However, as onsite SI was common before COVID-19, the ecological validity of these previous studies might have been compromised. The present study was based on the hub and home settings that resemble the norm of SI working conditions in the COVID-19 era, thereby improving its ecological validity. Comparing the performance of numbers in SI from English into Chinese by professional interpreters working from a hub and from home could provide evidence on whether the two modes have similar or different influences on the cognitive loads of interpreters.

6.2.1 Self-reported Cognitive Load

In addition to measuring cognitive load indirectly by inferring SI performance, the current study also incorporated a self-reported cognitive load scale for participants to rate the cognitive load of their task. Self-reported rating scale of cognitive load is a subject measurement tool that reflects retrospective perceptions of cognitive load. Research participants have shown themselves to be capable of indicating numerically the perceived mental difficulty of a task (Paas et al. 2003). Paas scale has been found to be a reliable cognitive load measurement (Chen et al. 2011; Naismith et al. 2015;

Szulewski et al. 2017). This self-reported rating scale survey method was chosen because it can be used in multiple different locations, be it home or hub.

6.3 Method

6.3.1 Participants

All participants were recruited by mainland China-based translation agencies that forwarded the CVs of participants to the researcher of this study. The CVs of participants indicated that they all hold at least a Master's degree in translation and interpreting or language-related disciplines. The participants were 43 English/ Mandarin interpreters (31 female and 12 male). Table 6.2 shows the distribution of genders between the two settings (Figs. 6.1 and 6.2).

All participants worked as freelance English/ Chinese conference interpreters, with professional experiences ranging from 5 to more than 20 years. All participants are based in mainland China. Their CVs indicated that they have had experience in performing solo SI for 30 min non-stop in the online SI setting either from a hub or from home.

Table 6.2 Gender of Participants

Home		Hub	
Male	Female	Male	Female
5	14	7	17

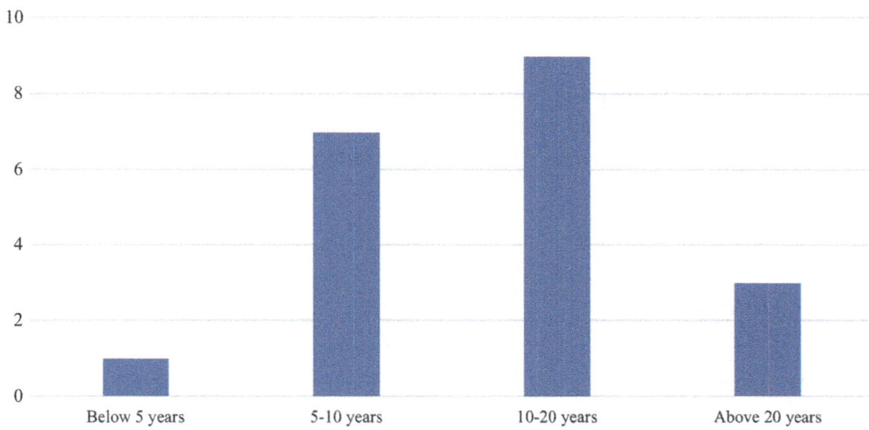

Fig. 6.1 Years of SI experience: Home

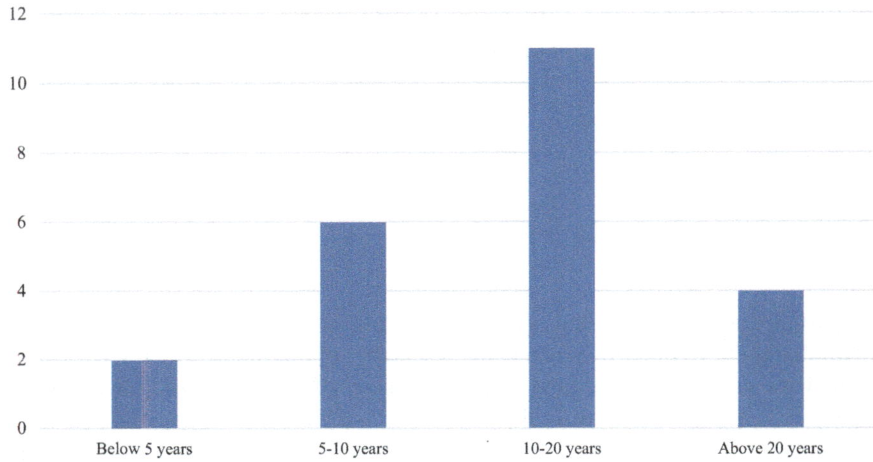

Fig. 6.2 Years of SI experience: Hub

Translation agencies responsible for recruitment informed the participants that they would perform a solo SI task for 30 min from English into Mandarin either from a hub or their home for an English speaker on the topic of China's Belt and Road Initiative in the Russian Far East. All interpreters (23 work from a hub, 20 work from home) received financial compensation directly from the recruiting agencies, which charged the researcher for SI fees, hub rentals, and service fees. The participants had to sign a confidential agreement and a consent release form allowing the researcher to report data from the recordings for non-commercial purposes. The participants were assured of their anonymity.

The experiment took place in August 2020. Summer has always been a "low season" for the conference-interpreting profession, and it was easier to arrange such an undertaking with agencies and interpreters than in high seasons. Owing to the ongoing pandemic, agencies and interpreters might have been motivated to try new modes of working that could constitute the new normal even after the end of the pandemic. Agencies had to have a hub and be able to coordinate the RSI of multiple interpreters.

6.3.2 Materials

The experimental speech was modified from an actual speech delivered in English at a Belt and Road Initiative event that took place in Hong Kong. The speaker of the experimental speech was a male Caucasian with a detectable Russian accent. The total length of the experimental presentation was almost 26 min at a speaking pace of an average of 116 English words per minute. The speaker spoke in front a video camera with an external microphone in a university studio normally reserved for

Table 6.3 Numbers in the two segments

	Segment 1	Segment 2
Simple whole numbers	1000 m	180 m
Complex whole numbers	1.08 million	230 thousand
Percentage	17.2%	15.3%
Year	2018	2019

the production of online lectures for course delivery during the COVID-19 campus closure. After the production of the video, it was saved as an MP4 file to be sent to agencies. The presentation contained two segments for the analysis of this study, segment 1# began at 3′12″ after the start of the presentation and segment 2* began at 21′45″. Table 6.3 shows both segments contained four types of numbers: simple whole numbers, complex whole numbers, decimals, and years (Desmet et al. 2018).

6.3.3 *Procedure*

Interpreters who worked from home received a Zoom link to login to the platform 30 min before the scheduled start time and were told to use either a laptop or desktop computer. Wi-Fi connection and Bluetooth headphones were not allowed for those who worked from home. Agency technicians assisted the interpreters remotely to test their headphones and microphones and gave the interpreters a countdown before the presentation started. The technicians were also responsible for recording the SI soundtracks. At the end of the presentation, the Paas scale appeared on the computer screens of the interpreters. The technicians informed the interpreters verbally to take a picture of the screen using their cellphone and circle the number that best represented the efforts required for the SI task before sending the picture back to the technicians using instant messaging apps. Once the technicians received the Paas scale from the interpreters, they informed the interpreters to logout. Interpreters who worked from hubs were told to arrive half an hour before the scheduled start time. They could see a large TV screen in front of them outside of the booth after being seated in the booth. The rest of the procedure was the same as for those working from home. At the end of the experiment, agencies sent all SI recordings and photos of the Paas scale from the interpreters to the author of this paper for analysis.

6.3.4 *Coding of Translated Numbers*

All recordings of the Mandarin SI were transcribed by iflyrec.com, a Chinese online transcription service. Similar to Cheung (2016), two native Mandarin-speaking checkers compared the transcriptions to the audio recordings to ascertain the accuracy of the transcriptions of the two segments. Instead of using a binary approach to

Table 6.4 Translated numbers that were categorized as approximations

	Segment 1		Segment 2
1000 m	N.A	180 m	About 100 m and more than 100 m
1.08 million	One million plus, about 1 million, and above 1 million	230 thousand	Few hundred thousand, about two hundred thousand, and more than two hundred thousand
17.2%	Above 17%, above 10%, (about) 17%, and a dozen %	15.3%	Above 15%, (about) 15%, more than 15%, and dozen %
2018	Two years ago	2019	Last year

classify correctly from incorrectly translated numbers, this study adopted a descriptive approach to categorize all translated and omitted numbers in the two segments. Two coders coded the numbers separately, and a third coder then grouped the codes into five categories, namely, correct, approximation, omission, incorrect, and unintelligible.

Correctly translated numbers had to be a direct transcoding from English, that is, having all digits in the same order and the correct order of magnitude of the source language numbers. The numbers 2018 and 2019 were an exception as translations containing just the last two digits (i.e., 18 or 19) were coded accurate.

Translated numbers that were coded as approximations either contained at least the first digit of the numbers and an accurate order of magnitude or an accurate translation of the order of magnitude. Table 6.4 lists all translated numbers in the two Mandarin SI segments that were coded as approximation.

Omission refers to all numerical digits and the degree of order missing in the rendition. However, an omission may not necessarily be an indication of an incorrect or incomplete meaning. For instance, an interpreter rendered the first sentence in segment 1 ("…airport now has a 1,000-m runway, in addition to a shorter runway that was built during the Soviet era") in a way that could be translated into English as "the airport now has two runways, one long and one short, one new and one old." Such a rendition gets the accurate message across. However, the number 1,000 was missing in the translation, which was eventually coded an "omission."

Translated numbers coded as incorrect had one of the following features: (1) incorrect first digit (e.g., 17.2% was translated into 70.2%), (2) incorrect order of the digits (e.g., 180 was translated into 810 or 118), or (3) incorrect order of magnitude (e.g., 230 thousand was translated into 23 thousand). The direct transcoding approach, an attempt to translate all digits into the target language, is the common feature that all incorrect numbers shared.

The code unintelligible was for translated numbers that were difficult to decipher. In several occasions exclusive to the home group, the audio volume in the recording where the interpreters uttered the numbers in Chinese dropped suddenly, resulting in unintelligible audio signals. Unintelligible parts also included instances when interpreters sounded as if they were mumbling or coughing, thereby making the numbers incomprehensible. Unintelligible is unlike omission, rather it is a noise that replaces where a number is supposed to be. For instance, the second part of the last sentence in segment 2 ("...this number is quite remarkable and represents a growth rate of 15.3% compared to the year before) was rendered as "this number is a good growth rate from last year" and was thus coded as omission. However, an unintelligible count was given to the rendition that goes "this number is quite good and represents [unintelligible] percent growth rate from last year." Instances like these could be due to technical glitches, latency, physiological conditions of the interpreters, or an attempt to mask a potentially incorrect translation.

6.4 Results and Discussions

6.4.1 Cognitive Load Results of the Paas Scale

There was a significant difference in the Paas scales for the hub (M = 5.130, SD = 0.868) and home (M = 5.750, SD = 0.850) conditions; $t(41) = -2.355$, $p < 0.05$. The perceived cognitive load for those who worked from a hub was significantly lower than for those who worked from home.

The heightened perceived cognitive load of interpreters working from home may have resulted from the increased level of fatigue caused by the high stress level (Roziner and Shlesinger 2010) arising from, among others, the sense of isolation in the home setting. Technicians are normally present in the hub to help interpreters resolve different technical problems, including but not limited to issues that affect the audio quality of the source language. Audio quality is vital to spoken language interpreters, because when audio quality deteriorates, interpreters' performance may suffer. While an onsite technician may not be able to resolve sound-related problems right away, interpreters working in a hub may not feel as helpless as those who work from home. Internet connection and ambient noise may also contribute to the significantly higher perceived cognitive load that participants of the home group felt.

Internet connection may also be a concern to interpreters working from home. Internet connection is vital for both interpreters working from a hub and from home to deliver professional services. Professional hubs are usually equipped with permanent Internet connection, whereas interpreters working from home may experience various connection problems. Unstable connection may affect the transmission of both the source target languages. Internet connection affects the quality of source language transmission that interpreters depend on to produce target language renditions. Connection glitches that distort or delay source language transmission may also affect interpreter's comprehension, leading potentially to errors and omissions in the rendition. Similarly, unstable connection may lead to undesirable audio quality in the renditions that SI listeners receive. Unstable connection is normally not the fault of the interpreters. However, if an interpreter's connection becomes unstable when working from home, then the listening experience of both clients and listeners would mostly be negatively affected, resulting in a negative perception of the interpreter's performance and potentially jeopardizing their employment prospect.

Ambient noise may also increase the stress level of interpreters. While some microphones may have noise cancellation functions, they may still pick up background noise, such as a screaming child, construction works, passing trains, sirens, and so forth. Professional hubs are normally soundproof and capable of minimizing the disturbance of those noises. Unless interpreters can find a soundproof space to work from home, it may be difficult for them to isolate those other noises. When working from home, interpreters may be under stress of staying constantly alert to noises beyond their control. All these conditions could potentially increase their stress level and result in a higher perceived cognitive load, which could influence performance. How the two groups differed in terms of their performance of numbers is discussed in the following section.

6.4.2 Accuracy Rate: Home Versus Hub

The home group did not differ significantly in terms of overall accuracy rate from the hub group. The percentages of correct translations were calculated for the four numbers in the translations for each segment and across both segments. A change score was calculated by subtracting the segment 2 percentage correct from the segment 1 percentage correct. The two groups of interpreters were compared on these variables using independent samples t-tests. As shown in Table 6.5, both groups completed an average of over 81% of the segment 1 translations correctly (t (41) = -0.25, $p = 0.803$). Likewise, the two groups completed an average of more than 25% of the numbers in segment 2 correctly (t (41) = 0.30, $p = 0.763$). Both groups decreased significantly in the accuracy of their translations from segment 1 to segment 2. As indicated by the negative Segment Change scores shown in Table 6.5, the decrease in accuracy between the two groups did not differ significantly (t (41) = 0.37, p = 0.716).

In addition to having similar overall accuracy rates in segment 1, the two groups also handled each of the four numbers in segment 1 similarly. As Fig. 6.3 shows, the two groups had a very similar percentage of correct number renditions of the

Table 6.5 Percentage of correct number rendition between interpreters working from hub versus from home

Percentage of accurate number translations	Hub (n = 23)		Home (n = 20)				
	Mean	*SD*	*Mean*	*SD*	*t*	*df*	*p*
Segment 1	81.52	11.22	82.50	14.28	−0.25	41	0.803
Segment 2	28.26	8.61	27.50	7.69	0.30	41	0.763
Segment change	−53.26	11.44	−55.00	19.19	0.37	41	0.716

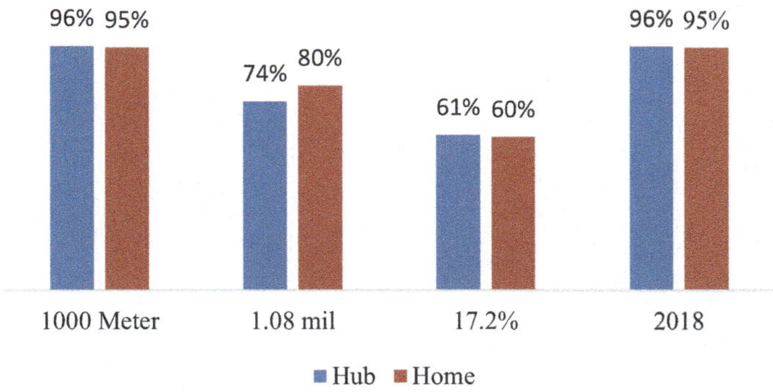

Fig. 6.3 Accuracy per number in segment 1 between the two groups

four numbers in segment 1, which was just 3 min into the SI task. The average accuracy rates of 1,000 m and 2018 were above 90% for both groups. The translation of 1,000 m and 2018 could be translated into Chinese by transcoding. However, the other two numbers were problematic. The average accuracy rates of the translation of 1.08 million and 17.2% were below 90% for both groups.

Accuracy rates suffered for numbers that required extra mental efforts. Translating 1.08 million into Mandarin could be a challenge because the Chinese language groups large numbers in multiples of *wan* (ten thousand), for example, 1 million is 100 *wan* in Chinese. There is also the need to say "zero" before the final unit digit for numbers such as 108. Therefore, extra mental arithmetic might be needed to translate 1.08 million to 108 *wan* (one-hundred-zero-eight ten-thousand) in Mandarin. Mental arithmetic requires a number of steps to complete (see Timarová 2005) that may demand the attention and cognitive resources of the interpreters while they are tackling the ongoing SI task. The translation of the number 17.2% could also be problematic because interpreters needed to rearrange the word "percent" and the numerical digits. The idiomatic translation of 17.2% in Mandarin is by-a-hundred seventeen point two (percent 17.2). The rearrangement needed to translate from English into Mandarin might be taxing to the short-term memory of some interpreters. The translation of 17.2% had the lowest correct counts among the four numbers in the hub group (61%) and home group (60%).

Fatigue resulting from performing the SI for a lengthy period may have resulted in a decrease of accuracy in numbers. The accuracy rates of all four numbers for both groups were above 50% in segment 1. However, overall accuracy rates plummeted in segment 2. Vigilance decrement, or performance deterioration, links prolonged task performance to an increase in the level of fatigue and number of errors (Baldwin and Cisler 2018). As Fig. 6.4 shows, the average accuracy rates of the two groups ranged from 10 to 55%, probably because interpreters were almost 23 min into the task when they had to deal with segment 2. Similar to segment 1, numbers that required mental conversion (i.e., 230 thousand and 15.3%) had lower average accuracy rates than did the other two numbers in both groups. Only 10% of the home

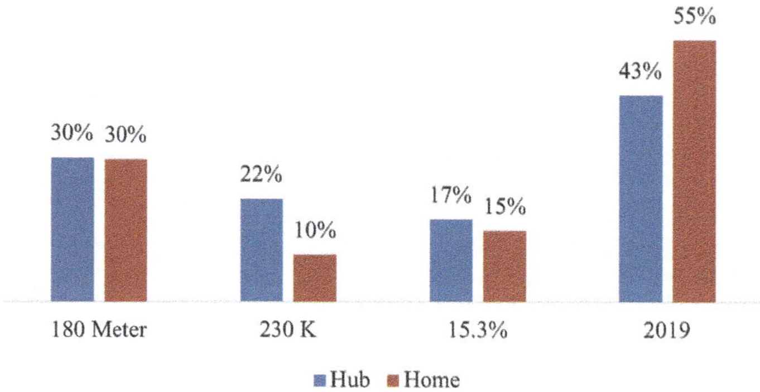

Fig. 6.4 Average accuracy per number in segment 2 between the two groups

group translated the number 230 thousand correctly, while it was 22% for the hub group. For the number 15.3%, only 15% of the home group translated correctly, while it was 17% for the hub group. This outcome is consistent with segment 1, where numbers that required mental conversion had the lowest accuracy rates. It is tempting to conclude at this point that working from a hub or home did not influence number accuracy in SI; instead, it was the duration of how long interpreters have been into the task that influenced accuracy. However, the two groups differed in the number of approximations.

The hub group had more counts of approximation while the home group had more counts of incorrect for the two numbers that required mental conversion. As Fig. 6.5 shows, for the number 230 thousand, the hub group had 6 counts of approximation and 4 counts of incorrect, while the home group had 2 counts of approximation and 9 counts of incorrect. As for the number 15.3%, the hub group had 7 counts of approximation and 2 counts of incorrect, while the home group had 1 count of approximation and 8 counts of incorrect.

The use of approximation to cope with numbers in SI may be considered a strategy to circumvent SI difficulties (Pinochi 2009) and could be acceptable (Korpal and Stachowiak-Szymczak 2020). However, whether approximation equals errors is inclusive. After comparing how translators and interpreters handled numbers differently, where the former translated all digits accurately and the latter occasionally handled numbers by omitting and rounding off, Kajzer-Wietrzny et al. (2021) suggested that approximation may have to do with interpreters' efforts in managing cognitive resources during the SI process. Desmet et al. (2018) labelled approximation as errors but acknowledged that approximation is a useful SI strategy. The assessment scale of Korpal and Stachowiak-Szymczak (2020) awards each translated number categorized as approximation 0.5 points, placing it between an accurately translated number that receives 1 point and 0 point for incorrectly translated.

Likewise, some interpreters may omit the numbers strategically or intentionally (Napier 2004) and instead use non-numerical representations such as "many" or "few" to substitute numbers in the target language. Some interpreters may have

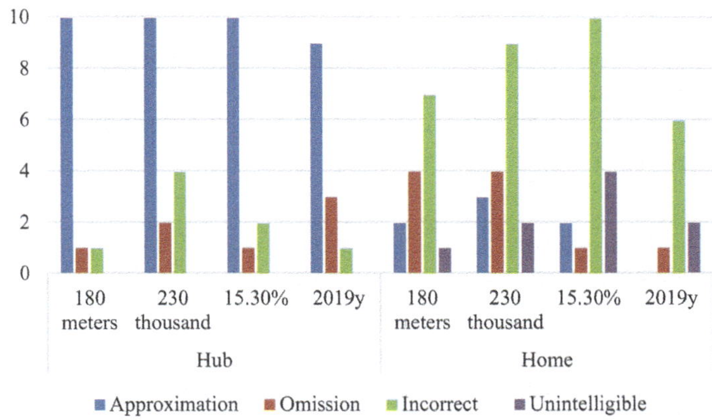

Fig. 6.5 Categories outside of the correct category in segment 2 between the groups

omitted the numbers because they could not remember or were overwhelmed by the numbers so they gave up on these to move on to what they could handle. It is difficult to ascertain what motivated the participants to omit numbers. Listeners may not notice these omissions regardless of interpreters' motivations. However, incorrect numbers and unintelligible mumbles in the target language are audible to listeners, whether or not they notice the inaccuracy or the unintelligibility is beyond the scope of this study.

The transcoding technique may be a double-edged sword when coping with numbers in SI. In this study, accurately translated numbers are those that are transcoded accurately. Likewise, incorrectly translated numbers are limited to the translation of numbers that were transcoded inaccurately. There are no instances of incorrect approximations or incorrect omissions in this study. Participants in studies that investigated the use of automatic voice recognition technologies in SI (e.g., Defrancq and Fantinuoli 2021; Desmet et al. 2018; Pisani and Fantinuoli 2021) tended to use the transcoding approach when given visual access to numbers, suggesting a tendency for interpreters to transcode when dealing with numbers.

The preference to transcode numbers may have to do with the perception that transcoding is relative resource effectiveness. Given that numbers could be challenging in the SI process, interpreters may "opt for a strategy that reduces overall cognitive processing demands" (Seeber 2011: 191). The transcoding approach may seem to reduce cognitive resources because there is only one way to transcode a number from one language into another. The approximation technique may seem to require more cognitive resources for decision making as interpreters have multiple options to approximate a number. That there are more inaccurately translated numbers in segment 2 than in segment 1 for both groups suggests a tendency for participants to "reduce willingness to exert effort" (Matthews et al. 2000: 207), probably due to fatigue. The higher incorrect counts of the home group in segment 2 suggest that they made more attempts to transcode than the hub group did. The higher incorrect counts also coincide with the significantly higher Paas scale scores of the home group than of the hub group. However, it is difficult to determine whether the home group's higher number of transcoding attempts was a result of their heightened perceived cognitive load or the heightened perceived cognitive load led to more attempts to transcode. However, the comparison between the two groups suggests that participants working in different settings (i.e., hub vs. home) adopt different coping strategies.

6.5 Conclusion

The experiment results are consistent with those of previous research on the negative effects of fatigue resulting from being on task for a lengthy period of time on SI performance. However, the significantly more approximation counts in the hub group suggest that those who worked from a hub were still able to exercise executive processing rather than minimizing executive processing. One of the reasons why the home group had significantly more incorrect counts in the second segment may be the strategy of minimizing executive processing. An incorrect rendition suggests that the interpreter attempted to directly map a number from one language into another. The use of the transcoding technique could minimize cognitive processing resources because there is only one way to transcode. On the other hand, more processing resources may be required to approximate numbers because there are multiple ways to approximate. The difference of Paas scale results between the two groups may corroborate how the groups handled numbers differently.

One of the limitations of this study is the lack of a direct comparison of interpreters' cognitive load between the two conditions. However, such comparison may not be necessary as the current study focused on how interpreters handled numbers in the two working conditions. Studies that investigate whether working from home requires more cognitive resources than working in the hub condition could measure the cognitive load of the interpreters directly. A strength of the current study is the simplicity of the design, which did not require substantial logistic resources. Both simple and complex approaches are essential to help understand if there are differences in interpreters' performance between working from home and working from a hub. As most participants had been professionally active pre COVID, it is conceivable that they had had more onsite experience than home experience at the time of this experiment. Subsequently, working from home might have felt challenging. Future studies could recruit participants with similar amounts of hub and home experience. Another limitation is that participants were not asked if they encountered any technical problems during the SI process. It is therefore difficult to rule out if technical glitches caused the heightened perceived cognitive load reported by home group participants. Future studies could seek to understand if participants experience technical problems during the SI process.

Acknowledgements This project was funded by Project Number: P0041297 from the Department of Chinese and Bilingual Studies of the Hong Kong Polytechnic University.

References

AIIC. 2020. COVID-19 distance interpreting recommendations for institutions and DI hubs. https://aiic.org/site/world/about/inside/basic/covid.

Altman, J. 1994. Error analysis in the teaching of simultaneous interpretation: A pilot study. In *Bridging the gap: Empirical research of simultaneous interpretation*, ed. S. Lambert and B. Moser-Mercer, 25–38. Amsterdam/ Philadelphia: John Benjamins.

Baldwin, C., and D. Cisler. 2018. Neuroergonomic methods of assessing learning. In *Cognitive load measurement and application: A theoretical framework for meaningful research and practice*, ed. R. Zheng, 240–262. New York: Routledge.

Bolatov, A.K., T.Z. Seisembekov, A.Z. Askarova, R.K. Baikanova, D.S. Smailova, and E. Fabbro. 2021. Online-learning due to COVID-19 improved mental health among medical students. *Medical Science Educator* 31 (1): 183–192.

Braun, S., and A. Clarici. 1996. Inaccuracy for numerals in simultaneous interpretation: Neurolinguistic and neuropsychological perspectives. *The Interpreters' Newsletter* 7: 85–102.

Čeňková, I., R. Meylaerts, E. Hertog, A. Szmalec, and W. Duyck. 2014. Simultaneous interpreting and working memory executive control. *Interpreting* 16 (2): 139–168.

Chauliac, M., L. Catrysse, D. Gijbels, and V. Donche. 2020. It is all in the "Surv-Eye": Can eye tracking data shed light on the internal consistency in self-report questionnaires on cognitive processing strategies? *Frontline Learning Research* 8 (3): 26–39.

Chaves, S. 2020. Remote simultaneous interpreting hubs or platforms: What's the best option? *The ATA Chronicle* (July/August 2020): 25–28.

Chen, S., J. Epps, and F. Chen. 2011. A comparison of four methods for cognitive load measurement. In *Proceedings of the 23rd Australian Computer-Human Interaction Conference*, ed. C. Paris, N. Colineau, V. Farrell, G. Farrell, and W. Huang, 76–79. New York: Association for Computing Machinery.

Cheung, A.K.F. 2001. Code-mixing and simultaneous interpretation training. *The Interpreters' Newsletter* 11: 57–62.

Cheung, A. K. F. 2003. Does accent matter? The impact of accent in simultaneous interpretation into Mandarin and Cantonese on perceived performance quality and listener satisfaction level. In *Evaluación de la calidad en interpretación de conferencias: investigación*, ed. A. Collados Aís, M. Fernández Sanchez, and D. Gile, 85–96.

Cheung, A.K.F. 2008. Simultaneous interpreting of numbers: An experimental study. *Forum* 6 (2): 23–38.

Cheung, A.K.F. 2009. Numbers in simultaneous interpreting: An experimental study. *Forum* 7 (2): 61–88.

Cheung, A. K. F. 2011. 漢英同傳中刪減與增譯現象的案例分析 [Omissions and additions in Chinese into English simultaneous interpreting: A case study]. *中國翻譯 [China Translators Journal]* 2011 (6): 42–46.

Cheung, A.K.F. 2012. Omission in simultaneous interpreting: Word order differences1. *Forum* 10 (2): 19–33.

Cheung, A.K.F. 2014. Anglicized numerical denominations as a coping tactic for simultaneous interpreting from English into Mandarin Chinese: An experimental study. *Forum* 12 (1): 1–22.

Cheung, A.K.F. 2015. Scapegoating the interpreter for listeners' dissatisfaction with their level of understanding: An experimental study. *Interpreting* 17 (1): 46–63.

Cheung, A.K.F. 2016. The effectiveness of summary training in consecutive interpreting (CI) delivery. *Forum* 14 (1): 1–18.

Cheung, A.K.F. 2022a. Listeners' perception of the quality of simultaneous interpreting and perceived dependence on simultaneous interpreting. *Interpreting* 24 (1): 38–58.

Cheung, A.K.F. 2022b. COVID-19 and interpreting. InConext: Studies in Translation and Interculturalism, 2(2): 9-13.

Chew, S.K.M., and A.K.F. Cheung. 2022. Media interpreting into Malaysian Sign Language: Adaptations and strategies. InConext: Studies in Translation and Interculturalism, 2(2): 112-136.

Chmiel, A., P. Janikowski, and A. Lijewska. 2020. Multimodal processing in simultaneous interpreting with text: Interpreters focus more on the visual than the auditory modality. *Target* 32 (1): 37–58.

Defrancq, B., and C. Fantinuoli. 2021. Automatic speech recognition in the booth: Assessment of system performance, interpreters' performances and interactions in the context of numbers. *Target* 33 (1): 73–102.

Desmet, B., M. Vandierendonck, and B. Defrancq. 2018. Simultaneous interpretation of numbers and the impact of technological support. In *Interpreting and technology*, ed. C. Fantinuoli, 13–27. Berlin: Language Science Press.

Fedorenkova, N. 2020. Six remote simultaneous interpreting platforms and Zoom. *The ATA Chronicle* (November/December 2020): 14–21.

Gile, D. 2009. *Basic concepts and models for interpreter and translator training*. Amsterdam/Philadelphia: John Benjamins.

Hild, A. 2015. Discourse comprehension in simultaneous interpreting: The role of expertise and redundancy. In *Psycholinguistics and cognitive inquiries into translation and interpreting*, ed. A. Ferreira and J. W. Schwieter, 67–100. Amsterdam/Philadelphia: John Benjamins.

Jones, R. 2002. *Conference interpreting explained*. Manchester: St. Jerome Publishing.

Kajzer-Wietrzny, M., I. Ivaska, and A. Ferraresi. 2021. 'Lost' in interpreting and 'found' in translation: Using an intermodal, multidirectional parallel corpus to investigate the rendition of numbers. *Perspectives* 29 (4): 469–488. https://doi.org/10.1080/0907676X.2020.1860097.

Korpal, P., and K. Stachowiak-Szymczak. 2018. The whole picture: Processing of numbers and their context in simultaneous interpreting. *Poznan Studies in Contemporary Linguistics* 54 (3): 335–354.

Korpal, P., and K. Stachowiak-Szymczak. 2020. Combined problem triggers in simultaneous interpreting: Exploring the effect of delivery rate on processing and rendering numbers. *Perspectives* 28 (1): 126–143.

Kurz, I. 2002. Physiological stress responses during media and conference interpreting. In *Interpreting in the 21st century*, ed. G. Garzone and M. Viezzi, 195–202. Amsterdam: John Benjamins. https://doi.org/10.1075/btl.43.19kur.

Lamberger-Felber, H. 2001. Text-oriented research into interpreting-Examples from a case-study. *HERMES-Journal of Language and Communication in Business* 26: 39–64.

Liu, M., D.L. Schallert, and P.J. Carroll. 2004. Working memory and expertise in simultaneous interpreting. *Interpreting* 6 (1): 19–42.

Ma, X., and A.K.F. Cheung. 2020. Language interference in English-Chinese simultaneous interpreting with and without text. *Babel* 66 (3): 434–456.

Massaro, D.W., M.M. Cohen, A. Gesi, R. Heredia, and M. Tsuzaki. 1993. Bimodal speech perception: An examination across languages. *Journal of Phonetics* 21 (4): 445–478.

Matthews, G., D. Davies, S. Westerman, and R. Stamers. 2000. *Human performance: Cognition, stress and individual differences*. Philadelphia, PA: Psychology Press.

Mazza, C. 2001. Numbers in simultaneous interpretation. *The Interpreters' Newsletter* 11: 87–104.

Mead, P. 2015. Numbers. In *Routledge encyclopedia of interpreting studies*, ed. F. Pöchhacker, 286–288. New York: Routledge.

Meuleman, C., and F. Van Besien. 2009. Coping with extreme speech conditions in simultaneous interpreting. *Interpreting* 11 (1): 20–34.

Moser-Mercer, B. 2003. Remote interpreting: Assessment of human factors and performance parameters. Joint project, International Telecommunication Union (ITU). Ecole de traduction et interprétation, University of Geneva (ETI).

Moser-Mercer, B. 2005. Remote interpreting: The crucial role of presence. *Bulletin VALS-ASLA (swiss Association of Applied Linguistics)* 81: 73–97.

Moser-Mercer, B., A. Künzli, and M. Korac. 1998. Prolonged turns in interpreting: Effects on quality, physiological and psychological stress (pilot study). *Interpreting* 3 (1): 47–64.

Naismith, L.M., J.J. Cheung, C. Ringsted, and R.B. Cavalcanti. 2015. Limitations of subjective cognitive load measures in simulation-based procedural training. *Medical Education* 49 (8): 805–814.

Napier, J. 2004. Interpreting omissions: A new perspective. *Interpreting* 6 (2): 117–142.

Neagu, A., and R. Georgescu. 2020. Riding the high-tech wave: Conference interpreting and the 'geeky' edge. In *The translator, the interpreter and the dialogue of languages in the digital age*, ed. A. Neagu, 36–52. Newcastle upon Tyne: Cambridge Scholars Publishing.

Paas, F., J. Tuovinen, H. Tabbers, and P. van Gerven. 2003. Cognitive load measurement as a means to advance cognitive load theory. *Educational Psychologist* 38 (1): 63–71.

Peper, E., V. Wilson, M. Martin, E. Rosegard, and E., and R. Harvey. 2021. Avoid Zoom fatigue, be present and learn. *NeuroRegulation* 8 (1): 47–47.

Pinochi, D. 2009. Simultaneous interpretation of numbers: Comparing German and English to Italian. *An Experimental Study. the Interpreters' Newsletter* 14: 33–57.

Pisani, E., and C. Fantinuoli. 2021. Measuring the impact of automatic speech recognition on number rendition in simultaneous interpreting. In *Empirical studies of translation and interpreting*, ed. C. Wang and B. Zheng, 181–197. New York: Routledge.

Plevoets, K., and B. Defrancq. 2016. The effect of informational load on disfluencies in interpreting: A corpus-based regression analysis. Translation and interpreting studies. *The Journal of the American Translation and Interpreting Studies Association* 11 (2): 202–224.

Reithofer, K. 2020. Intelligibility in English as a lingua franca–The interpreters' perspective. *Journal of English as a Lingua Franca* 9 (2): 173–193.

Riccardi, A. 2005. On the evolution of interpreting strategies in simultaneous interpreting. *Meta: Journal des traducteurs/Meta: Translators' Journal* 50 (2): 753–767.

Rosendo, L.R., and M.C. Galván. 2019. Coping with speed: An experimental study on expert and novice interpreter performance in the simultaneous interpreting of scientific discourse. *Babel* 65 (1): 1–25.

Roziner, I., and M. Shlesinger. 2010. Much ado about something remote: Stress and performance in remote interpreting. *Interpreting* 12 (2): 214–247.

Seeber, K.G. 2011. Cognitive load in simultaneous interpreting: Existing theories—new models. *Interpreting* 13 (2): 176–204.

Seeber, K. G., L. Keller, R. Amos, and S. Hengl. 2019. Expectations vs. experience: Attitudes towards video remote conference interpreting. *Interpreting* 21 (2): 270–304.

Seeber, K.G., L. Keller, and A. Hervais-Adelman. 2020. When the ear leads the eye–the use of text during simultaneous interpretation. *Language, Cognition and Neuroscience* 35 (10): 1480–1494.

Simon, D.M., and M.T. Wallace. 2018. Integration and temporal processing of asynchronous audiovisual speech. *Journal of Cognitive Neuroscience* 30 (3): 319–337.

Song, S., and A.K.F. Cheung. 2019. Disfluency in relay and non-relay simultaneous interpreting: An initial exploration. *Forum* 17 (1): 1–19.

Stachowiak-Szymczak, K., and P. Korpal. 2019. Interpreting accuracy and visual processing of numbers in professional and student interpreters: An eye-tracking study. *Across Languages and Cultures* 20 (2): 235–251.

Sugino, C. 2021. Student perceptions of a synchronous online cooperative learning course in a Japanese women's university during the COVID-19 Pandemic. *Education Sciences* 11 (5): 231–249.

Szulewski, A., A. Gegenfurtner, D.W. Howes, M.L. Sivilotti, and J.J. van Merriënboer. 2017. Measuring physician cognitive load: Validity evidence for a physiologic and a psychometric tool. *Advances in Health Sciences Education* 22 (4): 951–968.

Timarová, Š. 2005. Working memory. In *Routledge encyclopedia of interpreting studies*, ed. F. Pöchhacker, 443–446. New York: Routledge.

Timarová, Š, I. Čeňková, R. Meylaerts, E. Hertog, A. Szmalec, and W. Duyck. 2014. Simultaneous interpreting and working memory executive control. *Interpreting* 16 (2): 139–168.
Ziegler, K., and S. Gigliobianco. 2018. Present? Remote? Remotely present! New technological approaches to remote simultaneous conference interpreting. In *Interpreting and technology*, ed. C. Fantinuoli, 119–139. Berline: Language Science Press. https://doi.org/10.5281/zenodo.1493299.

Andrew K. F. Cheung is Associate Professor of the Department of Chinese and Bilingual Studies of The Hong Kong Polytechnic University. He holds a Ph.D. from the University of East Anglia. He is a member of the editorial boards of Babel and the Translation Quarterly. He is a member of the *Association internationale des interprètes de conférence* (AIIC). His research interests include quality perception of interpreting and corpus-based interpreting studies.

Chapter 7
Remote Simultaneous Interpreting and COVID-19: Conference Interpreters' Perspective

Marta Buján and Camille Collard

Abstract The COVID-19 pandemic brought face-to-face meetings to a halt almost overnight. Shortly afterwards, however, gatherings were moved online and remote communication tools enabled interpreters to resume servicing meetings. Remote simultaneous interpreting (RSI) has now boomed and its widespread use has brought about fundamental changes in conference interpreting. While distance interpreting had been around for years, particularly in certain settings such as court or health interpreting (Ozolins 2011; Braun and Taylor 2012), or when remote participants occasionally took part in face-to-face conferences (Braun 2015; Ziegler and Giglioblanco 2018; TDFI-AIIC 2018), most interpreters were suddenly confronted with new and challenging working conditions. This chap will present how conference interpreters coped with this new reality. It will lay out their view on working conditions, how they perceived the impact of RSI on the interpreter's performance, the main issues and opportunities identified in RSI, as well as their outlook on the future role of RSI in the profession. These findings are part of a wider survey-based study conducted one year into the pandemic, between March and April 2021. The survey collected valid data from 849 respondents, all of them conference interpreters with at least 5 years of professional practice, from 19 countries.

Keywords Remote simultaneous interpreting · Distance interpreting · Conference interpreter's perspective · Working conditions · COVID-19

M. Buján (✉)
WTO, 154 Rue de Lausanne, 1211 Genève, Switzerland
e-mail: m.bujan@aiic.net

C. Collard
ESIT, 8 avenue de Saint-Mandé, 75012 Paris, France

K. Liu and A. K. F. Cheung (eds.), *Translation and Interpreting in the Age of COVID-19*, Corpora and Intercultural Studies 9,
https://doi.org/10.1007/978-981-19-6680-4_7

7.1 Introduction

The World Health Organization characterized COVID-19 as a pandemic on March 11th 2020 (WHO 2020). As a consequence, lockdowns and travel restrictions ensued worldwide, bringing the conference and meeting industry to a halt. The impact of COVID-19 and related restrictions has been felt across all industries and geographies. For conference interpreters, it meant that work assignments were cancelled one after the other, with virtually no work left during the strictest lockdown phase. Shortly afterwards, many face-to-face meetings were replaced with platform-based videoconferences, and remote simultaneous interpreting (RSI) took hold to become the predominant way of work during the pandemic months. However, RSI assignments and working conditions varied greatly. After investing in new equipment, many interpreters worked from their home-based work stations, whereas others mostly serviced meetings from hubs set up either by private companies or international organizations. The industry and the trade underwent a complete overhaul. Conference interpreters had to adapt to radically different ways of working, away from delegates, sometimes also from their boothmates, adjusting turn-length to cope with the constraints of remote interpreting, dealing with technology-related issues, etc. While certain colleagues struggled to adapt and wanted to go back to the pre-COVID situations as soon as possible, others spotted new opportunities in the new arrangements. In any case, most conference interpreters were hardly aware of how colleagues in other markets or regions were coping with the new normal.

That is why, roughly a year into the COVID-19 pandemic, this survey aimed at gathering information about how conference interpreters worked in RSI with regard to market developments, working conditions, technical setup, and team work. The survey also collected the respondents' views on the pros and cons of RSI. This chap presents the results of the survey with regard to the interpreters' perspective on RSI. The statistics pertaining to market developments, working conditions, technical setup, and teamwork will be published in an upcoming paper. With 946 responses collected from professional conference interpreters from 7 regions and 19 countries, this is, to the best of our knowledge, the largest survey-based study on remote simultaneous interpreting conducted so far. Therefore, the responses collected are extremely relevant to providing an accurate depiction of practitioners' habits and their perspective on RSI at the time. We would like to thank the 946 experienced professional interpreters who took time to complete our survey between March 10th and April 11th 2021. We are particularly thankful for the help provided by professional associations, organizations, and individuals in disseminating the survey. The high rate of responses clearly points to the significance of this topic among professional interpreters, who today are still discussing about the optimal conditions necessary to provide the same high-quality interpreting services both on-site and on RSI.

7.2 Literature Review

Remote interpreting (RI) refers to situations in which interpreters are not located in the same place as participants in the meeting, whom they can only see on a screen, without a direct view of the meeting room or the speaker (Mouzourakis 2006; Braun 2015). A distinction is drawn between RI and videoconference interpreting, in which interpreters are in the main room where the meeting is taking place, but have to occasionally interpret a speaker taking the floor via a video link from a different location. They both fall under the generic term of distance interpreting. Distance interpreting is the umbrella term for technology-mediated interpreting in settings in which "interpreters are physically separated from some or all of their clients and use communication technologies such as tele- and videoconferencing to deliver their services" (Braun 2019: 2). Figure 7.1 below shows a diagram representing various modalities of distance interpreting, according to Braun (2019).

Whereas remote interpreting has expanded enormously during COVID-19 due to the impossibility of holding meetings face-to-face (Hoyte-West 2022), it was nothing new (Ziegler and Gigliobianco 2018; Albarino 2019; Bond 2019). Remote interpreting was already a well-established practice in health and court interpreting (Braun 2019). As for conference interpreting, several remote interpreting experiments have been carried out by major international organizations since the 70's (Mouzourakis 2006). Feasibility studies were conducted by the European Telecommunications Standard Institute, the United Nations, the International Telecommunications Union in collaboration with the ETI (University of Geneva) and Europeans institutions (Böcker and Anderson 1993; Moser-Mercer 2003; Mouzourakis 2006; Roziner and Shlesinger 2010; Braun 2019). The rationale behind some of those studies was to determine the feasibility of remote interpreting, as organizations were seeking ways to cut down on interpreting costs, mainly related to travel expenses and DSA (daily subsistence allowance). Also, in order to try to avoid long trips for very short meetings or to solve interpreters' availability-related issues. In the EU, a major concern was also the proliferation of languages to be interpreted and space-related constraints to accommodate all the booths/interpreters needed (Mouzourakis 2006).

However, conference interpreters had been reluctant, when not outright opposed, to take remote interpreting as a standard practice before COVID-19 (TFDI-AIIC

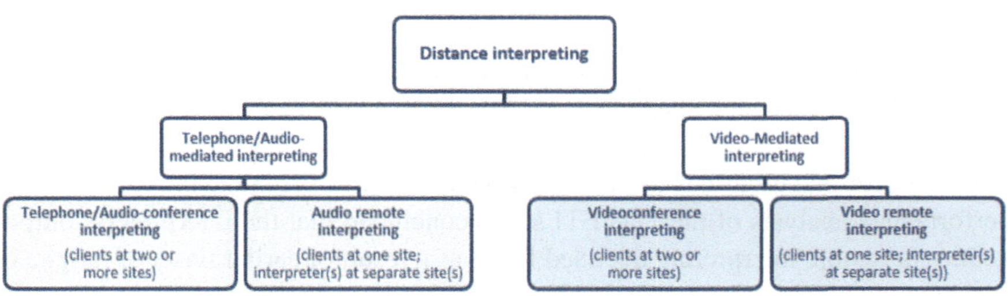

Fig. 7.1 Modalities of distance interpreting (Braun 2019: 2)

2018; AIIC 2018). Traditionally, they pointed to technical challenges related to sound quality or to the stability of the internet connection. In addition, participating conference interpreters reported more difficulties to concentrate due to a certain feeling of alienation. A number of physical complaints were also made (headaches, eye-redness, back pain, etc.) (Mouzourakis 2003). As these challenges were pointed out across experiments, it was not possible to pin them down on a particular setting or organization (Moser-Mercer 2005; Mouzourakis 2006). In more recent studies conducted at the UN and the EU institutions, practitioners pointed to a negative effect on teamwork when working remotely, as well as concerns related to data privacy (Hoyte-West 2022).

Simultaneous interpreting is a highly cognitive demanding task, so any additional complexity is likely to have a negative impact (Braun 2019). Working conditions have adapted over time to ensure a high-quality service while protecting the health and well-being of interpreters (Moser-Mercer et al. 1998). Distance interpreting is no exception. As remote interpreting seems to be more challenging, the interpreter must make more efforts to maintain the output quality, which results in early-onset fatigue (Moser-Mercer 2003) and a more rapid decline in quality (Roziner and Schlesinger 2010). That is why shorter turns are generally recommended when working remotely.

The feeling of alienation due to the condition of remoteness (Mouzourakis 2006) has been found to strongly correlate with lack of motivation in remote interpreting. This feeling of not being present in the gathering seems to be associated with the view of the meeting room rather than to the view of the speaker (Moser-Mercer 2005). Furthermore, interpreters feel they have less control over their work in remote interpreting (Moser-Mercer 2003), which results in a higher level of stress. According to Moser-Mercer (2005), changes in normal working conditions will lead to loss of quality; remote interpreting has an impact on memory, production and listening efforts. She also points out the possibility that a new generation of interpreters might be better prepared to adapt to the new conditions of remote interpreting.

Whereas conference interpreters consistently point to the same challenges associated with remote interpreting, there seems to be a gap between their subjective perceptions and findings stemming from data collected at experiments (Roziner and Schlesinger 2010; Braun 2019). Furthermore, some studies comparing the quality of remote and onsite interpreting yield conflicting results: the ITU/University of Geneva study (Moser-Mercer 2003) and the one conducted by the European Parliament, as reported in Roziner and Shlesinger (2010). The ITU/ETI study (Moser-Mercer 2003) analysed the performance of six conference interpreters over several days of on-site and remote interpreting. The European Parliament study, conducted in 2004 and reported in Roziner and Shlesinger (2010), involved 36 interpreters also working on-site and remotely over a period of two weeks. Both studies monitored the interpreters' performance as well as their emotional responses to remote interpreting. The performance analysis of the ITU/ETI study concluded that the interpreters' output quality in remote interpreting declined faster as a result of earlier onset of fatigue in in this modality (Moser-Mercer 2003). In the European Parliament study, however, no statistically significant difference was found between interpreters' performance working on-site or remotely (Roziner and Shlesinger 2010).

Roziner and Shlesinger (2010) argued that meeting the same quality standards in remote interpreting is harder than in onsite interpreting. As a matter of fact, both studies (Moser-Mercer 2003; Roziner and Schlesinger 2010) showed that interpreters perceived distance interpreting as more stressful. Moser-Mercer (2005) contended that a higher level of stress is due to an increased difficulty in processing information, which in turn leads to fatigue. More cognitive resources have to be allocating to understanding the input speech to the detriment of other stages in the process, such as output. The literature clearly points to interpreting problems being magnified in the distance modality, e.g., in terms of lexical activation (Braun and Taylor 2012; Braun 2013, 2014).

A further relevant study was conducted by Seeber et al. (2019). They surveyed interpreters' attitudes and expectations with regard to their remote interpreting work at the 2014 FIFA World Cup. The authors relied on two questionnaires, circulated among interpreters before and after the assignment. They found out a significant shift in interpreter's attitudes towards remote interpreting. Although most interpreters felt initially apprehensive about working remotely and held rather negative views on remote interpreting, they reported being mostly satisfied with their own performance and the experience as a whole after the assignment. They didn't perceive RI to be more stressful either. It should be noted, however, that remote interpreting services are provided in widely disparate conditions. The experience of working at a hub, with satellite duplex video links, co-located with colleagues and supported by a team of technicians throughout is hardly comparable to interpreting via an on-line platform, from home, separated from one's boothmate and having to cope with poor sound quality compounded by speakers lacking appropriate equipment.

Most of these studies were conducted before the COVID-19 pandemic, when remote interpreting still played a minor role in conference interpreting as a whole. Therefore, the relevance of these results in the current environment might be called into question. An online survey conducted in Turkey in the early months of 2020, just before the pandemic broke out, still showed that interpreters were not very keen on adopting remote interpreting (Kincal and Ekici 2020). Respondents declared to have a strong preference for on-site interpreting for a variety of reasons, such as networking opportunities, the possibility of meeting speakers and participants, and the sense of being physically part of the event. Research has demonstrated that communication is inherently multimodal (Adami 2016), so comprehension is enhanced when listeners can draw information from various modalities such as gestures, proxemics, face movements, etc. (Buján 2019). Interpreters therefore rely on a range of multimodal and contextual sources to fully comprehend what the speaker actually means, in order to fully grasp the pragmatic meaning of the speech beyond the mere semantics of the words uttered (Seleskovitch and Lederer 2014; Setton 1999). Hence, remote interpreting requires more strenuous efforts as many of those sources are either limited or non-existent (Ziegler and Gigliobianco 2018; Braun 2019). An additional difficulty identified in remote interpreting pertains to the frequency range of the incoming voice of speakers. When the frequency range transmitted falls short of the 125–15,000 Hz required to fully display the nuances of human prosody, the interpreters' output quality is bound to decrease as they are unable to compensate for the missing input by resorting to interpreting techniques such as changes in voice-to-ear span or additional pausing (Ziegler and Gigliobianco 2018).

Input signal quality issues may also have an impact on interpreters' health. Professional associations have been very vocal sounding the alarm about possible health issues experienced by interpreters when working remotely. The Canada AIIC Regional Bureau (2021) conducted a survey among 51 active conference interpreters employed by the Federal Translation Bureau in January 2021. 70% of the respondents reported having suffered auditory injuries serious enough to force most of them to take time off work. Furthermore, 97% of respondents argued they were unable to perform to the same quality standards as in on-site interpreting when working remotely. Consequently, professional associations have advocated for adapting working conditions in remote interpreting to protect interpreters' wellbeing while ensuring high-quality services. Broadly speaking, interpreters' associations call for shorter and fewer interpreting sessions (AIIC 2021).

7.3 Methodology

7.3.1 Aim of the Study and Research Questions

Given the lack of research into remote interpreting after COVID-19, this survey-based study reported here was launched to find out how conference interpreters had adapted to the new reality brought about by the pandemic. The design of the survey was guided by the following research questions:

- Which new working habits, if any, have conference interpreters adopted throughout the world as RSI became widespread?
- Is the situation on the private market different from that of the institutional market?
- How do conference interpreters feel about RSI?

We decided to focus solely on remote simultaneous interpreting (RSI) because of its widespread use and the fundamental difference between this modality and on-site simultaneous interpreting. Therefore, our survey targeted interpreters who had already worked as traditional booth-based simultaneous conference interpreters before the pandemic. We were interested in looking into various settings: interpreting remotely from home, from a hub, and from the interpreter's traditional workplace.

7.3.2 Design and Implementation of the Survey

The survey included 61 questions. In order to ensure the relevance of the data collected to compare conference interpreting before and after COVID-19, respondents with less than three years of experience as conference interpreters or those for whom conference interpreting was not the main source of income were filtered out at the beginning of the survey. In addition, a minimum of 5 days of work in RSI since COVID-19 broke out was a prerequisite for taking this survey. The survey was divided into the following sects.

Interpreter's profile. This sect aimed at gathering interpreters' demographic information and professional profile, including their age, region, years of experience, membership of a professional association, language combination, professional status (staff, freelance, retired), type of market (institutional, private), amount and modality of work before and after the pandemic broke out.

Working conditions in RSI as compared to on-site interpreting. This sect collected data on the number and length of sessions per day in RSI, along with team strength, fees, and travelling.

Section C focused on technical conditions, including what platforms were mostly used, specific training received (if any), equipment used by speakers, place of work (hub, home, client premises), and equipment and internet connection used by interpreters.

Section D delved into team work in RSI assignments, enquiring about communication with colleagues in the team, coordination and handover between boothmates, organization and length of turns.

Finally, Sect E, which is the main focus of this chap, collected the interpreter's views of RSI. Questions revolved around the interpreters' assessment of their own performance, working conditions, user's expectations, and their overall feeling about RSI. We invited respondents to identify major challenges and opportunities arising from this new working environment and what their outlook was on the future of the profession.

The survey was open from March 10th to April 11th 2021. 946 responses from 7 regions and 19 countries were received. After filtering out non-eligible participants and removing invalid data, 849 valid responses were used for analysis. For the sake of consistency and to ensure a common understanding of key terms by all participants, a number of definitions were provided in the introduction to the survey:

RSI: ICT-enabled conference simultaneous interpreting of distant speaker(s)/signer(s), where the interpreter has a video-mediated view of that speaker/signer. It also includes audio RSI, where the interpreter has no view of the speaker (although telephone interpreting is not included in this survey). The interpreter may be co-located with some participants and interpreters in the meeting.

Hub-based RSI: The interpreter provides RSI services from a hub, i.e., a room equipped with interpretation booths and remote interpretation equipment. The interpreter is co-located with at least some other interpreters from the team. Hubs can be either external/private (rented from a dedicated company for the event, outside the client's/employer's premises) or institutional, i.e., at the client's/employer's premises (e.g., international organizations, etc.).

Home-based RSI: The interpreter provides RSI services from their home or from a dedicated office (e.g., co-working spaces). The interpreter is by herself or himself, not co-located with the other interpreters and participants.

Boothmate: Although boothmates are not necessarily physically in the same booth in remote interpreting, the term *boothmate* is kept for ease of reference.

7.4 Results of the Survey and Discussion

7.4.1 Respondents' Profile

The respondents consisted of people from all age groups. The group with the fewest respondents was the below-30-years group. This was to be expected, as people from this age group have only recently started their careers and a minimum of three years of experience as conference interpreter was required to complete the survey. Most respondents were over 40 years old (Fig. 7.2) and had been working as conference interpreters for more than 15 years (Fig. 7.3).

With regard to their regular place of work (Fig. 7.4), the overwhelming majority of respondents (68%) were based in Europe. Brussels, Geneva and Paris stood out as the places with the highest number of responses, not surprisingly given the size of the conference interpreting market in these countries. The Americas was the second region with the highest number of respondents (19%), although well behind Europe, followed by Asia Pacific and Africa and Arab countries, both regions with a similar response rate (6 and 5% respectively).

79% of respondents were members of a professional association. 59% were AIIC members, candidates or pre-candidates. Only 21% of respondents were not members of any professional association (Fig. 7.5).

Furthermore, 87% of respondents claimed to work only as freelancers, whereas 9% of respondents worked as staff interpreters and 4% were retired (Fig. 7.6).

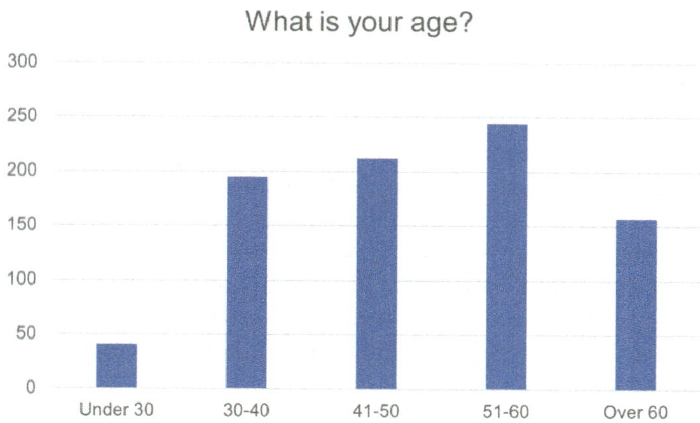

Fig. 7.2 Respondents' age

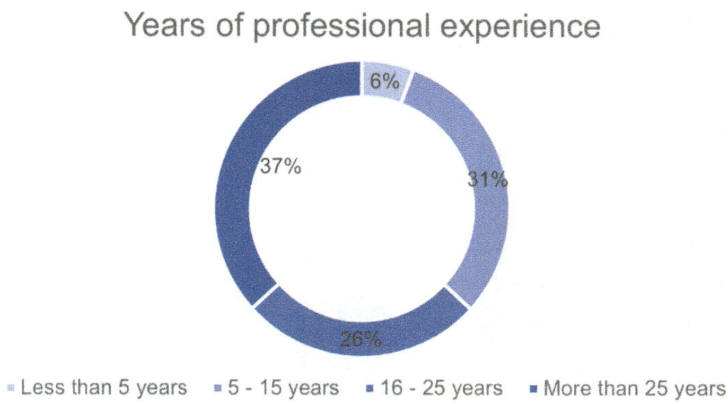

Fig. 7.3 Respondents' professional experience as conference interpreters

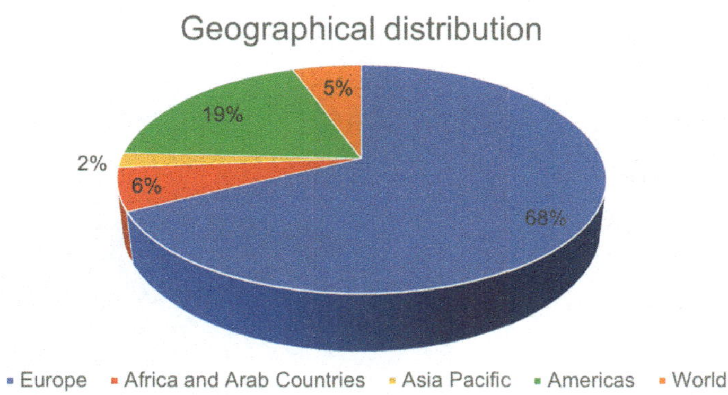

Fig. 7.4 Regions in which respondents were based

As for the type of market respondents drew their clients from, 61% claimed to provide conference interpreting services both for the institutional and private market. 23% reported to work exclusively for the private market, while 16% only had institutional clients (international organizations, EU institutions or government agencies) (Fig. 7.7).

7.4.2 Overview of Main Results

The survey clearly showcased the huge impact of the pandemic on the conference interpreting industry: While remote interpreting allowed interpreters to keep working during the crisis, 68% of respondents had worked fewer days and 46% had fewer clients.

When it comes to working conditions, the study showed that recommendations by AICE (2020) and AIIC (2021) in terms of working hours were mostly followed:

Fig. 7.5 Membership of professional associations among respondents

Fig. 7.6 Respondents' professional status as conference interpreters

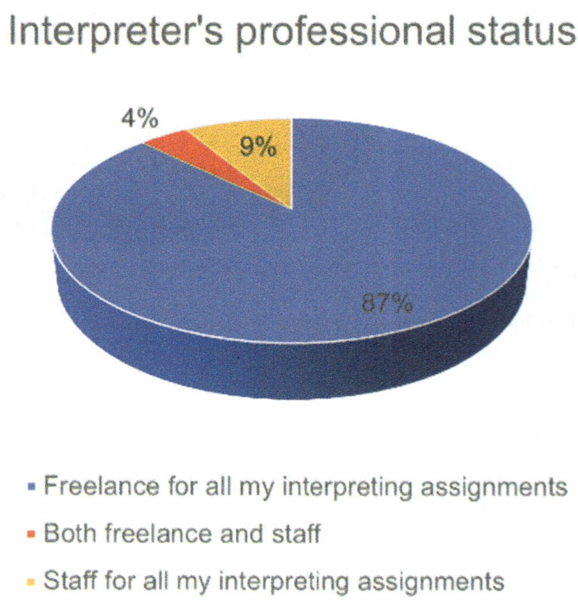

shorter sessions for 75% of respondents, while 62%of respondents claimed to take shifts of 20 min or less. However, some technical conditions do not seem to meet the recommendations: only 7% of respondents reported that external microphones were always used by participants taking the floor. Similarly, 75% of respondents sometimes or always worked from home, while only 26% preferred home-based RSI to working in a hub, mostly for technical reasons (96.3%).

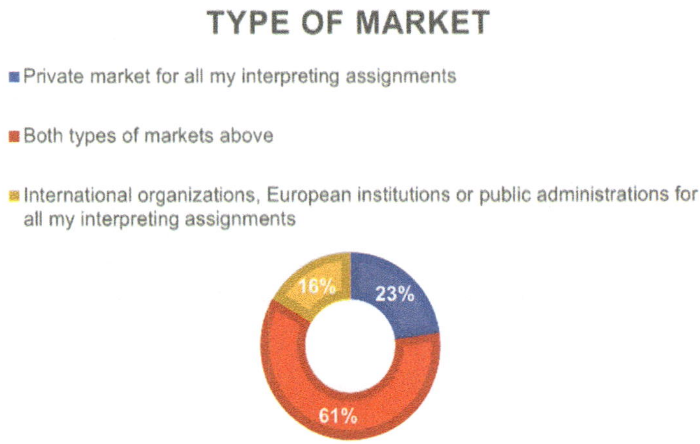

Fig. 7.7 Respondents' interpreting services market

According to the responses collected, teamwork still seems to matter in RSI: 77% of respondents stated that they sometimes or always helped their boothmate. As most of the time they were not in the same booth nor working with connected consoles, 74% of respondents resorted to "makeshift" solutions to listen to their colleague (through another device or platform, or by joining the conference as participants).

7.4.3 Interpreters' Perspective on RSI

50% of respondents thought that they performed below on-site standards in RSI. Interestingly, both seasoned and less experienced interpreters recorded similar answers. 50% of respondents with more than 15 years of experience as conference interpreters considered they performed worse in RSI, while only 3% thought they did better. 47% did not notice any difference in terms of performance between RSI and on-site interpreting. For interpreters with 15 years of experience or less, those figures were 49%, 4% and 47% respectively (Fig. 7.8).

As for interpreters' perception of working conditions, 74% of respondents thought that working conditions were worse in RSI than in on-site interpreting. The main arguments laid down to explain why RSI is more challenging were as follows: poor sound quality, weakened teamwork, increased difficulty to communicate with booth partners and loss of non-verbal communication cues by speakers. Interestingly, even respondents claiming to work only for international institutions (as staff or freelance interpreters) overwhelmingly considered RSI working conditions were worse than on-site interpreting (89% of a sample size of 142 respondents) (Fig. 7.9), despite enjoying the same fees (or even higher) and shorter working hours. Only 2 respondents from this subset stated that they deemed working conditions in RSI to be better thanks to shorter working hours, and less commuting.

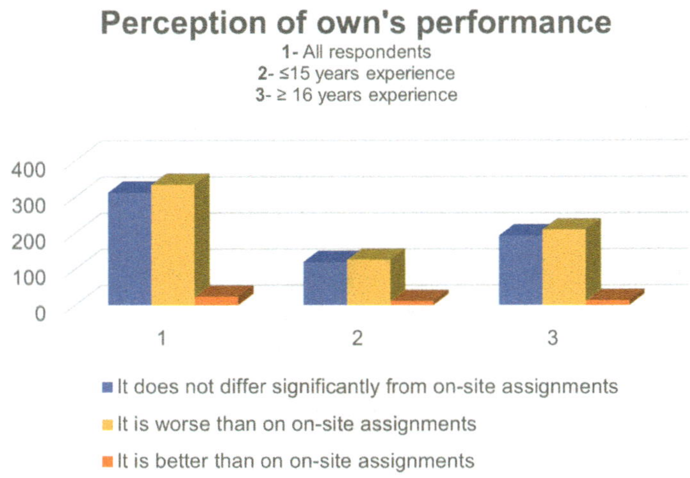

Fig. 7.8 Respondents' perception of own performance in RSI

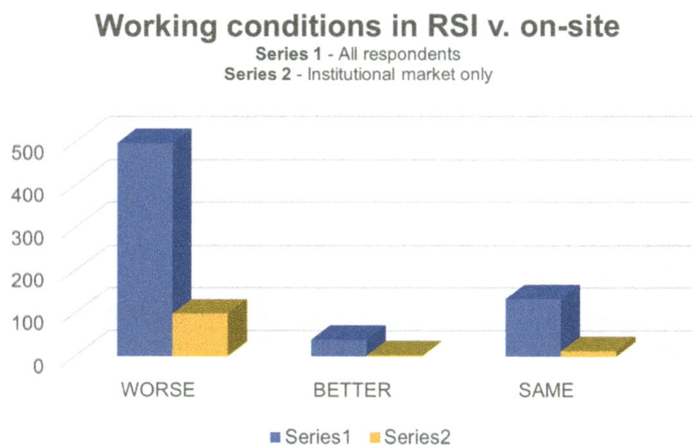

Fig. 7.9 Respondents' claims on working conditions in RSI v. on-site interpreting

Only 21% of interpreters working exclusively for the institutional market reported working from home sometimes, whereas 65% never did and 14% did so only rarely. Even though they usually worked in the same room as their boothmates (albeit in separate booths) and allegedly had easier access to technical support throughout the meetings, they still claimed teamwork is hampered by RSI. In addition, 93% of them considered that this modality is more difficult, which is a higher than the respondents claiming RSI to be more challenging (83%) (see Fig. 7.10). When breaking responses down by years of experience, we found a remarkable degree of consistency. 83% of respondents with 16 or more years of experience found RSI more difficult, as did 82% of interpreters with 15 or less years of experience as conference interpreters.

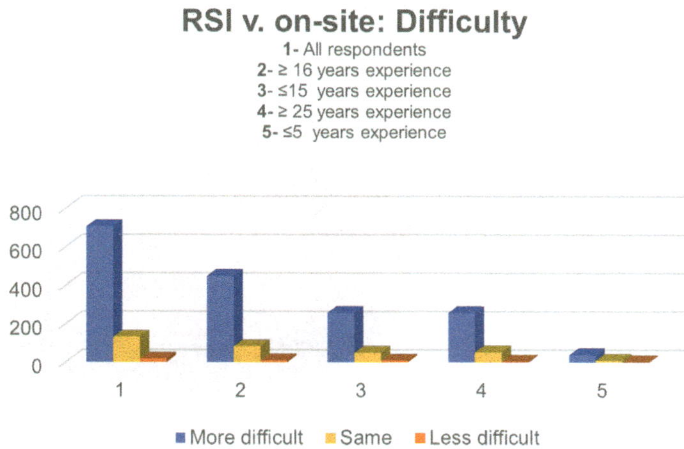

Fig. 7.10 Difficulty of RSI v. on-site interpreting

When we focused solely on the most and the least experienced respondents, their responses turned out to be the same. 83% of seasoned interpreters (over 25 years of experience) and all the interpreters with a conference interpreting career spanning less than 5 years describe this modality as more difficult (Fig. 7.10). Despite increased difficulty and worse conditions and performance, 67% of respondents feel that users' expectations are the same or higher.

When it comes to challenges related to RSI, most respondents reported experiencing technical issues, mainly related to poor sound quality as a result of speakers not using the right equipment or not having a stable internet connection. Professional issues, mainly linked to market disruption, was the second major concern for respondents as a whole, whereas health issues came as their second main worry for those working only for the institutional market. As for the advantages linked to RSI, responses were less clear-cut. Many interpreters stated they saw no advantage at all, whereas others referred to positive elements, such as less travelling/commuting, shorter working hours, better work-life balance or less harm to the environment as a result of fewer trips. Despite most respondents making negative comments about RSI, though, roughly one year into the pandemic and after several months working on RSI in a wide variety of assignments and settings, 57% of respondents stated they would like to keep working on RSI (Fig. 7.11).

Comments made on the non-compulsory box at the end of the survey paint a more nuanced picture. While most respondents do not see RSI favourably, the majority are convinced that it is here to stay. The collected remarks can be divided into three broad categories. Positive comments about RSI highlighted that it opens up new business opportunities, as fewer costs for clients mean that they can now afford providing interpreting services for meetings that previously did not resort to this service. Better work-life balance was another recurrent advantage linked to RSI, as well as a higher degree of flexibility and the possibility to service multiple assignments on a single

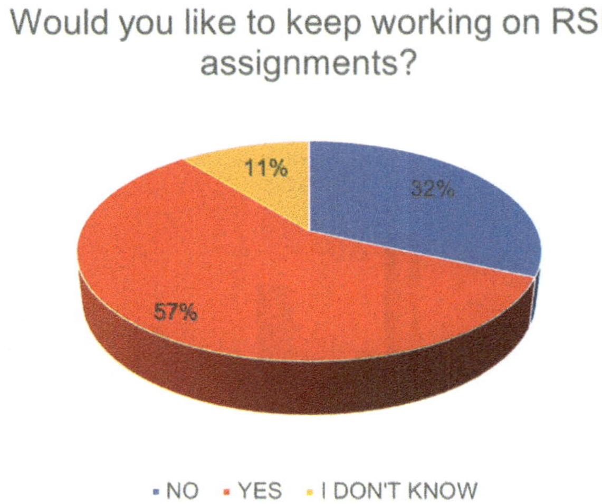

Fig. 7.11 Interpreters' willingness to keep working on RSI

day. Interestingly, one respondent saw RSI as a way to put off being replaced by AI-based interpreting services, given that RSI drives down interpreting-related costs and therefore makes the AI technological push less urgent and compelling. Even interpreters who expressed a negative opinion of RSI admitted that it had allowed them to earn a living during the pandemic. Finally, many saw it as a more environmentally-friendly form of interpreting, as it involved less travelling. Many respondents pointed to the fact that it was no longer necessary to travel long distances for shorter meetings, neither for interpreters nor for delegates.

On the negative side, hardline critics argued that RSI takes away all the pleasurable aspects of conference interpreting and leaves only the difficulties. While the fewer number of trips involved was seen as a major advantage by many respondents, others claimed to miss going to new places and sharing time with colleagues away from home. Most mentioned the missing human factor in RSI as a major drawback and pointed out to the loss of networking opportunities as a result. Another disadvantage frequently laid down had to do with the fact that RSI makes teamwork harder, as well as learning from colleagues. Many respondents feared that interpreters would increasingly be viewed as robots who can simply be switched on/off, as ever less visible by users, who may end up thinking of interpretation as just a plug-and-play feature of RSI platforms. A major concern was the uberization of the profession, whereby platforms would end up taking the lion's share of the business (and profits), while severely underpaying interpreters. It was argued that this would inevitably lead to lower quality standards which would ultimately make interpretation services redundant. As a matter of fact, many interpreters viewed the RSI business model as detrimental to interpreters, given that it opened up the trade to unfair competition and unqualified interpreters. In addition, many considered that RSI did away with the notion of domicile. Many respondents worried about privacy and confidentiality issues. Others remarked that home-based RSI ate away at interpreters' income, as most overheads now fell on the interpreter (internet connection, equipment, utilities, etc.). Almost all interpreters reported sound quality as a major hurdle in RSI; they worried about the effects of toxic sound on their physical and mental health, which they felt were being severely underestimated. Other difficulties mentioned were higher cognitive load, lack of technical support and the fact that RSI technology was not yet mature.

Finally, a third category of comments could be described as showing a pragmatic approach. Many interpreters, regardless of how they felt about RSI, acknowledged that it was here to stay. Therefore, they argued that instead of moaning about it, conference interpreters should embrace it and focus on securing decent working conditions and on protecting the interpreters' health and wellbeing. Educating participants and speakers at remote meetings was considered paramount in order to reduce the difficulties inherent to RSI (poor sound quality, poor internet connection, etc.). Many described RSI as a necessary evil, and some advocated for research to be conducted on the input sound frequency range (in Hz) delivered through platforms and in various RSI settings. The findings of these studies can help provide evidence to take informed decisions on fees, working hours, team strength, etc. Most seemed to share the view that RSI is best suited for shorter bilingual meetings, but not for multilingual conferences. International organizations and AIIC were called upon to take the lead and establish evidence-based conditions for RSI. Most claimed that RSI should be a fallback option but not the new mainstream mode of interpreting.

7.5 Conclusion and Further Research

This survey sheds some light on how the conference interpreting profession has evolved during the pandemic, mainly as a result of the enormous shift brought about by RSI. Despite past reluctance to take up distance interpreting among conference interpreters, they quickly adapted to the new circumstances and transitioned to remote interpreting almost overnight. Not only did that involve a change in working practices, but a considerable investment in the necessary equipment, above all for those who worked from home.

The survey confirmed that interpreters were called to work in different RSI settings: from home, from a purpose-built hub offered by private providers or from institutional hubs (i.e., repurposed conference rooms/booths at international organizations, etc.). The differences in terms of market developments, working conditions, teamwork, and technical setup will be discussed in a forthcoming paper, but we can already report a clear tendency to work shorter hours and fewer sessions, particularly in the institutional market. Despite the wide range of working conditions, technical setups and fees, respondents showed remarkable consistency in their assessment and perception of RSI, which clearly leans on the negative side. Regardless of their market and years of experience, respondents overwhelmingly considered RSI to be more difficult. Worth noticing is that this is the case for both novices and seasoned interpreters. This would seem to contradict Moser-Mercer (2005) hypothesis about less experienced interpreters being more likely to better adapt to this new modality as they have less entrenched working habits. Other findings from previous studies, however, are borne out by the survey. For example, the feeling of alienation and of not being present in the meeting is one of the major difficulties linked to RSI (Mouzourakis 2006). Also, they perceived RSI as being more challenging than on-site interpreting mainly as a result of poor sound quality and higher complexity (teamwork, communication with boothmates, technology issues, etc.) (Braun 2019). Furthermore, respondents consistently claimed to experience more stress and fatigue in RSI (Moser-Mercer 2003, 2005).

As for the research questions, the survey clearly demonstrates that conference interpreters have developed new working habits, such as shorter shifts and creative ways to enable handover and to communicate with booth partners. When it comes to differences between the institutional and the private market, the far more widespread use of home-based interpreting in the latter stands out. Furthermore, while some interpreters in the private market point to new business opportunities opened up by RSI as a major advantage, colleagues working exclusively for international organizations tend to be less sanguine about the benefits of RSI. Moreover, other positive aspects of RSI, such as better work-life balance or less commuting are also not so strongly felt among interpreters working for international organizations, who mostly still have to commute to work. On the contrary, this group of interpreters is less affected by problems related to home-based RSI, such as lack of a proper workspace, lack of technical support or the use of multiple devices to communicate with boothmates. Despite all these differences, feelings about RSI reported by respondents are very consistent, as are comments freely made by some respondents. There is hardly any difference in the type of issues stated by respondents, neither based on the type of market nor, incidentally, between members and non-members of AIIC.

The overview provided by the findings in this survey pictures the situation as it was in March–April 2021, one year into the pandemic, where RSI was dominant and practices began to settle. However, responses are bound to change over time as the situation evolves. RSI is becoming an additional standard modality to provide conference interpretation services along with interpreting at on-site and increasingly frequent hybrid meetings. It would therefore be interesting to run a similar survey again in some time to compare the results and to draw a more accurate picture of the shift taking place in the conference interpreting trade. Will fears reported by interpreters regarding market disruption come true? Are health-related risks linked to RSI more accurately defined? Do interpreters feel more positive about RSI now that they are more used to it? Have working conditions settled and applied consistently both in the private and the institutional markets? Has the technology matured enough to do away with problems related to sound quality? Are participants in meetings using the right equipment? These questions can only be answered by similar research projects in the future. For the time being, and quoting one of the respondents, what distinctly emerges from this survey is that RSI during COVID-19 was a “life-saver and game-changer”.

References

Adami, E. 2016. Multimodality. In *Oxford handbook of language and society*, ed. O. García, N. Flores, and M. Spotti, 451–472. Oxford: Oxford University Press.

AICE. 2020. Resumen: indicaciones acerca de la Interpretación Simultánea Remota (ISR). https://www.aice-interpretes.com/enlaces/archivoenlace4363.pdf. Accessed 22 April 2022.

AIIC. 2018. AIIC position on distance interpreting. https://aiic.org/document/4837/AIIC_position_on_TFDI_05.03.18.pdf. Accessed 22 April 2022.

AIIC. 2021. AIIC COVID-19. Distance interpreting recommendations. https://aiic.org/site/world/about/inside/basic/covid. Accessed 22 April 2022.

Albarino, S. 2019. UN to host bake-off for remote interpreting platforms, NMT, speech-to-text. *Slator*. https://slator.com/un-to-host-bake-off-for-remoteinterpreting-platforms-nmt-speech-to-text/. Accessed 22 April 2022.

Böcker, M., and D. Anderson. 1993. Remote conference interpreting using ISDN videotelephony: A requirements analysis and feasibility study. In *Proceedings of the human factors and ergonomics society, 37th annual meeting*, 235–239.

Bond, E. 2019. EU gives in-principle green light to use of remote interpreting platforms. *Slator*. https://slator.com/eu-gives-in-principle-green-light-to-use-of-remote-interpreting-platforms/. Accessed 22 April 2022.

Braun, S. 2013. Keep your distance? Remote interpreting in legal proceedings: A critical assessment of a growing practice. *Interpreting* 15 (2): 200–228.

Braun, S. 2014. Comparing traditional and remote interpreting in police settings: Quality and impact factors. In *Traduzione e interpretazione per la società e le istituzioni*, ed. M. Viezzi and C. Falbo, 161–176. Trieste: Edizioni Università di Trieste.

Braun, S. 2015. Remote interpreting. In *Routledge handbook of interpreting*, ed. H. Mikkelson and R. Jourdenais, 352–367. London/New York: Routledge.

Braun, S. 2019. Technology and interpreting. In *Routledge handbook of translation and technology*, ed. M. O'Hagan, 271–288. London: Routledge.

Braun, Sabine, and Judith L. Taylor. 2012. Video-mediated interpreting in criminal proceedings: Two European surveys. In *Videoconference and remote interpreting in criminal proceedings,* ed. Sabine. Braun and Judith L. Taylor, 69–98. Cambridge/Antwerp: Intersentia.

Buján, M. 2019. The function of face gestures and head movements in spontaneous humorous communication. *European Journal of Humour Studies* 7 (2): 1–29.

Canada AIIC Regional Bureau. 2021. Distance interpreting during the pandemic. A survey of official interpreters employed by the federal Translation Bureau. https://aiic.org/uploaded/web/Interpreter%20survey%20report%20FINAL.pdf. Accessed on 22 April 2022.

Hoyte-West, A. 2022. No longer elite? Observations on conference interpreting, Covid-19, and the status of the post-pandemic profession. *Orbis Linguarium* 20 (1): 71–77.

Kincal, S., and E. Ekici. 2020. Reception of remote interpreting in Turkey: A pilot study. *RumeliDE Dil Ve Edebiyat Araştırmaları Dergisi* 21: 979–990.

Moser-Mercer, B. 2005. Remote interpreting: Issues of multisensory integration in a multilingual task. *Meta* 50 (2): 727–738.

Moser-Mercer, B., A. Künzli, and M. Korac. 1998. Prolonged turns in interpreting: Effects on quality, physiological and psychological stress. *Interpreting* 3 (1): 47–64.

Moser-Mercer, Barbara. 2003. Remote interpreting: Assessment of human factors and performance parameters. *AIIC Webzine, Summer 2003.* https://aiic.org/document/516/AIICWebzine_Summer2003_3_MOSER-MERCER_Remote_interpreting_Assessment_of_human_factors_and_performance_parameters_Original.pdf. Accessed 22 April 2022.

Mouzourakis, Panayotis. 2003. That feeling of being there: Vision and presence in remote interpreting. https://www.academia.edu/25852376/That_feeling_of_being_there_Vision_and_presence_in_remote_interpreting. Accessed 22 April 2022.

Mouzourakis, Panayotis. 2006. Remote interpreting. A technical perspective on recent experiments. *Interpreting* 8 (1): 45—66.

Ozolins, U. 2011. Telephone interpreting: Understanding practice and identifying research needs. *Translation and Interpreting* 3 (2): 33–47.

Roziner, Ilan., and M. Shlesinger. 2010. Much ado about something remote. Stress and performance in remote interpreting. *Interpreting* 12 (2): 214—247.

Seeber, Kilian G., L. Keller, R. Amos, and S. Hengl. 2019. Expectations versus experience. Attitudes towards video remote conference interpreting. *Interpreting* 21 (2): 270–304.

Seleskovitch, D., and M. Lederer. 2014. *Interpréter pour traduire*, 5th ed. Paris: Les Belles Lettres.

Setton, R. 1999. *Simultaneous interpretation: A cognitive-pragmatic analysis*. Amsterdam: Benjamins.

TFDI-AIIC. 2018. Distance interpreting. Survey results. https://aiic2.in1touch.org/uploaded/web/TFDI_DI_survey_full_FINAL_09.18.pdf. Accessed 21 July 2022.

World Health Organisation. 2020. Director general's opening remarks at the media briefing on COVID-19. https://www.who.int/director-general/speeches/detail/who-director-general-s-opening-remarks-at-the-media-briefing-on-covid-19-11-march-2020. Accessed 22 April 2022.

Ziegler, K., and S. Gigliobianco. 2018. Present? Remote? Remotely present! New technological approaches to remote simultaneous conference interpreting. In *Interpreting and technology*, ed. C. Fantinuoli, 119–139. Berlin: Language Science Press.

Marta Buján Ph.D in Linguistics, MA in Conference Interpreting, staff interpreter at the WTO, member of AIIC. She has combined her career as a conference interpreter with lecturing in interpreting, translation and linguistics at various universities in the UK, France at Spain. Her research includes multimodality, cognitive linguistics, humour studies, and remote simultaneous interpreting.

Camille Collard obtained her Ph.D in Translation Studies at Ghent University in 2019. She is currently head of the Master in conference interpreting and the Master of Translation studies at Ecole Supérieur d'Interprètes et de Traducteurs (ESIT) in Paris. As a member of the Clesthia research group, she carries out corpus-based research on cognitive processes in simultaneous interpreting (ear-voice span, numbers and disfluencies), as well as survey-based research on remote simultaneous interpreting.

Chapter 8
Reconceptualising Interpreting at the United Nations

Marie Diur and Lucía Ruiz Rosendo

Abstract This chapter provides an overview of the characteristics of conference interpreting at the United Nations (UN) and focuses on the research undertaken thus far in terms of testing procedures and working conditions. Drawing on the analysis of archival documents, on our experience as interpreters and on our knowledge of the testing procedures at the UN, we specifically examine the impact of COVID-19 on working and testing procedures and explore the challenges and opportunities brought about by the pandemic, as well as the need for international organisations, in particular, and the conference interpreting profession, in general, to accept and adapt to new circumstances, particularly to the organisation of online exams and to the increasing use of Remote Simultaneous Interpreting (RSI). Finally, the chapter offers some recommendations for future research.

Keywords Conference interpreting · United Nations · Admission exams · Working conditions · RSI · COVID-19

8.1 Introduction

The COVID-19 pandemic has drastically changed working methods for many professions, and interpreting has not been immune to these changes. Through the analysis of archival documents, coupled with our experience as interpreters and interpreter trainers, as well as the first author's experience as Chief Interpreter of the United Nations Office at Geneva (UNOG), we have been able to identify two areas in which the pandemic has had the greatest effect on the work carried out by interpreters at

M. Diur (✉)
United Nations Office at Geneva (UNOG), Palais des Nations, 1211 Genève, Switzerland
e-mail: marie.diur@un.org

L. Ruiz Rosendo
Faculty of Translation and Interpreting, University of Geneva, Bd du Pont d'Arve 40, 1205 Geneva, Switzerland
e-mail: Lucia.Ruiz@unige.ch

K. Liu and A. K. F. Cheung (eds.), *Translation and Interpreting in the Age of COVID-19*, Corpora and Intercultural Studies 9,
https://doi.org/10.1007/978-981-19-6680-4_8

the UN: admission exams and the interpreter's work in the different UN headquarters (Geneva, New York, Vienna and Nairobi). Regarding admission procedures, prior to being admitted into the UN as a conference interpreter, candidates need to be tested, as is the case in most international organisations. Such admissions exams were conducted onsite until 2019, but the pandemic accelerated work on an online testing procedure (which was already in the pipeline pre-pandemic). As far as the impact of the pandemic on the work carried out by interpreters goes, it is worth noting the increasing use of Remote Simultaneous Interpreting (RSI) platforms for large multilingual meetings, despite the numerous challenges encountered when using such platforms.

In the first part of this chapter, we examine remote interpreting as an increasingly frequent interpreting method, particularly after the outbreak of the COVID-19 pandemic, and then focus on the transition towards RSI in the context of the UN. The second part focuses on the move to online testing procedures put in place at the UN in order to guarantee interpreter turnover. Although online exams had already been considered prior to the outbreak of COVID-19, the pandemic has accelerated their implementation. We examine the many changes brought about by the pandemic in this analysis of new working conditions and of online tests. By providing a description of all these changes and challenges, we aim to improve our current understanding of the interpreting needs that had and still have to be met by the UN as an international organization.

8.2 Remote Interpreting

In pre-pandemic times, in-person meetings were the norm for international organisations. However, the COVID-19 pandemic made it difficult, and in many cases even impossible, to travel to meetings, leading to many meetings being cancelled, while others had to be held remotely. This had a significant impact on the interpreting community (ESIT 2021): on the one hand, particularly during the initial stages of the pandemic, interpreters saw a considerable decrease in their working days and were faced with a great deal of uncertainty as to the immediate future of the profession; on the other hand, they had to adapt to new working methods. More specifically, there was an increasing need to recruit interpreters for settings where users were geographically separated but still needed to communicate with each other. One of the main repercussions was the acceleration of the use of technology in interpreting which, according to Braun (2019), has recently evolved at a much faster pace than in previous decades. This is particularly the case in the fields of distance interpreting, technology-supported interpreting and machine interpreting.

The diversification and evolution of technology was necessary to allow for remote interpreting (also known as distance interpreting), understood as "forms of interpreter-mediated communication delivered by means of information and communication technology" (Fantinuoli 2018: 4) in which interpreters are physically separated from their users. Remote interpreting prosaically refers to the work carried out by interpreters from a remote location without a direct view of the room but with a view of the speakers on a screen. It has traditionally been defined as a method that "facilitates access via telephone/audio or video link to a remotely located interpreter or team of interpreters by clients who are together at one site" (Braun 2019), but this definition has since evolved to include other settings, e.g. when all the interpreters and the users are at different locations, or when the interpreters work from the same place but the delegates are connected from different countries. This latter configuration is usually the case at international organisations such as the UN, in which the interpreters work from the booths located in the headquarters but the delegates connect from elsewhere.

The nature of interpreting adopted by international organizations, including the UN, was remote interpreting, also called "video remote interpreting", "remote simultaneous interpreting" (RSI) and "distance interpreting", the latter being a broader term that sometimes refers to the same reality.

Whilst RSI has been the object of widespread scepticism amidst the interpreting community, since the beginning of COVID-19, the International Association of Conference Interpreters (AIIC) has developed an evolving position on the matter. As a consequence of the many technological and societal changes that have been accelerated since the outbreak of the pandemic, AIIC has embraced remote interpreting, understanding "the potential it offers to bring multilingualism to a wider sphere" (AIIC 2019). Indeed, some tests have shown that RSI can be implemented without breaching professional associations' deontological codes and norms (see for example Causo 2011: 202).

Along these lines, it is worth noting that AIIC has authored different reports and guidelines on RSI to help interpreters understand the implications of the different types of remote interpreting: in 2020, the association drafted a reference guide following the AIIC RSI seminar held in Geneva by AIIC Switzerland on 29 February 2020. This guide makes the distinction between two types of distance interpreting: teleconference interpreting and remote interpreting, along the lines of the definitions included in the AIIC Position paper on distance interpreting (AIIC 2018) and of the AIIC COVID-19 Distance Interpreting Recommendations for Institutions and DI Hubs (AIIC 2020a) which stipulates that the type of interpreting both depends on the location of the interpreters and of the participants:

> If the interpreters are located together with some active participants, with other active participants appearing remotely, they are performing teleconference interpreting.
>
> If the interpreters are all located together (team co-location) but no participants are at the same location, they are performing remote interpreting, here remote hub interpreting (also referred to as a distance interpreting hub).
>
> If the interpreters are working together by booth (booth co-location) but not with the rest of the team, they are performing remote interpreting in a single-booth hub.
>
> Set-ups also exist where interpreters work individually but are able to communicate with boothmates (virtual booth) or teammates (virtual team) (AIIC 2020b: 4).

RSI, as a modality, has historically been considered controversial, mainly due to the "reduced sensory input available to interpreters working in this modality" (AIIC 2019). In fact, studies show that interpreting from a different location to all or some of the participants creates a number of challenges (e.g. Braun 2014). Braun (2014: 163) recalls that interpreting is a "highly strategic cognitive-linguistic process of discourse comprehension and production … in which the interpreter forms his/her (own) understanding of the source text and produces his/her version of this in the target language", and posits that working remotely adds another layer of complexity. In her study, she comes to the conclusion that interpreting challenges are magnified by RSI working conditions, regardless of the interpreter's training, their experience or the quality of their equipment. As Russo, Iglesias Fernández, and Braun (2020: 235) posit, RSI is a double-edged sword: on the one hand, it can "increase the efficiency and sustainability of interpreting service provision" but, on the other hand, it raises questions about interpreting quality, communication dynamics, interpreter training and skills, working conditions, and remuneration. In their overview of studies carried out about the impact of RSI on the interpreter's performance, René de Cotret et al. (2020) come to the conclusion that this layer of complexity stems from the lack of virtual presence, the feeling of alienation and the reduced social presence (already identified by Braun (2012)), the decline in interpreter's performance and the need to allocate greater resources to the comprehension stage.

Whilst its use has soared during the COVID-19 pandemic, RSI is not a new phenomenon, and has been the object of some inquiry in the literature for some time. Even though, before the COVID-19 pandemic, RSI platforms were not used at international organisations, videoconference interpreting has been widely used in other settings, such as court (Devaux 2018) and medical scenarios. This being said, international institutions have been displaying interest in RSI for several decades, in that they saw it as a means to meet "linguistic demand and mitigat[e] logistical difficulties associated with displacing large teams of interpreters" (Braun 2019: 276).

Consequently, RSI has been tested in these organisations in the past (see Ruiz Rosendo 2021; Ziegler and Gigliobianco 2018 for a detailed description of these tests). The first tests were undertaken by UNESCO in 1976, and then by the UN (Mouzourakis 1996): in both cases, the interpreters found videoconferencing conditions to be inferior to those of simultaneous interpreting in a standard meeting room. In 1999, the International Telecommunications Union (ITU) conducted a study on interpreters' perception of and attitudes towards RSI: its main finding was that the interpreters reported a loss of control and increased fatigue, although the physiological stress measurements did not reflect this self-reported data. In the twenty-first century new studies were carried out to test RSI: in 2004 the conclusions of the test conducted at the European Parliament showed that the interpreters were satisfied with the quality of interpreting, although they reported increased fatigue and a feeling of alienation (Roziner and Shlesinger 2010). A decade later, in 2014, Seeber et al. (2019) analysed the attitudes of interpreters who provided video remote conference interpreting during the 2014 FIFA World Cup™ and found that the interpreters' attitudes towards RSI, as experienced during that event, were, in general, positive, probably due to the technological advances of recent years. In 2019, the European

Commission and the Council of Europe tested several RSI platforms, and found that they could be deployed successfully in smaller meetings with only two languages, whereas meetings with many participants and multiple languages present significant complications which can make it difficult to run these meetings smoothly using RSI platforms. A common result of these studies is the interpreters' overall belief that RSI is more stressful than onsite interpreting.

Murgu (2021), in her study about stress and performance in RSI, adds other studies carried out in the academic field, such as those conducted at the University of International Studies in Rome and at the *Ecole Supérieure d'Interprètes et de Traducteurs* (ESIT), as well as further studies in the professional field carried out in Turkey and by the Canadian Association of Professional Employees. The results of the academic studies show that interpreters consider training in RSI platforms to be an essential factor in boosting performance, and that they consider that handling technical problems can be an issue during assignments. The findings of the professional studies in Turkey and Canada show that interpreters believe their performance is worse in RSI and that they experience higher levels of stress when working remotely. It is worth noting, however, that studies that have included a clinical component have not found significant changes in stress hormone values nor increases in stress levels; the perceived increase in stress is likely to be a negative self-perception by the interpreter, probably due to a lack of control of the situation during an RSI assignment. There have also been large, funded projects that have examined the impact of different video-mediated interpreting formats in specific settings, such as the AVIDICUS project in the legal setting. This project revealed that video-mediated interpreting exacerbates interpreting problems (more lexical activation problems and over-elaboration tendencies) and accelerates the onset of fatigue, as well as engendering a sense that the human element and engagement with the users has been lost.

8.3 RSI at the UN

As we have seen in the previous section, the main differences between in-person and remote meetings is that in the former, participants are located in the conference room and interpreters work from the booths installed in those rooms, while technicians have full control over the audio equipment being used, whereas in remote meetings, the interpreters and participants are not co-located. In the case of the UN, remote meetings require the use of RSI platforms that are integrated into the UN on-premises Audio Visual Systems (United Nations Global Marketplace 2020) and can be located anywhere in the world.

When the pandemic broke out in 2020, each of the four UN duty stations (New York, Geneva, Vienna and Nairobi) created a Remote Interpretation Task Force to conduct preliminary, limited-in-scope tests of different RSI platforms, with a view to using them in meetings during the crisis. Later on, more extensive live testing was carried out during real meetings. These tests enabled the organization to learn about how the platforms work and to identify potential problems that may arise and which would need to be addressed. One major problem encountered was that the quality of the audio feed from remote participants varies greatly, as it depends upon the equipment they use, particularly the microphone, as well as their internet connection. Based on experience gathered during testing, the task forces drafted documents containing recommendations about the microphones and equipment that should be used by remote participants during remote meetings, in order to help them achieve the best possible sound quality.

In order to familiarize speakers with this new modality, several awareness campaigns were launched, including video messages and infographics. Information sessions with delegates were also organized. It was important to explain to the audience that, for interpretation to take place, high quality audio is essential, as the risk of damage to interpreters' hearing increases as audio quality deteriorates. UN interpreters themselves participated in videos explaining the dos and don'ts, what kind of microphone to use and which ones to avoid and the reasons to use an ethernet cable instead of Wi-Fi. Those self-explanatory videos are now publicly available and some are also shown prior to the start of meetings.

In addition, training courses for new and existing moderators were organized. Several technical aspects were emphasized during those training sessions, such as the importance of having optimal audio quality for interpreters or the necessity of cooperation between interpreters and moderators. Some shadowing exercises were also put in place in order to show how a sound that may seem fine to a passive listener is sub-par for an interpreter. By the same token, a disclaimer has also been added on the website, as it is important for participants to understand that working conditions with RSI differ from normal working conditions, and that sound that is deemed sufficient for passive listeners will not necessarily be sufficient for interpreters. Importantly, existing RSI platforms do not currently meet ISO standards on sound and image quality for simultaneous interpretation, including ISO requirements for different modes of distance interpreting (ISO 2603, ISO 4043, ISO 20108, ISO 20109). It has also been argued that interpreting a remote speaker requires greater cognitive effort and causes higher levels of stress and fatigue. For all these reasons, working conditions were modified and adapted for UN staff and freelance interpreters in order to take into account potential health hazards. Meeting duration was reduced from three to two hours and for a three-hour hybrid meeting with a platform, the maximum duration of remote interventions would not exceed 30 min.

8.4 Admission Exams at the UN

8.4.1 Background

Similar to other international organizations, such as the European Union, in order to become a UN accredited interpreter candidate, one must sit and pass an admission exam that tests simultaneous interpreting (SI). The first generation of self-taught interpreters worked only in consecutive interpreting (CI). Then came the second generation, in the period covering the two decades from 1960 to 1980. During those years, a large number of trainees or associate interpreters, mostly coming from other sections of the conference services, were recruited and received a three-month training provided by the UN. They were then required to pass an exam. This training programme was closed at the beginning of the 1980s because, due to the implementation of the programme, all the vacancies in the interpreting section had been filled; there were fewer internal candidates and an increasing number of interpreters were being trained in interpreting schools in Europe and the United States (Baigorri Jalón 2004).

During the 1990s, the Language Competitive Examination (LCE) was introduced to establish a roster of successful candidates from which to fill present and future vacancies. Indeed, UN Regulations expressly prohibit the recruitment of candidates outside the LCE process (see Diur 2014; Ruiz Rosendo and Diur 2017a, b) for a detailed description of the LCE). Those candidates who opted to become a freelance interpreter were not requested to pass the LCE but the freelance test that was organised to that effect. Therefore, since the 1990s, the UN has held two different admission exams: the LCE to recruit staff interpreters, and the freelance test to accredit those interpreters who want to work at the UN as freelancers.

Until 2019, both exams were organized in situ at different examination centres, with no possibility of sitting the exam online. The main shortcoming of such an in-person testing scheme was that it was impossible for some candidates to sit the exam for financial and geographical reasons. In fact, the number of examination centres was rather limited, and many candidates had to travel at significant personal expense. Freelance exams were not publicly announced so only a number of freelancers were aware of the dates and modalities of the tests. Therefore, the UN decided to reconceptualise the admission exams and administer online exams. The rationale was to make the process more democratic, transparent and inclusive while improving geographical representation among candidates.

8.4.2 The GLR and the CELP

Whilst the reconceptualization of the UN admission exams had been on the table since before the pandemic, the outbreak of COVID-19 accelerated the process and obliged the UN to swiftly renegotiate the whole concept and structure of the exams after the outbreak of the pandemic, and both the freelance exam and the LCE moved online. The freelance exam is now called the Global Language Roster exam (GLR), while the LCE is now entitled the Competitive Examination for Language Positions (CELP). GLR exams are organized regularly in order to add interpreters to the roster (used by the four duty stations to recruit freelancers), while the CELP is used to recruit staff interpreters. It is worth noting that both tests are similar in procedure, technological needs and assessment criteria although the level tested is different.

In different resolutions adopted by the UN General Assembly, in particular Resolution 73/346 of 16 September 2019, it was reaffirmed that multilingualism was "a core value of the Organization [that] contributes to the achievement of the goals of the United Nations, as set out in Article 1 of the Charter of the United Nations" (UN General Assembly 2019: 1). The General Assembly also requested the Secretary General to continue his efforts to hold competitive examinations for the recruitment of language staff sufficiently in advance in order to fill current and future vacancies in the language services in a timely manner (A/C.5/76/L.4) and to continue to make every effort to enhance access to competitive examinations for applicants in all regions, including by organizing remote examinations and by bringing, to the extent possible, examination sites closer to their locations in order to allow the greatest number of potentially qualified candidates to participate in them.

In order to organise tests on line, it was necessary to find a platform that would allow candidates from different regions of the world to sit a UN exam remotely. The platform chosen was Vidcruiter, which was, at the time, a platform already being used by Human Resources in the UN New York Duty Station for recruitment purposes. The platform, however, needed to be customized and adapted to interpretation needs and some technical improvements were required. Several rounds of testing by staff interpreters in all four duty stations took place, and mock exams were organised to make sure that the platform answered the organization's needs. During these tests, it was immediately identified that staff interpreters would need to be trained in the use of the platform, since it was necessary to have more than one interpreter per booth acquainted with its use and functions.

Feedback from all testers was then used to customize and adapt the platform with the developers. As remote testing was new at the UN, staff interpreters in charge of organizing remote testing needed to know what to do, for example, if a candidate had a technical problem during a test or if, all of a sudden, the internet connection failed or became too erratic. Several guides and tutorials were made available for all different stakeholders: organisers, coordinators, evaluators and candidates. The purpose of these guides and tutorials was to allow all actors to easily monitor and follow the online exam, be it pre-selection exams, GLR exams or CELPs. A webpage was created with tutorials and instructions on how to proceed. Clear marking criteria were devised. Those criteria are communicated to all candidates prior to the remote testing and are available on the testing platform. The message reads as follows:

Your performance will be evaluated using the following criteria:

- Delivery: the extent to which the vocal output flows smoothly, is evenly paced, clearly enunciated and inspires confidence, as demonstrated by clear pronunciation, control of pace, breathing and pauses, and use of appropriate volume, tone and intonation.
- Accuracy: extent to which all levels of meaning of the original are conveyed, as demonstrated by effective analysis of argument/message, adequate transmission of the main ideas and sufficient detail, effective summarization and recasting of sentences.

- Target language quality: the extent to which lexical, grammatical and syntactical choices are effective and the appropriate register is used, as demonstrated by appropriate word choices, correct grammar and idiomatic syntax.

Online exams are not devoid of difficulties, such as the institution's need to create a robust technical infrastructure. The challenges of sitting an online exam are manifold, and can include slow network speed, connectivity issues or poor technical infrastructure development (Alsadoon 2021). Therefore, candidates receive a series of instructions about the equipment and technical setup in order to take the exam and are provided with a checklist that they need to cover. In order for the candidates to get acquainted with the platform and to double check their technical set-up, mock exams are held. The mock test is mandatory, as it is important to make sure that all candidates know the platform and to avoid a situation where they encounter problems on the day of the exam. Failure to take the mock exam means that the candidate will be excluded from the pre-selection test. Mock exams are indispensable because it is the only way for candidates to make sure that their technical set-up meets expectations and requirements.

The structure of the online CELP differs from the former LCE: the examination process, as was the case before, still consists of two parts: Part 1 is used to test interpretation skills and Part 2 is a competency-based interview. However, Part 1 now includes a pre-selection test (the pre-selection test is included both for the GLR exam and the CELP). Only candidates who are successful in the pre-selection test will be invited to sit the online interpretation exam, and candidates are informed of their eligibility or non-eligibility by email. Candidates are responsible for identifying and securing a location suitable for them to complete the examination, as having a good internet connection is of crucial importance.

Approximately two weeks before the pre-selection test and the online exam session, all eligible candidates are obliged to complete a mock test to ensure that their equipment and internet connection are acceptable. The mock test will not be evaluated and is only intended to help candidates familiarize themselves with the platform and check their set up. If technical problems were to arise during Part 1 of the exam (pre-selection and test), a retake is organized. Retakes are an integral part of the exam process, since technical problems can always occur where an internet connection is needed.

Another challenge identified in the literature on online exams is managing candidates who try to cheat. According to research, cheating in an online setting is considered easier than doing so in an onsite exam (Comas-Forgas et al. 2021). Consequently, and in line with Xiong and Suen's (2018) suggestions, the UN has implemented an identity authentication procedure via webcam. In practice, this requires candidates to appear on video while interpreting in order to discourage cheating.

Both the CELP and GLR exams are centrally marked by the Board of Examiners, which is made up of senior interpreters from all four duty stations. The assessment criteria for the new exams are the same as for the LCE: excellent passive comprehension of the two source languages, accuracy in interpretation into grammatically correct target language, an ability to construct complete sentences, an understanding of appropriate style and register, an ability to keep up with speed, intelligent editing of logically redundant words and phrases, an ability to cope with difficult or dense passages, and good diction and delivery.

8.5 Conclusions

The COVID-19 pandemic has had an impact on both the interpreting method and the acceleration of the transition to online admission tests at the UN. Regarding the former, the pandemic drastically changed the way that meetings and events were held. One of the more complex aspects of holding meetings in an online and/or hybrid format was to continue to provide six languages in simultaneous interpretation, and how to address the challenges stemming from the use of RSI.

The learning curve has been very steep for all actors involved: organizers, delegates and interpreters. They all had very little time to adapt to the new situation and learn how to use these platforms for meetings. Interpreters find that their work has been made more difficult by the often poor sound quality, caused by the use of unsuitable microphones and equipment by remote participants, and by the fact that the audio feed is transmitted via the public Internet with low bandwidth. The experience can therefore be frustrating, particularly because interpreters require above average sound quality in order to be able to do their job, since they have to speak and listen at the same time. This level of sound quality is difficult to achieve in remote meetings.

Furthermore, international organisations are based on the principle of multilateralism, defined as a "process of organizing relations between groups of three or more states" (Britannica 2006), also understood as "coordinating relations among three or more states in accordance with certain principles" (Ruggie 1992: 568). This means that delegates have to meet and to speak to discuss together and, importantly, should be able to see each other to discuss complex ideas and to interact effectively. Therefore, despite the fact that advances in communications technology has rendered it possible to hold international meetings throughout the pandemic, it is debatable whether or not online international meetings, and therefore RSI, will replace in-person meetings in the long term. This possibility is particularly questionable, given that many delegates are increasingly seeing that these remote meetings are not a replacement for in-person meetings. Indeed, in our opinion, many interpreting users are looking forward to a time when they can once again meet in person and have face-to-face discussions.

With regard to the admission exams, the UN, which had already envisaged switching to online exams, had to accelerate the process due to the pandemic. Since its inception, the online system has been an efficient, fair, transparent, and inclusive process. Several GLR and CELP tests have since been conducted and it seems fair to conclude that remote testing, at least as done by the UN, does work. Additionally, it has fulfilled its objective of increasing inclusivity and allows the participation of candidates from regions that were not able to sit UN exam before. Although exams are now online, the skills tested and the requirements are still the same. It should also be added that, due to the pandemic, candidates have, in the majority of cases, had experience working online using RSI platforms, and are, therefore, accustomed to the use of such platforms. Given the new changes to the interpreting market, schools and universities will probably need to follow suit and adapt to the changing landscape, including this new way of testing in their curriculum.

It would be desirable for research in the field of interpreting at international organizations to explore the challenges faced by interpreters as a consequence of the changes stemming from the increasing use of RSI platforms. This is a topic that will require a great deal of further analysis, particularly regarding the impact of RSI on the interpreter's wellbeing. Further analysis is also required in order to verify whether or not current interpreter training programmes properly prepare interpreter students for what they will face in the profession, such as the use of said RSI platforms and sitting online exams to be admitted into international organizations as a freelance or as a staff interpreter.

Disclaimer The views expressed herein are those of the author and do not necessarily reflect the views of the United Nations.

References

AIIC. 2018. AIIC position paper on distance interpreting. https://aiic.ch/wp-content/uploads/2020/04/aiic-position-on-distance-interpreting-05032018.pdf.

AIIC. 2020a. AIIC Covid-19 distance interpreting recommendations for institutions and DI Hubs. https://aiic.ch/wp-content/uploads/2020a/04/aiic-covid-19-intro-distance-interpreting-recommendations-for-institutions-and-di-hubs.pdf.

AIIC. 2020b. Reference guide to Remote Simultaneous Interpreting (RSI). https://aiic.ch/wp-content/uploads/2020b/05/aiic-ch-reference-guide-to-rsi.pdf.

AIIC. 2019. AIIC and distance interpreting. https://aiic.org/site/world/about/profession/distanceinterpreting

Alsadoon, H. 2021. Challenges of deploying online exams. *Revista Rom Nească Pentru Educaţie Multidimensională* 13 (1): 403–415.

Baigorri Jalón, Jesús. 2004. Interpreters at the United Nations: A history. Trans. A. Barr. Salamanca: Ediciones Universidad de Salamanca.

Braun, S. 2014. Comparing traditional and remote interpreting in police settings: Quality and impact factors. In *Traduzione e interpretazione per la società e le istituzioni*, ed. M. Viezzi and C. Falbo, 161–176. Trieste: Edizioni Università di Trieste.

Braun, S. 2019. Technology and interpreting. In *The Routledge handbook of translation and technology*, ed. M. O'Hagan, 271–288. London: Routledge.

Braun, S. 2012. Recommendations for the use of video-mediated interpreting in criminal proceedings. In *Videoconference and Remote Interpreting in Criminal Proceedings*, ed. S. Braun and J.L. Taylor, 301–328. Antwerp/Cambridge: Intersentia

Britannica. 2006. Multilateralism. https://www.britannica.com/topic/multilateralism.

Causo, J.E. 2011. Technical guidelines for remote interpretation. In *Videoconference and remote interpreting in criminal proceedings*, ed. S. Braun and J.L. Taylor, 301–306. Guilford: University of Surrey.

Comas-Forgas, R., T. Lancaster, A. Calvo-Sastre, and J. Sureda-Negre. 2021. Exam cheating and academic integrity breaches during the COVID-19 pandemic: An analysis of internet search activity in Spain. *Helyon* 7 (10): e08233.

Devaux, J. 2018. Technologies and role-space: How videoconference interpreting affects the court interpreter's perception of her role. In *Interpreting and technology*, ed. C. Fantinuoli, 91–117. Berlin: Language Science Press.

Diur, M. 2014. *Preparing candidates for the United Nations Language Competitive Examination (LCE)*. Masters diss.: Université de Genève.

ESIT. 2021. ESIT research project on remote simultaneous interpreting. https://ec.europa.eu/education/knowledge-centre-interpretation/news/esit-research-project-remote-simultaneous-interpreting_en.

Fantinuoli, C. 2018. Interpreting and technology: The upcoming technological turn. In *Interpreting and technology*, ed. C. Fantinuoli, 1–12. Berlin: Language Science Press.

Mouzourakis, P. 1996. Videoconferencing: Techniques and challenges. *Interpreting* 1 (1): 21–38.

Murgu, D. 2021. Approaching stress and performance in RSI: Proposal for action to take back control. *Translation and Interpreting Technology Online*, 68–75.

René de Cotret, F., A.A. Beaudoin-Julien, and Y. Leanza. 2020. Implementing and managing remote public service interpreting in response to COVID-19 and other challenges of globalization. *Meta* 65 (3): 618–642.

Roziner, I., and M. Shlesinger. 2010. Much ado about something remote: Stress and performance in remote interpreting. *Interpreting* 12 (2): 214–247.

Ruggie, J.G. 1992. Multilateralism: The anatomy of an institution. *International Organisation* 46 (3): 561–598.

Ruiz Rosendo, L., and M. Diur. 2017a. Admission exams at international organisations: The United Nations' Language Competitive Examination. *CLINA. An Interdisciplinary Journal of Translation, Interpreting and Intercultural Communication* 3 (2): 33–52

Ruiz Rosendo, L., and M. Diur. 2017b. Employability in the United Nations: An empirical analysis of interpreter training and the LCE. *The Interpreter and Translator Trainer* 11 (2–3): 223–237.

Ruiz Rosendo, L. 2021. Interpreting for international organisations. *ENTI, Encyclopaedia of Translation and Interpreting*. https://www.aieti.eu/enti/interpreting_international_institutions_ENG/.

Russo, M., E. Iglesias Fernández, and S. Braun. 2020. Introduction. *The Interpreter and Translator Trainer* 14 (3): 235–239.

Seeber, Kilian G., L. Keller, R. Amos, and S. Hengl. 2019. Expectations vs. experience: Attitudes towards video remote conference interpreting. *Interpreting* 21 (2): 270–304.

UN General Assembly. 2019. Resolution A/RES/73/346. https://documents-dds-ny.un.org/doc/UNDOC/GEN/N19/284/46/PDF/N1928446.pdf?OpenElement.

United Nations Global Marketplace. 2020. Remote Simultaneous Interpreting (RSI) platform. https://www.ungm.org/Public/Notice/120055.

Xiong, Y., and H.K. Suen. 2018. Assessment approaches in massive open online courses: Possibilities, challenges and future directions. *International Review of Education* 64 (2): 241–263.

Ziegler, K., and S. Gigliobianco. 2018. Present? Remote? Remotely present! New technological approaches to remote simultaneous conference interpreting. In *Interpreting and technology*, ed. C. Fantinuoli, 119–139. Berlin: Language Science Press.

Marie Diur joined the UNOG as Chief of the Interpretation Service in 2017, after nearly ten years at UNOV, initially as Chief of the French Booth and then as Chief Interpreter. Marie worked as a freelance interpreter at different UN agencies, the European Union, and the private market up until 2001 when she joined the UN as a Staff Interpreter. Marie has been an AIIC member since 1992, and a visiting examiner in interpretation schools in France and Belgium. She finished her doctoral work at the University Pablo de Olavide in 2015. Marie is the former chair of the IAMLADP Taskforce on Interpreting Issues and is the UNOG Outreach Focal Point for Interpretation.

Lucía Ruiz Rosendo is an associate professor at the University of Geneva's Interpreting Department. She is also a conference interpreter working in the institutional market in Geneva. She finished her doctoral work at the University of Granada in 2006 and worked at the University Pablo de Olavide from 2004 to 2015. She currently teaches in the MA in Conference Interpreting and the MAS in Interpreter Training (University of Geneva). Her main areas of research are interpreting in conflict zones and scenarios, interpreting at international organisations and interpreter training. She is an active member of AIIC.

Chapter 9
Humanitarian Interpreting in the Age of COVID-19

Lucía Ruiz Rosendo and Maura Radicioni

Abstract This chapter describes the study of humanitarian interpreting as an emerging discipline within Translation and Interpreting Studies. Its aim is to chart the rapidly expanding volume of literature on humanitarian interpreting and describe the state of the field in the age of COVID-19 pandemic. It first provides an overview of the impact of the pandemic on the provision of humanitarian aid, as a general topic, to then focus on humanitarian interpreting. The chapter offers some background information on the definition of "humanitarian interpreting", as framed within the broader field of crisis translation, to subsequently address the challenges that humanitarian organizations and their interpreters face in their efforts to meet the needs posed by multilingual and multicultural communication, especially after the outbreak of the pandemic. It concludes with some recommendations for future research in the field of humanitarian interpreting.

Keywords Humanitarian aid · Humanitarian interpreting · Crisis translation · Health emergency · COVID-19

9.1 Introduction

Humanitarian crises are defining elements of the current international geopolitics. They are a direct consequence of wars, conflicts, displacements, and migrations, as well as major health emergencies, as the current war in Europe and the recent COVID-19 pandemic have clearly shown. In these challenging contexts, the aim of humanitarian action is to relieve suffering in conflict-affected areas through the delivery of aid and the protection of populations in need. As such, it is a practice encompassed in the more general notion of humanitarianism, which refers to "those practices formally described as "humanitarian", such as humanitarian relief or aid, and the far more controversial (military) humanitarian intervention" (Radice 2016:

L. Ruiz Rosendo (✉) · M. Radicioni
Faculty of Translation and Interpreting, University of Geneva, Geneva, Switzerland
e-mail: Lucia.Ruiz@unige.ch

K. Liu and A. K. F. Cheung (eds.), *Translation and Interpreting in the Age of COVID-19*, Corpora and Intercultural Studies 9,
https://doi.org/10.1007/978-981-19-6680-4_9

103). In this context, humanitarian action refers to assistance that is based on the principles of humanity, impartiality, neutrality and independence, as enshrined in International Humanitarian Law (IHL).

Within the framework of what Holly Reed (2001) defines as complex humanitarian emergencies, the communication needs of civilian populations are increasingly and rapidly felt. These are populations who are often displaced from their homes and who almost always witness a deterioration of their living conditions. The COVID-19 pandemic is one such complex humanitarian emergency, and it has had a tremendous impact on the provision of humanitarian aid and on the work carried out by interpreters and cultural mediators as humanitarian actors. Indeed, interpreting and cultural mediation have, historically, been instrumental in facilitating communication between people who speak different languages and come from different linguistic and cultural backgrounds.

This chapter provides a summary of research undertaken in the field of humanitarian interpreting, crisis communication and crisis translation. It further surveys the impact of the pandemic on humanitarian action, in general, and on humanitarian interpreting, in particular. Finally, the chapter suggests sources for further reading and offer recommendations for future research. The aim of this discussion is to provide an account of the challenges that interpreters encounter as humanitarian workers, particularly when faced with an unexpected emergency such as a pandemic.

9.2 Humanitarian Interpreting

Research on interpreting in conflict and post-conflict scenarios began to grow at a rapid pace in the 2000s, following both the growing use of interpreters and cultural mediators in challenging contexts to facilitate communication and their ensuing visibility. The need to investigate the factors influencing their work in various regions and contexts has been highlighted by several scholars (e.g. Palmer 2007; Inghilleri 2009; Baker 2010; Footitt and Kelly 2012; Ruiz Rosendo and Persaud 2016; Ruiz Rosendo and Barea Muñoz 2017). As revealed by the increasing number of contemporary studies devoted specifically to the role of interpreters in complex humanitarian settings, in all scenarios related to conflict, violence and war, and health crises, interpreters do not only enable communication but become active partners in the process of mediation and conflict resolution, often providing humanitarian assistance to refugees and people in need in their capacity as all-round aid workers.

Various aspects have been investigated in the literature, ranging from historical, ethnographic, and sociolinguistic perspectives on the relationship between migration and translation (Inghilleri 2017), to the fundamental role played by translation as a form of intercultural communication in migration contexts (Cronin 2006), and the link between identity and language in a global society (ibid.). Linguistic practices emerging from migration contexts (and from the narratives of such contexts) and their relation to translation have also been the subject of study, alongside related issues of identity, role, power, and agency (Polezzi 2012). Researchers usually focus on war-related contexts, highlighting the complex ethical, organizational, and psychological implications of interpreters' work in these contexts. In this respect, there has been an increasing focus on the role of interpreters working in conflict zones for the military (Inghilleri 2010; Ruiz Rosendo 2020a), journalists on missions abroad (Palmer 2007), as well as complex scenarios directly or indirectly related to conflict and migration, including asylum-seeking procedures (Inghilleri 2003; Pöllabauer 2004) (for a detailed description of the studies carried out in the field of translation and interpreting in conflict and post-conflict scenarios, see Ruiz Rosendo 2020b).

There are, in addition, further studies that examine the role of translators and interpreters in the context of non-governmental organizations (NGOs); these include works by Tesseur (2018), who analyses the role of professional and non-professional translators at Amnesty International; Delgado Luchner (2018), who sheds light on the language practices of Caritas Switzerland and the Fédération genevoise de coopération; Radicioni (2019), who investigates the role of cultural differences in the language and cultural mediation practices enacted by the cultural mediators working for the Italian humanitarian medical NGO Emergency; and Montalt (2020), who analyses the role of translators and of translation in the context of Doctors Without Borders (MSF) and Translators Without Borders (TWB), focusing on how communication in humanitarian crises can be further improved.

The positionality of interpreters working in humanitarian contexts has also been the subject of scholarly investigation. The research conducted by Delgado Luchner and Kherbiche (2018) focuses on the positionality of interpreters working for the International Committee of the Red Cross (ICRC) and the United Nations High Commissioner for Refugees (UNHCR). The issue of positionality has also been addressed by Todorova (2016, 2017) in her studies on her experience as an interpreter working for the UNHCR in Kosovo and Macedonia.

Fewer studies have been centred on training programs specifically designed to meet the needs of interpreters working in conflict and post-conflict related contexts. Tipton (2011) focuses on emergent learning relationships between civilian interpreters and military personnel in situations of violent conflict, and Ruiz Rosendo (2022) deals with the creation of communities of practice in the context of military training and capacity-building missions deployed by Western armed forces in countries in conflict, specifically the learning relationships built between Spanish military officers deployed in Afghanistan and civilian interpreters who worked for them. The same topic has been investigated by Radicioni and Ruiz Rosendo (2022) in their study on the community of practice emerging between the cultural mediators employed by the NGO Emergency at its outpatient clinic in a highly degraded and migration-intensive area in southern Italy. Studies by Bergunde and Pöllabauer (2019) on the design and development of a training curriculum and handbook for interpreting trainees and trainers within the context of asylum hearings, Delgado Luchner and Kherbiche's (2019) work on the development of pedagogical tools to better equip humanitarian interpreters to solve ethical dilemmas, as well as the research by Ruiz Rosendo, Barghout, and Martin (2021) on the effectiveness of a training program targeted at United Nations staff interpreters who go on field missions are also worth mentioning.

Given the growing interest shown by scholars and professional organizations in the role of interpreters working in humanitarian contexts and the need to address their training needs in an interdisciplinary manner, it is worth acknowledging the definition of "humanitarian interpreting" by Delgado Luchner and Kherbiche (2018: 423), which reads as follows:

> Humanitarian interpreters work in conflict or post-conflict settings, or amongst populations displaced by conflict; their work environment falls within the legal framework of IHL [International Humanitarian Law] and International Refugee Law; they are exposed to human suffering because of the mandate of the organizations they work for and the settings in which their interpreting services are required: detention visits, interviews with victims of conflict, refugee status determination interviews, etc.; [and] the beneficiaries of their services often fall in the category of "protected persons" according to IHL; humanitarian interpreters play a role in enabling beneficiaries to access their rights

In helping beneficiaries to access their rights, humanitarian interpreters are actually aid workers, and the language used in mediation and the cultural intermediaries using it can, rightly, be framed within the broader context of humanitarian aid provision, with humanitarian interpreting being seen as a form of such aid. This is clearly shown, for instance, in the study by Radicioni (2019), in which cultural mediators contribute to overcoming the cultural differences between migrant patients and the local authorities, as well as providing them with social and health guidance. Cultural mediation is considered as a form of humanitarian aid provision in its own right, and in this case, through their work, the cultural mediators help migrant patients exercise their right to health.

9.3 Crisis Communication and Crisis Translation

The studies mentioned in the previous section have a common denominator: they all deal with communication and interpreting/cultural mediation practices performed in contexts of crises and emergencies. From this perspective, a fruitful interdisciplinary debate with disaster science offers common ground to address the notion of crisis communication and, within the latter, the role and challenges of crisis translation. Seeger et al. (1998: 7) provide a useful definition of a crisis, understood as "a specific, unexpected, non-routine event or series of events that creates high levels of uncertainty and a significant or perceived threat to high priority goals". These can be triggered by natural hazards, pandemics, or man-made disasters, including terrorism and conflict (Glade and Alexander 2016). Crises happen within multilingual and multicultural societies (Cadwell 2014; Cadwell and O'Brien 2016; O'Brien and Cadwell 2017): consequently, they lead to displacement of people and global economic migration across the world, creating the subsequent need for migrants or displaced persons to adapt to new contexts. Language plays a prominent role in both cross-boundary and local crises (O'Brien and Federici 2019), as does the ability to communicate effectively with migrants and refugees or long-time foreign residents with limited proficiency in their local language. Without proper communication in the right language, crises can have far-reaching long-term or temporary implications on the health and safety of residents and migrants. These implications can have profound cascading effects, as defined by Pescaroli and Alexander (2015: 64–65):

> …the dynamics present in disasters, in which the impact of a physical event or the development of an initial technological or human failure generates a sequence of events in human subsystems that result in physical, social, or economic disruption. Thus, an initial impact can trigger other phenomena that lead to consequences with significant magnitudes.

Faced with the cascading effects of a crisis, "crisis communication" becomes paramount. Seeger et al. (2016: 13) define it as follows:

> …the ongoing process of creating shared meaning among and between groups, communities, individuals, and agencies, within the ecological context of a crisis, for the purpose of preparing for and reducing, limiting, and responding to threats and harm.

Scholars have only recently started to acknowledge the complexity of communication mediated by interpreters or translators in crisis settings. This is especially the case in the context of "cascading disasters" (Pescaroli and Alexander 2015) and in rapidly evolving scenarios (Pescaroli and Alexander 2016), which can trigger other crises far from the area in which they originated. While the need for translation and interpreting is widely recognized, cross-border multilingual communication in crisis settings is understudied (Federici 2016). The settings concerned are varied and characterized by the need for swift action in difficult circumstances in "all forms of communication in extreme conditions, be they conflicts, disasters, emergencies, or crisis" (Federici 2016: 2). In this respect, another relevant definition that adds to the above is that of "crisis translation", as suggested by Federici et al. (2019a, b: 3):

> Crisis translation is understood as the transfer of written information from one linguistic and cultural system to another in the context of an adverse event that enables affected communities and responders to be prepared for crises and disasters, improve resilience, and reduce the loss of lives.

In their study, they further specify that crisis and disaster communication must be multimodal and multilingual, and, as such it is enabled through multichannel, inter- and intra-lingual translation due to the transboundary nature of modern-day crises (ibid.). In a later paper, O'Brien and Federici (2019: 131) complemented the definition provided above and specified that:

> […] crisis translation [should be intended] as a specific form of communication that overlaps with principles of risk communication […] as much as with principles of emergency planning and management […]

Though needed as a key element of disaster management, translation is rarely used in the field and has been underresearched so far (Federici 2019a; b). To this end, one initiative worth consideration is the EU-funded INTERACT project (International Network on Crisis Translation), which is aimed at researching translation in crisis scenarios. Starting by acknowledging that, in situations of crisis, the delivery and exchange of multilingual information needs to be clear, timely and accurate to effectively respond to disasters, the project provides ten policy recommendations to improve crisis communication through the integration of translation in national, international, or regional crises. The project highlights that, when translation is missing from crisis communication policy, the communication of multilingual information is unlikely to be fully or systematically implemented in a response, nor will it be considered during planning and preparedness stages.

Let us now consider the role of training. In crisis settings, mediation, arbitration, or humanitarian aid discussions take place between parties who do not share the same language or culture. Hence, individuals such as translators, interpreters, and cultural mediators are brought in to help negotiate the multiple languages and cultures and to aid the communication process (Moser-Mercer et al. 2014). Although there are some interpreter training programs put in place to increase the relevance and adequacy of interpreting in crisis settings (see, for example, Doğan 2016; Bulut and Kurultay 2001), in most cases training is lacking, and the individuals facilitating communication are non-professional interpreters and translators. As stressed by Federici and Al Sharou (2018), crisis translation relies predominantly on volunteers, who provide a service which prevents communication issues from turning into communication crises. Further evidence on this is provided by Filmer and Federici's (2018) study on migrants landing at the ports of Sicily, Italy, where the authors highlight that language brokers perform tasks that include translation, interpreting, social service, and advocacy, without necessarily having received training in any of these areas.

Most of the studies focusing on crisis translation/interpreting deal with health emergencies. Notable studies include those carried out by Greenstone (2010) and Powell and Pagliara-Miller (2012) on how to manage the physical and mental health risks when working in crisis situations, and on the need for medical teams and interpreters to work together in health crises, respectively. O'Brien and Cadwell's (2017) study also focuses on a health crisis: in this study, examining the readability of health-related information in the 2014 Ebola crisis in Kenya, the authors come to the conclusion that written modes of communication, even in the case of translated texts, might not be the best solution for some countries and cultures. Fewer studies have investigated the language and translation/interpreting practices employed by medical humanitarian organizations dealing with emergency situations, such as the COVID-19 pandemic.

9.4 The Impact of COVID-19 on Humanitarian Action

The COVID-19 pandemic has compounded existing humanitarian needs for the most vulnerable populations, who are also at heightened risk of poor health conditions and of suffering secondary impacts: the outbreak of the pandemic occurred amidst other cascading health and humanitarian crises and extreme weather events, and this outstripped the humanitarian capacity response in different countries (Voûte and Guevara 2020). Lau et al. (2020: 4) posit that previous epidemics have shown that "indirect health effects often exceed the morbidity and mortality caused directly by the disease", what they call "indirect mortality and morbidity". Hirata et al. (2021: 24) mention different indirect or secondary impacts stemming from a pandemic, such as:

> …economic instability and livelihood disruptions, food insecurity and malnutrition, health system stress/collapse, expanded need for psychological support, educational delays, increased child labor, hindered access to basic services, and the rise of violence and abuse.

Other impacts include the disruption of live-saving health services and prevention programs (Lau et al. 2020), the disruption of childhood vaccination and further economic deprivation (Pritchard et al. 2020). To understand the magnitude of the current humanitarian crisis, these authors underline that two billion people live in fragile and conflict-affected states and that, by 2019, 70.8 million people had been driven from their homes. This means that one in every 45 people worldwide needed humanitarian assistance in 2020.

In an already trying context, the COVID-19 pandemic substantially and rapidly transformed the way in which humanitarian aid was delivered, due to travel restrictions and lockdowns, lack of human resources and a lack of medical supplies. Therefore, the pandemic forced humanitarian organizations to adapt in extraordinary ways, facing up to the challenge of adjusting to new ways of working whilst trying to maintain the quality of their programs to meet the needs of vulnerable populations and to ensure the safety and security of communities and staff alike (Lawson-McDowall et al. 2021). More specifically, the barriers to an effective response in vulnerable areas were: the overcrowded living conditions experienced by migrants and refugees; limited movement and consequent limited access to public health; the impossibility of observing social distancing and self-isolation; limited access to drinking water, adequate sanitation and hygiene, and food and income; the existence of pre-existing major diseases, such as HIV and tuberculosis; the endemic lack of healthcare providers, which has been aggravated by travel restrictions; and poorly functioning healthcare systems and limited public health infrastructure. In addition, the pandemic spread in areas already severely affected by ongoing conflict and political instability, mass displacement, natural disasters and extreme poverty. In many of these areas, governments and armed groups placed even more restrictions on humanitarian organizations as they tried to access the populations in need (Brubaker et al. 2021).

The virus also spread in refugee camps, where medical resources were already scarce and disease-prevention recommendations were difficult or almost impossible to implement (Vonen et al. 2021). Migrants, including internally displaced persons (IDPs), asylum seekers and refugees, did not have access to social protection mechanisms (British Red Cross 2020), and in many cases this was true even before the pandemic. Moreover, mistrust and a lack of access to information jeopardized efforts to control the pandemic (Pritchard et al. 2020). This was particularly the case in camps where refugees, who already faced constant language-related difficulties when accessing healthcare services (Vonen et al. 2021), did not always have access to information about the pandemic, preventive measures, and their rights and entitlements. Indeed, the lack of translation of communication materials, together with the spread of misinformation, was one of the challenges that migrants had in West and Central

Africa, according to the report by the British Red Cross (2020). This report also highlights that information sources in refugee camps were predominantly informal networks and social media forums.

In short, whilst the pandemic had an impact on the worldwide population, people living in areas already ravaged by conflict and in refugee camps were disproportionately affected. The pandemic undoubtedly exacerbated humanitarian crises and presented humanitarian workers with yet more challenges when performing their job, due to their reduced ability to respond not only to the pandemic, but also to urgent community needs.

Faced with this situation, the adaptation of humanitarian aid has been a major cause of concern, inasmuch as accessing vulnerable populations and delivering aid has been significantly more challenging (Driss 2020). Importantly, COVID-19 guidance has not necessarily been as "applicable to humanitarian settings where living and working conditions as well as socio-economic environments are very different" (Singh et al. 2020: 1). Since such guidance was not context-specific, humanitarian organizations were obliged to be innovative to deal with the disease. Furthermore, given that the pandemic altered the relationships between local and international humanitarian organizations (Brubacker et al. 2021), the role of local actors (local NGOs, community-based organizations and community volunteers) was key in building community trust and ensuring the mobilization of messaging in risk prevention (British Red Cross 2020). Local actors were also crucial in ensuring that interventions were adapted to local needs, priorities and contextual challenges (Lau et al. 2020). In fact, these authors argue that poor communication and a lack of cultural awareness during past epidemics, such as the Ebola epidemic in West Africa, fuelled fear and mistrust towards healthcare providers, and discouraged local populations from seeking healthcare. Against this backdrop, the role of humanitarian interpreters and cultural mediators was essential in helping vulnerable populations overcome language and cultural barriers and access COVID-19-related information.

9.5 The Impact of COVID-19 on the Work of Humanitarian Interpreters

The COVID-19 pandemic has shown to an even greater extent how timely, trusted, and accurate health-related information needs to be. As Civico (2021: 1) points out, "the COVID-19 pandemic took most governments around the world by surprise and pushed them to address many issues that had long been neglected. Among them, communication proved to be a particularly challenging matter." Communication proved to be even more challenging in communities characterized by their dependence on humanitarian aid.

As previously highlighted, literature on disaster and crisis response recognizes the need for timely, trusted, and accurate communication. This is especially true for unfamiliar ideas such as those that emerged during the COVID-19 pandemic (e.g., cocooning, social distancing, or behaviour change). As Zhang and Wu (2020: 526–527) posit:

> … language barriers may affect the international circulation of epidemic prevention materials, thus hampering emergency rescue operations in the affected communities. Therefore, it is necessary to include multilingual logistics in national emergency preparation, response and recovery plans.

Along these lines, Moser-Mercer et al. (2021: 6) highlight the importance of effective communication in any crisis scenario:

> In humanitarian, conflict, post-conflict/early recovery and protracted refugee contexts, communication is key to ensuring coordination of relief operations, the provision of essential services related to WASH (water-sanitation-health), protection, food security and Education in Emergencies (EiE), whether within the borders of countries in crisis or in those hosting the forcibly displaced.

To account for the new situation, humanitarian NGOs had to adapt their interpreting and cultural mediation practices in order to avoid situations where people misunderstood instructions or were excluded from participating in preparedness, response and recovery efforts. Mathews et al.'s (2022) study examining the experiences and challenges of sign language interpreters during the pandemic in Ireland and the United Kingdom is one such example, showing that public briefings and national campaigns were important elements of crisis communication and that interpreting was an essential element of this process.

Another health-related study conducted on crisis communication in a health emergency is Wang (2019), which focuses on translation in the COVID-19 emergency in Wuhan and illustrates the tasks carried out and the challenges encountered by government and external volunteer translators. Other authors have stressed the importance of translation in facilitating communication between foreign populations and emergency responders after natural disasters such as earthquakes (Munro 2013; Cadwell 2019), particularly when making language services available to foreign nationals in the response phase.

It is worth mentioning that studies on the impact of the pandemic on the work carried out by interpreters who work for humanitarian organizations are few and far between. The findings of a preliminary survey that we carried out of reports drafted by the CCHN and the ICRC show that, even though there has been some publications on the impact of COVID-19 on humanitarian action, its impact on interpreters has not been the focus of any studies so far. A case scenario that illustrates how cultural mediators and interpreters (as humanitarian actors in their own right) had to adapt to the new challenges imposed by the pandemic is described in Radicioni and Ruiz Rosendo's forthcoming study. It focuses on the measures taken by the NGO Emergency in Italy, which provides free medical care and surgical treatment to civilian victims of conflicts, war, land mines and poverty in war-torn scenarios outside Italy, as well as free medical care, assistance, and social guidance to individuals in need in Italy. The NGO employs cultural mediators for its activities in Italy within the context of *Programma Italia*. They work at outpatient clinics and mobile units scattered throughout the country and speak Italian, English, French, Arabic, Spanish, Romanian, and a few African languages (Esan, Bini, as well as Pidgin English), among others. With the outbreak of the COVID-19 pandemic, *Programma Italia*'s activities for the provision of general medicine, nursing, and psychological support services, both face-to-face and in remote, were not interrupted, and the cultural mediators working for the NGO continued providing healthcare and social guidance to migrants. However, all activities had to be adapted to safeguard Emergency's staff and patients alike. Drawing on the organization's experience in treating patients with Ebola in Sierra Leone in 2014 and 2015, Emergency collaborated with national and local health authorities to manage the coronavirus outbreak and launched new initiatives, while continuing to provide its traditional services in different modalities. A stronger focus on communication was chosen so that information would reach beneficiaries in a timely and culturally appropriate manner, and mediators played a pivotal role in the process.

A major concern was that migrants could not easily understand and implement information due to language barriers and fake news about the disease, which had started circulating within the local population. One of the main goals of the new communication approach was, therefore, to provide people with the necessary information to implement COVID-19 protective measures and convince them of the importance of cocooning and leaving their homes only if strictly necessary. Providing correct information, e.g., about social distancing and mobility, through various communication channels was, therefore, essential. Various actions were implemented to this end, resulting from both a bottom-up and a top-down approach stemming from central decisions made by the NGO. Triage facilities, coordinated by cultural mediators working alone or with a nurse, were set up in front of almost all *Programma Italia* outpatient clinics to provide patients with COVID-19-related information and direct them to the most appropriate local health companies and hospitals.

One bottom-up initiative was the use of WhatsApp groups, which were specifically targeted at vulnerable groups of the population, migrants above all, informing them about safety and social distancing rules, behavioural norms as regards mobility and the need to stay at home, and referring them to the competent public health services. An extremely effective communication initiative was the creation of videos produced by cultural mediators in various languages (e.g., Pidgin English, Punjabi, Wolof, French, Bengali, Russian, Arabic and Romanian), which aimed at providing correct information to non-Italian speakers and to make sure that minimum safety standards were respected. The videos were disseminated on YouTube, Facebook, and WhatsApp, and they were shown by various social groups managed by migrant communities living in Italy. The effectiveness of the videos, soon proven with the first video produced in Pidgin English, confirms O'Brien and Cadwell's (2017) assumption that meaning can be created not only through written words but also through images, icons, and sounds.

Another effective measure implemented within *Programma Italia* was carried out in Polistena, in the South of Italy, and consisted of the implementation of a rapid swab service for the most vulnerable groups, including migrants, who were most at risk of infection. Rapid antigenic swabs were administered at a drive-in tent, where Emergency health professionals gave medical and nursing support, and cultural mediators provided information and orientation to migrants. Importantly, in all the activities implemented by Emergency, cultural mediators served as actual aid workers, as they flexibly took on new roles and developed new initiatives to communicate with foreign patients with the overall aim of guaranteeing beneficiaries' right to health.

Programs to train humanitarian interpreters have also been affected by the pandemic, in that the few existing initiatives had to be adapted to the new situation. It is worth noting that most training programs were residential until the outbreak of the pandemic, but the lockdown and travel restrictions forced the coordinators of such programs to move fully online. This was the case of the joint training program organized by the University of Geneva's Faculty of Translation and Interpreting (FTI) and the ICRC. Until 2020, several courses had been organized in the field in different regions in Africa, Asia and the Middle East. The pandemic led the organizers to develop an online course concept to continue with the training of humanitarian interpreters using a learning management system. Although the modular structure of the course did not essentially change, there was a need to record the lectures and role plays which would be analysed, as well as to rethink the conceptual rationale of the different activities and group work. This was also the case with the joint program organized by the FTI and the CCHN to train interpreters who work in humanitarian negotiation, which was designed from the outset (in 2020) as an online course.

9.6 Conclusions

In this chapter, our aim has been to contribute to current debates surrounding the challenges faced by humanitarian interpreters when confronted with a health emergency, specifically the COVID-19 pandemic. Any health emergency can have an impact on the work performed by humanitarian actors, including interpreters and cultural mediators. Given the importance that effective communication has in any crisis situation, the work of these interpreters and mediators is essential for building trust, overcoming potential miscommunication problems, as well as disseminating all information regarding the measures taken by the authorities to control the spread of the disease. This is particularly crucial for migrants and refugees, who typically face difficulties in accessing healthcare due to the fact that they do not speak the local language.

The main difficulty faced by humanitarian interpreters and cultural mediators after the outbreak of the pandemic was the lack of realistic measures that could be implemented in the settings in which migrants and refugees lived. This indicates that many of the solutions put in place were the result of improvised decisions made under time pressure. However, one of the challenges that we faced in our research and when delving deeper into the topic was the scarcity of information about the impact of the pandemic on humanitarian interpreters. Therefore, more research is needed to more systematically analyse the work performed by such interpreters when confronted with a pandemic, as well as their needs and the challenges that they have experienced. The importance of further investigation in this field lies in the need to distil the experiences from past activities and actively take them into account in future actions and behaviours, in order to avoid making the same mistakes again. On this matter, it would be encouraging to see more joint research among scholars, interpreters and humanitarian organizations.

References

Baker, M. 2010. Interpreters and translators in the war zone. *The Translator* 16 (2): 197–222.

Bergunde, A., and S. Pöllabauer. 2019. Curricular design and implementation of a training course for interpreters in an asylum context. *Translation and Interpreting* 11 (1): 1–21.

British Red Cross. 2020. Rapid response insights: The primary humanitarian impacts of COVID-19. https://www.redcross.org.uk/-/media/documents/about-us/international/rapid-response-primary-impacts-covid-19.pdf.

Brubaker, R., A. Day, and S. Huvé. 2021. *COVID-19 and humanitarian access: How the pandemic should provoke systemic change in the global humanitarian system.* Centre for Policy Research: United Nations University.

Bulut, A., and T. Kurultay. 2001. Interpreters-in-aid at disasters: Community interpreting in the process of disaster management. *The Translator* 7 (2): 249–263.

Cadwell, P. 2019. Trust, distrust and translation in a disaster. *Disaster Prevention and Management* 29 (2): 157–174.

Cadwell, P., and S. O'Brien. 2016. Language, culture, and translation in disaster ICT: An ecosystemic model of understanding. *Perspectives. Studies in Translation Theory and Practice* 24 (4): 557–575.

Cadwell, P. 2014. Translation and interpreting needs in the great east Japan earthquake of 2011. In *Proceedings of the XXth FIT world congress* (Vol. II), 752–760.

Civico, M. 2021. *COVID-19 and language barriers.* Ulster: Ulster University. https://www.ulster.ac.uk/__data/assets/pdf_file/0010/931492/REAL21-4.pdf.

Cronin, M. 2006. *Translation and identity.* Oxford/New York: Routledge.

Delgado Luchner, C. 2018. Contact zones of the aid chain: The multilingual practices of two Swiss development NGOs. *Translation Spaces* 7 (1): 44–64.

Delgado Luchner, C., and L. Kherbiche. 2018. Without fear or favour? The positionality of ICRC and UNHCR interpreters in the humanitarian field. *Target* 30 (3): 415–438.

Delgado Luchner, C., and L. Kherbiche. 2019. Ethics training for humanitarian interpreters working in conflict and post-conflict settings. *Journal of War and Cultural Studies* 12 (3): 251–267.

Doğan, A. 2016. Anybody down there? Emergency and disaster interpreting in Turkey. In *Mediating emergencies and conflicts: Frontline translating and interpreting*, ed. F.M. Federici, 44–53. London: Palgrave Macmillan.

Driss, H. 2020. The effects of the Covid-19 pandemic on humanitarian aid operation in Jordan. *Capstone Collection* 3223. https://digitalcollections.sit.edu/capstones/3223.

Federici, F.M., and K. Al Sharou. 2018. Moses, time and crisis translation. *Translation and Interpreting Studies* 13 (3): 486–523.

Federici, F.M., S. O'Brien, P. Cadwell, J. Marlowe, B. Gerber, and O. Davis. 2019a. INTERACT recommendations on crisis communication policies. https://reliefweb.int/report/world/international-network-crisis-translation-recommendations-policies.

Federici, F.M., S. O'Brien, B. Gerber, and P. Cadwell. 2019b. *The international humanitarian sector and language translation in crisis situations. Assessment of current practices and future needs.* London; Dublin; Phoenix, AZ: INTERACT The International Network on Crisis Translation.

Federici, F. M. 2016. Introduction: A state of emergency for crisis communication. In *Mediating emergencies and conflicts. Frontline translating and interpreting*, ed. F.M. Federici, 1–29. New York, NY: Palgrave Macmillan.

Filmer, D.A., and F.M. Federici. 2018. Mediating migration crises: Sicily and the languages of despair. *European Journal of Language Policy* 10 (2): 229–253.

Footitt, H., and M. Kelly. 2012. *Palgrave studies in languages at war*. London: Palgrave/Macmillan.

Glade, T., and D.E. Alexander. 2016. Classification of natural disasters. In *Encyclopedia of natural hazards,* ed. P. Bobrowsky, 78–82. Berlin: Springer.

Greenstone, J.L. 2010. Use of interpreters with crisis intervention teams, behavioral health units, and medical strike teams: Responding appropriately and effectively. *International Journal of Emergency Mental Health* 12 (2): 79–82.

Hirata, E., M. Peach, and S. Tobing. 2021. The faith-based advantage: A case study on the adventist development and relief agency's response to humanitarian impacts of COVID-19 as a faith-based organization. *Christian Journal for Global Health* 8 (1): 24–33.

Inghilleri, M. 2009. Translators in war zones: Ethics under fire in Iraq. In *Globalisation, political violence and translation*, ed. E. Bielsa and C.W. Hughes, 207–221. London: Palgrave Macmillan.

Inghilleri, M. 2010. You don't make war without knowing why. *The Translator* 16 (2): 175–196.

Inghilleri, M. 2017. *Translation and migration. New perspectives in translation and interpreting studies*. London and New York: Routledge.

Inghilleri, M. 2003. Habitus, field and discourse. Interpreting as a socially situated activity. *Target* 15 (2): 243–268.

Lau, L.S., S. Guyer, M.C. Greene, R.T. Moresky, L.F. Roberts, S.E. Casey, S.P. Kachur, M. Zard, F.M. Fouad, and W. Zeng. 2020. Preventing and mitigating indirect health impacts of COVID-19 on displaced populations in humanitarian settings. https://www.publichealth.columbia.edu/sites/default/files/knowledge_brief_1.pdf.

Lawson-McDowall, J., R. McCormack, and S. Tholstrup. 2021. The use of cash assistance in the Covid-19 humanitarian response: Accelerating trends and missed opportunities. *Disasters* 45 (S1): 216–239.

Mathews, E., P. Cadwell, S. O'Boyle, and S. Dunne. 2022. Crisis interpreting and deaf community access in the COVID-19 pandemic. *Perspectives* (online first).

Montalt, V. 2020. Medical translation in crisis situations. In *Intercultural crisis communication translation, interpreting and languages in local crises*, ed. F.M. Federici and C. Declercq, 105–126. London, UK: Bloomsbury.

Moser-Mercer, B., L. Kherbiche, and B. Class. 2014. Interpreting conflict: Training challenges in humanitarian field interpreting. *Journal of Human Rights Practice* 6: 140–158.

Moser-Mercer, B., S. Qudah, M.N.A. Malkawi, J. Mutiga, and M. Al-Batineh. 2021. Beyond aid: Sustainable responses to meeting language communication needs in humanitarian contexts. *Interpreting and Society* 1 (1): 5–27.

Munro, R. 2013. Crowdsourcing and the crisis-affected community: Lessons learned and looking forward from mission 4636. *Journal of Information Retrieval* 16: 210–266.

O'Brien, S., and P. Cadwell. 2017. Translation facilitates comprehension of health-related crisis information: Kenya as an example. *Journal of Specialised Translation* 28: 23–51.

O'Brien, S., and F.M. Federici. 2019. Crisis translation: Considering language needs in multilingual disaster settings. *Disaster Prevention and Management* 29 (2): 129–143.

Palmer, J. 2007. Interpreting and translation for western media in Iraq. In *Translating and interpreting conflict*, ed. M. Salama-Carr, 13–28. Amsterdam: Rodopi.

Pescaroli, G., and D.E. Alexander. 2016. Critical infrastructure, panarchies and the vulnerability paths of cascading disasters. *Natural Hazards* 82: 175–192.

Pescaroli, G., and D.E. Alexander. 2015. A definition of cascading disasters and cascading effects: Going beyond the 'toppling dominos' metaphor. *planet @ risk* 3 (1): 58–67.

Polezzi, L. 2012. Translation and migration. *Translation Studies* 5 (3): 345–356.
Pöllabauer, S. 2004. Interpreting in asylum hearings: Issues of role, responsibility and power. *Interpreting* 6 (2): 143–180.
Powell, C., and C. Pagliara-Miller. 2012. The use of volunteer interpreters during the 2010 Haiti earthquake: Lessons learned from the USNS COMFORT operation unified response Haiti. *American Journal of Disaster Medicine* 7 (1): 37–47.
Pritchard, J., A. Collier, M. Mundenga, and S.A. Bartels. 2020. COVID in crisis: The impact of COVID-19 in complex humanitarian emergencies. *Journal of Military, Veteran and Family Health* 6 (2): 70–82.
Radice, H. 2016. The responsibility to protect as humanitarian negotiation: A space for the "politics of humanity"? *International Politics* 53 (1): 101–117.
Radicioni, M., and L. Ruiz Rosendo. forthcoming. Interpreting in times of Covid-19: Cultural mediation as a means of effective multilingual communication. In *Translation in times of cascading crises*, ed. F. Federici and S. O'Brien. London: Bloomsbury Publishing.
Radicioni, M., and L. Ruiz Rosendo. 2022. Learning dynamics between cultural mediators in humanitarian healthcare: A case study. *JosTrans* 37: 139–159.
Radicioni, M. 2019. Cultural differences in interpreter-mediated medical encounters in complex humanitarian settings: The case of emergency ONG Onlus. In *Handbook of research on medical interpreting*, ed. I.E.T. de V. Souza and E. Fragkou, 165–187. Hershey, Pennsylvania: IGI Global.
Reed, H., Roundtable on the Demography of Forced Migration, Committee on Population, National Research Council. 2001. Demographic assessment techniques in complex humanitarian emergencies: Summary of a workshop. http://www.nap.edu/catalog/10482.html.
Ruiz Rosendo, L. 2020a. Interpreting for the Afghanistan Spanish Force. *War & Society* 39 (1): 42–57.
Ruiz Rosendo, L. 2020b. Translating and interpreting in conflict. In *The Oxford handbook of translation and social practices*, ed. M. Ji and S. Laviosa, 45–65. Oxford: Oxford University Press.
Ruiz Rosendo, L. 2022. Interpreting for the military: Creating communities of practice. *JosTrans* 37: 16–34.
Ruiz Rosendo, L., and M. Barea Muñoz. 2017. Towards a typology of interpreters in war-related scenarios in the Middle East. *Translation Spaces* 6 (2): 182–208.
Ruiz Rosendo, L., and C. Persaud. 2016. Interpreting in conflict zones throughout history. *Linguistica Antverpiensia* 15: 1–35.
Ruiz Rosendo, L., A. Barghout, and C. Martin. 2021. Interpreting on UN field missions: A training programme. *The Interpreter and Translator Trainer* 15 (4): 450–467.
Seeger, M.W., T.L. Sellnow, and R.R. Ulmer. 1998. Communication, organization, and crisis. *Annals of the International Communication Association* 21 (1): 231–276.
Seeger, M.W., T.L. Sellnow, and R.R. Ulmer. 2016. *Communication and organizational crisis.* Westport, CT: Greenwood Publishing Group.
Singh, N.S., O. Abrahim, C. Altare, K. Blanchett, C. Favas, A. Odlum, and P.B. Spiegel. 2020. COVID-19 in humanitarian settings: Documenting and sharing context-specific programmatic experiences. *Conflict and Health* 14 (79): 1–9.
Tesseur, W. 2018. Researching translation and interpreting in non-governmental organisations. *Translation Spaces* 7 (1): 1–19.
Tipton, R. 2011. Relationships of learning between military personnel and interpreters in situations of violent conflict. *The Interpreter and Translator Trainer* 5 (1): 15–40.
Todorova, M. 2016. Interpreting conflict mediation in Kosovo and Macedonia. *Linguistica Antverpiensia* 15: 227–240.
Todorova, M. 2017. Interpreting at the border: "Shuttle interpreting" for the UNHCR. *Clina* 3 (2): 115–129.
Vonen, H.D., M.L. Olsen, S.S. Eriksen, S.S. Jervelund, and T.A. Eikemo. 2021. Refugee camps and COVID-19: Can we prevent a humanitarian crisis? *Scandinavian Journal of Public Health* 49: 27–28.

Voûte, C., and M. Guevara. 2020. Policy brief on humanitarian impacts. *The Lancet Countdown on Health and Climate Change*, December 2020. https://www.msf.ch/sites/default/files/2020-12/lancet_countdown_policy_brief_msf.pdf.

Wang, P. 2019. Translation in the COVID-19 health emergency in Wuhan. A crisis manager's perspective. *The Journal of Internationalization and Localization* 6 (2): 86–107.

Zhang, J., and Y. Wu. 2020. Providing multilingual logistics communication in COVID-19 disaster relief. *Multilingua* 39 (5): 517–528.

Lucía Ruiz Rosendo is an associate professor at the University of Geneva's Interpreting Department, Faculty of Translation and Interpreting. She is also a conference interpreter working in the institutional market in Geneva. Her research has been published in *Linguistica Antverpiensia, Target, War and Society, The Interpreter and Translator Trainer* and *Armed Forces and Society*, among others, as well as edited collections, including the *Oxford Handbook of Translation and Social Practice*. She teaches in the MA in Conference Interpreting and the MAS in Interpreter Training (University of Geneva). Her main areas of research are interpreting in conflict zones and scenarios, interpreting at international organisations and interpreter training. She is also the coordinator of the FTI-ICRC (International Committee of the Red Cross) programme to train ICRC interpreters who work in the field and the co-coordinator of the FTI-UNOG course "Interpreting in UN field missions". She also collaborates with the Centre of Competence on Humanitarian Negotiation (CCHN), in which she provides specialised training and counselling for professional and non-professional interpreters who work in different humanitarian organisations, such as the ICRC, UNHCR, WFP, MSF Switzerland, and HD.

Maura Radicioni is currently pursuing a Ph.D. degree in Interpreting Studies at FTI, University of Geneva (Switzerland), with a research project on humanitarian interpreting. She obtained her MA in Conference Interpreting from the University of Bologna, DIT at Forlì (Italy) in 1997. Since then, she has worked a conference interpreter and interpreter trainer. She was lecturer in English-Italian liaison and conference interpreting at the Forlì-based DIT of the University of Bologna from 2003 to 2019, with teaching assignments also at the University of Macerata and Università Politecnica delle Marche. From July to October 2017, she was involved as a trainer in the first humanitarian interpreting pilot course carried out in Italy, jointly organized in blended-learning mode by the University of Bologna DIT and the University of Geneva FTI.

Chapter 10
Teamwork in the Virtual Booth—Conference Interpreters' Experiences with RSI Platforms

Márta Seresi and Petra Lea Láncos

Abstract Remote simultaneous interpreting (RSI) platforms existed well before the COVID-19 pandemic, but their use skyrocketed when social distancing and mandatory quarantine restrictions made it practically impossible to organize on-site events with live interpretation. This new working method has a clear impact on interpreters' workload. In a traditional booth setting, conference interpreters can rely on their boothmates when it comes to problem solving. Scholarly literature on the subject is relatively scarce, but it seems to confirm that interpreters heavily rely on each other when reproducing names, numbers and lists, communicating with clients and technicians while in the booth, as well as providing emotional support. In a virtual booth, however, communication between partners can be obstructed, and non-verbal communication is entirely impossible. In our research, we conducted semi-structured interviews with trained conference interpreters to examine how in-booth communication works on RSI platforms, what kind of difficulties may arise, what strategies interpreters use to overcome these difficulties and how RSI platform developers could change platforms to allow for a smoother simultaneous interpreting experience for interpreters and the audience alike. Results suggest that trained and experienced interpreters are capable of finding strategies to deal with most of the arising difficulties, very often in a more autonomous way than in a traditional setting. However, the emotional importance of having a boothmate seems to emerge more explicitly than in our previous study about boothwork.

Keywords Simultaneous interpreting · Teamwork · Boothmate · Cooperation · Handover

---

M. Seresi (✉)
Department of Translation and Interpreting, Eötvös Loránd University (ELTE), Budapest, Hungary
e-mail: seresi.marta@btk.elte.hu

P. L. Láncos
Faculty of Law and Political Sciences, Pázmány Péter Catholic University (PPKE), Budapest, Hungary
e-mail: lancos.petra.lea@jak.ppke.hu

K. Liu and A. K. F. Cheung (eds.), *Translation and Interpreting in the Age of COVID-19*, Corpora and Intercultural Studies 9,
https://doi.org/10.1007/978-981-19-6680-4_10

10.1 Introduction

When defining simultaneous interpretation, we usually refer to two main elements. On the one hand, in the case of simultaneous interpretation, the speech production of the speaker and the interpreter takes place almost simultaneously. On the other hand, we also emphasize the technical conditions without which simultaneous interpretation cannot take place. For a very long time, under technical conditions, we meant that interpreters were seated in an interpreting booth, listening to the room through earphones, speaking into a microphone, and taking turns every 20–30 min or so (Nolan 2005). The professional standards of the International Organization of Conference Interpreters (AIIC) states that "two interpreters per booth" are required to cover one language pair each (AIIC 2000).

This definition was taken for granted right until the SARS-Cov-2 coronavirus outbreak in 2019 made it necessary to physically separate interpreters, speakers and audience members of an event from each other. In these cases, booth partners cooperate in special ways, but are normally physically separated from each other. Interpreters will either work from home or log in from a remote workstation. It may also be the case that they convene in an interpreters' hub, but sit alone in their booth, or they may even sit in the same booth, separated by plexiglass. We have seen several examples of these solutions both in the national markets and in international or EU institutions. What these solutions have in common is that the booth partners' usual cooperation in a single-space booth is unfeasible due to pandemic precautions.

It is worth noting that on the national markets there has always been a need for employing single interpreters for shorter or even longer jobs to save costs (Seresi 2019; Bouhmid 2019). Meeting such needs, of course, also raises quality and ethical issues. In light of all this, it is worth reviewing why simultaneous interpreters work in pairs, but sometimes even in trios or more in the international or EU context, and exactly what kind of cooperation takes place between them. Building on our earlier survey-based research, we elaborate on the forms of cooperation between booth partners and their specific needs in a simultaneous interpreting context. Then we turn to possibilities of booth partner cooperation in various remote interpreting situations introduced in the wake of the corona virus pandemic. Working with semi-structured interviews we asked interpreters about their experiences with working remotely alone or with a'booth partner', the forms of cooperation they developed, their specific needs arising on the job that had not been met and recommendations for further developing remote interpreting tools to improve cooperation, and thereby also delivery.

10.2 Boothwork in the Scholarly Literature

The scholarly literature underlines that simultaneous interpretation is a very strenuous activity. The interpreter must simultaneously monitor, interpret, and analyse the speaker's speech production, translate, and reproduce what is uttered, while also planning and editing their own speech production (Moser-Mercer et al. 1998). Often the interpreter must use three or four working languages within the span of half an hour. In addition, due to the cognitive complexity of the task, the simultaneous interpreter may experience a level of stress that is comparable to that affecting air traffic controllers (Zeier 1997). Therefore, at certain intervals, the interpreter must rest and pass the microphone to their partner.

It is generally suggested in the literature that an interpreter should not undertake simultaneous interpretation alone for a stretch of time longer than 40 min (Moser-Mercer et al. 1998). Typically, those who work in pairs will pass the microphone after 30 min, although partners may switch as frequently as every 15 min, depending on the difficulty of the topic and the speaking style of the speaker. In their 1998 research, Moser-Mercer et al. found that after 30 min, there was a discernible increase in the number of errors made by interpreters, in particular, confusing, grave errors. Surprisingly, these errors went unnoticed by the interpreters themselves, presumably because they no longer had the energy to monitor their own performance under the pressure of the high cognitive load. Overwhelmed interpreters merely found that the original speech they were interpreting became more difficult after thirty minutes, when in reality, this was not the case.

Being able to switch and rest is not the only reason why interpreters work in pairs, however. The passive interpreter also plays an important role, as long as they are in the booth or are somehow 'accessible' to the active interpreter. Assistance provided by the booth partner may be divided into three main categories: assistance in interpreting, practical assistance, and emotional support.

The type of assistance most often cited by simultaneous interpreters is the *assistance in interpreting* (Seresi and Láncos 2020). The passive interpreter cooperates with the active partner to enhance the quality of delivery by helping solve word-level problems, jotting down numbers, names or terms quickly, or by quietly waving and nodding (Gile 1995). Based on their interviews with Thai interpreters Rattanabutr and Rangponsumri further list boothmates' assistance in pointing out mistakes made by the partner while interpreting (Rattanabutr and Rangponsumri 2016).

The booth partner may further assume a role in assisting their partner with documents, in case the speaker has provided the interpreters with a written version of his speech, a table with the data he wants to list etc. Under these circumstances, the active interpreter must not only share their attention between listening and interpreting but must focus their attention on information arriving visually. In such cases, it is helpful when the passive partner organizes the documents, annotates them, hands them over or points out parts of the text that the speaker is mentioning, especially if they skipped or supplemented a part of the speech (Rohonyi 2016).

The *assistance* provided by the boothmate may also be *of a practical nature.* For example, the partner can be of assistance if unexpected technical problems arise or when a last-minute document must be procured. The passive interpreter will also take action when someone enters the booth during the conference and will be available if the active interpreter suddenly experiences a coughing fit, feels ill or is unable to work for other reasons. (Seresi and Láncos 2020).

Finally, it is worth mentioning the *emotional support* provided by the boothmate. This may take the form of simple gestures, such as bringing each other coffee or water (Bouhmid 2019; Seresi and Láncos 2020), or by encouraging the partner with non-verbal cues while they are working (Seresi and Láncos 2020).

Nevertheless, assistance provided by the boothmate is not always perceived as helpful by their partner. Some interpreters find it more confusing when their partner tries to help: it distracts them, or they themselves are reluctant to ask for help (Rohonyi 2018). Some interpreters are nervous when their colleagues are present and hear how they work (Gile 1995). That's why in her 2020 paper, Christova identifies emphatic productive, emphatic unproductive (or even destructive) and non-emphatic interactivity strategies among simultaneous interpreters (Christova 2020). In their interviews Rattanabutr and Rangponsumri gathered information on uncooperative boothmate behaviour such as unwillingness to help, not listening to the speaker, leaving the booth or sleeping in the booth as well as intrusive and distracting behaviour, such as trying to attract the working interpreter's attention by touching them, holding a note to their face or trying too hard to help (Rattanabutr and Rangponsumri 2016).

According to the findings of a previous survey (Chmiel 2008), 45% of interpreters leave the booth when it is not their turn to work. And even when they stay, they prefer to solve a puzzle, play on the phone, read a book or the news, look up terms for their own turn or prepare for the next speech. Yet even those who leave the booth or stay without assisting their partner, typically pay attention to the speakers in the room and their partner's production at the beginning of the event in order to get a better picture of what is being discussed. In particular, these interpreters focus on the terminology employed, so that the terms are used in accordance with the vocabulary of conference participants and consistently with their partner (Chmiel 2008). They can also gauge their partner's skills and decide to whether or not it is 'safe' to leave the booth or participate more actively and be available to take over in case the partner cannot deliver.

Thus, while booth partners do not always provide assistance to the active interpreter, and conversely, interpreters are not always open to accepting help from their partner, there are quite a few reasons as listed above, for AIIC standards to foresee that interpreters work in pairs. These are incidentally also the reasons why most interpreters refuse to work alone.

10.3 The Turn Towards Remote Interpreting During the Times of the COVID-19 Pandemic

Early attempts at remote interpreting, and related research started in 1970s (Tripepi Winteringham 2010). Remote interpreting was initially rejected by interpreters, who saw in this new form of interpreting a marked decline in working conditions and, as a corollary, a potential deterioration in quality and a significant reduction in the social prestige of the profession.

Interpreters felt that they had been exiled to a remote workstation, where conditions were more difficult, since visual information was limited, they did not necessarily see the audience's reactions, and in case problems arose, it was difficult for them to contact their clients (Mouzourakis 2006). For all these reasons, they reported feelings of alienation and fatigue (Moser-Mercer 2005). They also feared that the prestige of the profession would plummet if interpreters were transferred from high-level negotiations and high-prestige clients to a workstation set up in the basement of a separate building (Hurdiss-Jones 1989). Over time, the technical equipment supporting remote interpreting became more widely available, and beyond criticisms regarding incomplete visual information, among interpreters using cheaper tools, often without the help of a technician, more and more complaints about sound quality were voiced (Seresi 2016).

However, interpreters' reservations about the quality of remote simultaneous interpretation were not confirmed by research (Roziner and Shlesinger 2010). It should also be noted that prior to the lockdown measures introduced because of the pandemic, even when working remotely, interpreters worked side by side, in an environment that mimicked a real booth.

The Covid-19 outbreak at the beginning of 2020 rapidly turned into a full-blown pandemic, which proved to be devastating for several branches of the national economies. Indeed, with national restrictive measures implemented to protect the health and life of citizens, such as lockdowns, travel restrictions, cancelling of large events, prohibitions on assembly, provisions governing the mandatory use of masks etc. organizing international events involving interpreting seemed unfeasible. In the spring of 2020 interpreters routinely saw their assignments cancelled, including not only engagements at EU and international institutions, but those that would have taken place in their country of residence as well.

Following a few months of virtually no interpreting work, events were moved to existing or newly developed platforms enabling simultaneous interpreting. This created new job opportunities for simultaneous interpreters, who at the same time had to face an unprecedented challenge: they had to work far away from not only their clients but also from their partner, typically from their own homes, using their own equipment. In this set up, there could be no question of resorting to the usual forms of cooperation with the boothmate. With our series of interviews recorded in January 2021, we investigated the difficulties faced by interpreters 'migrating' to remote interpreting platforms. From our semi-structured interviews, a myriad of new developments, difficulties, and advantages emerged: in this article, we explore the many forms of virtual cooperation between boothmates.

10.4 Methodological Approach

Lockdown type restrictions in the first wave of COVID-19 in Hungary were ordered in March 2020. We conducted our research in January 2021, when interpreters were already beginning to get used to the "new normal" of working remotely, having gained sufficient experience in interpreting on RSI (remote simultaneous interpreting) platforms.

We opted for a qualitative research method (Creswell 2009). On the one hand, the possible number of participants in interpreting research is usually limited (Gile 1998), making the use of quantitative research methods and the formulation of universally valid findings extremely difficult. On the other hand, our main objective was to gain insight into interpreters' individual behaviour and to identify possible factors of interest in a situation that has never occurred before in the history of conference interpreting. These considerations explain why our choice fell upon the use of a qualitative method (Duflou 2016), that is, on making semi-structured interviews.

Interviews allow researchers to gather information about situations in which the research participants cannot be directly observed (Creswell 2009), which is very often the case when interpreters work at confidential events. During an on-line event, organizers have even more control over those who can join as observers and do not necessarily wish to share the limited bandwidth available with outsiders. In these circumstances, asking interpreters about their experiences in an interview setting seemed a quick and feasible solution for gathering data.

Using ZOOM, we asked 10 experienced Hungarian conference interpreters about their experiences. All interpreters invited to participate in our research have been active interpreters on the Hungarian and international markets for over 10 years. Interpreting being their main source of income, during the pandemic, they switched to using RSI platforms as soon as possible.

Each semi-structured interview took 20–30 min and each participant was asked the same 5 standard questions: 1. What RSI platforms have you used so far? 2. Did you always work with partner? If not, why? 3. What difficulties did you encounter when working with a partner? 4. What solutions did you come up with to meet these challenges? 5. What are your recommendations for developing RSI platforms?

The interviews were semi-structured, for participants could deviate from the suggested topics and could freely mention anything that occurred to them in connection with the use of RSI platforms. The conversations were recorded and we took notes. As we wanted to identify the main factors of interest in connection with boothwork in a virtual setting, we used a thematic approach to analyse our data (Creswell 2009). Using a basic qualitative analysis, we identified the recurring themes and organized the responses we gathered by these major topics (e.g., "Listening to Each Other;" "Handover;" "Providing Assistance," "The partner as hindrance," etc.). Below, we review the responses concerning virtual cooperation with the boothmate in the RSI setting.

10.5 The Responses

At the beginning of each conversation, we asked participants to list RSI platforms they had worked with and asked whether they take on RSI assignments without a partner. We then inquired about the difficulties of cooperating with the 'boothmate' virtually. In the course of the interviews, respondents identified a number of difficulties in working removed from their partner. These problems fall into three major categories: listening to the partner, handing over the microphone, and providing assistance. Nevertheless, our participants have come up with viable solutions to these difficulties, which are also described below. Finally, we asked them how RSI platforms should be improved.

10.5.1 RSI Platforms Used by the Participants

We first asked about the RSI (or other ITC) platforms used by the participants (Table 10.1). Our participants have already gained online interpreting experience with a wide variety of platforms. Participants named the following platforms: Zoom (7 mentions), VoiceBoxer (5), Kudo (5), Interactio (4), Interprefy (4), Skype (3), Webex (2), Facebook Stream (1), MS Teams (1) and Google Meet (1).

In order to perform the assignment in the best possible quality, in some cases these platforms had to be combined with each other (e.g., Webex with Zoom or MS Teams, possibly running Skype on 2 devices). Sometimes the combination of different platforms was due to the client's unwillingness to invest in a proper RSI platform. During the interviews, some participants qualified these solutions as "home tuning" or "low-cost". One participant described the technical challenges of this period as follows: "Everybody must first shoot themselves in the foot to understand how important it is to use the appropriate platforms and devices."

Table 10.1 Platforms mentioned by the participants

Platform mentioned	Out of 10
Zoom	7
VoiceBoxer	5
Kudo	5
Interactio	4
Interprefy	4
Skype	3
Webex	2
Facebook stream	1
MS teams	1
Google meet	1
Combining several platforms	2

Table 10.2 Working online without a boothmate

Working without a boothmate	Out of 10
Never	3
Only for assignments shorter than 2 h	2
Only for assignments shorter than 90 min	2
Only for assignments shorter than 1 h	2
Only for consecutive assignments	1

Two participants also mentioned that in addition to the platforms they were already actively using, they also took a course on using another platform. In fact, it was quite typical in this period that interpreters sought to expand their skills, since they felt that they could only remain active in the market if they adapted quickly to the new circumstances.

10.5.2 RSI Without a Partner

In the second question, we asked participants whether they had experience in RSI interpreting without a partner (Table 10.2). Three answered in the negative, but only one participant said that they would never, under any circumstances, undertake an interpretation assignment alone. When asked under which circumstances respondents would undertake online interpreting assignments alone, five interviewees answered they would do so only in case of shorter assignments [less than two hours (2), less than one and a half hours (2) and less than 60 min (2)]. Three interpreters mentioned that in the case of consecutive interpreting, it is not customary to work with a partner on the Hungarian market.

When asked if it was difficult to work alone in an online setting, almost everyone replied that it was not, since they knew the client well (3) or already had a routine in using RSI platforms (1). Only one interpreter mentioned that it was hard to work this way, as the success of the whole event depended on them and their technical background (internet connection, computer).

10.5.3 Listening to the Partner

As already indicated in the introduction, boothmates pay attention to each other's interpretation, for it is only this way that they can guarantee consistent terminology, help their partner by jotting down numbers and words if the other runs into a difficulty, and continue interpreting coherently when their partner turns off their microphone. However, listening to each other can be difficult when interpreters do not work side by side.

Table 10.3 Listening to boothmate

Listening to boothmate	Out of 10
Being at the same venue	7
Using 2 devices	6
Using 3 devices	2
Listening to each other on the RSI platform	2
Not listening to each other at all	2

Surprisingly, even in the times of the pandemic, the majority of our participants, seven out of ten answered that their primary solution to this problem was to interpret from the same place (Table 10.3). This place is usually the home of one of the interpreters, or sometimes an ad hoc workstation set up by the client. This shows how much interpreters rely on seamless cooperation. However, this solution also has its drawbacks: on the one hand, in an epidemic situation, interpreting in the same airspace is highly risky. On the other hand, when the same internet connection is used in an apartment to run the RSI platform, a possible technical breakdown could jeopardize the work of both interpreters. Finally, it may be very confusing to hear our partner's output both from the headset through the RSI platform and at the same time, in reality.

Another frequently mentioned solution is when interpreters are not physically in the same place, but are in constant contact with each other. In such cases, it is essential to use several devices at the same time: six participants mentioned using two devices (laptop plus tablet or phone), and two respondents use up to three devices. This solution enables interpreters to remain in constant audio or video contact, hearing each other work and allowing for seamless handovers. The downside to this is that the two devices they operate also require two earphones. All this is costly and the solution only works if partners remember to mute and activate microphones on the right devices at the right time. This obviously entails additional cognitive load for interpreters and can only be confidently managed with proper routine.

Only two interpreters who responded to our January 2021 survey mentioned that they were listening to their partner through the RSI platform they were already using without operating an additional device. Since then, however, based on the feedback received from interpreters, some RSI platforms have been further developed to allow interpreters to listen to each other. Nevertheless, there are still platforms where this is out of the question. Yet even on platforms where it is possible to listen to the partner, a typical problem was that it was impossible to listen to both the speaker and the partner at the same time. Thus, the interpreter was either informed of his partner's solutions or what was said in the'room'. This is not always enough, however, for interpreters to develop a consistent terminology or to assist each other. In cases where it was possible to listen to two channels at the same time, these were not transmitted in separate ears of the interpreter, and their volume could not be adjusted separately either. Consequently, listening to the partner and the room was more often than not a distraction.

The last "solution" mentioned by two participants was not listening to each other at all. This approach may be down to the fact that initially, interpreters did not really know these platforms and the cognitive load involved in simultaneous interpreting online was too great to start using extra devices as well. However, a clear drawback of this solution is the inconsistent use of terminology among interpreters (who have no idea what terminology their partner is using), as well as the threat that at the time of handover, half or even entire sentences will be lost, since the partner is not aware at which point they are cued in.

10.5.4 Handover

In a previous study about boothwork we completed before the COVID-19 pandemic (Seresi and Láncos 2020), 96% of the 80 participating interpreters indicated that they actively cooperate with their partner during the handover (e.g. by making eye contact, gesturing when they are ready to take over or hand over the microphone). This was the most common form of collaboration identified in our research on boothmates' cooperation. However, such non-verbal communication is clearly impossible when interpreters are not in the same room.

All 10 participants interviewed in this study reported (see Table 10.4) that they had used an application for managing the handover (e.g. Messenger, WhatsApp etc.). In most cases, they sent each other a series of messages in a sort of countdown ("1 min"–"OK"–"Now") or, for the sake of simplicity, sent emoticons they had agreed on beforehand, in order to indicate that they were ready to hand over the microphone.

Only one participant mentioned using the chat function of the RSI platform for this purpose. In this case, however, interpreters must be careful not to enter messages into the general chatbox, for everyone to see. Under the cognitive load of simultaneous interpretation, it is difficult to pay attention to selecting the right chatbox and it may be easier to use a separate device, such as a phone application.

In the event that boothmates are unable to listen to each other or have no other means of communication, a solution may be to discuss in advance exactly when they will hand over the microphone (this was also mentioned by three respondents), hoping that they will not cut into each other's words. Another solution is to monitor whether the partner's microphone is on: if not, it is time to take over.

Table 10.4 Organizing microphone handover

Organizing microphone handover	Out of 10
Using chat application on mobile phone	10
Using the RSI platform's chat	1
Agreeing on exact time and handing over the microphone without indicating it to the boothmate	3
Monitoring whether the other microphone is turned on/ boothmate is speaking	2

Participants mentioned a lot of difficulties in connection with handing over the microphone:

- In many cases, only the active or, on the contrary, the passive interpreter can initiate the transfer, so in the event of an error, the partner cannot override it if their 'boothmate' has pressed the wrong key.
- Handing over the microphone is a multi-step process, so there is more room for error.
- The interpreter working from home may not notice that they had made a mistake during the handover, and it is difficult to draw their attention to this error.
- Only the technician can override it if someone has pressed the wrong button (while in a traditional booth, the partner can intervene with one move).
- The partner may not notice the handover message in time.
- In an emergency situation, the interpreter cannot see whether or not the partner is available to take over.
- Even in obvious emergency situations (such as a sudden coughing fit), the partner cannot simply take over the microphone without requesting the handover.
- In case of streaming, partners may hear the original sound with a different delay, making a smooth handover particularly difficult.

Most of the above difficulties cannot be overcome with creative solutions, therefore, the further development of RSI platforms will be necessary to improve the performance and cooperation between virtual boothmates.

10.5.5 Assisting the Virtual Boothmate

In a traditional setting, the passive interpreter assists their active partner. In our previously mentioned study, 93% of the 80 interpreters participating in the survey responded that they assist their partner by jotting down numbers and names, 86% help navigate documents discussed and 82% help by looking up difficult terms, just to mention a few of the most important forms of cooperation between boothmates (Seresi and Láncos 2020). Such cooperation however, is not feasible when interpreters are working from a separate location.

The main problem seems to be that the active interpreter is unable to ask for help, since listening and speaking associated with simultaneous interpretation leaves no capacity to ask for help by typing in the question in the chat function of the RSI platform or in a separate device. Nevertheless, several interpreters mentioned that they still try to help their partner, and do so proactively. This is because they already know each other well enough to know which areas they are more proficient in than their peers. The problem, however, is that it is not possible to know if their partner will notice the help appearing in the chat. Message notifications may irritate or even frighten the active interpreter, who may think they are being alerted to a technical or other problem. This can cause a lot of stress; as one participant noted: "I don't know if I will ever be able to respond calmly to technical problems."

In fact, typing and sending a message is much more time-consuming than gesturing in the booth or pointing to a word: by the time the message arrives, it may not even be relevant anymore. In addition, it can be particularly unprofessional to accidentally send a helpful message to the general chatbox for everyone to see, as one of the participants reported.

Just like when interpreting in the booth, on an RSI platform, the partner may be less than helpful and even make the assignment more difficult. This is particularly so, when the partner is inexperienced with RSI, is less flexible, or easily panics. One of our participants, for example, admitted that in the beginning they were so stressed by having to work online that they were actually happy to interpret alone, "because at least that way I could control everything".

In the online context the question of whether the passive partner is available during their break is just as relevant as in the traditional booth setting. Three participants noted that when working on an RSI platform, they are afraid to leave the room for fear they must suddenly take over due to technical problems on their partner's side; something that actually occurred with one of our participants. Meanwhile, the reverse may also happen: there were those who reported that they had wanted to switch urgently, but sent messages to their partner in vain, who was nowhere to be found. One of the participants revealed in confidence that they had even double-booked the day and worked on another online event during their 'breaks' and as such, were not available to step in for their partner when necessary. Meanwhile, their clients knew nothing of this double-booking.

While in traditional settings it may be a problem that the partner fails to pass the microphone, in RSI situations it is hardly typical for the active interpreter to "hog the mic". "There's no such thing as someone going with the flow and forgetting to hand over," one of our participants said. Meanwhile, in the case of traditional conference interpreting, just after arriving late to the event (47%), this was the most frequently cited irritating behaviour (45%) on the part of the partner (Seresi and Láncos 2020). The fact that such behaviour is extremely rare in online settings, may be down to the fact that working on RSI platforms is much more burdensome. In fact, several participants mentioned that they switch more often than usual: "if the sound quality is poor, as frequently as every 5 min".

Lastly, when considering boothmates' cooperation, it is also worth mentioning emotional support. Especially those partners who work together often, besides providing professional assistance, they also support each other emotionally in the cognitively demanding and highly stressful situation of simultaneous interpreting. 88% of the 80 interpreters interviewed in our previous research said that they bring coffee and water for their partner, and several interpreters also mentioned that if they undertake shorter assignments without a partner, they miss the support and cooperation of their boothmate, including the conversations during the breaks (Seresi and Láncos 2020).

Four of the ten participants mentioned that they missed discussing the event with their partner after working online, having no opportunity to 'vent'. Three participants mentioned that it is a very strange feeling to work with someone for hours and then turn off the computer at the end of the event, suddenly finding themselves alone at home, as if just waking up from a dream. However, only three participants reported that they would call each other at the end of the event. Another interpreter only says goodbye to their partner in a chat message, while three participants claimed that they did not miss conversations with colleagues at all. Individual preferences varied greatly on this point.

10.5.6 Suggestions for the Development of RSI Platforms

Our last question concerned the improvements participants would like to see on RSI platforms. Surprisingly, while participants had typically elaborated passionately and at length on their difficulties and experiences, they often gave uncertain, varied answers to this question. Of course, it is most probably easier to identify a problem than to suggest a solution. Nevertheless, answers to this question were also received, as summarized in Table 10.5.

Overall, our 2021 interviewees want platforms to make available multiple communication (visual and audio) channels so that they can better communicate with their partner, with the participants and the technician, while also being aware of what is happening on the 'floor' and listening to their colleagues. At the same time, interpreters would like to see simpler and more user-friendly layouts, which of course, would be a great challenge for developers, should further channels be included in an improved version of the given platform.

The most popular solution would be to set up hubs (workstations designed for remote interpretation), as this would transfer some of the necessary communication channels from the virtual space to the physical reality, increasing transparency and enabling the joint physical presence of interpreters. However, one participant remarked that they were afraid that if interpreters started working from hubs, "they

Table 10.5 Possible development of RSI platforms

Suggestions	Out of 10
Hubs	4
Chat function should be more transparent	3
Relay should be more user-friendly	3
Handover should be simpler	2
Interpreters should hear each other	2
Interpreters should see each other	2
Interpreters should be able to verbally communicate with each other	1
Handover should be standardized	1
One device should be enough	1
Platforms should be more user-friendly	1
Interpreters shouldn't see each other	1

would stay that way forever". Two participants noted that there was no technical development that could make up for what is lost: one of the respondents stressed that they did not become an interpreter to work from home, and if RSI is here to stay, they will choose another profession. According to three of our ten participants, there is no need for further improvements, as developers have already done all that could be technically achieved in this situation. Instead, clients must be educated about the RSI context and how this changes expectations towards interpreters, or simply return to on-site conferences.

10.6 Summary

In our research built on semi-structured individual interviews conducted in January 2021, we sought to answer the question of how cooperation between simultaneous interpreters changes when interpreters work using RSI platforms. From the trends that emerged from the interviews, it is clear that in a virtual environment, it is difficult to listen to the partner, handover is less smooth, and it is very difficult, and sometimes impossible, to help the active partner effectively. Consequently, many participants decided to not even try to cooperate: they gave up listening to each other and did not even try to ask for or provide help. It is most probably down to these reasons that, contrary to our expectations, interpreting alone in an RSI context did not feel significantly more difficult to interpreters than RSI interpreting with a partner.

Despite the difficulties identified, none of the participants reported that they were unable to perform one or several of their assignments due to these difficulties. Thus, we can say that qualified conference interpreters are able to cope with working on RSI platforms. At the same time, there is no doubt that in these cases they are more or less left to their own devices in every sense of the word, facing a greater cognitive burden. As a result, interpreters are forced to develop and apply new strategies to try and restore cooperation in the RSI context. At the same time, when cooperation strategies require too much effort on their part, they may choose to rather solve the task alone. While they can work on their own as well, they nevertheless prefer to work with a physically accessible boothmate in a traditional, on-site setting.

In light of the above, it is no surprise that despite the pandemic, most participants decided to work online from the same place and are adamant about returning to the traditional setting of on-site simultaneous interpretation as soon as possible. In this respect, interpreters are not alone: clients are also keen on going back to organizing physical events. As one of the participants said: "There was not a single event that didn't end with the line: we hope, we'll see each other in person next time. In fact, they go to conferences because of the breaks."

Should health, environmental or economic reasons prevent this, many interpreters find the creation of hubs to be an acceptable solution. From these centres, which are specifically designed for remote interpreting, they could work collaboratively, albeit remotely, in their familiar interpreting booth.

References

AIIC. 2000. *Professional standard*. www.aiic-mxac.com. Accessed 11 Aug 2021.

Bouhmid, M. 2019. *Impact of working remotely from the booth partner in the videoconference-based interpreting setting: Comparative study between voiceboxer and Kudo platforms*. TR7P81 MA research project, London Metropolitan University.

Chmiel, A. 2008. Boothmates forever? On teamwork in a simultaneous interpreting booth. *Across Languages and Cultures* 9 (2): 261–276.

Christova, E. 2020. Interactivity of simultaneous interpreters as actors of a cognitive event. *Journal of Siberian Federal University. Humanities & Social Sciences* 13(3): 375–384.

Creswell, J.W. 2009. *Research design: qualitative, quantitative, and mixed methods approaches*. Los Angeles: Sage.

Duflou, V. 2016. *Be(com)ing a conference interpreter. An ethnography of EU interpreters as a professional community*. Amsterdam/Philadelphia: John Benjamins Publishing Company.

Gile, D. 1995. *Basic concepts and models for interpreter and translator training*. Amsterdam: John Benjamins.

Gile, D. 1998. Observational studies and experimental studies in the investigation of conference interpreting. *Target* 10 (1): 69–93.

Hurdiss-Jones, F. 1989. A teacher's view of and fears for the future of the interpreting profession. In *The theoretical and practical aspects of teaching conference interpretation*, ed. L. Gran and J. Dodds, 159–160, Udine, Campanotto Editore.

Moser-Mercer, B. 2005. Remote interpreting: issues of multi-sensory integration in a multilingual task. *Meta* 50 (2): 727–738.

Moser-Mercer, B., A. Künzli, and M. Korac. 1998. Prolonged turns in interpreting: effects on quality, physiological and psychological stress. *Interpreting* 3 (1): 47–64.

Mouzourakis, P. 2006. Remote interpreting—a technical perspective on recent experiments. *Interpreting* 8 (1): 45–66.

Nolan, J. 2005. *Interpretation. Techniques and exercises*. Clevedon, Buffalo, Toronto: Multilingual Matters LTD.

Rattanabutr, P., and N. Rangponsumri. 2016. Teamwork in simultaneous interpretation. *Journal of Translation and Interpretation in Thailand* 1 (2): 61–87.

Rohonyi, B. 2016. Birkózás az írott szöveggel szinkrontolmácsolás közben 2. rész [Wrestling with the written text during simultaneous interpreting Part 2.]. *Fordítástudomány* 18(1): 31–49.

Rohonyi, B. 2018. *A szöveggel támogatott szinkrontolmácsolás vizsgálata angol–magyar nyelvi irányban* [Simultaneous interpreting with text in HU-EN relation]. PhD thesis, ELTE.

Roziner, I., and M. Shlesinger. 2010. Much ado about something remote: stress and performance in remote interpreting. *Interpreting* 12 (2): 214–248.

Seresi, M., and P. Láncos. 2020. Szinkrontolmácsok együttműködése a tolmácskabinban [Simultaneous interpreters' cooperation in the interpreting booth]. *Fordítástudomány* 22 (2): 30–43.

Seresi, M. 2016. *Távtolmácsolás és távoktatás a tolmácsképzésben [Remote interpreting and distance education in interpreter training]*. Budapest: ELTE Eötvös Kiadó.

Seresi, M. 2019. A tolmácsolás szakmai standardjainak kialakulása és érvényesülése a gyakorlatban [Interpreters' professional standards: Origins and practical implementation]. In *Diszciplínák találkozása—nyelvi közvetítés a XXI. században*, ed. Sz. Szoták, 135–145. OFFI: Budapest.

Tripepi Winteringham, S. 2010. The usefulness of ICTs in interpreting practice. *The Interpreters' Newsletter* 15: 87–99.

Zeier, H. 1997. Psychophysiological stress research. *Interpreting* 2 (1/2): 231–249.

Márta Seresi (Ph.D.) is a Senior Lecturer at the Department of Translator and Interpreter Training at Eötvös Loránd University, Budapest, where she teaches consecutive and simultaneous interpretation between Hungarian and French. She also organises international virtual classes for students of the European Masters in Conference Interpreting (EMCI) program in cooperation with the European Union's institutions' interpreting services. She also participates in the work of the ELTE Doctoral Program of Translation. Her main area of research is remote interpreting. She is currently the Vice-Chair of WG7 (Language professionals) in the European Union's LITHME COST Action. She is also an accredited freelance conference interpreter of the European Institutions and works regularly for the EU institutions in Brussels and Luxembourg.

Petra Lea Láncos (LLM, Ph.D., habil.) graduated from Pázmány Péter Catholic University in 2003. She has been an Associate Professor at the Department of European Law at Pázmány Péter Catholic University (Budapest) since 2009. Besides her academic career, she also worked at the Office of the Commissioner for Fundamental Rights (2013-2014) and the National Media and Infocommunications Authority (2015-2016). Currently, she works at the Constitutional Court of Hungary (since 2019), as freelance interpreter for the EU institutions (since 2011), and as Editor of the Hungarian Yearbook of International Law and European Law (since its establishment in 2013). Her research interests are language rights, legislation and codification in EU law and EU soft law.

Chapter 11
COVID-19 and the Configuration of Materiality in Remote Interpreting: Is Technology Biting Back?

Deborah Giustini

Abstract This chapter explores the interrelation between COVID-19, remote interpreting, and technology in affecting the provision of interpreters' services. Drawing upon and extending scholarship that examines the articulation of interpreters' work and materiality, the chapter adopts a sociological perspective rooted in practice theory. This approach assumes that socially situated phenomena, or practices, are the result of a complex socio-material context where habits, activities, and relationalities are arranged. Leveraging data from language industry sources and surveys, the chapter takes technology as its focus and discusses its role in arranging such elements in remote interpreting during the COVID-19 pandemic. In doing so, it sheds light on some of the challenges and opportunities that are emerging in the field, including how interpreters and the industry have adapted to the spread of remote work. The chapter integrates innovative theoretical lenses to remote interpreting studies, contributing a non-anthropocentric view to the role of materiality in the interpreting industry that problematizes the development of technology-mediated production and consumption behaviours.

Keywords Remote interpreting · Technology · Practice theory · Social practice · COVID-19

11.1 Introduction

This chapter, informed by practice theory and interpreting research, contributes on these fronts by examining the relationship between remote interpreting and technology during the COVID-19 pandemic. The interpreting and translation literature contains growing theoretical contributions that highlight the centrality of technology in the performance of translators' and interpreters' work (Braun 2015; O'Hagan 2016; Caldwell et al 2018; Olohan 2020). Since the spread of COVID-19, scholarly and industry views have devoted attention to the traction of both remote interpreting

D. Giustini (✉)
KU Leuven, Blijde Inkomststraat 21, Erasmushuis, box 3318, 07.26, 3000 Leuven, Belgium
e-mail: deborah.giustini@kuleuven.be

K. Liu and A. K. F. Cheung (eds.), *Translation and Interpreting in the Age of COVID-19*, Corpora and Intercultural Studies 9,
https://doi.org/10.1007/978-981-19-6680-4_11

and innovative technological solutions as interpreters work from home (Seeber and Fox 2021). This chapter builds upon and extends this knowledge through a practice theory approach. Practice theory deals with the social world as both structure and agency funnelled into an array of "practices," the mutually influencing elements that compose everyday life, such as skills, meanings, norms, goals, emotions, and materiality (Reckwitz 2002). As an expanding body of research grounded in social theory, practice theory deals extensively with organizations and workplaces (Schatzki 2002; Nicolini 2012) including of translation and interpreting (Olohan 2020; Giustini 2021, 2022).

Without producing a reductionist account of remote interpreting, the chapter offers a productive avenue of enquiry by discussing some key elements that reveal the deep articulation between this practice and technology. Using data from language industry sources and surveys, this is complemented by emerging scholarly overviews of remote interpreting during the COVID-19 pandemic, including the role of technology in shifting habits in the interpreting industry. It is necessary to clarify that the chapter, for space reasons, only focuses on spoken, remote conference interpreting, illustrating its arguments by referring specifically to simultaneous interpretation. Comprehensive discussions of technology, sign language and public service interpreting may be accessed elsewhere (e.g., Brunson 2008; Napier et al. 2017). Furthermore, for disambiguity purposes, the chapter adheres to the ISO 20108:2016 definition of remote interpreting, "interpreting of a speaker in a different location from that of the interpreter, enabled by information and communications technology". Braun (2015) further distinguished remote interpreting by the type of technology used (videoconference, over the phone, teleconference) and by the participants' location. This distinction is not needed for the chapter scope, which uses instead remote interpreting to indicate an encompassing technological setup regardless of the parties' physical location or type of conduit.

11.2 Remote Interpreting and COVID-19

On 11 March 2020, the WHO declared COVID-19 a pandemic. Its consequences have been widespread, especially in the labour market. Several sectors, including interpreting, adapted to working remotely to overcome the challenges of social distancing and infection risks. As most events pivoted to the virtual world, remote interpreting demand grew up to 95% to address the needs of industries, international organizations, and corporations (Nimdzi 2021). The European Language Industry Survey (European Language Service Industry 2020, 2021) and the three FIT Europe (Fédération Internationale des Traducteurs, International Federation of Translators) (2020) surveys, indicated that COVID-19 has been a game-changer for language service providers (LSPs), buyers, and freelancers across the translation and interpreting sectors. The ELIS surveys show that 65% of LSPs and 38% of freelancers have moved online all their jobs. The FIT Europe surveys report that the pandemic has affected the business of 96.8% of respondents: 58.1% indicated their business had fallen off a cliff; 38.7% that it had slowed down; 44.1% expected their income to drastically drop within three months. General concerns across surveys include unilateral rates cut, ongoing instability, and securing work after the end of the pandemic.

Scholarly views equally reflect on such challenges, as interpreters across the globe have adapted their working methods to respond to shifting market demand and business modes. These are especially questioning the potential of the COVID-19 restrictions to act as a catalyst for remote interpreting as a "new" working model in the industry, with concerns ranging from the low reliability of many remote solutions, to cheaper, but most worryingly also inferior working conditions (Seeber and Fox 2021; Matsushita 2020; Crezee and Major 2020).

11.3 Placing Technology in Translation and Interpreting Studies

In the context of interpreting and translation production, scholars have discussed the "materialities of communication" (Littau 2016), the human-technology interaction that mediates the accomplishment of language work. The theoretical coordinates of this translation-oriented research explore the significance of technological artefacts that support translation work (O'Hagan 2016). Olohan (2011) identified this relationship as the "dance of agency", or the dialectics of resistance and accommodation that goes through translators' interaction with materiality, such as the use of translation memories (TMs) and adjustments to the increasing use of technology in their daily working tasks. Leveraging the same metaphor, Ruokonen and Koskinen (2017) and Caldwell et al. (2018: 303) argued that translators experience a "symbiotic, if sometimes uncomfortable, dance of agency" with technology in their working life, often resisting advances such as machine translation due to negative experiences of use, threats of substitution, and deskilling, resulting in shared cultural repertoires of a "love/hate" struggle for technology.

Sociomaterial conceptualizations of technology are also evident in interpreting studies, particularly those examining simultaneous interpreting. Technologies have supported simultaneous interpreting since the 1920s through the development of sound transmission systems and have evolved at a fast pace. Computers and the Internet with its rich availability of topical information, for example, shifted the way interpreters prepare their assignments and deal with aspects such as the complexity of areas they work in (Kalina 2009), as well as terminological management and material retrieval during the interpretation (Costa et al. 2018). Remote interpreting is arguably the technological development which has most changed the organization of interpreters' work (Fantinuoli 2018; Braun 2015). The reasons for its introduction are manifold: economic aspects, availability and organizational issues, and more recently, health safety linked to the COVID-19 pandemic. In fact, remote interpreting overcomes the need for interpreters to attend on-site, mitigating potential supply shortfalls by eliminating time and costs associated with mobility. Interpreters benefit from remote options as they can offer their services despite geographical and client budget limitations, e.g., when clients cannot accommodate for their travel. Remote interpreting also facilitates access to professionals of rare languages or in areas where face-to-face interpreters might be unavailable (Braun 2015). However, research shows that remote interpreting comes with several downsides, including faster fatigue onset, lexical activation issues, stress, sound shocks, concentration problems, and over-elaboration as part of interpreters' strategies to cope with problems in situations of altered acoustic and visual input (Braun 2017, 2019). Apart from measurable physiological and ergonomic factors, interpreters may not experience "the right feel for the situation" because of their lack of physical interaction with the event, speakers, and audience (Ziegler and Gigliobianco 2018: 120).

The spread of remote interpreting also goes hand in with professionals being available "at the push of a button", or the "industrialization" of interpreting (Carl and Braun 2018). This has sparked debate on the feasibility and sustainability of its working conditions, which might negatively affect how the profession and interpreter status are perceived by the general public (Fantinuoli 2019). Pym (2011) stressed that this resistance reveals not only legitimate concerns over worsening working conditions, but also the unspoken danger of interpreters falling behind and losing market power, autonomy over work, and ability to dictate labour price. As Olohan (2011) argued, it is vital that the social (stakeholders in the interpreting industry) and the technological (e.g., the cloud-based interfaces for remote interpreting) be reciprocally "tuned" to achieve the interactive stability of the service and fair working conditions.

These warnings appear timely as the global COVID-19 led demand for flexible, digitalized communication services increasingly pushes interpreters out of the social contract: stakeholders such as software vendors, organizations and users can justify the implementation of technology to achieve labour control and cost reduction. The 2022 take of the European Language Industry Survey, covering the 18 months of the pandemic, shows that 77% of language professionals are still concerned about price pressure; 65% are "wary" of the economic climate, due to the consolidated tendency to outsource remote interpreting services for lower fees. Cronin and Delgado Luchner (2021), drawing upon Moulier-Boutang (2011) frame these pandemic-led developments of remote interpreting within the wider shift towards the digitalization and remotization of work of the contemporary economic model of cognitive capitalism. Cognitive capitalism streamlines information, communication, and knowledge through technological systems to hasten the circulation of services for increasing their value and generating income. The promotion of remote interpreting helps to insert the interpreter into this seamless, virtual circuit of information, rendering her immobile (e.g., to travel costs) and slicing up her work (e.g., into minutes or hours rather than half or full working days) for lucrative upscaling. In this sense, technology supports the exploitation of interpreting through an extractivist economic logic that can subjugate interpreters' work (Cronin and Delgado Luchner 2021).

These framings contribute a non-anthropocentric perspective, sharpening our understanding of remote interpreting as a "situated activit[y] involving embodied, embedded cognition within a network of mutually interdependent 'actors and factors'", as economic concerns and technological systems (Ehrensberger-Dow and Massey 2017: 104). This same sensitivity is reflected in practice theory, an ontology indicating that material arrangements contribute to making up the site of the social, that is, human coexistence (Schatzki 2002). The next section introduces a practice-based approach to remote interpreting during the COVID-19 pandemic.

11.4 Practice Theory

Practice theory is an ontology that accounts for how social order endures and changes through "practice." Stemming from the philosophical and sociological work of Wittgenstein, Heidegger, Bourdieu, and Giddens among others, practice theory gained renewed international resonance through its "second wave," the influential writings of Theodore Schatzki (1996) and Andreas Reckwitz (2002). Its epistemology sees social phenomena not as structures external to, and imposed upon, human agency. Instead, attention is given to practices as constituting the social order, transpiring across time and space. Notwithstanding some variations, a practice is defined as spatially-temporally dispersed sets of doings and sayings organized by common understandings (Schatzki 2010), or a routinized type of behaviour dependent on tacit knowledge, which emphasizes the "material" character of action as anchored in embodiment and artefacts (Reckwitz 2002). Examples are publicity, commuting, cooking, camping, and teaching, while Olohan (2020) and Giustini (2019, 2021, 2022) included translation and conference interpreting.

Despite differences between social theorists, practices are made of some basic organizing elements. Schatzki's influential version argued that practices are composed by: (i) practical understandings of what to say and do (skills); (ii) rules; (iii) teleoaffectivity, or sets of goals, values, and emotions which individuals embrace; and (iv) materiality, meaning artefacts, objects, and technology; these elements compose the "stuff of social life" (2010: 125). Which elements, for example, compose the practice of remote interpreting? Clearly, practical understanding: interpreting skills are required, knowledge of foreign languages, communicative competence, good memory, mental dexterity, general knowledge, analytical skills, and the capacity to perform publicly and under pressure (AIIC 2020b). This mastery in turns rests upon social conventions, or norms. Practice theory promotes the idea that behaviours, rather than being the expression of an individual's capacities and attitudes, is the observable expression of collective meanings. To exemplify, most interpreters have a shared convention, that performing a "proper interpretation" means conveying the speakers' message. These understandings have a social history, which involves the organization of the profession, its deontology, cultural representations, and institutional interventions. Finally, since practices are reproduced through social grounds of action, they are also inherently relational, involving the coordination and intersubjective negotiation of participating individuals (Nicolini and Monteiro 2016). This is evinced in the teamwork of remote simultaneous interpreting, which requires at least two interpreters due to performing fatigue; in the pivot role (the interpreter from whom other booths take relay), or in coordinating with the speakers. Additionally, the understanding that interpreters work to facilitate communication and use strategies for performing optimally and receive payment in return is a teleoaffective convention of the practice, no less than the practice's deontological norms and ethics.

Practice theorists importantly argue that human activity is interwoven with materiality, which "structure(s) what actions can and might be carried out when, where, how, and for what ends" (Schatzki 2010: 136). A notable integration of such perspective is Maeve Olohan's (2020) book *Translation and Practice Theory*, which theorizes the socio-material complexities of commercial translation. Following Schatzki and Reckwitz, Olohan's "performative ontology" (2020: 5) shows that translation practices are supported by the "infrastructures" (entities such as the Internet), "devices" (the "things in action" that are actively and visibly mobilized) and "resources" (energy systems or data networks such as TMs). Evidently, remote interpreting requires material components: devices as virtual booths/consoles, headphones, microphones; the technological infrastructure of the computer; and resources such as stable Internet connection, on which much business depends in pandemic times. These linkages points to a relational, agentic process between remote interpreting and the material interfaces which inform the organization and production of interpreters' embodied schemas of behaviour.

11.5 Practising Remote Interpreting in COVID-19 Times

Materiality supports the stability and evolution of practices (Schatzki 1996). The elements that uphold practices can be re-evaluated and linked through artefacts, objects, and technology for the re-invention of more sustainable practices (Laakso et al. 2021). This happens when a practice faces the "tension between the reproduction of current systems and normal ways of life ('stability') and the emergence of alternatives that can form the seeds for transition ('change')" (Geels et al. 2015: 6). The COVID-19 pandemic encapsulates this argument. Already in pre-COVID-19 times, the interpreting profession had faced a "technological turn" (Fantinuoli 2018), meaning that it was transformed by the flourishing of innovations, such as web-based platforms for remote simultaneous interpreting. However, interpreting showed stability in preferring the provision of traditional onsite services. Before the pandemic, moving most of interpreting to the digital world seemed unfeasible; today, it is the dominant norm (Nimdzi 2021). The obliged shift to remote work, alongside the race to technological implementation, reconfigured interpreting as a "more sustainable" business practice in line with public health concerns during the pandemic. The infrastructure of material and cloud-based technologies, as interpreting interfaces or the objects used to work from home (e.g., headphones, laptops) co-constituted new working modalities for stakeholders. These developments allowed the practice to strengthen and circulate widely: remote interpreting and technology spurred each other and became entangled in a dynamic that constitutes renewed ways of doing interpreter work and related patterns of consumption.

11.5.1 Skills and Technology

Interpreting studies scholars emphasize worrisome developments of technology use as a result of the economic pressure to contain costs and enhance productivity, including discourses of replacement of interpreters' role and deskilling (Fantinuoli 2019; DePalma and Sargent 2013). There are certain general trends in employment that are becoming commonplace in the interpreting industry, such as cost reductions, fast turnarounds, and lowering working conditions. These trends reached unexpected proportions during the pandemic, as the impossibility of face-to-face meetings and the widespread use of technology accelerated them considerably (Hoyte-West 2022). One phenomenon is especially relevant for the present debate: the relation of skills and technology (Acemoglu and Restrepo 2019). This relation revolves around the splitting of labour into manual, routine, low-paying jobs which are easier to match by machines; and high-paying jobs, requiring greater skill level which machines cannot outperform. The activities less susceptible to automation are in fact tied to intellectual and creative skills. This phenomenon is relevant because interpreting carries a bag of expertise that is complex to be fully substituted by technology, thus falling into the latter category. Interpreting requires real-time cognitive exercises in decision-making while accommodating speech components, communication intelligibility, emotions, and cultural references. Notwithstanding, due to the COVID-19 crisis interpreters have been expected to tune to technologies to carry out the job, developing an open attitude towards upskilling in their use as a means to stabilize their actions by securing the technical competence needed for performing (Hoyte-West 2022). These competencies include handling several virtual environments, each with its own specificities (e.g., handover function); controlling the technological and material tools that make remote interpretations possible (e.g., setting up microphones, headphones, browsers); and intervening in case of breakdowns. Furthermore, remote interpreting requires the adjustment of communication strategies in view of virtual conversations without getting accustomed with the event (e.g., entering the booth, taking a seat, arranging personal belongings), while also lacking some major tactile, visual, and kinetic clues that help understanding speakers and messages.

From these examples, we evince that materiality contributes to knowing and doing in practice, helping to embody and convey mastery (Gherardi and Nicolini 2003), as well as stabilizing human action by giving it focus, shape, and direction (Svabo 2009). The COVID-19 pandemic brought this interrelation to a new level, with interpreters refining their abilities to react appropriately to new situations, and technology playing a coordinating role in the performance. In other words, technology necessarily participates in remote interpreting just as human beings—the interpreters—do, as "resources which enable and constrain the specificity of a practice" (Reckwitz 2002: 208) and which redefine the sensemaking of the competent practitioner.

Notably, materiality also interlinks with practices' teleological ("end-oriented") and affective ("feeling-oriented") dimension, constituting the conditions for practitioners' activities by expressing goals and emotions in their daily iterations (Shove et al. 2012). Interpreting (and by extension, remote interpreting) has a teleoaffective structure which guides practitioners to fulfilling both internal and external aims. Interpreters achieve external aims such as making a profit from their labour, securing commissions, and preserving professional reputation by meeting the internal aims of the practice, i.e., maximal effectiveness of communication, an "oughtness" characterizing acceptable performance. This oughtness, however, also exhibits irregularities "occasioned by breakdowns and dangers" (Schatzki 2002: 74) caused by contextual challenges of the interpretation. These include analysing the message, processing between languages, digesting technical topics and terminology, constraints of intelligibility and speed, cultural references, stress deriving from public exposure of the performance, and the high-stakes nature of settings. Interpreters strive to guarantee communication by crisis-saving strategies such as omissions, additions, weakening, and strengthening the message content (Monacelli 2009).

These dangers are enhanced by remote interpreting and its wide use in COVID-19 times. Research and professional practice are replete with reports of acceptable technological functionality in remote interpreting, but with the more-than-occasional disruption in sound/video feed quality, platforms operability, and bandwidth interruptions (Corpas Pastor and Gaber 2020; Braun 2019). Importantly, in remote interpreting the responsibility of troubleshooting appropriate technical arrangements falls with the interpreter. Despite the AIIC's guidelines (2020a) that platform providers exempt interpreters from any technical responsibility during an event, everyday practice seems often permeated by the opposite assumption (Simon et al. 2010; American Translators Association 2021). These teleological directions might impede interpreters to uphold communication aims when materiality collapses.

Alongside, affectivity—the emotions and moods steering behaviour—also shapes practices. Collard and Buján's (2021) survey of 850 staff and freelance interpreters in 19 countries during the pandemic reported that 67% of respondents faced emotional struggles to adjust to the working conditions of remote interpreting while 83% considered this shift as "difficult". Studies on remote interpreting and COVID-19 (Midões 2021) and practice-based studies of affect in simultaneous interpreting (Giustini 2019) show that technology channels specific emotional processes, as interpreters' feeling of "lack of control" during remote interpreting assignments. This is due to interpreters' sense of augmented risk in the remote environment, where they cannot fully anticipate or solve technical debacles (Ziegler and Gigliobianco 2018; Braun 2019). The almost complete reliance on virtual systems during the pandemic is likely to exacerbate interpreters' stress over crisis management against technological breakdowns.

11.5.2 Stakeholders: A Reconfigured Relationship

In practices, change also occurs by technological innovations, and the actors supporting such innovations. This results in renewed arrangements in the policies, values and visions, institutions, and regulatory instruments that are part of a practice's landscape (Mazur et al. 2015; Barnes et al. 2018). The move towards virtual events and technologies in interpreting gained great prominence during the pandemic, prompting the "consumption side"—institutions such as the UN and the European Parliament, and actors such as the private sector, software developers and vendors—to adapt to the new reality of the "production side", or interpreters working from home or from hubs (Hoyte-West 2022).

For the consumption side this arrangement appears overwhelmingly positive. Software developers and vendors benefit from the pandemic as a major point of investment and validation of Software-as-a-Service (SaaS), i.e., virtual interpreting technology such as web conferencing platforms. SaaS companies have become global leaders in the remote interpreting market by serving a variety of industries, institutions, and multinational companies (Nimdzi 2021; Corpas Pastor 2022). For instance, Interprefy has tripled its business in the second quarter of 2020 (Slator 2020). In 2021, Interactio and KUDO have closed a Silicon Valley evaluation series A round (a company's first significant round of venture capital financing, with stock sold to investors) of respectively $30mln and $21mln, leading to significant business expansion, product engineering, and marketing growth (TechCrunch 2021; Multilingual 2021). Investments of this size are a major expansion point for the whole interpreting industry, but they also illustrate how technology accounts for change in a practice, as these constitute and modulate each other.

Concerning the production side, technological solutions have allowed interpreters to stay in business throughout the pandemic. However, we should also be aware that SaaS companies are profit-oriented and promote an industry shift based on agile, just-in-time remote interpreting services (European Language Service Industry 2020, 2021). This business model is already typical of much of the contemporary economy, spanning from organizations to "gig" work performed through digital labour platforms. It exposes workers, including interpreters and translators, to risks related to precarious employment status and income level, lack of work-life balance, social protections, bargaining power, and dependence on the platform and SaaS for the allocation of work (Fırat 2021; Moorkens 2020). Pre-pandemic, scholars had already highlighted the uneasy alliance between technology and unfavourable changes to the interpreting profession, including downgrading fees and social esteem (Pöchhacker 2011; Fantinuoli 2018). A 2019 European Commission-sponsored survey conducted in Italy, Spain and the UK shows that most buyers in the private and public sector prefer remote interpreting for the ability to book interpreters at a short notice; no need for either party to relocate; economic value (cheaper costs); and easier access to professionals beyond geographical and physical limitations. Additionally, 40% of buyers indicated that a fair price for a full-day session of remote interpreting should be Euro 200, while 24.1% indicated Euro 100. CSA Research (2020) also indicates that 65% of interpreters surveyed during the pandemic foresee buyers' increasing demand for remote interpreting, resulting in scarce good-paying jobs and uncertainty about the sector's future. The European Language Service Industry (2022) reinforces these findings, indicating that notwithstanding the language industry's transition throughout two years of pandemic disruption, freelance interpreters do not see substantial improvements. 20% of interpreters reported that they need to supplement their earnings with another professional activity, despite the remote interpreting market having reached a saturation point.

Industry data overall shows that the demand of remote interpreting worldwide is indeed growing as one of the main inputs of the knowledge economy, but that much of it is already stuck at the lower end of the market, where technology and remote interpreting are used as a major selling point for cheapening interpreters' labour (European Language Service Industry 2021; Slator 2021; Collard and Buján 2021). This articulation demonstrates that buyers exploit the opportunity to access an expanding interpreting market tailored to their needs and capacity to dictate labour price through the expansion of technological developments. From a practice-based perspective, the ethos of remote interpreting (particularly in COVID-19 times) can be conceptualized as technocentric, due to its redirecting business solutions and stakeholders' relations. Since practices are an interdependent system, alterations in one element, such as the material forces of technology, leave an imprint on other social elements, such as economic interests and practitioners' working conditions.

11.5.3 Technology and (Dis)embodiment

Practices integrate bodily and material know-how into human activity as the ways in which people know what to do and how to "dwell" in a situation (Schatzki 2002). In this frame, a distinctive issue emerges alongside the way technology orients embodiment in remote interpreting: "invisibility." Most remote interpreting systems create a complex material ecology where participants get congruent visual access to each other. This ecology, however, does not afford visibility to all participants. Whereas visual props such as slides and speakers are visible to the interpreter through the video transmission, interpreters are not generally shown via video feed. As Pöchhacker (2009) noted, already simultaneous interpreting technology in the 1920–1940s pushed interpreters away from the rostrum and into booths, making them less physically visible to users. Remote interpreting and the COVID-19 pandemic exacerbated this arrangement, both in the basic definition of the interpreter's invisible role as the metaphorical "relayer" of words rather than as the active co-participant in the interaction (Angelelli 2004) but also downplaying her "physical and professional visibility" (Dam and Zethsen 2013: 246).

First, the technology of remote interpreting connects interpreters and users through the interpretation act. However, it also separates interpreters' embodied presence from other event participants, creating additional difficulties. On site, interpreters can intervene if experiencing difficulties, for instance by leaving the booth, discreetly going up to the speaker and asking to slow down. This is not entirely possible in remote interpreting. Interpreters can use the chat to signal problems to the organizers or speakers. However, the technical set up of many platforms and events often disables the speaker-interpreter chat, leaving interpreters to communicate only with the technician/moderator chat or interpreters' group chat. This necessitates the technician/moderator to constantly monitor the chat or be willing to call attention to the difficulty, without fearing that either party is perceived as insistent or as disrupting the event flow. Additionally, interpreters might be reluctant to intervene in case this exposes them to blacklisting as too critical, or because they might feel that users are indifferent to their difficulties. Thus, interpreters can be at loss when a situation requires intervention. Various degrees of intervention—or what Angelelli called the "visibility of the interpreter at work" (2004: 29)—are essential for effective communication and compound interpreters' expertise, but risks deriving from the material ecology of remote interpreting can prevent interpreters from performing what makes sense to them as competent practitioners.

Secondly, interpreters' embodied presence and expert labour is hidden to view in the asymmetric materiality of SaaS technologies. As Angelelli (2004) suggested, interpreters, although having agency in the communicative event, are invested with a shadow quality that is often assigned to them by third parties. By assigning remote interpreters a shadow quality through their lack of physical visibility, the materiality of SaaS reproduces the instrumentalist idea that the interpreter is a disembodied presence that merely performs acts of cognitive transfer. Interpreters might feel their working relationship with stakeholders is "depersonalized" in remote interpreting, in a way that negatively affects their role and labour. Research exploring the challenges of remote interpreting in COVID-19 reports interpreters' growing increasing experiences of alienation and "atomization", the individualization of the interpreter's body and labour because of a "zoomified" world where they are pushed back into an invisible role (Cammoun-Claveria 2021).

The use of technology in remote interpreting seems to contribute to a negative re-enactment of invisibility of interpreters' work. Such reality assumes larger proportions if their embodied, skilled labour is "hidden" beneath the surface of the web and reaches listeners through the digital interpolation of technology. Following Gray and Suri's (2019) influential discussion of software interfaces' impact on contemporary work, interpreters too risk becoming part on an exploitative economic logic that makes them metaphorically "ghost workers", or an invisible workforce that powers communication labour through online means. The result is that clients interface with a professional figure whose work and presence are constrained by the technological configuration in which they both operate. Using a practice-based sensitivity, I define this process as the "dematerialization" of the interpreter as generated by the re-articulation of the relationships among materiality, embodiment, and interpreters' pragmatic activities. This entanglement stresses that the role of interpreters in remote work is an issue of "matter"—a recurring invisibility of both their body and labour which is co-constituted by technology. In other words, the sociotechnical density of remote interpreting re-orients interpreters' activities as the circulation of "transparent" communication, up to the point of making "dematerialization" a threat to the interpreters as technology assumes a political dimension against their labour.

11.5.4 Teamwork and Coordination

Materiality is also intertwined with social relations, as it helps practitioners to coordinate and cooperate, in turn stabilizing or destabilizing the regular order of performance (Svabo 2009). The example of teamwork in simultaneous interpreting is illustrative. Teamwork indicates interpreters' collective effort during the performance, as boothmates work in turns to contain the cognitive load and ensure full processing capacity. The passive interpreter helps the active interpreter, for instance by locating terminology or writing down information. Teamwork is also fundamental to monitor incoming and outgoing channels or taking over during an expected event. Overall, teamwork is pivotal for job quality, as often interpreters are judged by the booth performance. The COVID-19 pandemic has disrupted such routines. Due to the elevated risk of infection from sharing a booth for prolonged periods of time, interpreters have coordinated teamwork virtually during remote interpreting.[1] This affects teamwork through conjoining and disjoining effects.

Among the conjoining effects, technology helps interpreters to control turn length and handover remotely. Many interfaces have a timekeeping feature that is handy for turn-taking decisions and allows the active interpreter to send a warning to the boothmate to hand over. The boothmate accepts the request, the active interpreter confirms and switches off the microphone. The now-broadcasting interpreter switches on the microphone and starts the turn. Some interfaces also feature a countdown widget that appears alongside a handover request, which facilitates the procedure in a virtual environment where boothmates cannot see each other. The rendition can also be monitored by the non-broadcasting interpreter by adjusting the floor and the boothmate's volume levels.

Among the disjoining effects, there are constrained job facilitation and team spirit. Interpreters may experience detachment from the team they interpret with (Moser-Mercer 2005; Seeber et al. 2019) and miss activities such as meeting with colleagues or "walking to the job" in favour of distanced "work based on turn-taking" only (McKibbin 2021: 26). Furthermore, just like the interpreter needs the speaker's non-verbal behaviour to better grasp meaning, the boothmates need non-verbal cues to receive and provide support. In "traditional booth times" boothmates could check each other's bodily signals and intervene in case of strain. They would assist through tasks as terminological and document management, by writing down the needed

[1] During the pandemic, interpreters have also been assigned either to individual booths, to avoid sharing the same enclosed space, or have worked together at "remote interpreting hubs" (studios that provide conference level hardware and software according to industry standards) where they can access the information, computer technology, and network infrastructure.

information and showing it to the colleague, or physically pointing to scripts or slides. In remote interpreting, these routines are unavailable. Interpreters must write any suggestion via the platform in-built chat function, or attract the colleague's attention through other means, e.g., WhatsApp messaging. Establishing a separate teamwork channel outside the platform is often resorted to because of the "Big Brother effect", chats monitored by the technician and the organizer (Bouhmid 2019). Interpreters may avoid the chat to ask for help or to criticize the speaker with the boothmate for fear of repercussions by third parties. A "safe" booth environment becomes inexistent in platforms, so interpreters negotiate alternative protocols for optimal coordination. Furthermore, the AIIC (2020a) reports additional cognitive load and distractions resulting from multitasking in teamworking.

These examples direct to a practice-based conceptualization of remote teamwork. While technology participates in the performance of interpreting through shared arrangements such as handover and chat functions which are central to cooperation, it also produces ambiguous disturbances, such as surveillance, multitasking overload, and the carrying out of alternative routines which destabilize the regular order of things. While practice theory stresses that the "unstable mixtures" of materiality (Svabo 2009; Shove, Pantzar, and Watson 2012) generate possibilities for implementing new patterns of activity—as interpreters quickly devised and operationalized renewed forms of teamwork—innovation emerges also out of unease with material matters. The engagement with virtual environments points to interpreters' changing understanding of how to go about in the practice, as they are removed from traditional forms of collegiality and must renegotiate their capacity to act and engage with other agents —human or non-human.

11.6 Conclusion

The cross-reading of remote interpreting and technology through practice theory shows their multi-faceted convergence in interpreters' work. Alongside the changes driven by COVID-19, it suggests that we look for materiality-mediated activity and its role in creating performative alignments, coordination, but also disturbance and breakdowns in remote interpreting. Leveraging the strength of a practice-theoretical approach, the chapter offered fertile ground for the conceptualization of social and material interactions, meaning those technological entities which can both stabilize and destabilize interpreters' actions and relations.

The outcome of the four analytical examples illustrates how remote interpreting does not merely relate to the introduction of technology in the profession. Rather, it is a matter—both concretely and figuratively—of reconfiguring the interaction between technological solutions, meanings, and interpreters' ways of doing as the result of economic interests, industry developments, and current public health concerns. Overall, there seems to be a fracture line between positive technological innovation, and technology as "biting back" interpreters. In this analysis, the chapter stressed the order-producing but also the disrupting effects of technology in remote interpreting: the transmission of a professional way of doing and a shared repertoire of performing which goes hand in hand with negotiating the handling of new tools; dwindling working conditions; oscillating relationships with stakeholders; new coordination patterns; and the dematerialization of interpreters' visible labour. In this sense, technology plays a crucial role not simply because it affects the traditional enculturation and collectively established aspects of interpreting, but because it re-establishes action, giving it new elements to evolve around. Since the practice-theoretical perspective discussed herein is not exhaustive and the pandemic is still ongoing at the time of writing, further investigations may elaborate how materiality participates in the social action of interpreting, and how it is affecting the future of the interpreting industry beyond COVID-19.

References

Acemoglu, D., and P. Restrepo. 2019. Automation and new tasks: how technology displaces and reinstates labor. *Journal of Economic Perspectives* 33 (2): 3–30.

AIIC. 2020a. AIIC Covid-19 distance interpreting recommendations for institutions and DI Hubs. https://aiic.org/document/4839/AIIC%20Recommendations%20for%20Institutions_27.03.2020a.pdf. Accessed 7 Feb 2022.

AIIC. 2020b. What it takes. https://aiic.org/site/world/conference/whatittakes. Accessed 7 Feb 2022.

American Translators Association. 2021. ATA position paper on remote interpreting. https://www.atanet.org/advocacy-outreach/ata-position-paper-on-remote-interpreting/. Accessed 7 Feb 2022.

Angelelli, C.V. 2004. *Revisiting the interpreter's role: a study of conference, court, and medical interpreters in Canada, Mexico, and the United States*. Amsterdam: John Benjamins.

Barnes, J., R. Durrant, F. Kern, and G. MacKerron. 2018. The institutionalisation of sustainable practices in cities: how initiatives shape local selection environments. *Environmental Innovation and Societal Transitions* 29: 68–80.

Bouhmid, M. 2019. Impact of working remotely from the booth partner in the videoconference-based interpreting setting: Comparative study between voiceboxer and kudo platforms. https://tinyurl.com/yckz9a2b. Accessed 21 Feb 2022.

Braun, S. 2015. Remote interpreting. In *Routledge encyclopedia of interpreting studies*, ed. F. Pöchhacker, 346–348. London: Routledge.

Braun, S. 2017. What a micro-analytical investigation of additions and expansions in remote interpreting can tell us about interpreter's participation in a shared virtual space. *Journal of Pragmatics* 107: 165–177.

Braun, S. 2019. Technology and interpreting. In *The Routledge handbook of translation and technology*, ed. M. O'Hagan, 271–288. London: Routledge.

Brunson, J.L. 2008. Your case will now be heard: sign language interpreters as problematic accommodations in legal interactions. *Journal of Deaf Studies and Deaf Education* 13 (1): 77–91.

Cadwell, P., S. O'Brien, and C.S.C. Teixeira. 2018. Resistance and accommodation: factors for the (non-)adoption of machine translation among professional translators. *Perspectives* 26 (3): 301–321.

Cammoun-Claveria, R. 2021. Évolution Dans L'aliénation: Craintes Fondées ou Réticences d'une Profession Réfractaire? In *100 Years of conference interpreting: A legacy*, ed. K. G. Seeber, 274–278. Cambridge Scholars.

Carl, M., and S. Braun. 2018. Translation, interpreting and new technologies. In *The Routledge handbook of translation studies and linguistics*, ed. K. Malmkjaer, 374–390. London: Routledge.

Collard, C., and M. Buján. 2021. ESIT research project on remote simultaneous interpreting. https://www.researchgate.net/publication/350957508_First_overview_of_results. Accessed 1 Mar 2022.

Corpas Pastor, G. 2022. Technology solutions for interpreters: the VIP system. *Herměneus. Revista De Traducción e Interpretación* 23: 91–123.

Corpas Pastor, G., and M. Gaber. 2020. Remote interpreting in public service settings: technology, perceptions and practice. *SKASE Journal of Translation and Interpretation* 13 (2): 58–78.

Costa, Hernani, Gloria Corpas Pastor, and Isabel Durán-Muñoz. 2018. Assessing terminology management systems for interpreters. In *Trends in E-tools and resources for translators and interpreters,* ed. Gloria Corpas Pastor and Isabel Durán-Muñoz, 57–84. Leiden: Brill.

Crezee, Ineke, and George Major. 2020. Our work as interpreters in these unprecedented times. *International Journal of Interpreter Education* 12(1): 2. https://tigerprints.clemson.edu/ijie/vol12/iss1/2.

Cronin, M., and C.D. Luchner. 2021. Escaping the invisibility trap. *Interpreting and Society* 1 (1): 91–101.

CSA Research. 2020. COVID-19 freelancer survey data. https://csa-research.com/Featured-Content/For-LSPs/Industry-Data-and-Resources/Freelancer-2-Survey. Accessed 1 Mar 2022.

Dam, H.V., and K.K. Zethsen. 2013. Conference interpreters—the stars of the translation profession? A study of the occupational status of Danish EU interpreters as compared to Danish EU translators. *Interpreting* 15 (2): 229–259.

DePalma, Donald A., and Benjamin B. Sargent. 2013. *Translation services and software in the cloud: How LSPs will move to cloud-based solutions.* Lowell: Common Sense Advisory.

Ehrensberger-Dow, M., and G. Massey. 2017. Socio-technical issues in professional translation practice. *Translation Spaces* 6 (1): 104–121.

FIT Europe. 2020. Results from FIT Europe's COVID-19 "Take 3" survey. https://fit-europe-rc.org/en/results-from-fit-europes-covid-19-take-3-survey/. Accessed 27 Jan 2022.

European Commission. 2019. The remote interpreting services: future or present survey. https://www.shiftinorality.eu/en/system/files/download/Report%20IO3_SHIFT.pdf. Accessed 31 January 2022.

European Language Service Industry. 2020. European language industry survey 2020 before & after COVID-19. https://ec.europa.eu/info/sites/default/files/2020_language_industry_survey_report.pdf. Accessed 30 Jan 2022.

European Language Service Industry. 2021. European language industry survey. https://ec.europa.eu/info/sites/default/files/about_the_european_commission/service_standards_and_principles/documents/elis_2021_european_language_industry_survey.pdf. Accessed 30 Jan 2022.

European Language Service Industry. 2022. 2022 European language industry survey. https://slator.com/2022-european-language-industry-survey/. Accessed 17 Mar 2022.

Fantinuoli, Claudio. 2018. Computer-assisted interpreting: Challenges and future perspectives. In *Trends in E-tools and resources for translators and interpreters*, ed. Gloria Corpas Pastor and Isabel Durán-Muñoz, 153–174. Leiden: Brill.

Fantinuoli, Claudio. 2019. The technological turn in interpreting: The challenges that lie ahead. https://tinyurl.com/3v53bszu. Accessed 21 Jan 2022.

Fırat, G. 2021. Uberization of translation: Impacts on working conditions. *The Journal of Internationalization and Localization* 8 (1): 48–75.

Geels, F.W., A. McMeekin, J. Mylan, and D. Southerton. 2015. A critical appraisal of sustainable consumption and production research: the reformist, revolutionary and reconfiguration positions. *Global Environmental Change* 34: 1–12.

Gherardi, S., and D. Nicolini. 2003. To transfer is to transform: The circulation of safety knowledge. In *Knowing in organizations: a practice-based approach*, ed. D. Nicolini, S. Gherardi, and D. Yanow, 204–224. New York: Sharpe.

Giustini, D. 2019. "It's not just words, it's the feeling, the passion, the emotions": an ethnography of affect in interpreters' practices in contemporary Japan. *Asian Anthropology* 18 (3): 186–202.

Giustini, D. 2021. "The whole thing is really managing crisis": practice theory insights into interpreters' work experiences of success and failure. *The British Journal of Sociology* 72 (4): 1077–1091.

Giustini, Deborah. 2022. Embedded strangers in one's own job? Freelance interpreters' invisible work: a practice theory approach. *Work, Employment and Society.* https://doi.org/10.1177/2F09500170211059351.

Gray, M.L., and S. Suri. 2019. *Ghost work: how to stop silicon valley from building a new global underclass.* Boston: Harcourt.

Hoyte-West, A. 2022. No longer elite? Observations on conference interpreting, Covid-19, and the status of the post-pandemic profession. *Orbis Linguarum* 20 (1): 71–77.

Kalina, S. 2009. Dolmetschen im Wandel–neue Technologien als Chance oder Risiko. In *Tagungsband der internationalen Fachkonferenz des Bundesverbandes der Dolmetscher und Übersetzer*, ed. W. Baur and F. Mayer, 393–401. Berlin: BDÜ.

Laakso, S., R. Aro, E. Heiskanen, and M. Kaljonen. 2021. Reconfigurations in sustainability transitions: a systematic and critical review. *Sustainability* 17 (1): 15–31.

Littau, K. 2016. Translation and the materialities of communication. *Translation Studies* 9 (1): 82–96.

Matsushita, K. 2020. The results of an online survey on remote interpreting under COVID-19. *Japan Association for Interpreting and Translation Studies Journal* 20: 125–146.

Mazur, C., M. Contestabile, G.J. Offer, and N. Brandon. 2015. Assessing and comparing German and UK transition policies for electric mobility. *Environmental Innovation and Societal Transitions* 14: 84–100.

McKibbin, K. 2021. Looking forward: COVID-19 and its impact on working interpreters. https://digitalcommons.wou.edu/theses/69. Accessed 25 Feb 2022.

Midões, A. T. L. 2021. Adapting to remote interpreting training in times of COVID-19–an experimental study. https://recipp.ipp.pt/bitstream/10400.22/17361/1/Alberto_Mid%C3%B5es_MTIE_2020.pdf. Accessed 25 Feb 2022.

Monacelli, C. 2009. *Self-preservation in simultaneous interpreting: surviving the role.* Amsterdam: John Benjamins.

Moorkens, J. 2020. "A tiny cog in a large machine": digital taylorism in the translation industry. *Translation Spaces* 9 (1): 12–34.

Moser-Mercer, B. 2005. Remote interpreting: Issues of multi-sensory integration in a multilingual task. *Meta: Translators' Journal* 50(2): 727–738.

Moulier-Boutang, Y. 2011. *Cognitive capitalism.* Polity.

Multilingual. 2021. KUDO closes $21 million in an oversubscribed series A funding round. https://multilingual.com/kudo-closes-21-million-in-an-oversubscribed-series-a-funding-round/. Accessed 17 February 2022.

Napier, J., R. Skinner, and G.H. Turner. 2017. "It's good for them but not so for me": inside the sign language interpreting call centre. *Translation & Interpreting* 9 (2): 1–23.

Nicolini, D. 2012. *Practice theory, work, and organization: an introduction.* Oxford: Oxford University Press.

Nicolini, D., and P. Monteiro. 2016. The practice approach in organizational and management studies. In *The Sage handbook of process organization studies*, ed. A. Langley and H. Tsoukas, 110–127. London: Sage.

Nimdzi. 2021. The Nimdzi Interpreting Index. https://www.nimdzi.com/interpreting-index-top-interpreting-companies/#Key-trends-and-developments. Accessed 3 Feb 2022.

O'Hagan, M. 2016. Response by O'Hagan to "Translation and the materialities of communication." *Translation Studies* 9 (3): 322–326.

Olohan, M. 2011. Translators and translation technology: The dance of agency. *Translation Studies* 4 (3): 342–357.

Olohan, M. 2020. *Translation and practice theory.* London: Routledge.

Pöchhacker, F. 2009. Conference interpreting: Surveying the profession. *Translation and Interpreting Studies* 4: 172–186.

Pöchhacker, F. 2011. Conference interpreting. In *The Oxford handbook of translation studies*, ed. K. Malmkjær and K. Windle, 307–324. Oxford: Oxford University Press.

Pym, A. 2011. What technology does to translating. *Translation & Interpreting* 1: 1–9.

Reckwitz, A. 2002. Toward a theory of social practices: a development in culturalist theorizing. *European Journal of Social Theory* 5 (2): 243–263.

Ruokonen, M., and K. Koskinen. 2017. Dancing with technology: translators' narratives on the dance of human and machinic agency in translation work. *The Translator* 23 (3): 310–323.

Schatzki, T.R. 1996. *Social practices: a Wittgensteinian approach to human activity and the social.* Cambridge: Cambridge University Press.

Schatzki, T.R. 2002. *The site of the social: a philosophical account of the constitution of social life and change.* University Park: Penn State University Press.

Schatzki, T.R. 2010. *The timespace of human activity: on performance, society, and history as indeterminate teleological events.* Lanham: Lexington Books.

Seeber, Kilian G., Laura Keller, Rhona Amos, and Sophie Hengl. 2019. Expectations vs. experience: attitudes towards video remote conference interpreting. *Interpreting* 21 (2): 270–304.

Seeber, K.G., and B. Fox. 2021. Distance conference interpreting. In *The Routledge handbook of conference interpreting*, ed. M. Albl-Mikasa and E. Tiselius, 491–507. London: Routledge.

Shove, E., M. Pantzar, and M. Watson. 2012. *The dynamics of social practice: everyday life and how it changes.* London: Sage.

Simon, Julie, Beverly Hollrah, Mary Lightfoot, Richard Laurion, and Leilani Johnson. 2010. Steps toward identifying effective practices in video remote interpreting. http://www.interpretereducation.org/wp-content/uploads/2011/06/VRIStepsReportApril2010_FINAL1.pdf. Accessed 2 Feb 2022.

Slator. 2020. Remote interpretation technology provider interprefy witnesses exponential growth during global lockdown. https://slator.com/remote-interpretation-technology-provider-interprefy-witnesses-exponential-growth-during-global-lockdown/. Accessed 2 Feb 2022.

Slator. 2021. Interpreters wonder how to charge for recorded remote simultaneous interpreting. https://slator.com/interpreters-wonder-how-to-charge-for-recorded-remote-simultaneous-interpreting/. Accessed 2 Feb 2022.

Svabo, C. 2009. Materiality in a practice-based approach. *The Learning Organization* 16 (5): 360–370.

TechCrunch. 2021. Interactio, a remote interpretation platform, grabs $30M after seeing 12x growth during COVID-19. https://tinyurl.com/52t2d494. Accessed 17 Feb 2022.

Ziegler, K., and S. Gigliobianco. 2018. Present? Remote? Remotely present! New technological approaches to remote simultaneous conference interpreting. In *Interpreting and technology*, ed. C. Fantinuoli, 119–139. Berlin: Language Science Press.

Deborah Giustini is a postdoctoral researcher and lecturer at KU Leuven. She is Editorial Board Member of Interpreting and Society, International Advisory Board Member of the British Journal of Sociology, and Executive Council Member of the International Association of Translation and Intercultural Studies. Her research interests include digitalization, work practices, and professional expertise in knowledge-intensive sectors as the language industry.

Part III
Translation and Interpreting Teaching in the Age of COVID-19

Chapter 12
Hybrid Mode of Teaching in the Translation Classroom: Students' Perceptions and Experiences

Kanglong Liu, Ho Ling Kwok, and Wenjing Li

Abstract The outbreak of COVID-19 has brought numerous problems and challenges for teaching and learning. This is also the case with translation teaching, where translation teachers and students need to adapt to new teaching modes to cope with the "new normal" brought by the pandemic. To meet the different needs of students, various Hong Kong universities have implemented a hybrid mode of teaching in which students can choose to attend classes in person or online. However, hybrid teaching can be more challenging than pure face-to-face or online teaching because the teacher must coordinate students from different attendance modes and cater to their needs. For this reason, this study aimed to systematically examine students' perceptions of hybrid teaching in translation courses by focusing on three aspects: technology capabilities, beliefs and learning experiences. Data were collected from surveys and in-depth interviews to identify the views of students from different attendance mode. The results show that the hybrid mode is appropriate for teaching translation, although there are some limitations that could be improved. Some important implications and suggestions were provided on maximising the effectiveness of this new mode of teaching.

Keywords Hybrid mode of teaching · Translation · Technology · Beliefs · Learning experiences

12.1 Introduction

A hybrid mode of teaching combines different learning environments or instruments to accommodate both face-to-face and online students (Linder 2017). This new teaching mode has become more prevalent due to the emergence of COVID-19, a highly contagious disease that developed into a pandemic in different countries in early 2020 (Centre for Health Protection 2022; World Health Organization 2021). National lockdowns and school closures are being implemented around the world

K. Liu (✉) · H. L. Kwok · W. Li
The Hong Kong Polytechnic University, Hong Kong, China
e-mail: kl.liu@polyu.edu.hk

K. Liu and A. K. F. Cheung (eds.), *Translation and Interpreting in the Age of COVID-19*, Corpora and Intercultural Studies 9,
https://doi.org/10.1007/978-981-19-6680-4_12

to control this infectious disease, which poses a challenge to teaching and learning globally (UNO 2020). To minimize the impact of the epidemic on teaching and learning, there has been a dramatic increase in the use of online teaching, especially in higher education institutions (Dwivedi et al. 2020; Paudel 2021; International Association of Universities 2020). Online teaching is inevitably a "new normal" under the pandemic.

As the COVID-19 outbreak has slightly stabilised in some regions, such as Hong Kong, a hybrid teaching mode has emerged. Face-to-face teaching was restored and online instruction was maintained for international students still affected by travel restrictions. The hybrid mode allows students to attend classes offline or online to meet their preferences and needs. However, the hybrid mode is more than a mere combination of face-to-face and online teaching because teachers can be challenged by coordinating students from different attendance modes and catering to the needs of these two distinct groups of students simultaneously. Unlike interpreting courses which are highly dependent on the instruments including microphones, monitors and tape recorders and requires constant interaction, translation courses typically consist of lectures, practice sessions and the use of online resources to aid the translation process, and are therefore a good testing ground for hybrid teaching models. To the best of our knowledge, no research has attempted to investigate the effectiveness of hybrid mode in translation teaching settings. This study aims to systematically examine students' perceptions of hybrid teaching in translation classrooms in order to fill such a gap, which may also provide some insights into the adoption of hybrid teaching mode in translation teaching and even other disciplines.

12.1.1 Hybrid Mode of Teaching: Concepts and Challenges

With the advances in technology in this digital era, the combination of face-to-face and online modes of teaching has widely been adopted to meet the needs of students with different learning styles and preferences. Although previous studies have investigated the effectiveness of different teaching approaches that integrate online and face-to-face elements, most of them focused on blended teaching,[1] i.e., the combination of face-to-face instruction with technology-mediated activities outside a traditional classroom at an appropriate balance (Graham 2006; Linder 2017). In the context of the COVID-19 pandemic, in order to minimize the risk of COVID-19 transmission through social contact while maintaining continuity of education (Li et al. 2021; Rasheed et al. 2020), a teaching approach different from blended learning, i.e., the hybrid mode of teaching has become more prevalent. By definition, the hybrid mode of teaching in this study "utilises technology to create a variety of learning environments for students" (Linder 2017: 11) and accommodates both

[1] Many articles with the title "hybrid mode" actually refer to blended teaching. To prevent confusion, the term "hybrid mode" or "hybrid teaching" denotes a class that accommodates both face-to-face and online students in the remainder of this chapter.

face-to-face and online attendance modes in a class. It retains the traditional face-to-face teaching characteristics of live, synchronous human interaction while providing students with different attendance options. Ostensibly, the hybrid mode is simply a synchronic integration of face-to-face and online teaching.

Moving traditional face-to-face lessons online, however, is not easy to achieve in the first place. Many studies have reported the challenges faced by students, teachers, and educational institutions in the sudden adoption of online instruction (Nisiforou et al. 2021; Trust and Whalen 2020; Sahu 2020). Students need adequate self-regulation ability and digital literacy to succeed in the online mode of learning (Broadbent 2017). In addition, although online instruction offers students more flexibility in learning, students generally reported a lack of interactions with teachers and their peers which would be considered a valuable experience in the traditional face-to-face mode (Dziuban and Moskal 2011). Pure online learning mode may also result in a high drop-out rate and a low excellence rate (Moskal et al. 2013). Teachers also face challenges in managing technology and preparing appropriate online teaching resources (Brown 2016; Trust and Whalen 2020). Institutions face challenges in providing supportive services and tailoring assessment and evaluation (Sahu 2020; Broadbent 2017; Porter and Graham 2016). The hybrid mode can even be more challenging than pure face-to-face or online instruction as teachers must coordinate students from different attendance modes. However, as most previous studies only investigated the challenges and effectiveness of the online mode of teaching, limited research has been conducted on hybrid teaching. In the following, we will review two main considerations in the successful transition from pure face-to-face teaching to online mode discussed in previous literature: technological and pedagogical aspects (Herring et al. 2016). Besides, the different beliefs that affect one's acceptance of a new teaching mode will also be reviewed. It is believed that a systematic review of these aspects will help shed light on the adoption of hybrid teaching mode in translation courses.

12.1.2 Hybrid Mode of Teaching: Main Considerations

12.1.2.1 Technological Aspect

Hybrid mode of teaching offers students options of both online and face-to-face attendance. To ensure a successful transition from traditional face-to-face mode to hybrid mode of teaching, several issues should be paid attention to. To begin with, technology capabilities are particularly relevant to online attendance in hybrid mode. Computer literacy, which refers to knowledge and ability to proficiently use a computer and relevant technology, and technological preparedness, which indicates the readiness of necessary computer hardware (e.g. microphones, camera) and software (e.g. presentation programme, video conferencing software), are two prerequisites for online attendance (Paudel 2021). Further, Cox and Marshall (2007) found that teachers' proficient use of information and communication technologies could facilitate automation and interactivity in classrooms. In contrast, the technical problems that arise at any time can be the major weakness of online lessons (Angelova 2020). Therefore, online students' experience in the hybrid classroom is highly correlated with the technological capabilities of the parties involved.

12.1.2.2 Pedagogical Aspect

Besides technological issues, different teaching activities and assessments in hybrid mode also deserve special attention as they affect students' learning experiences and outcomes. It should be pointed out that not all teaching activities can be conducted using a hybrid mode. For example, practicum in medical health discipline and experiments in science discipline can hardly be replaced by online instruction. In the context of translation teaching and learning, online teaching seems more viable as translation classes typically consist of lectures given by the instructors, practice sessions and students making use of various online resources to complete translation tasks. In addition, students do not need special equipment to complete their studies, other than the use of a personal computer. This makes online mode possibly applicable to translation teaching, which provides a desirable testing ground for investigating the use of hybrid teaching mode in this study. However, researchers also highlighted the importance of interaction in translation teaching, such as nurturing collaboration skills, checking understanding of translation knowledge, practising target language skills, and improving translation skills through translation projects (Muijs and Reynolds 2011; Burns and Myhill 2004; Li et al. 2015; Alfer 2017). Kiraly (2000: 17) regarded translation education as "a dynamic, interactive process based on learner empowerment". In comparison, inadequacy in interaction and communication can lead to a sense of isolation (Tümen Akyildiz 2020). Although in-class interaction is possible in hybrid teaching, the ways of interaction and communication are not necessarily the same as in traditional face-to-face classes, as teachers also need to cater to the online group by using messaging function in video conferencing software. In this sense, both teachers and students need to adapt to changes in interaction mode and class dynamics. The effectiveness of this interaction in the translation classroom and how students' learning experiences are affected needs further investigation.

In addition, the hybrid teaching mode gives rise to assessment issues, as students attend classes in different modes, some in person and some online. For example, although group work is often utilized in translation instruction to allow students to learn about peer perspectives and translation methods (Liao 2014), students tend to perform individual tasks rather than group work (Angelova 2020). This is because individual reports and projects are less dependent on synchronous communication tools and therefore easier to set up. In contrast, the different attendance modes under hybrid teaching make group work quite challenging. The difficulty in managing groups and synchronous assessments seems to make assessments requiring synchronous methods far less common in online education (Turnbull et al. 2021). Thus, it is worth exploring whether the restricted implementation of particular assessment methods in hybrid mode affects student learning.

12.1.2.3 Students' Beliefs

Moreover, students' beliefs can shape their behavioural intentions. While extant studies have identified students' positive beliefs toward incorporating online elements in teaching, such as improved satisfaction and motivation in learning (Huang and Hong 2016; Moskal et al. 2013), not all the beliefs are positive. From the psychological viewpoint, shifting to hybrid mode of teaching means that students and teachers are forced to cope with changes, which might cause emotional reactions or resistance due to fear and doubts about new directions (Fullan 2004). In this sense, students' beliefs and perceived usefulness of hybrid teaching mode may hint at one's intention to accept or resist the sudden change of the teaching mode, thus affecting the learning outcomes (Pham et al. 2021). At the same time, the subsequent learning experiences can alter their beliefs and intention to continue learning online (Zhao et al. 2022). These suggest that students' beliefs about hybrid teaching mode and actual experiences are interrelated with each other.

12.1.3 Research Questions

Based on the foregoing review, we can see that with the inevitable constraints of the online mode, technological readiness, adaptation and appropriate adjustment of instructional activities, and students' beliefs influence successful change and educational outcome. In this study, we mainly address the following three research questions:

RQ1: How do students perceive the technology capabilities of themselves, their teachers and the university?

RQ2: What are students' beliefs about using hybrid teaching mode in translation courses?

RQ3: Do students from different attendance modes view their learning experiences of hybrid teaching in the translation classroom differently?

The findings are expected to reveal the pros and cons of hybrid teaching mode in translation settings from students' perceptions. Students' perceptions may also help provide insight into the effectiveness of this new teaching mode for the continuation of translation teaching during the pandemic, and the potential of the hybrid mode to become a new trend of education in the future.

12.2 Method

12.2.1 Design

This study adopted a mixed-methods design to investigate students' perceptions of the hybrid teaching mode in the translation classroom. This design allows a more comprehensive understanding of the research questions by explaining the survey results with follow-up interview data and gaining more insight from the integration of two sets of data (Creswell and Creswell 2018).

12.2.2 Participants

A total of 69 students majoring in translation at The Hong Kong Polytechnic University were recruited as participants in the survey (see Table 12.1). All of them reported having attended at least one translation course in hybrid mode before the survey. Among these participants, 48 (69.6%) reported face-to-face (f2f) as their major attendance mode (i.e., f2f group), while 21 (30.4%) reported online as their major attendance mode (i.e., online group) in the hybrid teaching classes. For the f2f group, they were aged 20 to 29 ($M = 23.3$, $SD = 2.0$). Among them, 42 (87.5%) were female, and 5 (10.4%) came from an undergraduate programme. For the online group, they were aged 20 to 24 ($M = 22.0$, $SD = 1.1$). Among them, 16 (76.2%) were female, and 12 (57.1%) came from an undergraduate programme. All participants took part in the survey voluntarily.

Six participants from the survey study were recruited to participate in the follow-up interview (Table 12.2), three from an undergraduate (UG) programme and three from a postgraduate (PG) programme. They were all female between the ages of 21 and 25.

Table 12.1 Demographic information of the survey participants

	Face-to-face (f2f) (N = 48)	Online (N = 21)
Age (years)	23.3 (*SD* = 2.0)	22.0 (*SD* = 1.1)
Gender		
Female	42 (87.5%)	16 (76.2%)
Male	6 (12.5%)	5 (23.8%)
Education level		
Undergraduate (UG)	5 (10.4%)	12 (57.1%)
Postgraduate (PG)	43 (89.6%)	9 (42.9%)

Table 12.2 Details of the interviewees

	Programme	Age	Primary attendance mode	Approximate proportion of attending classes in different modes (f2f: online)
Interviewee 1	UG	21	f2f	7:3
Interviewee 2	UG	21	f2f	4:1
Interviewee 3	UG	21	Online	0:1
Interviewee 4	PG	22	f2f	1:1
Interviewee 5	PG	24	f2f	7:3
Interviewee 6	PG	25	f2f	7:3

12.2.3 Instruments

The questions for the student survey were constructed by reviewing previous literature, including the Theory of Planned Behavior (Ajzen 1991), students' attitudes towards online lectures (Angelova 2020), the experience of distancing learning (Paudel 2021; Gruzdev et al. 2021), teaching and assessment methods (Burns and Myhill 2004; Vygotskiĭ 1978; Turnbull et al. 2021).

The questionnaire consisted of 12 questions (see Appendix 12.1), covering four areas: (1) demographic information (gender, age, education level, primary attendance mode); (2) technology capabilities (computer literacy and technological preparedness); (3) beliefs (participants' belief, perceived adaptability and perceived viewpoints of others before and after the adoption of hybrid teaching); (4) learning experiences (course delivery, students' conditions in class, communication, assessment method, etc.). Most of the questions were close-ended. Participants were asked to answer the questions based on their primary attendance mode in the hybrid teaching classroom. The survey was conducted online.

The semi-structured interview was designed to probe deeper into the various issues revealed by the quantitative survey results. In particular, the interview questions focused on the "what," "how," and "why" of students' perceptions of hybrid teaching. Interviewees were not limited to answering the questions based on their primary attendance mode. Instead, they were asked to freely express and to compare their experiences using different modes of attendance in a hybrid teaching class.

12.2.4 Procedures

The survey data were gathered using the Google Form near the end of the semester. Informed consent was obtained prior to conducting the survey. The time to complete the questionnaire was approximately 15 min.

We contacted the survey participants who indicated their interest in engaging in the follow-up interview, and obtained informed consent from the interviewees individually. The interviews were conducted online using Cantonese or Mandarin, which are two languages that both interviewer and interviewee felt comfortable with. The conversations were recorded for data analysis. The interview lasted for approximately 30–45 min for an individual participant.

12.2.5 Data Analysis

Descriptive statistics of the survey data were calculated based on students' primary attendance mode, namely the f2f group and online group. The audio-recordings of in-depth interviews were transcribed and treated as supplementary information to the survey results.

12.3 Results

12.3.1 Technology Capabilities

Before probing into students' beliefs and learning experiences of the hybrid teaching mode in the translation classroom, the survey first garnered students' perceptions of technological capabilities of different involved parties (Fig. 12.1). A high majority of students strongly agreed or agreed that they have enough computer literacy (f2f: 77.1%; online: 85.7%), with only a few having problems obtaining enough suitable devices for lessons (f2f: 16.7%; online: 23.8%). Nearly all respondents agreed that their teachers had the computer literacy for holding hybrid lessons (f2f: 87.5%; online: 95.2%). Over 70% of the respondents considered the technical support provided by the university and the instruments equipped for hybrid classrooms sufficient and appropriate. In brief, these survey results demonstrated that students, teachers and the university have appropriate technological capabilities in response to the adoption of hybrid teaching.

Although students held a positive view of the technological readiness of different parties in the survey, they still encountered some technological problems during the hybrid mode of teaching, as indicated by the interviewees. For example, interviewee 5 (f2f) complained that the equipment in a few classrooms did not function well occasionally. Another problem is related to teachers' awareness. Interviewee 1 (f2f) and 4 (f2f) reported that a few teachers were not familiar with the screen and sound sharing settings of some video conferencing platforms. This caused online students to be unable to hear the correct sound channel or see the correct computer screen. Furthermore, they mentioned that teachers sometimes neither noticed the problem nor the messages sent by online students in the chat box of video conferencing platforms, resulting in limited interaction with online students.

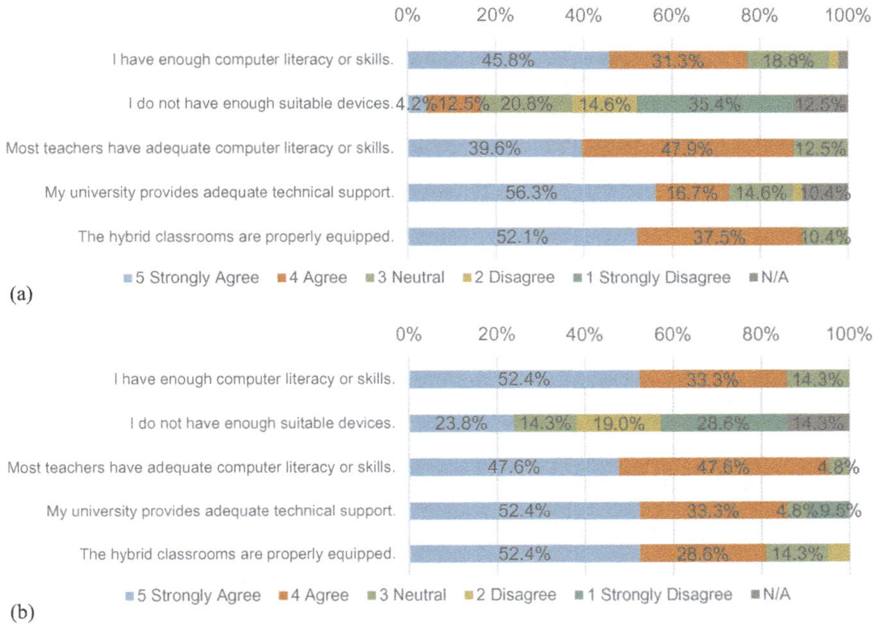

Fig. 12.1 Technology capabilities of using hybrid teaching mode in translation courses: **a** face-to-face group; **b** online group

12.3.2 Beliefs

Figure 12.2 shows students' general beliefs, perceived adaptability and perceived classmates' and teachers' standpoints of hybrid teaching mode in translation courses before the semester began and after a semester of hybrid teaching. For the f2f group, after a semester in hybrid mode, a slight increase in the number of positive responses was observed. Interviewee 2 (f2f) was one of them. Initially, she believed that "face-to-face teaching must be the best". Later, she found that the learning experiences of the hybrid mode was better than she expected, because the university's advanced equipment greatly bridged the gap between online and face-to-face learning experiences. The hybrid mode also allowed her to attend the class in either mode flexibly based on her needs.

For the online group, 90.5% of respondents initially believed that their classmates and teachers viewed the hybrid mode positively. However, this proportion slightly dropped to 80.9% after the hybrid mode was implemented for one semester. Respondent 3 (online) stated that "online students are more likely to be ignored by teachers than offline students," although this did not pose a major problem for her. "Especially when a class had more offline students, the teacher would talk happily with the students in the class and forget about the online students" (Interviewee 4, f2f). This may disappoint some online students who value class interaction. In general,

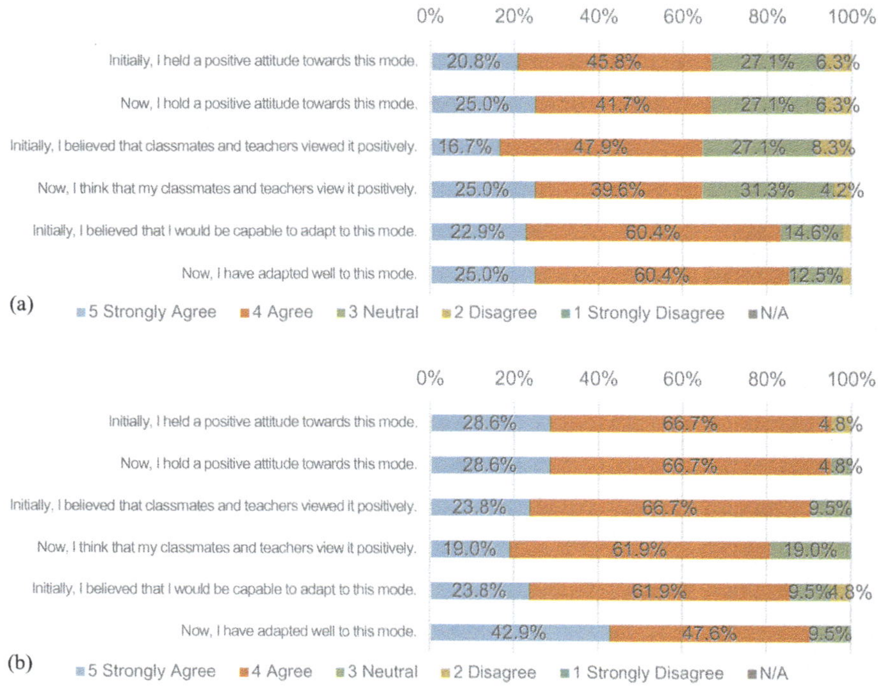

Fig. 12.2 Beliefs towards hybrid teaching mode in the translation courses before and after hybrid teaching: **a** face-to-face group; **b** online group

students who preferred to attend hybrid classes in an online mode are more positive about hybrid teaching than students who take hybrid classes primarily in an offline mode.

12.3.3 *Learning Experiences*

Figure 12.3 presents students' learning experiences about the hybrid teaching mode.

From the perspective of course delivery, interviewees mentioned in-class translation teaching activities under the hybrid mode, such as lectures, game-based quizzes, Q&A, group discussions with mini-presentations and individual translation exercises. According to the survey, 66.7% of online group respondents reported reduced interactive activities, while only 41.7% of f2f group respondents held the same viewpoint. In contrast, only about 23% of respondents in both groups claimed that practice-based learning had decreased. In addition, nearly half of the survey respondents reported that they received more resources from their teachers in the hybrid teaching mode. The most frequently cited resource by the interviewees was recorded lectures.

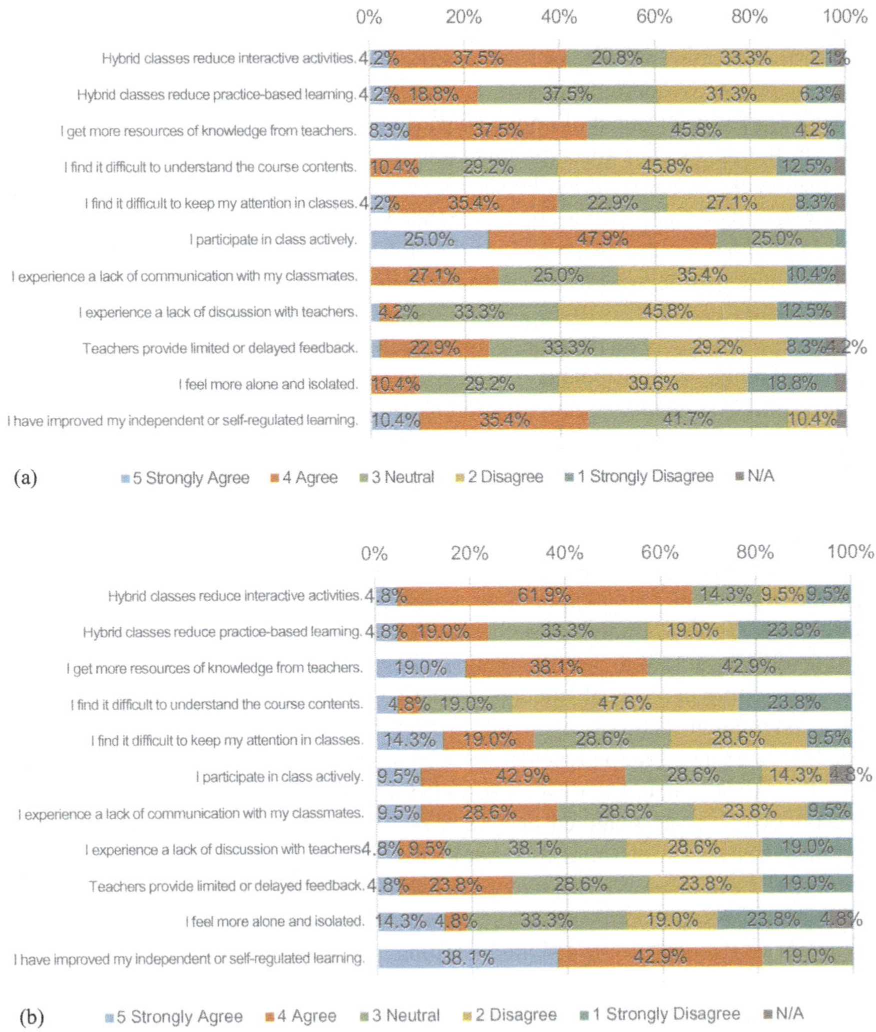

Fig. 12.3 Students' experiences of hybrid teaching mode in translation courses: **a** face-to-face group; **b** online group

As for student engagement in hybrid classes, the survey revealed that using hybrid mode did not influence students' understanding of course contents. Compared with the online group, respondents from the f2f group participated in class more actively (f2f: 72.9%; online: 52.4%). Unlike most survey respondents, Interviewee 3 (online) was more active in the online mode. She explained, "When answering teachers' questions, you did not feel embarrassed, and you did not need to show your face, so it [online mode] probably made me more engaged in class". Interviewee 2 (f2f) sometimes responded via the video conferencing platform even though she attended the class offline. Besides, a slightly higher proportion of offline students claimed to have difficulty concentrating in classes (f2f: 39.6%; online: 33.3%), while four out of six interviewees reported that they were more concentrated when attending hybrid classes face-to-face instead of online (Interviewee 1, 4, 5, 6, f2f).

From the perspective of communication, the face-to-face attendance mode has its advantages. As revealed by the survey statistics, compared to the online group, fewer respondents in the f2f group experienced a lack of interaction with classmates (f2f: 27.1%; online: 38.1%), a lack of discussion with teachers (f2f: 6.3%; online: 14.3%), limited or delayed feedback from teachers (f2f: 25.0%; online: 28.6%), and feeling more isolated (f2f: 10.4%; online. 19.1%). Interviewees reflected that online students needed to rely on messaging apps to talk to classmates and emails to contact teachers. Unlike offline students who can have instant discussions with their peers in class, online students' communication is delayed.

Still, online attendance mode was prominent in promoting students' independent and self-regulated learning. Over 80% of respondents in the online group reported increased independence and self-regulation in learning, while the same applied to only 45.8% of respondents in the f2f group. This may be due to the fact that offline students are directly "monitored" by the teacher in the classroom, while online students' immediate facial expressions or reactions are not easily visible. As interviewee 4 (f2f) said, "Under online mode, you are basically alone and need to rely on yourself". Interviewee 3 (online) also believed that online attendance mode was more demanding in terms of students' initiative of learning than the offline mode.

For assessment methods, as mentioned by the interviewees, open-book exams, closed-book exams, group presentations and individual assignments are all feasible under the hybrid mode. Figure 12.4 revealed that a large proportion of both groups of respondents strongly agreed or agreed that individual assignments could facilitate their translation learning in general (f2f: 83.3%; online: 85.7%) and was an appropriate form of assessment under the hybrid mode (f2f: 83.3%; online: 90.4%). Comparatively, respondents were more conservative about the effectiveness of exams and group assignments for translation learning and their suitability under the hybrid mode.

Interviewee 2 (f2f) and 3 (online) explained that although group work such as presentations and group assignments was feasible under the hybrid mode, the communication within the group was difficult under the hybrid mode. In the case of individual work, students have less difficulty completing assignments because they do not have to experience the same communication problems with other students as they do when undertaking group work. Furthermore, compared with an exam with time restrictions, individual assignments allowed students to work on a translation earnestly and carefully by searching for the cultural meaning of the terms, thus facilitating students' acquisition of related translation skills (Interviewee 3, online).

Regarding the overall evaluation of the hybrid mode (Fig. 12.5), about 90% of the respondents were satisfied with their overall experience of using hybrid mode in translation classes, and only a few felt that their learning in hybrid classes was less effective (f2f: 10.5%; online: 19.1%) and that the hybrid teaching mode could not

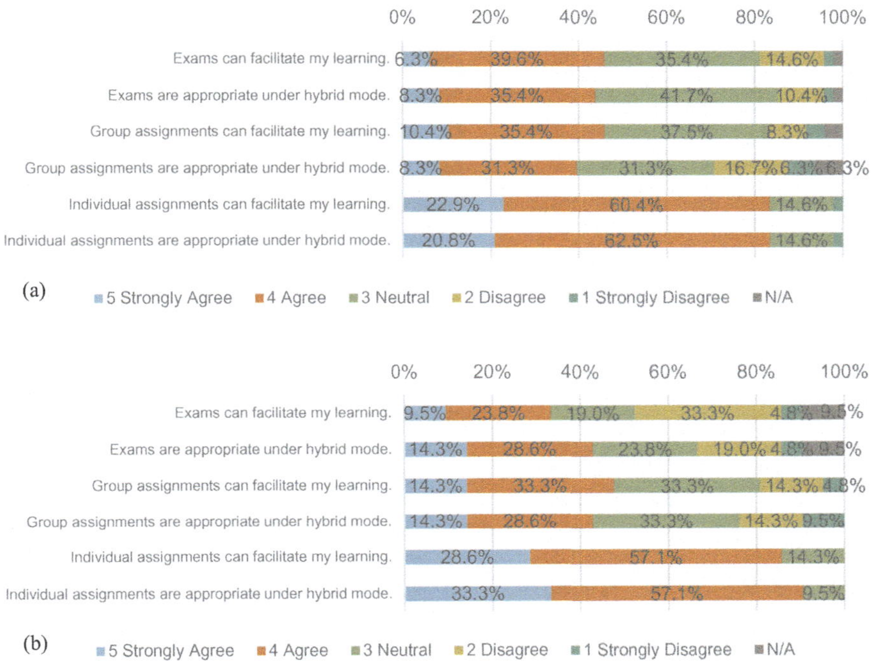

Fig. 12.4 Assessment methods used under hybrid teaching mode in translation courses: **a** face-to-face group; **b** online group

guarantee the quality of teaching and learning (f2f: 25.1%; online: 19.0%). Surprisingly, a higher proportion of respondents from the online group did not find any difficulties in using hybrid teaching (f2f: 62.5%; online: 85.7%) and regarded it as a suitable method for translation courses (f2f: 48.0%; online: 76.2%) than from the f2f group.

Interviewees agreed that the hybrid mode is appropriate for teaching translation, as long as teachers are able to manage both offline and online students. Interviewee 1 (f2f) struggled with using the hybrid mode as she observed that some teachers neglected the online students. Interviewee 2 (f2f) experienced more interactive classroom activities after shifting to the hybrid mode, so she appreciated this teaching mode. Interviewee 4 (f2f) "hoped that the university could provide training to teachers" on how to teach using hybrid mode.

Regarding students' preferences for the teaching mode (Fig. 12.6), the majority of respondents identified the hybrid mode of teaching the most preferred mode (f2f: 58.3%; online: 71.4%). Similar results were observed in the interviews. Five interviewees also considered the hybrid mode as their preferred choice because it could meet the different needs of student.

With respect to the qualities needed for a successful hybrid mode of teaching (Fig. 12.7), the majority agreed on the importance of students' self-motivation (f2f:

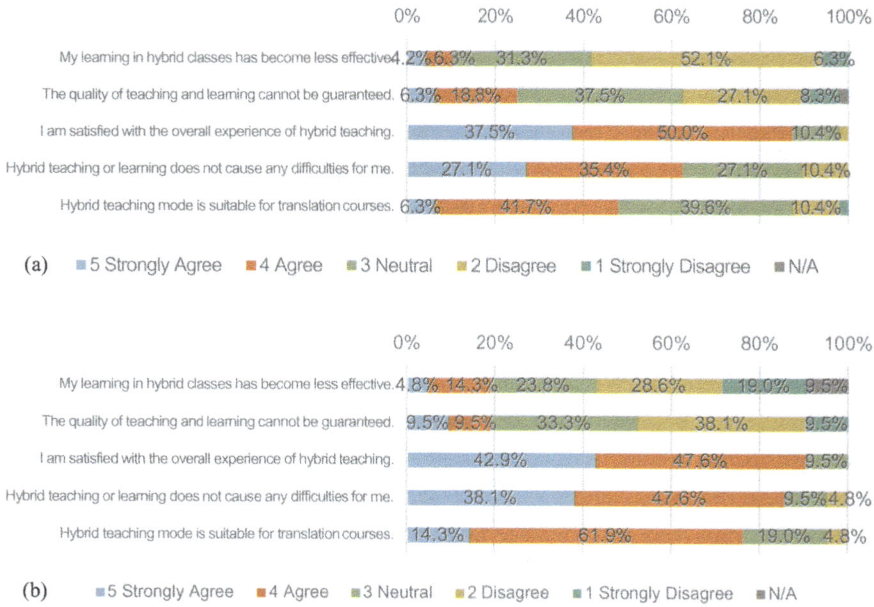

Fig. 12.5 Overall comments of using hybrid teaching mode in the translation courses: **a** face-to-face group; **b** online group

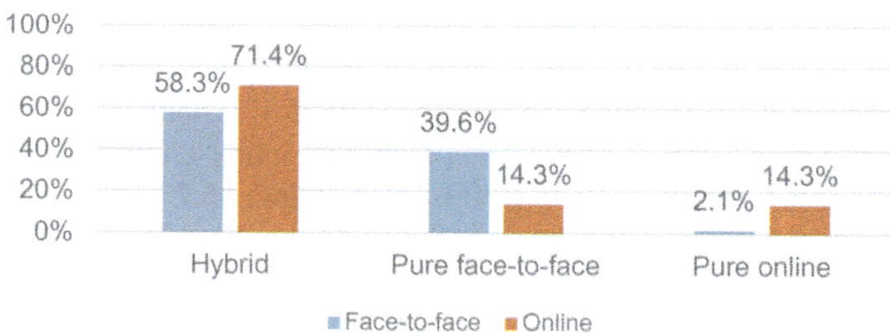

Fig. 12.6 Preferred teaching modes by the two groups

87.5%; online: 81.0%) and time-management skills (f2f: 77.1%; online: 71.4%). Importantly, students' independence was the only quality that a higher proportion of respondents in the online group (81.0%) considered more important than in the f2f group (66.7%). Interviewee 4 (f2f) also noted that online students should be self-disciplined.

There were apparent differences between the two groups in terms of the necessity of students' computer literacy and students' technological preparedness for a successful hybrid mode of teaching. More than half of the respondents in the f2f group considered them important, while less than 30% of the respondents in the

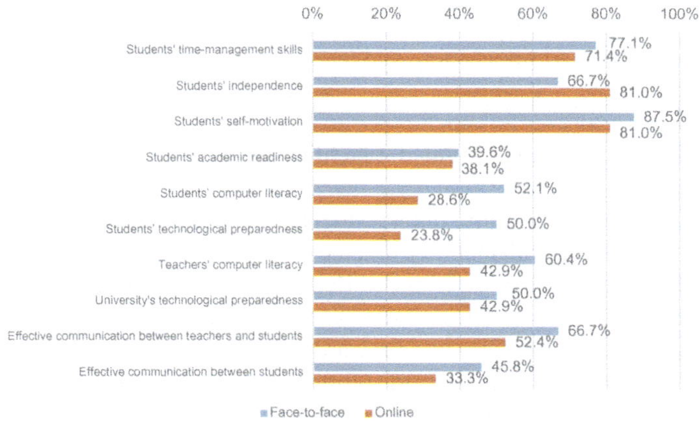

Fig. 12.7 The qualities required for a successful hybrid mode of teaching

online group held the same position. Interviewee 6 (f2f) emphasised the importance of technological preparedness for online attendance in the interview. The face-to-face mode was her primary attendance mode due to the anxiety she felt when she could not manage the online system well or could not log in to the video conferencing platform due to various technological issues.

12.4 Discussion

This study has examined the unique experiences of different attendance modes under hybrid teaching. In this section, we address the three research questions in detail and reveal the strengths and weaknesses of the hybrid mode. The implications of this study are also discussed.

12.4.1 Students' Perceptions of Hybrid Mode of Teaching

12.4.1.1 Technology Capabilities

Most respondents were satisfied with the technological capabilities of the students, faculty, and university, including computer literacy and readiness of equipment, to adopt the hybrid teaching mode. Still, some technical problems were identified during the interviews. As suggested by Angelova's (2020) study, online teaching mode is largely constrained by technology, which is a major weakness of online teaching. Under the hybrid mode, technical problems usually occur in the online attendance mode but not in the face-to-face mode, which leads to some unexpected problems and psychological burdens for online students and becomes a disadvantage of the hybrid mode. Therefore, teachers and universities need to pay special attention to technology issues in hybrid teaching and learning.

12.4.1.2 Beliefs About the Hybrid Teaching Mode

Generally speaking, the majority of respondents from both the f2f and online groups perceived their attitudes, adaptability, and the standpoints of their peers and teachers towards the hybrid teaching mode as positive, both before and after the implementation of the hybrid mode. These three aspects correspond to behavioural belief (i.e., one's attitude and predisposition towards hybrid learning behaviours), control beliefs (i.e., perceived competence and ability to demonstrate proper hybrid learning behaviours) and normative belief (i.e., perceived subjective norms of hybrid mode) in the theory of planned behaviors. These three beliefs can help predict a person's behavioural intentions (Ajzen 1991). Students' optimism about these beliefs indicates their acceptance of the sudden adoption of the hybrid mode in translation teaching.

The higher percentage of students holding positive beliefs in the online group compared to the face-to-face group can be explained by several possible reasons. First, some online students may be international students who were not in Hong Kong during the semester, and for whom the hybrid teaching mode has provided a pathway to continue their education. Second, the students who chose the unconventional online attendance mode may have been more open to changes, and thus held more positive beliefs about the hybrid teaching mode. In addition, as students indicated in the interviews, online attendance could also be a strategy for avoiding face-threatening communication when interacting with the teacher and classmates. Therefore, students of the online group have higher acceptance and lower resistance to the hybrid mode.

12.4.1.3 Learning Experiences Under the Hybrid Mode

The largest part of this study was to reveal students' learning experiences in terms of classroom dynamics (including course delivery, student engagement and communication) and assessment methods.

The use of various interactive activities can raise students' interest and engage them in the classroom. Learning will no longer be limited by teacher-oriented delivery of knowledge. As revealed in the interviews, game-based quizzes, discussions and class presentations are used in hybrid translation classes, which can be considered as interactive teaching and learning activities that allow teachers to check students' understanding of knowledge and exchange ideas (Muijs and Reynolds 2011). This is the advantage of the hybrid teaching mode. However, such benefit may be offset by teachers' neglect of online students. As mentioned by the interviewees, teachers sometimes failed to notice the written forms of communication that online students used in the classroom. The study corroborates previous findings that students face communication problems during online instruction (Gruzdev et al. 2021), which can lead to a sense of isolation (Tümen Akyildiz 2020). Also, while verbal communication allows for instant feedback, written communication has a longer response time and does not encourage student participation. As a result, online students may be less motivated to participate in class without close monitoring. Striking a balance between different forms of communication to ensure effective knowledge delivery and student engagement is the challenge of using the hybrid teaching mode. On the positive side, introverted students can benefit from written communication because they are not required to speak in front of the class, reducing their embarrassment and encouraging their participation.

For assessment methods, both groups recognised the importance and appropriateness of using individual assignments to enhance translation learning under the hybrid mode, which corroborates previous findings in online teaching (Angelova 2020; Turnbull et al. 2021). As with online teaching, the hybrid mode also favours asynchronous assessment approaches, such as individual assignments, but not synchronous or group-based assessment methods, such as exams and group projects. Considering there is no large difference in the ratings of perceived usefulness and appropriateness of assessment methods in the hybrid mode, it can be postulated that student learning is not much affected by the limitations of the assessment methods used.

The results reflect students' satisfaction with the use of the hybrid mode and their recognition of its applicability in translation courses. These indicate that the use of hybrid mode in translation teaching is off to a good start, although there is still room for improvement. As described by one interviewee, the hybrid mode is a "win–win" teaching mode for both international and local students. Flexibility is the biggest advantage of such a teaching mode which caters to both types of students.

12.4.2 Relationship Between Technology Capabilities, Students' Beliefs, and Learning Experiences

Based on the findings and the discussion above, hybrid mode of instruction needs to meet the basic requirements of technology capabilities, including computer literacy, technological preparedness and awareness, as it includes online teaching. Although students' initial beliefs about hybrid teaching mode have an impact on their learning experiences and outcomes (Pham et al. 2021; Ajzen 1991), different attendance modes can also cause students to experience different class dynamics (e.g., degrees of interaction, class participation, forms of communication). Such differences can create inequities experienced by students who choose to attend hybrid classes using different mode. These subsequent learning experiences can then influence their attitudes and intentions to continue with the new mode of learning (Zhao et al. 2022). The interaction between the three aspects, namely, technology capabilities, students' beliefs and learning experiences, is presented in (Fig. 12.8).

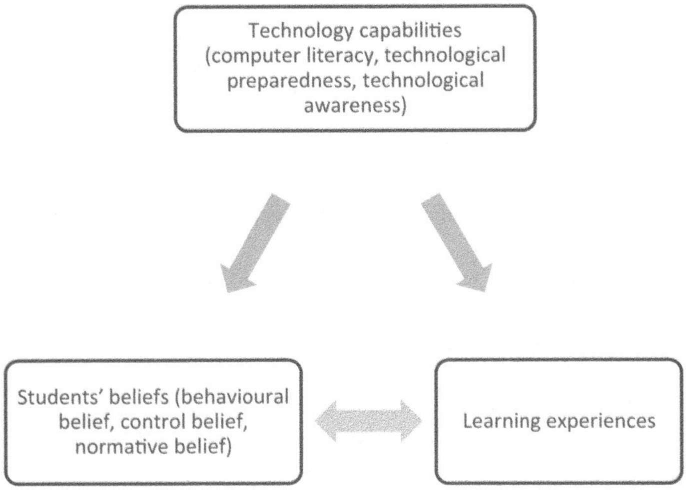

Fig. 12.8 Interaction between technology capabilities, students' beliefs and their learning experiences

12.4.3 Implications

Based on the interaction diagram depicting the relationship between the three major components (see Fig. 12.8), some recommendations and implications can be made to improve the implementation of hybrid teaching in translation classrooms. Some of these recommendations may also be applicable to other disciplines.

Teachers The teachers should have basic computer literacy to hold online teaching and tackle minor technical problems that might arise in teaching. They must also be aware of the need to ensure that course content is delivered correctly and successfully to online students. To go further, they can explore how to use appropriate technology and tools to facilitate translation teaching and learning, such as online interactive learning platforms, online corpora for data-driven learning (Liu 2015, 2020), machine translation for translation competence acquisition (Liu et al. 2022) and lecture recordings for review. Besides, to ensure fairness, teachers should make every effort to narrow the differences in learning experiences between the two attendance modes. Regarding communication problems, they can keep an eye on both groups of students in class by checking the chat box of video conferencing software from time to time, offering Q&A sessions, and providing some communication channels outside the classroom. It is recommended that they also use pedagogical approaches and teaching activities that can be carried out synchronously online and offline, such as lecture, online game-based quizzes, translation exercises, group discussions and presentations. Assessment methods and their weighing should also be carefully designed.

Universities Universities should ensure that hybrid classrooms are equipped with well-functioning instruments and computer software. Technical support, especially during class time, is essential. Universities can also provide training for teachers in digital literacy and hybrid pedagogy. Departmental forums can also be held for translation teachers to share their experiences and ideas. In addition, since students in the survey attribute the success of hybrid teaching more to self-related qualities, such as students' self-motivation, time-management skills and self-independence, the universities can support students' personal growth by providing relevant workshops to prepare them for the hybrid teaching mode.

12.5 Conclusion and Limitations

This study provides a preliminary understanding of the adoption of hybrid teaching through the lens of translation students. Particularly, perceived technological capabilities, students' beliefs and learning experiences under the hybrid teaching mode in translation classrooms were investigated through analysis of both quantitative and qualitative data. Our research yielded new ideas regarding the divergences brought by different attendance modes, as well as the pro and cons of the hybrid mode of teaching. Based on the findings, we can conclude that hybrid mode has the potential to be used in translation teaching or possibly other similar disciplines without practicums.

Despite the findings, our study has some limitations. Since this study was designed to preliminarily explore students' perceptions of a new teaching mode, the sample size was relatively small, and was based on students enrolled in translation courses. In the future, more students can be included in the survey which can be extended to interpreting courses. In addition, only students' perceptions of the hybrid mode of teaching were explored in this study. It should be noted that adopting a new teaching mode requires a concerted effort of different parties, i.e., students, teachers, and institutions. Future studies could also explore the perceptions of teachers and educational institutions about the hybrid teaching mode to gain a more comprehensive understanding of such a teaching method.

12.6 Appendix 12. 1

Survey

Personal Information

1. Gender
   - Male
   - Female
2. Age

   —

3. Education level

   - Undergraduate, year 1
   - Undergraduate, year 2
   - Undergraduate, year 3
   - Undergraduate, year 4
   - Master, year 1
   - Master, year 2

4. What is your major attendance mode in the translation courses that adopt hybrid mode of teaching?

   - Face-to-face
   - Online

Important Note

Please answer the rest of the questions based on your major attendance mode. If certain questions do not apply to you, please choose "N/A".

Technology capabilities

5. To what extent do you agree with the following statements about technology capabilities of using hybrid mode of teaching in translation courses?

	5 (Strongly agree)	4 (Agree)	3 (Neutral)	2 (Disagree)	1 (Strongly disagree)	N/A
a. I have enough computer literacy or skills to handle most of the technical problems that may arise in teaching						
b. I do not have enough suitable devices for classes, assessments, or interactions with classmates						

(continued)

(continued)

	5 (Strongly agree)	4 (Agree)	3 (Neutral)	2 (Disagree)	1 (Strongly disagree)	N/A
c. Most teachers have adequate computer literacy or skills to handle most of the technical problems that may arise in teaching						
d. My university provides adequate technical support that can solve my technical problems						
e. The hybrid classrooms are properly equipped in my university						

Beliefs

6. To what extent do you agree with the following statements about your perceptions about hybrid teaching mode in translation courses?

Before the first lesson of the hybrid class,

	5 (Strongly agree)	4 (Agree)	3 (Neutral)	2 (Disagree)	1 (Strongly disagree)	N/A
a. I held a positive attitude towards this new teaching mode in translation classes						
b. I believed that most of my classmates and teachers viewed this new teaching mode positively						

(continued)

(continued)

	5 (Strongly agree)	4 (Agree)	3 (Neutral)	2 (Disagree)	1 (Strongly disagree)	N/A
c. I believed that I would be capable to adapt to this new teaching mode						

7. Now

	5 (Strongly agree)	4 (Agree)	3 (Neutral)	2 (Disagree)	1 (Strongly disagree)	N/A
a. I hold a positive attitude towards this new teaching mode in translation classes						
b. I think that most of my classmates and teachers view this new teaching mode positively						
c. I have adapted well to this new teaching mode						

Learning experiences

8. To what extent do you agree with the following statements about your experiences of hybrid teaching mode in translation courses?

	5 (Strongly agree)	4 (Agree)	3 (Neutral)	2 (Disagree)	1 (Strongly disagree)	N/A
a. Hybrid classes reduce interactive activities (e.g. group discussions) during class						
b. Hybrid classes reduce practice-based learning						
c. I get more resources of knowledge from teachers through the hybrid teaching mode						
d. I find it difficult to understand the course contents						
e. I find it difficult to keep my attention in hybrid classes						
f. I participate in class actively (e.g. raising questions, answering questions or getting involved in discussions, etc.)						
g. I experience an overall lack of communication with my classmates						
h. I experience an overall lack of communication with teachers						

(continued)

(continued)

	5 (Strongly agree)	4 (Agree)	3 (Neutral)	2 (Disagree)	1 (Strongly disagree)	N/A
i. Teachers provide limited or delayed feedback in hybrid classes						
j. I feel more alone and isolated in hybrid classes						
k. I have improved my independent or self-regulated learning in hybrid classes						

9. To what extent do you agree with the following statements about assessment methods used under hybrid teaching mode in translation courses?

	5 (Strongly agree)	4 (Agree)	3 (Neutral)	2 (Disagree)	1 (Strongly disagree)	N/A
a. In general, exams can facilitate my learning in translation						
b. Exams are an appropriate assessment method						
c. In general, group assignments can facilitate my learning in translation						
d. Group assignments are an appropriate assessment method						

(continued)

(continued)

	5 (Strongly agree)	4 (Agree)	3 (Neutral)	2 (Disagree)	1 (Strongly disagree)	N/A
e. In general, individual assignments can facilitate my learning in translation						
f. Individual assignments are an appropriate assessment method						

10. To what extent do you agree with the following statements about overall comments of using hybrid teaching mode in translation courses?

	5 (Strongly agree)	4 (Agree)	3 (Neutral)	2 (Disagree)	1 (Strongly disagree)	N/A
a. My learning in hybrid classes has become less effective						
b. The hybrid mode cannot guarantee the quality of teaching and learning						
c. I am satisfied with the overall experience of using hybrid mode in translation teaching						
d. The hybrid teaching or learning mode does not cause any difficulties for me						
e. I think that the hybrid teaching mode is suitable for translation courses						

11. Please rank your preference for the teaching mode.

	1 (The most preferred)	2	3 (The least preferred)
a. Hybrid teaching mode			
b. Pure online teaching mode			
c. Pure face-to-face teaching mode			

12. Which of the following do you think are qualities needed for a successful hybrid mode of teaching? (can choose more than one option)

- Students' time-management skills
- Students' independence
- Students' self-motivation
- Students' academic readiness
- Students' computer literacy (i.e. knowledge and ability to use related technology efficiently)
- Students' technological preparedness (i.e. requirements of hardware and software)
- Teachers' computer literacy (i.e. knowledge and ability to use related technology efficiently)
- University's technological preparedness (i.e. requirements of hardware and software)
- Effective communication between teachers and students
- Effective communication between students.

References

Ajzen, I. 1991. Theory of planned behavior. *Organizational Behavior and Human Decision Processes* 50: 179–211.

Alfer, A. 2017. Entering the translab: translation as collaboration, collaboration as translation, and the third space of 'translaboration.' *Translation and Translanguaging in Multilingual Contexts* 3 (3): 275–290. https://doi.org/10.1075/ttmc.3.3.01alf.

Angelova, M. 2020. Students' attitudes to the online university course of management in the context of COVID-19. *International Journal of Technology in Education and Science* 4 (4): 283.

Broadbent, J. 2017. Comparing online and blended learner's self-regulated learning strategies and academic performance. *The Internet and Higher Education* 33: 24–32. https://doi.org/10.1016/j.iheduc.2017.01.004.

Brown, M.G. 2016. Blended instructional practice: a review of the empirical literature on instructors' adoption and use of online tools in face-to-face teaching. *The Internet and Higher Education* 31: 1–10. https://doi.org/10.1016/j.iheduc.2016.05.001.

Burns, C., and D. Myhill. 2004. Interactive or inactive? A consideration of the nature of interaction in whole class teaching. *Cambridge Journal of Education* 34 (1): 35–49. https://doi.org/10.1080/0305764042000183115.

Centre for Health Protection. 2022. *Frequently asked questions on Coronavirus Disease 2019 (COVID-19)*. Department of Health, HKSAR. https://www.chp.gov.hk/en/features/102624.html. Accessed 6 June 2022.

Cox, M.J., and G. Marshall. 2007. Effects of ICT: do we know what we should know? *Education and Information Technologies* 12 (2): 59–70. https://doi.org/10.1007/s10639-007-9032-x.

Creswell, J.W., and J.D. Creswell. 2018. *Research design: qualitative, quantitative, and mixed methods approaches*. Thousand Oaks, California: SAGE Publications Inc.

Dwivedi, Y.K., D.L. Hughes, C. Coombs, I. Constantiou, Y. Duan, J.S. Edwards, B. Gupta, et al. 2020. Impact of COVID-19 pandemic on information management research and practice: transforming education, work and life. *International Journal of Information Management* 55: 102211. https://doi.org/10.1016/j.ijinfomgt.2020.102211.

Dziuban, C., and P. Moskal. 2011. A course is a course is a course: factor invariance in student evaluation of online, blended and face-to-face learning environments. *The Internet and Higher Education* 14 (4): 236–241. https://doi.org/10.1016/j.iheduc.2011.05.003.

Fullan, M. 2004. *Leading in a culture of change: personal action guide and workbook*. San Francisco: Jossey-Bass.

Graham, C.R. 2006. Blended learning systems: definition, current trends, and future directions. In *The handbook of blended learning: global perspectives, local designs*, ed. C.J. Bonk and C.R. Graham, 3–21. San Francisco: Pfeiffer.

Gruzdev, I., E. Shmeleva, R. Kalinin, and K. Vilkova. 2021. Suddenly online: how Russian students switched to distance learning during the COVID-19 pandemic. In *Online teaching and learning in higher education during COVID-19: international perspectives and experiences*, ed. R.Y. Chan, K. Bista, and R.M. Allen, 134–149. New York, NY: Routledge.

Herring, M.C., M.J. Koehler, and P. Mishra, eds. 2016. *Handbook of technological pedagogical content knowledge (TPACK) for educators*. New York: Routledge.

Huang, Y.-N., and Z.-R. Hong. 2016. The effects of a flipped English classroom intervention on students' information and communication technology and English reading comprehension. *Educational Technology Research and Development* 64 (2): 175–193. https://doi.org/10.1007/s11423-015-9412-7.

International Association of Universities. 2020. *The impact of COVID-19 on higher education around the world: IAU global survey report*. Paris: International Association of Universities. https://www.iau-aiu.net/IMG/pdf/iau_covid19_and_he_survey_report_final_may_2020.pdf.

Kiraly, D. 2000. *A social constructivist approach to translator education: empowerment from theory to practice*. Manchester: St. Jerome Publishing.

Li, D., C. Zhang, and Y. He. 2015. Project-based learning in teaching translation: Students' perceptions. *The Interpreter and Translator Trainer* 9 (1): 1–19. https://doi.org/10.1080/1750399X.2015.1010357.

Li, Q., Z. Li, and J. Han. 2021. A hybrid learning pedagogy for surmounting the challenges of the COVID-19 pandemic in the performing arts education. *Education and Information Technologies* 26 (6): 7635–7655. https://doi.org/10.1007/s10639-021-10612-1.

Liao, P. 2014. *Theories, practices and research methods of translation teaching*. Taipei: Crane Publishing.

Linder, K.E. 2017. Fundamentals of hybrid teaching and learning. *New Directions for Teaching and Learning* 2017 (149): 11–18. https://doi.org/10.1002/tl.20222.

Liu, K. 2015. Investigating corpus-assisted translation teaching: A pilot study. In *Conducting research in translation technologies*, ed. P. Sánchez-Gijón, O. Torres-Hostench, and B. Mesa-Lao, 141–162. Oxford: Peter Lang Verlag.

Liu, K., H.L. Kwok, J. Liu, and A.K.F. Cheung. 2022. Sustainability and influence of machine translation: perceptions and attitudes of translation instructors and learners in Hong Kong. *Sustainability* 14 (11): 6399. https://doi.org/10.3390/su14116399.

Liu, K. 2020. *Corpus-assisted translation teaching: issues and challenges*. Singapore: Springer Singapore.
Moskal, P., C. Dziuban, and J. Hartman. 2013. Blended learning: a dangerous idea? *The Internet and Higher Education* 18: 15–23. https://doi.org/10.1016/j.iheduc.2012.12.001.
Muijs, D., and D. Reynolds, eds. 2011. *Effective teaching: evidence and practice*, 3rd ed. London: Sage.
Nisiforou, E.A., P. Kosmas, and C. Vrasidas. 2021. Emergency remote teaching during COVID-19 pandemic: lessons learned from Cyprus. *Educational Media International* 58 (2): 215–221. https://doi.org/10.1080/09523987.2021.1930484.
Paudel, P. 2021. Online education: benefits, challenges and strategies during and after COVID-19 in higher education. *International Journal on Studies in Education* 3(2):70–85. https://doi.org/10.46328/ijonse.32.
Pham, T.T.T., H.A. Le, and D.T. Do. 2021. The factors affecting students' online learning outcomes during the COVID-19 pandemic: a Bayesian exploratory factor analysis. *Education Research International* 2021: 2669098. https://doi.org/10.1155/2021/2669098.
Porter, W.W., and C.R. Graham. 2016. Institutional drivers and barriers to faculty adoption of blended learning in higher education. *British Journal of Educational Technology* 47 (4): 748–762. https://doi.org/10.1111/bjet.12269.
Rasheed, R.A., A. Kamsin, and N.A. Abdullah. 2020. Challenges in the online component of blended learning: a systematic review. *Computers & Education* 144: 103701. https://doi.org/10.1016/j.compedu.2019.103701.
Sahu, P. 2020. Closure of universities due to coronavirus disease 2019 (COVID-19): impact on education and mental health of students and academic staff. *Cureus* 12 (4): e7541–e7541. https://doi.org/10.7759/cureus.7541.
Trust, T., and J. Whalen. 2020. Should teachers be trained in emergency remote teaching? Lessons learned from the COVID-19 pandemic. *Journal of Technology and Teacher Education* 28 (2): 189–199.
Tümen Akyildiz, S. 2020. College students' views on the pandemic distance education: a focus group discussion. *International Journal of Technology in Education and Science* 4 (4): 322–334.
Turnbull, D., R. Chugh, and J. Luck. 2021. Learning management systems and synchronous communication tools: enablers of online education during COVID-19. In *Online teaching and learning in higher education during COVID-19: international perspectives and experiences*, ed. R.Y. Chan, K. Bista, and R.M. Allen, 39–49. New York, NY: Routledge.
UNO. 2020. *Education during COVID-19 and beyond*. Paris: The United Nations Educational, Scientific and Cultural Organization, UNESCO.
Vygotskiĭ, L. S. 1978. *Mind in society: the development of higher psychological processes*. M. Cole, V. Jolm-Steiner, S. Scribner, and E. Souberman (eds). Cambridge, Mass: Harvard University Press.
World Health Organization. 2021. Coronavirus disease (COVID-19). https://www.who.int/emergencies/diseases/novel-coronavirus-2019/question-and-answers-hub/q-a-detail/coronavirus-disease-covid-19. Accessed 6 June 2022.
Zhao, L., Ao, Y., Wang, Y., and Wang T. 2022. Impact of home-based learning experience during COVID-19 on future intentions to study online: a Chinese university perspective. *Frontiers in Psychology* 13. https://doi.org/10.3389/fpsyg.2022.862965.

Kanglong Liu is Assistant Professor of Department of Chinese and Bilingual Studies of The Hong Kong Polytechnic University. His research interests include corpus-based translation studies, language and translation pedagogy, *Hongloumeng* translation research. He is currently Associate Editor of Translation Quarterly, the official publication of the Hong Kong Translation Society. He has published widely in scholarly journals and authored the monograph *"Corpus-Assisted Translation Teaching: Issues and Challenges"* (Springer, 2020).

Ho Ling Kwok holds an MA in Linguistics from The Chinese University of Hong Kong. She currently works as a Research Assistant at The Hong Kong Polytechnic University. Her research interests include psychological approaches to translation and interpreting, corpus-based interpreting and translation studies, and translation teaching.

Wenjing Li is Teaching Fellow of Department of Chinese and Bilingual Studies of The Hong Kong Polytechnic University. Her research interests include literary translation, journalistic translation and translation pedagogy. Besides, she is also interested in the use of CAT tools and translation technology in translation teaching.

Chapter 13
Unmasking the In-Person Classroom: Cultural Advantages of Online Learning in the Chinese Context

Nancy Tsai and Damien Fan

Abstract As instructors who experienced first-hand the abrupt transition from face-to-face to online teaching in March 2020 in the US due to the COVID-19 pandemic, and who continue to adapt to various online platforms and technologies for the T&I classroom in Taiwan, we argue that the online classroom has specific cultural advantages summed up as the 4Cs: immediacy, privacy, intimacy, and democracy. We discuss how these advantages ring especially true for the Chinese classroom, because it is one not known for intimate interaction or lively discussion, but rather a mirror of Confucian class divide shaped by the legacy of the Chinese civil service exams. Findings from regular course evaluations and targeted feedback from students in the US and Taiwan support our argument. The goal is a more inclusive adoption of multimodal learning foregrounding "social presence" that transcends the black-and-white argument of "in-person" versus "online".

Keywords Online learning · Multimodal learning · Social presence theory · Democratized learning · Chinese culture · Confucian ideology

13.1 Introduction

It is not uncommon to look back nostalgically on a relationship and only recall how good it was, like the one we thought we had with the in-person classroom. Memory is unreliable and therefore a malleable excuse to turn to when not all is going well in a current relationship, like the one we are experiencing with the online classroom, expedited and exacerbated by the COVID-19 pandemic in early 2020. In fact, the human-screen relationship has already been propelled to unfathomable degrees of intimacy by the likes of the iPhone, Siri, and their swiping app-driven paradigms. But

N. Tsai (✉) · D. Fan
National Taiwan Normal University, Taipei, Taiwan
e-mail: ntsai@ntnu.edu.tw

D. Fan
e-mail: damienfan@ntu.edu.tw

K. Liu and A. K. F. Cheung (eds.), *Translation and Interpreting in the Age of COVID-19*, Corpora and Intercultural Studies 9,
https://doi.org/10.1007/978-981-19-6680-4_13

if creativity continued to flourish after pen and paper gave way to the typewriter, then computer, and now touch-and-swipe wireless screens, then it can hardly be said that the online classroom "sucks". One would think that Shakespeare himself might have tweeted if he could, maybe even crowdsourced his ideas online, given how attuned he was to the masses and what they liked. The resistance to the online classroom would then seem more like the outcome of overly romanticizing the in-person past, akin to overly romanticizing Shakespeare as a demi-god of high literature.

As instructors who lived through the abrupt switch from the in-person to online mode in mid-March 2020, during the panic-induced first days of looming lockdowns—and as instructors who have continued to toggle between online and in-person depending on fluctuating restrictions—we first present findings from general course evaluations not designed to specifically survey online learning experiences. Because the surveys cannot be said to artificially construct a "good" or "bad" experience, this lends them particular ecological validity. In addition, we also apply the findings of more targeted student feedback to further analyse perceptions of the online classroom as pandemic conditions evolve and restrictions shift. Next we propose the advantages of the online space observed, experienced, and summed up as the 4Cs: immediacy, privacy, intimacy, and democracy.

We then frame the advantages of the 4Cs as especially pertinent for the Chinese classroom, because, traditionally speaking, it is not known for intimate interaction or lively discussion, but one that is a mirror of Confucian class divide, spaced and maintained by one authority. The reason for resistance to online teaching by the instructor, in particular, will be examined as a residual reaction derived from the legacy of the Chinese civil service exams. This framing charges the online mode with a particular cultural dimension that is not apparent in discourse outside the East Asian cultures under influence from Confucianism. Our argument, in conclusion, is for a more inclusive adoption of multimodal learning premised on the social presence theory that foregrounds the human capacity to make a given space engaging, instead of a black-and-white argument of "in-person" versus "online" grounded in technical aspects.

13.2 Course Evaluations and Targeted Feedback

This section covers the courses we taught at an American institution with one of the first degree-granting T&I programmes in the country. They were conducted online from mid-March to mid-May, lasting eight weeks, commencing halfway through Spring 2020 when the WHO declared COVID-19 a pandemic. Since neither of the authors continued to teach in the US after Spring 2020, where the online classroom remained a fixture through Fall 2020 and Spring 2021, we could not see if the mode registered more conspicuously in the evaluations as time passed. We, therefore, also examine the general course evaluations for Spring 2021 and Fall 2021 at a university in Taiwan with a well-known T&I programme. Spring 2021 reflects the period when Taiwan experienced its first real threat by the pandemic after successfully maintaining in-person activities throughout most of 2020 when many parts of the world suffered from debilitating restrictions. From mid-May to the end of the semester in June, a total of four weeks, schools abruptly shifted online, mirroring the crisis mode in the US. The beginning of Fall 2021 was also online for three weeks because of the pandemic.

13.2.1 General Student Evaluations

13.2.1.1 Quantitative Scores (The US)

The courses taught online for the latter eight weeks of Spring 2020 include: Advanced Translation II into Chinese (Sections A & B; 2nd year); Intermediate Interpretation—Consecutive into Chinese (Section C; 1st year); Literary Translation into Chinese (mixed 1st and 2nd year); Advanced Interpretation–Consecutive into Chinese (Sections A & B; 2nd year); Advanced Interpretation–Simultaneous into Chinese (Sections A & B; 2nd year). Total student registration numbers for all courses was 64. Student makeup was majority overseas ethnic Chinese from China (42), followed by Taiwan (11) and Hong Kong (2), then ethnic Chinese educated outside the education systems of China (3) and Taiwan (1), then ethnic white American (2) or other ethnicity and nationality (Indian, 3). Official class size was 12 students per section, but at the time of registration, it could be higher or lower. The main platforms used were Canvas, Zoom, and GoReact. Neither Zoom nor GoReact was familiar to us prior to the shift online.

General course evaluations intend to capture student perception throughout the entire semester, which in this case saw a severe and abrupt classroom disruption due to the pandemic. The online shift was not a choice; it was forced upon both instructors and students. However, this seismic change and the supposed dire plunge in education quality registered little in the course evaluations we received back; neither in the quantifiable metrics of "course organization and effectiveness" (six questions) and "professor effectiveness" (six questions), nor in the qualitative section where students could comment.

Table 13.1 lists the ratings of the two overall evaluative indicators that sum up the twelve questions: Q7 "How would you rate the course overall? (0–5)" and Q13 "How would you rate the professor's effectiveness overall? (0–5)".

Though the response rate exceeds 60% for two courses only, it can be argued that the results are still a good representation of general perception of the courses and the instructor being highly effective because student evaluations are often seen as being driven by bias against the instructor. That is, students are likelier to respond in evaluations when they are dissatisfied rather than when they are content. But instead of reflecting the negative comments in public discourse concerning the online shift, these numbers paint the opposite picture. The most significant case concerns "Intermediate Interpretation—Consecutive into Chinese (Section C; 1st year)". It was argued at the time by scores of instructors how impossible it would be to teach

Table 13.1 Course evaluation scores (US)

Course	Response rate (responses/total)	Q7: Overall rating	Q13: Professor effectiveness
Advanced Trans. II into Chinese (A; 2nd)	33.3% (4/12)	4.8	5
Advanced Trans. II into Chinese (B; 2nd)	55. 6% (5/9)	4.4	4.6
Intermediate Interp—Consecutive into Chinese (C; 1st)	83.3% (10/12)	4.7	4.8
Literary Translation into Chinese (mixed)	41.7% (5/12)	4.8	5
Advanced Interp–Consecutive into Chinese (A&B; 2nd)	63.2% (12/19)	4.9	4.9
Advanced Interp— Simultaneous into Chinese (A&B; 2nd)	56.3% (9/16)	4.9	4.9

interpreting online; how "interpreting" relied on conspicuous human-to-human interaction to "work". However, the high response rate and high scores for both course and instructor demonstrates that "effectiveness" in teaching interpreting and the success of an interpreting course is not primarily driven by the modality used.

13.2.1.2 Qualitative Comments (The US)

Analysis of student comments suggest that the classroom modality mostly registers as an afterthought if the *content* is perceived to be meaningful and the organizational *structure* of the content effective. A case in point is the one comment in "Advanced Translation II into Chinese" that explicitly referred to the online switch. This comment did not fall under "strengths" of the course or what "improvements" were needed, two categories prompted by the evaluation. It was instead under a general prompt for the student to "explain your ratings". The student wrote: "[The instructor's] in-class activities were very useful and interesting. She kept the quality of her classes at a high level even after we switched our classes online. She is the only professor who didn't let this challenging situation affect her classes." Here "in-class" activities do not differentiate between online or in-person, suggesting that the modality is secondary when it comes to how students register their learning experience, which is perceived and expected to be instructor-initiated.

"Literary Translation into Chinese" provides even stronger support that the modality is secondary. This course was an elective that had never been offered before in the Chinese T&I programme. The latter half of this course—which coincided with the pandemic-induced online switch—was designed to use the "workshop" format popularized by the creative writing programme founded in 1936 at the University of Iowa (2022). This format calls for a roundtable discussion of the presenter's work by each participant. The catch is that the presenter cannot explain or defend the work until every participant has their say. This ensures that the presenter is exposed to initial varied interpretation and criticism of the work and that the participants are not interrupted by the presenter's claims of what the work is "supposed to mean". Arguably, to be successful, this format calls for in-person presence because it touches upon highly sensitive human emotions concerning ownership and interpretation of one's own work. "In-person" would also be especially pertinent for students originating from a Chinese context where expressing individual opinion is rarely encouraged and an "authoritative interpretation" is often expected, not to mention that none of the students participating had any experience in workshopping anyone's writing. However, the modality did not factor in any of the comments. No improvements were suggested and among the positive aspects that were described, effectiveness of the format/structure/organization were repeated and "workshopping" was described as "eye-opening" and a "strength". Instead of mentioning any rupture caused by the online switch, students looked forward to the class "every week" and were motivated to complete the homework "every week". One comment even cited the concept of "safe space" for discussion as a strength.

Similar positive feedback was observed in the comments for both "Advanced Interpretation Consecutive and Simultaneous" courses. One student "enjoyed every class". Others appreciated the "professor's preparation...and the excellent use of technology in the second half of the semester", "careful preparation for each class session", and "good curriculum design, professor's instructions, and feedback". This demonstrates that the instructor can transcend the supposed limits of the online space when the pedagogical structure and method is strong. In other words, the online space does not necessarily create deficient learning experiences; it could, however, expose or exacerbate weaknesses in the structure and method that existed *before* the online switch.

One negative comment does draw our attention to criticism of the online mode. For the course "Intermediate Interpretation—Consecutive into Chinese", a student wrote: "[Not ending on time] was especially frustrating when we were online because I had already been staring at a screen for 8 hours that day and just wanted to leave." This shows the physical stress placed on the learner when required to take classes online successively. But the comment actually places the emphasis on repeated physical stress and does not readily cite the online mode as compromising learning content, which is something that needs to be differentiated when we are examining instructor resistance to the online classroom. In fact, one comment of the strengths of this course stated: "It was a lot of fun." And: "I wish I had this class every day." There is room, therefore, to argue that the student can find the online mode physically taxing, but still find what was learned productive and fun. The two dimensions of "online"—the *surface* features of learning and the *content* of learning—are not the same and we should be wary of indiscrimination between them. After all, we neither celebrate nor blame the ergonomically-challenged wooden chairs and desks of the in-person classroom, where students sit eight hours a day, for the success or failure of a course.

13.2.1.3 Quantitative Scores (Taiwan)

Analysis of evolving student perception of the online classroom continued with general course evaluations in Taiwan. Courses examined include: Interpretation I (Spring 2021) and Interpretation II (Fall 2021). The first is a prerequisite for the latter and a significant number of the students remained the same from the first semester to the next. The total student number for Spring 2021 was 25; student makeup was mainly native Taiwanese (23), with one American-educated Taiwanese, and one overseas Vietnamese. For Fall 2021, the student number dropped to 15 due to seniors graduating in Spring 2021. All remaining students were native Taiwanese. However, the student body for the two semesters consisted of a mixed cohort of undergraduate freshmen to graduate students with varying levels of English from a number of different departments. These factors theoretically should accentuate the online challenge.

Because of prior experience with the online classroom in the US, we did not consider going online necessarily a deficiency in all circumstances. So at times the online mode was strategically chosen as the preferred one even when restrictions did not call for a switch. This happened once in Spring 2021, when GoReact was used to carry out the midterm exam in April before the forced shift online; and twice in Fall 2021, when WebEx was used to carry out the midterm exam and the mock midterm exam to walk students through all steps of the online exam. The online mode was chosen because it is much more efficient at testing a large student body in interpreting.

Table 13.2 lists the ratings of the six evaluative indicators. The four-week online shift in Spring 2021 did not make a dent in the scores, even though negative experiences nearing the end of an event may cloud the entire experience as negative (see "memory-experience gap" in Miron-Shatz et al. 2009). Nor did using online exams—a much criticized method—impact "grading and feedback". In fact, the score improved in Fall 2021.

13.2.1.4 Qualitative Comments (Taiwan)

Similar to the results from the American institution, none of the comments registered shifting online as negatively impacting learning. Of the 12 comments provided in the Spring semester of 2021, one student described looking forward to the course "every week". Notably, three students cited the last online class as being the most memorable because it was a "sharing circle" where each student was invited to share their feelings on the semester. Sharing of individual feelings is not usually encouraged and often suppressed in most Chinese classrooms. The cultural unfamiliarity of sharing and the often-criticized aspects of the screen creating "distance" and being "less human" should have significantly compromised the goal of the last class. But students commented how special they felt it was. This again demonstrates the human factor being the lead factor in impacting learning experiences. It leads us to believe that in a heavily instructor-oriented classroom like the Chinese one, if the instructor

Table 13.2 Course evaluation scores (Taiwan)

Main indicators	Interpreting I (Spring 2021)	Interpreting II (Fall 2021)
Course organization	5.0	5.0
Engages student interest	4.9	5.0
Teacher effectiveness	5.0	5.0
Teacher-student interaction	4.9	5.0
Grading and feedback	4.9	5.0
Overall satisfaction	4.9	5.0

Notes Response rate for Interpreting I was 60% (15 out of 25) and 67% (10 out of 15) for Interpreting II

does not see the online mode as a liability, and continues to channel both knowledge and emotions in an engaging manner, the students will not register the online classroom as a liability either.

13.2.2 Follow-Up Targeted Student Feedback (Taiwan)

At the end of Fall 2021, the 15 students in Interpreting II were asked to turn in a final report analysing their own performances and peer performances of the final exam, which was a staged conference event that simulated interpreting conditions. The students were asked to include four parts in their report; the third part was the embedded prompt to survey their online and in-person learning experiences (italics added):

1. One example & analysis of your own performance (when performing your role).
2. One example & analysis of someone else's performance (when observing as audience).
3. *Thoughts on online and in-person learning experiences in the last two semesters for this course.*
4. Other concluding thoughts (if any).

The word "thoughts" was deliberately chosen to avoid suggesting that the students should pick one over the other, an attempt to mitigate the instructor's own biases that may drive the formulation of constructs and questions. The duration of the "last two semesters" was made explicit because the students had taken Interpreting I with the same instructor. Asking them to look at a longer duration allowed for the evolution in thought. Table 13.3 shows the distribution of the orientation of those thoughts.

Table 13.3 Targeted student feedback (Taiwan)

Feedback	Frequency
Clear preference for online	2
Clear preference for in-person	3
Compared two; leans online	1
Compared two; leans in-person	3
Compared two; no clear preference	3
Not applicable (did not address question)	3
Responses/total (response rate)	12/15 (80%)

The in-person classroom does not enjoy absolute advantage because among the 12 valid answers, seven answers took a comparative approach without being prompted, suggesting that extensive experience of the two modes called for the students to perform a more level comparison. The three responses that were not applicable can even be said to render comparison moot—because the three students indeed did talk about their learning experiences, just without registering either modality, implying it is secondary, corresponding to our findings from the American institution. That would make 10 out of 15 answers not showing a clear preference.

However, the point of looking at targeted feedback is not to find a "winner" between online and in-person modalities by way of numbers. That exercise can be infinitely argumentative depending on how answers are labelled and grouped. It is unproductive for our purpose, which is to address the traditional power dynamics in the Chinese classroom. The pattern in the comments shows that students are more receptive to the online classroom two years into the pandemic. Even if the in-person classroom is overwhelmingly cited here by the students as being better at rendering "presence" (*linchang gan 臨場感*)—an advantage we do not deny—we have picked up on language used by the students that correspond to our aims of addressing power dynamics. Among the seven responses that took a level pros and cons approach, three talked about how the online mode offers equal space for all participants. Specifically: "All students can see and hear just as clearly because the distance is the same"; "everyone is on the same screen, given the same space, so people are more willing to talk" compared to in-person where "there is physical distance between the teacher and the students and the laddered rows where the students sit create distance too, so people feel less inclined to speak up"; "everyone has an equal opportunity to speak up" because "once the classroom falls silent, we know someone has to speak" and since it is obvious who has already spoken and who hasn't, the classroom "is less likely to be dominated by a few students" so "it is better for students who are usually more silent". These are qualities of the online classroom that can help the instructor reflect on the culturally charged space of the traditional in-person Chinese classroom and see their educational objectives in the online classroom in a different light.

13.2.3 Section Conclusion

General course evaluations are tested and tried institutional-level designs that attempt to capture the quality of education for all programmes and their courses, while not differentiating between in-person and online experiences. Thus it can be said to offer a more objective picture of how the online classroom *registers* in the student's reflective experience. Moreover, by analysing "narrative" provided by a targeted open-ended prompt, we can also offer a more nuanced qualitative interpretation of their experiences that eludes the more commonly used Likert scale, which may readily compute into statistical evidence, but may fail to offer insight to develop a potential solution or theoretical framework if statistical methods limit the interpretation of the data to be "inconclusive". In both general evaluations and targeted feedback, the supposed deficiencies or ineffectiveness of the online classroom did not readily translate into worsened negative experiences in our courses. This led us to formulate the advantages of the online classroom into the 4Cs: immediacy, privacy, intimacy, and democracy.

13.3 The 4Cs

We call the advantages of the online classroom the 4Cs: immediacy, privacy, intimacy, and democracy. The designation is an attempt to conceptualize our observations and the findings from course evaluations and targeted feedback. These largely fall under the reconfiguration of the conventional classroom space into the "screen", "grid", and "rooms" that enable "engagement" differently from the in-person classroom. This radical transformation of "space", and the new features technology has furnished this space with, allow for what we designate as the 4Cs. Because mainstream public discourse tends to see the online classroom as a makeshift means to get through the pandemic, we have chosen to compare the advantages of this online space with our past observations of the in-person classroom in Table 13.4. These advantages are regrouped according to the 4Cs in Table 13.5.

We undoubtedly did not theorize about the 4Cs before the pandemic hit; nor did we set out to teach by those principles explicitly when the online switch happened. But we have always seen the traditional in-person Chinese classroom as efficiently orderly but effectively oppressive, and always strived to find ways to break free from the silence it creates. When the backlash from instructors and students erupted against the online classroom, but its supposed deficiencies or ineffectiveness did not readily translate into worsened negative experiences in our courses, we sought to explain the resistance to the online classroom from a cultural dimension rather than technical one. Among the possible explanations, we believe a potent one to be the legacy of the Chinese civil service exams and the space and power dynamics it has engendered in the Chinese classroom. Because this is an ideological space, it cannot easily be captured by either quantitative scores or qualitative comments, so we apply

Table 13.4 Comparison of online and in-person classrooms

Dimensions	Comparison of online and in-person
The Screen (immediate; democratic)	Online: with mandatory "camera-on" request, all students are visibly present, on one screen, with names clearly displayed. In contrast, the in-person classroom is more conducive to day-dreaming, hiding behind laptops, falling asleep, texting. It is also harder to remember and call out names if the class is large.
The Grid (democratic)	Online: Level speaking platform in square space for every student because there is no back row hiding or front row hogging. In-person: Students up front get a better view and hear better. Some deliberately try to hide in the back; some may try to "save" the better seats in advance.
The Rooms (private; intimate)	Online: Virtual groups can be created; students can lead discussions in their own "breakout room" without interference from other groups. The instructor efficiently "releases" them from the rooms once time is up; they promptly reconvene in the virtual classroom to report their findings. In-person: Classroom may not be big enough for group discussion, resulting in groups interfering with one another. Discussions become loud and noisy because of interior echo.
Engagement—group (private; intimate)	Online: Instructor can virtually drop in on each group and engage with the group without affecting discussions in other groups. In-person: Instructor's conversation with one group is disruptive to another group; instructor's "looming" presence and movement becomes a distraction.
Engagement—individual (immediate; intimate)	Online: One-on-one engagement with an individual student is created by directly facing the student and seeing their face clearly without the distance between lectern and desk. In-person: Physical distance between the lectern and the student sitting in Row X is not conducive to inviting a student to elaborate on their thoughts; students "give up" more easily. The positioning of the instructor at the front or center of the classroom also imposes "authority", a barrier to dialogue.
Engagement—peer (democratic)	Online: Students are more comfortable sharing questions or thoughts with the class by texting in the chatroom. In-person: Some students are too shy to raise their hands; consistently only one or two extroverted students speak up.

(continued)

Table 13.4 (continued)

Dimensions	Comparison of online and in-person
Engagement—anonymous (immediate; private; democratic)	Online: Quick polling shows what students think about a certain proposition. In-person: Students are reluctant to raise their hands to reveal their affiliations; difficult and time consuming to count hands, especially when meekly half-raised.
Engagement—technical (immediate; democratic)	Online: Quick peer-to-peer, peer-to-instructor, instructor-to-peer content sharing of slides, translation examples, interpretation audio; allows students to take over and lead the discussion because they have technical command of the same screen. In-person: Only the instructor has command of the "lecture" space; cumbersome and time consuming for students to present their findings by coming to the lectern and attempting to make the file transfer or laptop connection work with the one screen up front.

Table 13.5 Advantages of the online classroom

The 4Cs	Advantages according to dimensions
Immediacy	– The Screen – Engagement–individual – Engagement–anonymous – Engagement–technical
Privacy	– The Rooms – Engagement–group – Engagement–anonymous
Intimacy	– The Rooms – Engagement–group – Engagement–individual
Democracy	– The Screen – The Grid – Engagement–peer – Engagement–anonymous – Engagement–technical

a particular theoretical lens in the next section, in an attempt to shed light on the education philosophy behind the resistance that may (un)wittingly make the online mode the scapegoat.

13.4 Space and Power in the Confucian Classroom

This section integrates the theoretical framework of the culturally-charged Confucian classroom to explain resistance to the online classroom, in particular by instructors in the Chinese context. In contrast to the notable Western or non-Chinese scholars who have participated in the creation of scholarship on Confucianism—especially lucid perspectives afforded to outsiders looking in—few, if any, can be said to have experienced being educated under a domestic Chinese education system that continues to draw its modus operandi from a particular construct of Confucianism that serves to reproduce class structure in support of imperial and, by extension, authoritarian rule. In fact, many Chinese scholars who have reached the status of professorship in elite institutions are likely the beneficiaries of such a system rather than its outcasts. Elman (1991) traced this system to the neo-Confucian orthodoxy of the Song dynasty; but since "neo" is not widely circulated outside the field of Sinology, we will not apply the term here. Instead we introduce the Chinese classroom and its ways of stratification as a lived-in experience by both authors, once students and now instructors, providing an auto-ethnographic account of the continued manifestations of "Confucianism", the umbrella ideology, in regulating space and power.

It would be imperative to point out that the Confucian ideology we are referring to as "Confucianism" is separate from "Confucius", the individual, human, scholar, and teacher. This distinction is important because, as Wu (2011) poignantly demonstrated by analysing the pedagogic discourse of Confucius in *The Analects*, Confucius the Human taught through dialogue. The production of knowledge was a co-operative result between student and teacher. Often it was the student who initiated the question, a far cry from the stereotyped Chinese classroom as one dominated by a lecturing teacher and silent (or silenced) students. What led to this epistemological break then? Between the pedagogical vision of acquiring knowledge by inquiry and the insidious suppression of questions and questioning, supplanted by rote memorization, imitation, and repetition in unified chorus. The chasm, we posit, was born from the creation of the Chinese civil service examinations (622; Tang dynasty) and its further institutionalization in late imperial China (1368–1911; Ming and Qing dynasties; Elman 2000).

Though often extolled to have created social mobility via an equalizing platform and corroborated by empirical scholarship showing "examinations of this period [circa 1148–1256] regularly served to recruit into the governmental service a very significant proportion of new blood [men with no family background of official service]" (Kracke 1947: 119), the exams mobilized a societal structure that in effect only consisted of a bureaucratic literati, the throne it professed to uphold, and the illiterate peasantry. The "throne" itself is but a beatified excuse for the reproduction of "the status quo" (Elman 2000: xxix), since real power did not necessarily rest in the hands of the emperor. The abolition of the civil exams in 1905, towards the last days of the Qing dynasty in the throes of modernization, did not end this reproduction of "the status quo". The exams continue to exist in their iterations as *gaokao* 高考 in China and *liankao* 聯考 in Taiwan, and subsequent other forms of exam-based assessments after the *liankao* system was officially retired in 2002 (Chin 2004). Our classrooms are thus compelled to continue the "tradition" of producing students who are trained to do well on exams, but who can scarcely define success or articulate self-worth beyond achieving high marks or passing exams refereed by the state (i.e. the authorities in power). Seen from this perspective, the collective acceptance of state-mandated mask-wearing and all forms of surveillance during the pandemic—the very context we situate our paper—would then not be a collective expression of consideration for others or the "common good"; rather, it would be the expression of minds that have forgotten how to question power because they have been trained in the classroom to attain it through exams upheld by the gatekeepers.

In the classroom, the traditional positioning of the instructor's lectern (or desk) up front, and the rows of students facing toward the lectern and blackboard, is arguably the same in both Chinese and Western contexts. The space designates the individual at the lectern with authority because this person will stand at a considerable distance from the subjects s/he addresses, whom are sitting. This is immediately a top-down structure created by the organization of space. Anyone who remembers being called upon to give a presentation for the first time will remember the nerves required to navigate this space—how the knees wobble, the voice shakes, the hands tremble—because the weight of power is alienating and the body needs to learn how to carry it and imbue the newly afforded space with authority. These characteristics of the modern-day traditional classroom are very similar regardless of the country or culture in which the classroom is located. Yet the practices carried out within this space can be remarkably different.

The authors of this paper recall, in situ, "bad" students being placed in the back rows; students with the top grades granted priority selection of seats in the third and fourth rows; the home teacher perched at the lectern surveilling the class from 12:30–13:00, enforcing "nap time", making sure everyone was face down and eyes closed at their desks; students with bright orange armbands policing the hallways peering in with their clipboards scoring the class on "orderliness" and "silence" at noon; students made to line up in the front of the classroom to receive corporeal punishment for subpar grades on a test; students asked to "self-surrender" to physical punishment because they did not meet their "own" goals of grade perfection (in which the whack becomes a symbolic tap on the open palm because the student came forth "voluntarily"); the young teacher driven to tears, crying in front of the class, because our weekly schoolwide ranking (not yearly, not national) in the subject she taught did not meet her expectations. In this in-person classroom, no one raised their hands to challenge the teacher; no teacher asked us to weigh in. The blackboard was always covered in formulas to take down; we memorized pre-fabricated "interpretations" of literary works—both classical and modern—and copied in silence. This is not nineteenth century China. These accounts cover elementary, junior, and senior high school in the late 1980s and 90s in Taiwan, which promoted (and continues to promote) itself as a beacon of democratic and progressive values. Yet the compliance of mind and body achieved through surveillance, self-surveillance, punishment, self-punishment, and psychological manipulation, all normalized as part of "education", is not at all dissimilar from Foucault's panopticon control, the "docile bodies" it produces, and the violence it conceals discussed in Ford's (2003) investigation of power in classroom organizational practices.

Some may argue that "things have changed". But is a mere thirty years enough to change what has been vividly satirized in fictional form for the last two hundred years and then some? From the fantastical stories in Pu Songling's *Strange Tales of a Chinese Studio* 聊齋誌異 (1740) to the satirical realism of Wu Jingzi's *Unofficial History of the Scholars* 儒林外史 (1750), to Lu Xun's *Kong Yiji* 孔乙己 (1919), a blunt caricature of the deficient student-scholar—the contortion of the mind by the exams has been shown to be woven into the fabric of Chinese life. The longing of *gongming* 功名 (the title bestowed by the exams) penetrates even the dreams of the population, taking on devout religious overtones (see Elman 2000: 295–370) of which any current-day Chinese parent who went to a temple to pray for their child's success in the Exam can relate to. If the body can remember and react to trauma and deprivation long after it ceases to exist, and pass it down to the next generation (Graff 2014; Stein et al. 2009), it would not be unreasonable to argue that for the last 500 years since the Ming dynasty, this distorted version of education—the physical and emotional toll it has taken on each student body—has been passed down to each generation of students and student-turned-teacher, and is a contributing factor to the heightened resistance or averse feelings towards the online classroom, which demands a level of immediate and intimate interaction that has been shunned and suppressed in the traditional classroom.

The transition from the in-person classroom to the online one exposes particular relations of power between teacher and student—manifested as "resistance"—because it represents a Foucauldian rupture, creating a fault line, "where the sediment of a discourse can be noticed more readily because it does not continue as expected" (Ford 2003: 7). In the Chinese case, the teacher can no longer expect to exercise the power provided by the traditions carried out in the in-person Confucian classroom—the sediment of Confucian pedagogical discourse. The teacher cannot wield space in the same way to intimidate, punish, or command the student as before; nor can the teacher use the traditional space to disengage from the student and hide the fact that the Confucian pedagogical discourse shaped by exams *never* demanded that the teacher engage in any critical or interactive way with the student in the classroom. "Silence" was expected, tolerated, and seen as a "cultural" feature of the Chinese classroom.

The online space strips "space" down to but a metaphorical function because physically everything is now "flat" on the screen. The teacher can no longer rely on the familiar organization of order and silence in the physical classroom to qualify their teaching as "normal". They are thrust to confront the eyes of the students staring back, waiting to be engaged. Silence here exposes their weakness rather than helping to hide it. And the teacher is at loss because "engaging" students is unfamiliar territory, a foreign demand. Blame is thus shifted to the technical platform. And because it is indeed more difficult to master the digital platform if one did not come of age circa 2007, when the iPhone ushered in the multi-app swiping paradigm, introspection is conveniently deflected. And the students? Arguably they did grow up accustomed to online reality and its navigation. But since power is a product of relations, the Chinese student is as much at loss as the Chinese teacher, because the student in the classroom can no more expect to hide behind silence than the teacher. Yet the Confucian pedagogical discourse shaped by exams *never* demanded that the student engage in any critical or interactive way with the teacher. The students sit despondently; their docile bodies waiting to be commanded. Blame is thus shifted to the technical platform; introspection is conveniently deflected.

Modern studies investigating learning environments in the Chinese classroom often fail to account for the implications of Confucianism as an ideology to uphold state power via exams; instead Confucianism is regarded or overlooked as a much less insidious form of "cultural heritage" that shapes Chinese students into silent and passive stereotypes in the West's eyes (see Tu 2001; Guo et al. 2017). One of the most statistically robust studies on major online education platforms used in China over the course of the pandemic pointed out that "due to the space distance of online teaching, the interaction between teachers and students is difficult to carry out", so if "the platform can provide rich interactive functionalities, it will be favored by more teachers and students" (Chen et al. 2020: 24). This presupposes that it was easier to carry out interaction between teachers and students in the Chinese classroom before the pandemic and that the onus is placed on the platform to develop technical features to simply "enable" interaction that is hindered by "distance". Yet anyone who has been a student in the Chinese education system or who has taught with the objective of trying to elicit student response in the Chinese classroom will know that the physical proximity of a teacher to a student often yields fear and silence rather than "rich" interaction. And if there is a response, it usually comes in the form of an echo, disciplined and in unison.

It can be argued that "Confucianism" cannot be captured statistically. It must be interpreted qualitatively by reading between the lines of the data, so the studies themselves cannot be faulted on this account. But it must also be pointed out that it may be challenging for Chinese studies to create constructs to capture the positive aspects of online education because the hegemonic existence of Confucian thought compels the subject to articulate the pre-pandemic in-person Chinese classroom as transparently "normal" (Gramsci 1971). It is a taken-for-granted ideological abstraction that conceals what actually took place in the pre-pandemic classroom. From there on, opinion proceeds from a bias against the online classroom. When investigating the effects of different classroom layouts on teacher practices, Martin (2002) characterized three different types of teachers: "the imprisoned, the free, and the simply confused" (153). The Chinese instructor (and student) can be said to fall under "the imprisoned": those whose "[h]abitual ways of seeing and thinking about classrooms create an obstacle to seeing alternative possibilities" (153).

Martin (2002) concluded that without training in environmental awareness, teachers "will be professionally impoverished and pedagogically impaired" (154). Indeed, twenty years later, the instructors in online classrooms could have benefited from Martin's prescient recommendation for training in specific environments. In our own classroom observations over the course of the pandemic, we, too, have observed that effective learning is not premised on the surface features of the space in which it takes place (though they may be facilitating factors). The general course evaluations and student comments complement this observation. Effective learning, rather, is premised on the teacher's cognitive capacity to create an interactive space with students—the teacher who is "free" in Martin's sense (2002: 153) to work *with* given physical features rather than see them as limitations. This is supported by Adelman and Walker (1974), who saw "the nature of talk, rather than structural arrangements, as the crucial indicator of openness" (103). They believed that open space designs or technical tools alone simply result in "innovation without change" if the "nature of talk" does not change, because "talk is the only readily available manifestation of the extent and process by which mutual understandings of what counts as knowledge in any context are transacted" (104). Similarly, Proshansky and Wolfe (1974) pointed out that it is not the physical setting itself that guarantees or inhibits "open" learning, but an open-education philosophy that makes way for it. The traditional Confucian classroom shaped by the legacy of the Chinese exam system was never guided by an "open-education philosophy" but rather a closed philosophy that aimed to maintain "the status quo". Therefore, when we as Chinese instructors say we long for the in-person classroom, we should be mindful and critical of what it is that we actually long for.

Though our own field is T&I and not specifically in educational theory, educational technology, or classroom design, it is uplifting to see that a number of findings, concepts, and theoretical arguments in these fields support our own observations of the limitations of the in-person Confucian classroom, which have led to the formulation of the 4Cs as advantages of the online classroom that may assist us in breaking free from ideological in-person confinements. Notable ones include Proshansky and Wolfe's (1974) findings close to fifty years ago which identified "the most glaring [deficiency]" of the traditional classroom to be "the lack of space for solitary activity" (570). This can be readily addressed by the "privacy" function we have designated as one the 4Cs in using online platforms. Though Cornelius and Herrenkohl (2004) saw the introduction of new tools as having the potential to transform power dynamics in the classroom, in their empirical study "*the teacher*'s support of student learning was *instrumental* in creating the relation of power between the student and the subject matter and in transforming the participant structure of the classroom" (476; italics added). The transformation in question is one where the participant structure becomes more democratic, which is the "democracy" function we have designated as another of the 4Cs the instructor can realize via the online mode. Poignantly, "democracy" is about giving space to challenge the status quo, something the Confucian classroom would do well to exercise.

13.5 Foregrounding Social Presence in Multimodal Learning

Extensive studies on computer-mediated communication (CMC) centred on social presence theory in the last four decades (see Cui et al. 2013) have also put forth the concepts of "immediacy" (Wiener and Mehrabian 1968) and "intimacy" (Argyle and Dean 1965), overlapping, if not exactly identical, with two designations of our 4Cs.

Supported by robust statistical analyses and constructs pertaining to interaction and perception, studies on social presence theory in CMC anchor the human factor and not the technical factor as driving perception of online learning experiences. In fact, these pre-pandemic studies are largely based on distance learning technology before Web 2.0, such as asynchronous email, texts, and bulletin boards—before students were conditioned by social media—and still they found a positive correlation between CMC and learning experience when "social presence" is factored in. This lends to the plausibility that our pandemic-induced use of synchronous videoconferencing platforms—some even with built-in simultaneous interpreting functions—can create equally positive experiences, if not actually "more social presence", as Cui et al. (2013: 679) projected. For this reason, we believe that foregrounding social presence in multimodal learning is the way forward.

As seen in the literature, the 4Cs we have observed as advantages of the online classroom—privacy, democracy, immediacy, and intimacy—have a strong basis in the social presence theory. Though the initial framing of the concept of "social presence" was given as "the degree of salience of the other person in the interaction and the consequent salience of the interpersonal relationship" (Short et al. 1976: 65), a rather abstract framing in the absence of ensuing empirical investigations concerning the construct, we see the research findings of Gunawardena and Zittle (1997) to be the most helpful in the context of the Confucian classroom. Specifically, they found that social presence could be cultured among participants and that the student's perception of the medium can be influenced by the social presence created by the instructor. In other words, in the hands of a skilled instructor, the subjective experience of the medium can be more social and more human, as shown in our "workshopping" and "sharing circle" examples.

This suggests that Chinese instructors may show a heightened awareness to social presence in the online classroom to break through traditional power dynamics in which both actors have explicitly been cultured to deny each other the qualities of privacy, democracy, immediacy, and intimacy. Findings combining the cultural factor of Confucianism and social presence theory would complement Tu's (2001) initial study on how Chinese students perceived social presence in an American classroom by examining how they perceive it in their own domestic Chinese classroom, a facet not yet covered but called for in his study. It could also explain why Wut and Xu (2021) found that the online learning environment was not conducive to establishing either cognitive social presence or affective social presence and why the "social presence phenomenon" (380) found in Gunawardena and Zittle (1997) were lacking in their study. Instead of contributing the absence entirely to the challenges presented by the online mode and the pandemic, social presence theory would account for the challenges created by the power dynamics inherent in Confucianism, which were not accounted for in Wut and Xu's (2021) study of Chinese students in Hong Kong.

The particular challenges of the T&I classroom in the Chinese context further illustrate the advantages of foregrounding the social presence theory in an online environment. As instructors of practice-oriented courses in T&I, we are not primarily tasked to introduce subject-matter knowledge or discipline-specific concepts. We are instead investigating varying ways of rendering a text or oral message into another language under specific conditions. That is to say, we are not introducing what climate change is, what NFTs are, what makes a city "smart", why relations between particular countries are "postcolonial". That knowledge is theoretically established prior to the task of translating or interpreting the literature, speeches, presentations, and panel discussions on those topics. However, the students who apply and we recruit in our MA programmes, to a great extent, are often recent graduates of four-year institutions with little or no professional experience in any field, and therefore have a very thin foundation on any of the professional discourses used in those fields, leading to the impression that translation or interpretation is inherently difficult to learn or teach, when the issue often lies in inadequate student profiles. On top of that, many of our students come with insufficient exposure to their non-native language (mostly English), exacerbating the difficulties in source language comprehension or target language production when either is in their non-native language.

The three respective student deficiencies in real-word knowledge, subject-matter knowledge, and language proficiency require the instructor to give intense oral instructions to address those deficiencies. The result is often one-way communication where, aside from the target translation or interpretation the student produces, the student has little room to engage in meaningful deliberation concerning the language product. Yet foregrounding the social presence theory would allow the instructors to be cognizant that the student must be afforded equivalent social presence to articulate the "learning problem" in order for learning to be meaningful. If we can change our focus from defining the language product to defining the learning problem, this can be further aligned with problem-based learning (PBL), which can also be effectively enacted in a multimodal classroom using everyday technologies (Ioannou et al. 2016). Moreover, precisely because the nature of our courses and challenges are primarily mediated through "talk"—talking about the source/target and interpreting/translating them; as opposed to lab experiments or the performing arts—we are already operating under reduced "extraneous cognitive processing" that may result from too much interactivity generated by multimodal technologies (Moreno and Mayer 2007: 321). This means as Chinese T&I instructors we are in an advantageous position to maximize the online mode to break free from cultural confinements imposed by the Confucian classroom, a unique conceptual vantage point compared to other disciplines and other cultural contexts weighing the advantages and disadvantages of the online classroom.

13.6 Conclusion

One of the largest-scale studies on the impact of the pandemic on higher education (Aristovnik et al. 2020)—a sample of 30,383 students from 62 countries—showed that satisfaction levels of online academic work and life were influenced by a network of complex factors, most discernible in socioeconomic terms and Internet-readiness (Oceania, North America, Europe often showing higher satisfaction and the African continent often showing the lowest); followed by student category (graduate level ranking higher than undergraduate); discipline (students in the social sciences had improved performances); and gender (males reporting more confidence in computer competencies than females) (7–10). This means that the online classroom can hardly be summed up as "sucks" and there is room for many particular angles of investigation into perceptions of the online mode.

Our particular angle of investigation is a cultural one that has permeated the lives of both Chinese instructors and students within an education system governed by a Confucian order in alignment with the goals of the Chinese civil service exams. On the surface, perceived dissatisfaction can be attributed to the online mode, blamed as an artificial obstruction interfering with human talent. However, upon accounting for the legacy of Chinese civil service exams in the context of Confucian order and power, the assumption that there was necessarily open talent prior to technical disruption can be deconstructed to reveal that in the instance of the Chinese context and classroom, the problem may not predominantly lie with the modality, but with the imprisoned human mind, or what Spence (1980) called "the strength and impermeability of the Confucian moral structure" (33)—with an emphasis on "structure" as "hierarchy" masked as "moral".

In concluding, it would be important to point out that the power dynamics seen in the Confucian classroom can be seen in other cultures as well, if not exactly in the present, then certainly in the past, whether in elite European public schools or in the classrooms dominated by Catholic order in old Quebec. Evidently, "empire" and "colonialism" are concepts from the West, and Foucault was not criticizing Chinese society when he surmised:

> that the real political task in a society such as ours is to criticize the working of institutions which appear to be both neutral and independent; to criticize them in such a manner that the political violence which has always exercised itself obscurely through them will be unmasked, so that one can fight them. (cited in Ford 2003: 5)

We thus offer this study as one of the cultural reasons that could explain what on the surface seems like a modern issue of technology, and look forward to future nuanced findings taking approaches similar to ours. There are no doubt limitations to this approach because we cannot apply statistical methods to produce validity scores on our theoretical interpretation of the data, for which the scope is limited. But we feel the findings here can be informative to the extent that they problematize the issue and complicate the argument for both instructors and students navigating the online classroom in different cultural contexts.

References

Adelman, C., and R. Walker. 1974. Open space—Open classroom. *Education 3–13*, 2 (2): 103–107. https://doi.org/10.1080/03004277408558953.

Argyle, M., and J. Dean. 1965. Eye-contact, distance and affiliation. *Sociometry* 28 (3): 289–304.

Aristovnik, A., D. Kerži, D. Ravšelj, N. Tomaževi, and L. Umek. 2020. Impacts of the COVID-19 pandemic on life of higher education students: A global perspective. *Sustainability* 12 (18): 8438 (1–34). https://doi.org/10.3390/su12208438.

Chen, T., L. Peng, B. Jing, C. Wu, J. Yang, and G. Cong. 2020. The impact of the COVID-19 pandemic on user experience with online education platforms in China. *Sustainability* 12 (18): 7329 (1–31). https://doi.org/10.3390/su12187329.

Chin, M.-C. 秦夢群. 2004. 大學多元入學制度實施與改革之研究[Study on the reform and implementation of diversified university admission]. *教育政策論壇 [Educational Policy Forum]* 7 (2): 59–84.

Cornelius, L.L., and L.R. Herrenkohl. 2004. Power in the classroom: How the classroom environment shapes students' relationships with each other and with concepts. *Cognition and Instruction* 22 (4): 467–498. https://doi.org/10.1207/s1532690Xci2204_4.

Cui, G., B. Lockee, and C. Meng. 2013. Building modern online social presence: A review of social presence theory and its instructional design implications for future trends. *Education and Information Technologies* 18 (4): 661–685. https://doi.org/10.1007/s10639-012-9192-1.

Elman, B.A. 1991. Political, social, and cultural reproduction via civil service examinations in late imperial China. *The Journal of Asian Studies* 50 (1): 7–28.

Elman, B.A. 2000. *A cultural history of civil examinations in late imperial China*. Berkeley: University of California Press.

Ford, M. 2003. Unveiling technologies of power in classroom organization practice. *Educational Foundations* 17 (2): 5–27.

Graff, G. 2014. The intergenerational trauma of slavery and its aftermath. *The Journal of Psychohistory* 41 (3): 181–197.

Gramsci, A. 1971. *Selections from the prison notebooks*. Trans. Q. Hoare and G. N. Smith. New York: International.

Gunawardena, C.N., and F.J. Zittle. 1997. Social presence as a predictor of satisfaction within a computer mediated conferencing environment. *American Journal of Distance Education* 11 (3): 8–26.

Guo, J., L. Yang, and Q. Shi. 2017. Effects of perceptions of the learning environment and approaches to learning on Chinese undergraduates' learning. *Studies in Educational Evaluation* 55: 125–134. https://doi.org/10.1016/j.stueduc.2017.09.002.

Ioannou, A., C. Vasiliou, and P. Zaphiris. 2016. Problem-based learning in multimodal learning environments: Learners' technology adoption experiences. *Journal of Educational Computing Research* 54 (7): 1022–1040.

Kracke, E.A. 1947. Family vs. merit in Chinese civil service examinations under the empire. *Harvard Journal of Asiatic Studies* 10 (2): 103–123.

Martin, S.H. 2002. The classroom environment and its effects on the practice of teachers. *Journal of Environmental Psychology* 22: 139–156. https://doi.org/10.1006/jevp.2001.0239.

Miron-Shatz, T., A. Stone, and D. Kahneman. 2009. Memories of yesterday's emotions: Does the valence of experience affect the memory-experience gap? *Emotion* 9 (6): 885–891. https://doi.org/10.1037/a0017823.

Moreno, R., and R. Mayer. 2007. Interactive multimodal learning environments. Special issue on interactive learning environments: Contemporary issues and trends. *Educational Psychology Review* 19: 309–326. https://doi.org/10.1007/s10648-007-9047-2.

Proshansky, E., and M. Wolfe. 1974. The physical setting and open education. *The School Review* 82 (4): 556–574.

Short, J., E. Williams, and B. Christie. 1976. *The social psychology of telecommunications*. London: Wiley.

Spence, J.D. 1980. *To change China: Western advisers in China, 1620–1960*. Harmondsworth: Penguin.

Stein, A.D., F.H. Pierik, G.H.W. Verrips, E.S. Susser, and L.H. Lumey. 2009. Maternal exposure to the Dutch famine before conception and during pregnancy: Quality of life and depressive symptoms in adult offspring. *Epidemiology* 20 (6): 909–915.

Tu, C.-H. 2001. How Chinese perceive social presence: An examination of interaction in online learning environment. *Educational Media International* 38 (1): 45–60. https://doi.org/10.1080/09523980010021235.

University of Iowa. 2022. History of writing at Iowa. https://writinguniversity.org/about-us/writing-iowa. Accessed 11 May 2022.

Wiener, M., and A. Mehrabian. 1968. *Language within language: Immediacy, a channel in verbal communication*. New York: Appleton.

Wu, Z. 2011. Interpretation, autonomy, and transformation: Chinese pedagogic discourse in a cross-cultural perspective. *Journal of Curriculum Studies* 43 (5): 569–590. https://doi.org/10.1080/00220272.2011.577812.

Wut, T..-M.., and J. Xu. 2021. Person-to-person interactions in online classroom settings under the impact of COVID-19: A social presence theory perspective. *Asia Pacific Education Review* 22: 371–383. https://doi.org/10.1007/s12564-021-09673-1.

Nancy Tsai is currently Assistant Professor at the Graduate Institute of Translation and Interpretation at National Taiwan Normal University. She holds a Ph.D. from the University of Ottawa, an MA from the Middlebury Institute of International Studies at Monterey, and an MFA in literary translation from the University of Iowa. She is also an accredited conference interpreter for the Federal Government of Canada. Her research interests include the integration of power relations, postcolonialism, and cultural studies in pedagogy, and discourse in translation and interpretation.

Damien Fan is currently Associate Professor at the Graduate Program in Translation and Interpretation of the College of Liberal Arts at National Taiwan University. He holds a Ph.D. and an MA from National Taiwan Normal University. He is an AIIC member. His research interests include conference interpreting pedagogy, neurolinguistics, and cognitive psychology.

Chapter 14
Teaching and Learning Translation and Interpreting in the Time of COVID-19: Preparation, Class Content and Activities and Assessment (The Slovak Case)

Soňa Hodáková and Emília Perez

Abstract This study provides a wide-ranging insight into the translation and interpreting (T&I) teaching and learning realities at Slovak universities in the wake of the COVID-19 pandemic outbreak. Identifying the key challenges in the changed training scenario after the transition from in-person to remote form, the authors of the study offer a comprehensive picture of the strengths and weaknesses of the training process from the perspective of both students and teachers. The identified key challenges, as well as their further development are analysed from a diachronic point of view—firstly a year after the pandemic outbreak (2021) and then at the end of the third wave of the pandemic (2022), just before returning to in-person on-site education. The presented results were obtained via empirical research conducted at all Slovak academic institutions providing certified training in the area of translation and interpreting. Consequent qualitative and quantitative analysis of the obtained data provides a rather complex perspective on the changed training and learning realities in Slovakia during the COVID-19 pandemic—with the main focus on student and teacher preparation, class content and activities and assessment. The findings of the study shed light on the effectiveness of selected strategies in remote academic training of to-be translators and interpreters and provide observations applicable in the further development of the educational process in the changed training reality.

Keywords Remote teaching · Learning · COVID-19 · Translation · Interpreting · Preparation · Class content · Activities · Assessment · Satisfaction · Adaptation

S. Hodáková (✉) · E. Perez
Department of Translation Studies, Constantine the Philosopher University, Nitra, Slovakia
e-mail: shodakova@ukf.sk

K. Liu and A. K. F. Cheung (eds.), *Translation and Interpreting in the Age of COVID-19*, Corpora and Intercultural Studies 9,
https://doi.org/10.1007/978-981-19-6680-4_14

14.1 Introduction

The unquestionable need for translators and interpreters, as well as their practical training and preparation, clearly have a long history, which, according to Pym (2011) and Müglová (2018), probably date back to ancient times. At the same time, the training of translators and interpreters has always had a primarily practical focus, based on the transmission of knowledge and skills and real practical experience. Institutionalised forms of T&I training reflect this dimension up to this day. Furthermore, a set of enhanced competences has developed in relation to changing social and communication needs (Djovčoš and Perez 2021), as well as dynamic technological development (Gromová and Müglová 2012). The last couple of decades have also seen an increased emphasis on enhancing specific intra- and interpersonal skills (see e.g. Kutz 2010; Kiraly 2013; Hurtado Albir 2015; European Master's in Translation 2017) which are being integrated into T&I curricula in order to prepare future graduates for various scenarios that can be experienced in their future career. The listed aspects have been reflected also in academic T&I education in Slovakia (Djovčoš and Perez 2021), currently being provided in the form of full-time training at five universities at both bachelor's and master's degree level. Before the arrival of 2020, all five universities had been providing T&I training solely in an in-person, on-site format, which, as in many countries across the globe, changed afterwards.

In March 2020, due to the COVID-19 pandemic outbreak in the country, all educational T&I activities transitioned into remote form in an online environment. After initial concerns and reservations of T&I teachers on whether and how all key competences could be equally enhanced remotely, both theoretical and practice-oriented disciplines were modified according to the new conditions and circumstances (Perez and Hodáková 2021). The main intention was to maintain the quality of teaching and learning, as well as to provide student development in all areas needed in their future careers. The aim of our research was to verify whether and to what extent this ambition has been achieved, how much teaching has changed under the influence of the pandemic, and which practices and strategies can be evaluated as examples of good practice in remote university education of translators and interpreters. Our main focus lies on student and teacher preparation, class content, activities, assessment and also workload and the extent of satisfaction with imparted theoretical knowledge and practical skills. In order to reflect not only on initial challenges but also on how teachers and students have adapted to the new conditions and circumstances, the authors of the study provide a diachronic perspective which compares the results of their research conducted a year after the pandemic outbreak and which was replicated at the end of the third pandemic wave before returning to on-site in-person teaching and learning.

14.2 Background

Searching for new possibilities and considering teaching and learning modifications have indeed become a necessity during the COVID-19 pandemic (Ali 2020). Despite being a challenging period, Hubscher-Davidson and Devaux (2021) believed it could be viewed as an "opportunity to rethink and enhance our teaching practices", concerns about the limitations of the online format in T&I training notwithstanding. In order to fulfil such perception, the authors of this study believe that it is important to identify the key factors and effects the changed T&I training scenario has imposed on both teaching and learning process as these can help to evaluate the strengths and weaknesses of necessary modifications.

Based on the results of our previous research collecting perspectives of T&I teachers and learners (Perez and Hodáková 2021), three key areas influencing the T&I teaching and learning process after the COVID-19 pandemic outbreak were identified. The first category—procedural factors—relates to the education process and its individual stages; the teaching process and its individual remote learning forms (synchronous, asynchronous); phases and elements in training; subject material; relayed knowledge, skills and competencies as well as evaluation of the education process. The second category—technical factors—covers the technical aspects of the education process and its individual stages, both for T&I teachers and students (e.g. availability of resources, communication methods, technical devices and manners of operation, etc.). The last category—psychosocial factors—relates to personal and interpersonal aspects that influence the process of remote learning and teaching (e.g. motivation, concentration, communication, social support, stress management, self-assessment, social contact, etc.). Previously identified factors (Perez and Hodáková 2021) serve as a basis for the present study which focuses on the effectiveness of applied strategies from a diachronic point of view.

In congruence with Hodges et al. (2020) and Hubscher-Davidson and Devaux (2021), the current study takes into account that initially introduced modifications of T&I training identified in their previous research might be results of a crisis solution rather than strategically planned design. Therefore, in the present study we focus on teachers' and students' adaptation to the changed training scenario. The study therefore offers a year-on-year comparison of the perspectives of T&I students and teachers on selected aspects of remote learning and, in doing so, we conducted two phases of research. The first one was conducted in February/March 2021, after almost a year-long interruption of in-person training. The second phase followed in February/March 2022, after almost two years of remote education, just before the students' return to the in-person mode. The study focuses on perceptions of the different stages of the learning and teaching process (preparation, classroom content activities and assessment) and satisfaction with the provided learning content (theoretical knowledge and practical skills) from the perspective of both students and teachers.

14.3 The Evolution of the Perception of Remote Teaching and Learning from the Perspective of Translation and Interpreting Students

In February/March 2021, we conducted an empirical, exploratory, quantitative–qualitative study focusing on the training process in the field of translation and interpreting studies amid the changed environment of the COVID-19 pandemic. We focused on the students' perspective, with the aim to identify, classify and analyse factors influencing the remote training (and learning) of students of translation and interpreting programmes in Slovakia (Perez and Hodáková 2021). Some of these factors later served as the basis for our comparative analysis between 2021 and 2022.

14.3.1 Research Samples and Methods

The first phase of the research in 2021 consisted of a semi-structured interview in the form of a focus group with five students of the master's study programme at the Faculty of Arts, Constantine the Philosopher University in Nitra (FA CPU). Based on the findings from the qualitative analysis, we identified the key factors that influenced remote training and learning according to students. In the second phase, qualitative findings from the interview were followed up with a questionnaire used in a subsequent quantitative analysis. First, it was piloted with 10 students at FA CPU and then distributed online to all universities in Slovakia which provide translation and interpreting study programmes. 208 questionnaires have been filled out.

14.3.1.1 Year 2021—Research Sample and Interview Procedure

Five students (4 females and 1 male) of the master's translation and interpreting study programmes at FA CPU in Nitra participated in the online focus group interview. The selection of subjects was intentional and stratified in order to ensure the most reliable representation of the reference population. The sex of the participants and the language combinations studied were representative of T&I students at FA CPU in Nitra. As one of the aims of the research was for subjects to compare individual aspects of remote training with in-person training, students in the later stage of their studies able to evaluate practical in-person training from before the pandemic had to be selected. The group interview lasted 90 min. It took place online via the Zoom platform, in a semi-structured form, i.e. with the moderator preparing basic topics and questions beforehand, and later adjusting their order and asking supplementary questions during the course of the interview as needed. Subsequently, an anonymous transcript of the interview was elaborated to serve as the basis for further analysis and survey design (Perez and Hodáková 2021).

14.3.1.2 Research Sample and Survey Design

In the following phase, an online questionnaire based on the key findings from the group interview was designed. It consisted of closed questions (multiple choice and Likert scale) and open questions providing an opportunity to freely express one's attitudes and opinions. Thus, the questionnaire provided not only quantitative but also qualitative data that strengthened our qualitative analysis of the individual factors. The questionnaire was distributed online to all universities in Slovakia providing T&I study programmes. It was aimed at at least second-year students of bachelor study programmes, as the aim was to compare in-person and remote forms of study, i.e. the respondents had to have attended at least one semester of their study in-person. To avoid undesirable distortion of data, the students did not state which university they attended. The final research sample consisted of 208 students with 59.6% attending a bachelor level study programme and 40.4% attending a master's level study programme (Perez and Hodáková 2021) (Fig. 14.1a).

In a follow-up study in early 2022, we were interested in how T&I students' perspectives on selected aspects of remote training and learning had evolved after more than two years of remote university education, i.e. just before their returning to in-person form of study. Only students in the 3rd year of a bachelor's degree and the 1st and 2nd year of a master's degree had the opportunity to compare full-time and remote learning in this period, therefore these students were selected for the survey from all Slovak universities that provide training of to-be translators and interpreters. A questionnaire was distributed to students in February/March 2022. It was largely based on the first questionnaire administered in 2021, but included some modified or added items reflecting the context towards the end of the third wave of the pandemic and imminent return to full-time study. The research sample consisted of a total of 55 T&I students from 4 Slovak universities, of which 36.4% were bachelor's degree students (3rd year) and 63.6% were master's degree students (1st and 2nd year) (Fig. 14.1b).

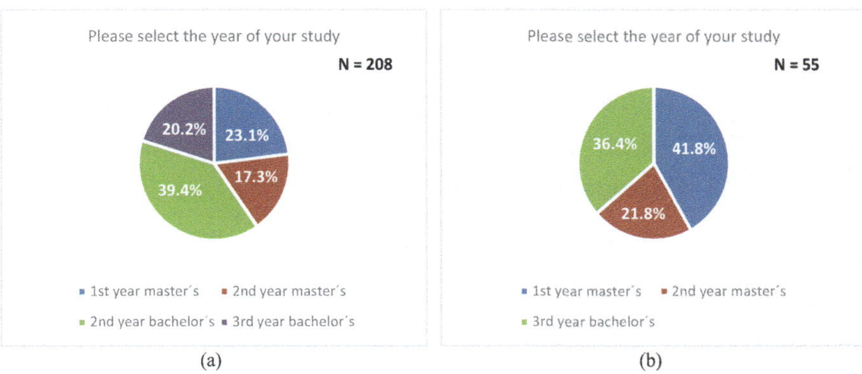

Fig. 14.1 Research sample of the questionnaire by year and level of study: **a** Year 2021; **b** Year 2022

14.3.2 *Data Analysis*

In the following section, we will focus on analysis of the data obtained by comparing year-on-year students' perspectives on the time invested into preparation for the remote mode and students' satisfaction with the provided learning content (acquired knowledge and skills).

14.3.2.1 Students' Preparation During Remote Training

Students in both observation periods (2021 and 2022) were asked to express the level of their agreement or disagreement with the statement, "I had to invest significantly more time to prepare for remote learning." (Fig. 14.2). In 2021, 26.4% of students disagreed with this statement. 50% reported that this statement was true for theoretical modules, and 48.1% agreed that it applied to practical modules focusing on language and culture. 39.4% of students had to invest more energy in preparing for practical modules focused on translation and 38.5% of students claimed to have had to invest more energy in preparing for practical modules focused on interpreting.

In 2022, 45.5% expressed disagreement with the same statement. According to 34.5% of students, the above statement is true for theoretical modules. 36.4% agreed it is applicable to practical modules focused on language and culture. 20% of students stated that they had to invest more time during the remote learning to prepare for practical modules focused on translation and 32.7% of students had to invest more time to prepare for practical modules focused on interpreting.

The year-on-year comparison shows that the number of students who did not have to invest more time in their preparation increased by 19.1%. At the same time, for all types of analysed modules (theoretical, practical modules focused on language

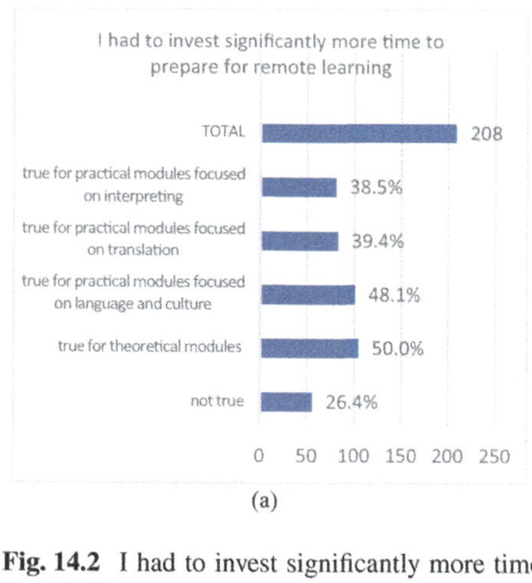

(a)

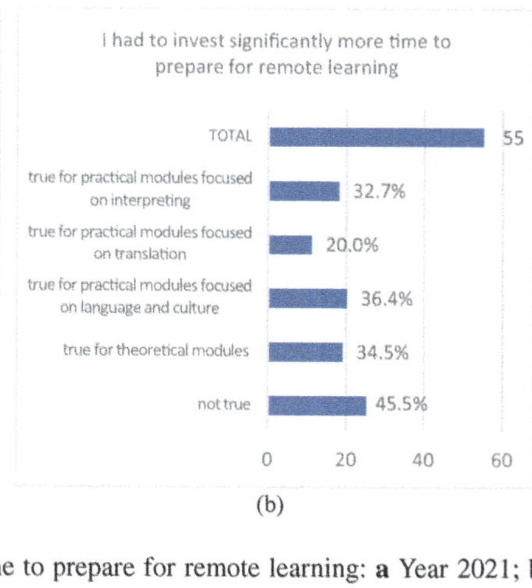

(b)

Fig. 14.2 I had to invest significantly more time to prepare for remote learning: **a** Year 2021; **b** Year 2022

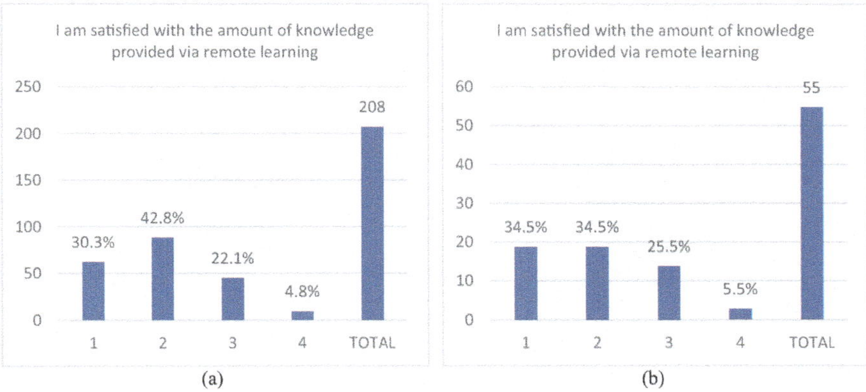

Fig. 14.3 I am satisfied with the amount of knowledge provided via remote learning[1]: **a** Year 2021; **b** Year 2022

and culture, practical modules focused on translation, practical modules focused on interpreting), the number of students who had to prepare more under the remote mode decreased. Based on the findings it can be suggested that the adaptation to the new learning scenario has been relatively successful on the part of students and that they have become accustomed to the preparation procedures and acquired effective time management. At the same time, however, factors on the part of teachers as well as their adapted methodological and didactic approach which will be discussed in the following sections, could certainly have influenced this aspect as well.

14.3.2.2 Students' Satisfaction with Knowledge Acquired During Remote Learning

Students in both observation periods (2021 and 2022) were asked to express their agreement or disagreement with the statement "I am satisfied with the amount of knowledge provided via remote learning" (Fig. 14.3).

In 2021, 30.3% strongly agreed and 42.8% somewhat agreed with the statement. On the other hand, 22.1% of the students rather disagreed and 4.8% did not agree at all. Thus, the majority of students (73.1%) expressed predominant satisfaction with the knowledge delivered via remote training.

In 2022, 34.5% of students expressed complete satisfaction with the knowledge they had acquired and 34.5% of students were equally satisfied. On the other hand, 25.5% were rather dissatisfied and 5.5% of the students were completely dissatisfied. Thus, the majority of students (69%) expressed predominant satisfaction with the knowledge delivered in remote mode, although we see a 4.1% decrease in satisfaction compared to 2021.

[1] Teachers and students evaluated their satisfaction on a scale from 1 to 4. 1—completely agree, 2—rather agree, 3—rather disagree, 4—do not agree at all.

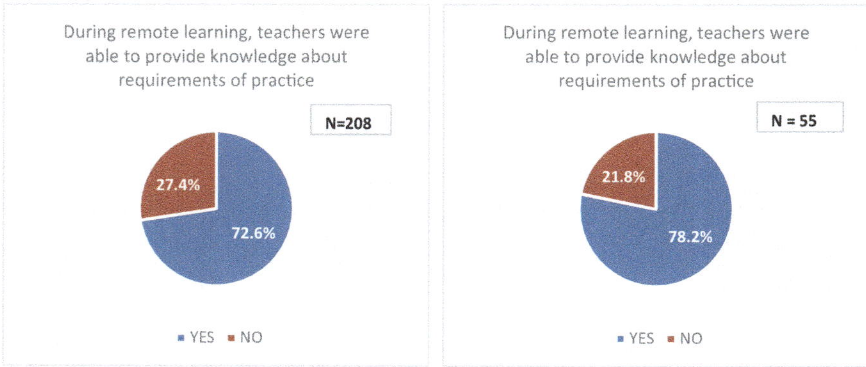

(a) (b)

Fig. 14.4 During remote learning, teachers were able to provide knowledge about requirements of practice: **a** Year 2021; **b** Year 2022

In relation to knowledge gained, students were also asked to comment more specifically on their satisfaction with their knowledge of the requirements of interpreting and translation practice. In both observation periods (2021 and 2022), students were asked to evaluate whether trainers were able to sufficiently deliver knowledge of the requirements of practice (professional matters, market demands, ethical, economic, administrative and legal aspects of T&I) during the remote sessions (Fig. 14.4). In 2021, 72.6% of students expressed trainers were able to deliver the aforementioned knowledge. Conversely, 27.4% of students expressed the view that trainers failed to deliver knowledge on current practice requirements.

In 2022, 78.2% of students felt that trainers were successful in providing knowledge on practice requirements, and in contrast 21.8% felt that trainers were not able to deliver this knowledge. The year-on-year comparison thus shows a 5.6% increase in student satisfaction with this aspect of teaching.

Overall satisfaction with knowledge acquired in general decreased slightly in 2022, which may be related to the fact that students have already completed two years of study almost exclusively in remote mode and may have more doubts about the extent and depth of the knowledge they have acquired.

In contrast, satisfaction with knowledge in relation to practice requirements increased slightly in 2022, which may indicate that teachers have managed to take better account of the professional aspect in their teaching and made better use of the opportunities offered by the online form of teaching—e.g. by providing guest lectures by foreign speakers, inviting practitioners, organising online workshops and webinars, etc.

14.3.2.3 Student Satisfaction with Skills Acquired During Remote Learning

In addition to their opinion on satisfaction with delivered knowledge, students were also asked to evaluate the practical skills they had acquired during the observed periods (2021 and 2022) (Fig. 14.5). In 2021, 19.7% were completely satisfied and 42.8% were somewhat satisfied with the practical skills acquired during remote training. Conversely, 28.8% were rather dissatisfied and 8.7% were completely dissatisfied. Thus, again, the majority of students (62.5%) expressed predominant satisfaction. However, overall satisfaction with practical skills acquired was lower than with acquired theoretical knowledge.

In 2022, 21.8% of students expressed overall satisfaction with the skills they had acquired remotely and 40.0% of students were somewhat satisfied. Conversely, 30.9% were rather dissatisfied and 7.3% of students were completely dissatisfied. Overall, the majority of students (61.8%) expressed their predominant satisfaction with the practical skills they had acquired during remote training. In this aspect, the result is comparable to the situation in 2021, as only a marginal decrease can be seen in overall satisfaction (by 0.7%). However, as in the previous year, students were less satisfied with the level of practical skills acquired compared to the acquired theoretical knowledge.

A possible rationale for the lower satisfaction with the practical skills acquired during remote training can be found in the qualitative responses of the students in the questionnaire. In the responses to the open-ended questions in the 2022 questionnaire, students often indicated greater confidence in the practical skills acquired in relation to translation competence compared to interpreting competence. Concerns about the lack of acquired interpreting competence were mainly related to the fact that the online interpreting training did not, in their opinion, meet all the parameters of an authentic interpreting situation (stress, stage fright, public speaking anxiety, etc.).

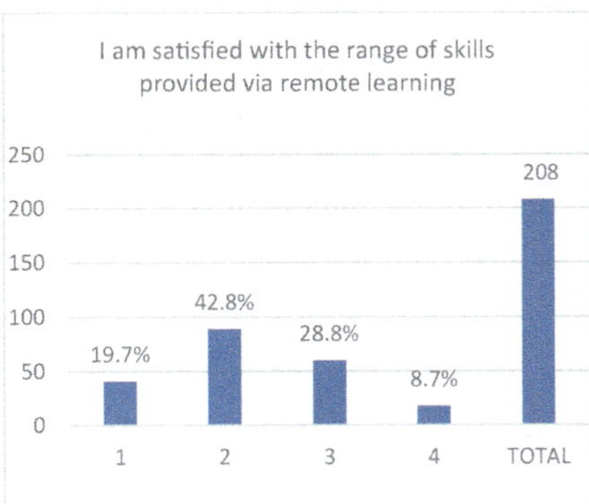

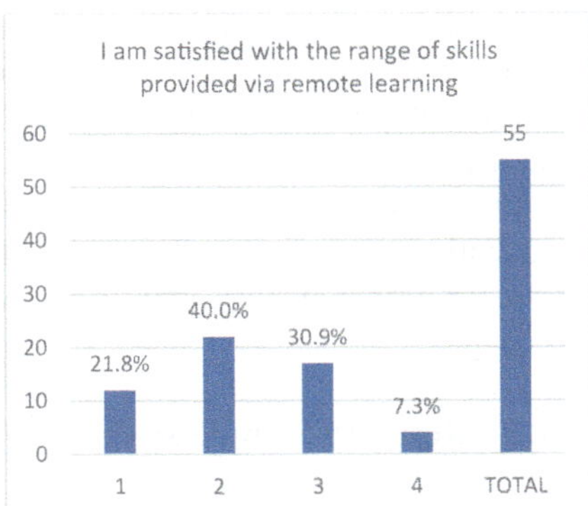

Fig. 14.5 I am satisfied with the range of skills provided via remote learning: **a** Year 2021; **b** Year 2022

14.4 Development of Perceptions of Remote Training: Perspective of Translation and Interpreting Teachers

In February/March 2021 the authors of this study also conducted an empirical, exploratory, quantitative–qualitative study focused on the translation and interpreting training process in the changed environment of the COVID-19 pandemic from teachers' perspective.

14.4.1 Research Samples and Methods

The first phase of the research consisted of a semi-structured interview in the form of a focus group with five teachers at the Faculty of Arts, Constantine the Philosopher University in Nitra (FA CPU). Based on the findings from the qualitative analysis we identified the key factors that influence remote training and learning according to teachers. In the second phase, the qualitative findings were followed up with an interview with a questionnaire to be used in a subsequent quantitative analysis. First, it was piloted with 3 teachers at FA CPU and afterwards distributed online to all universities in Slovakia that provide translation and interpreting study programmes. 33 questionnaires were filled out (Perez and Hodáková 2021).

14.4.1.1 Year 2021—Research Sample and Interview Procedure

Five T&I teachers at FA CPU in Nitra (4 females and 1 male) participated in the online focus group interview. The selection of subjects was intentional and stratified in order to ensure the most reliable representation of the reference population. Gender representation was proportionate to the composition of translation and interpreting teachers and the participation of teachers with diverse length of teaching experience was ensured (ranging from 3 to 40 years of experience). The group interview lasted 90 min. It took place online via the Zoom platform, in a semi-structured form, i.e. the moderator had prepared basic topics and questions beforehand, but adjusted their order and added more questions in the course of the interview as was needed. Subsequently, an anonymous transcript of the interview was elaborated to serve as the basis for further analysis and survey design (Perez and Hodáková 2021).

14.4.1.2 Research Sample and Survey Design

In the following phase an online questionnaire using findings from the group interview was designed. It consisted of closed questions (multiple choice and Likert scale) and open questions providing an opportunity to express respondents' attitudes and opinions. The questionnaire was distributed online to all universities in Slovakia providing T&I study programmes. To avoid distortion of data, the teachers were required not to state their university affiliation. The final research sample consisted of 33 T&I teachers. 54.5% of the teachers in the research sample provide theoretical modules, 33.3% modules focused on language and culture, 69.7% provide practical modules focused on translation and 48.5% practical modules focused on interpreting (Fig. 14.6a). In total 97% of the teachers reported that they mainly used a synchronous form of training (i.e. online interactive class with students in real time) during remote training, while the asynchronous form (i.e. without real-time interactive participation of the teacher) was reported as the preferred mode by only one teacher delivering theoretical modules (Perez and Hodáková 2021) (Fig. 14.7a).

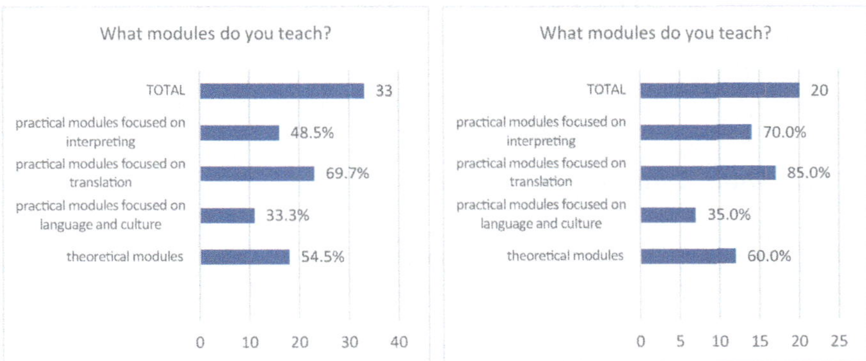

(a) (b)

Fig. 14.6 What modules do you teach: **a** Year 2021; **b** Year 2022

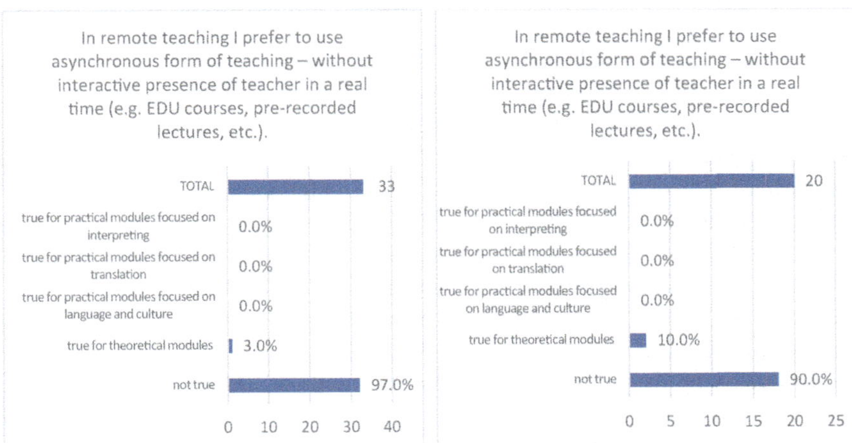

(a) (b)

Fig. 14.7 In remote teaching I prefer to use asynchronous form of teaching—without interactive presence of teacher in a real time (e.g. EDU courses, pre-recorded lectures, etc.): **a** Year 2021; **b** Year 2022

In a follow-up study in early 2022, the authors of this study were interested in how T&I teachers' perspectives on selected aspects of distance training had evolved over the course of time, after more than two years and just before the return to the in-person training format. With this aim, a questionnaire was distributed to T&I teachers at the relevant Slovak universities in February/March 2022. It was largely based on the 2021 questionnaire, but included several modifications and added items reflecting the context of the ending third wave of the pandemic and the imminent return to face-to-face teaching. The research sample consisted of a total of 20 T&I teachers. 60% of them were providing theoretical modules, 35% practical modules focusing on language and culture, 85% delivered practical translation modules and 70% practical interpreting modules (Fig. 14.6b).

90% of the teachers reported that they mainly use the synchronous form in remote training. Two teachers (10%) preferred the asynchronous form for theoretical modules (Fig. 14.7b).

14.4.2 Data Analysis

In the following section, we will focus on analysis of data obtained by comparing teachers' perspectives on the different stages of the teaching process (preparation, classroom activities, assessing students' performance) and teachers' satisfaction with the mediated learning content (theoretical knowledge and practical skills) on a year-to-year basis.

14.4.2.1 Preparation for Remote Training

In the questionnaire in both observation periods (2021 and 2022), teachers were asked to indicate their agreement or disagreement with the statement, "I had to invest significantly more time to prepare for remote training" (Fig. 14.8). In 2021, 24.2% of teachers disagreed with this statement. 39.4% of teachers had to invest more time in preparing for theoretical modules, and 21.2% in preparing for practical modules focusing on language and culture. 42.4% of teachers reported that they had to invest more time in preparing for practical translation modules and 36.4% of teachers in preparing for practical interpreting modules in the context of remote teaching.

In 2022, 20% of teachers reported that preparing for remote teaching did not take more time compared to in-person teaching. 35% of teachers reported that more time was taken up by preparing for theoretical modules. 20% of teachers had to invest more time in preparing for practical modules focusing on language, and 40% of teachers had to invest more time in preparing for practical modules focusing on translation. 60% of the teachers reported they had to spend more time preparing for practical interpreting seminars. In a year-on-year comparison, a slight decrease in the proportion of teachers who spent more time on preparation for remote teaching

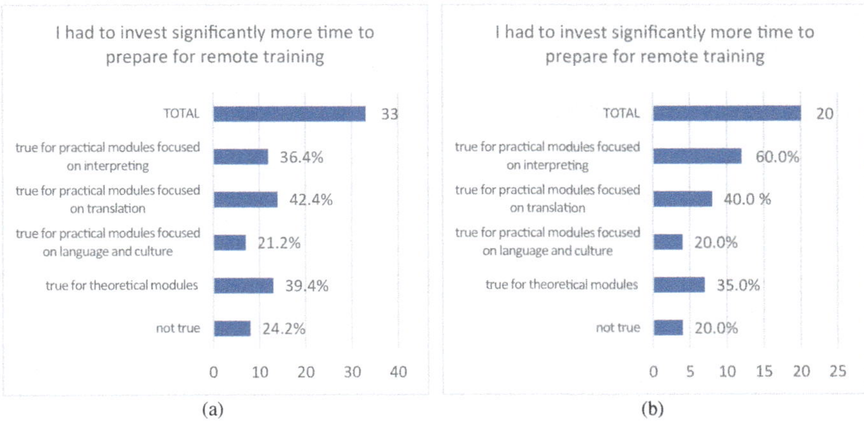

Fig. 14.8 I had to invest significantly more time to prepare for remote training: **a** Year 2021; **b** Year 2022

compared to in-person teaching can be observed. In both periods (2021 and 2022), the same number of teachers (12, i.e. 36.4% in 2021/60% in 2022) indicate that preparing for practical interpreting modules in remote mode required more time.

14.4.2.2 The Need to Modify Activities and Lessons

In addition to preparation for training, our research was also interested in whether and to what extent teachers had to modify classroom activities and lessons during remote teaching (Fig. 14.9). In 2021, 36.4% of teachers reported that there was no need to fundamentally modify activities and lessons. 27.3% of teachers had to modify lesson content in theoretical modules, 24.2% in practical language and culture modules, 27.3% in practical translation modules, and 30.3% in practical interpreting modules.

In 2022, 50% of teachers reported that there was no need to modify classroom activities and lessons because of remote mode of teaching. 15% of teachers had to make content modifications in theoretical modules, the same amount of 15% modified activities and lessons in practical modules on language and culture, 20% in practical translation modules, and 30% in practical interpreting modules.

In a year-on-year comparison, an overall increase in the proportion of teachers who were not forced to modify classroom activities (by 13.6%) is shown. At the same time, the number of teachers who had to substantially modify activities and lessons in all types of modules decreased—by 12.3% for theoretical modules, by 9.2% for practical language and culture modules, by 7.3% for practical translation modules, and by 0.3% for practical interpreting modules.

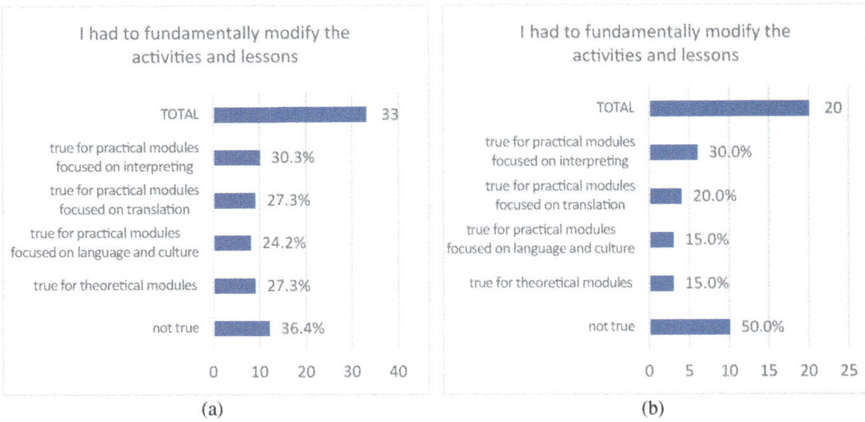

Fig. 14.9 I had to fundamentally modify the activities and lessons: **a** Year 2021; **b** Year 2022

14.4.2.3 The Need to Modify Assessment Tools

In connection with the transition to remote teaching, we were also interested in whether modification of assessment tools was required (e.g. oral exam, written exam, test, presentation, seminar thesis) in comparison with the assessment tools teachers used in the in-person teaching (Fig. 14.10). In 2021, 42.4% of teachers reported that they did not have to change assessment tools to a great extent in their modules. The same number of teachers (42.4%) had to change assessment tools for theoretical modules, and 24.2% of teachers were forced to change assessment tools for practical modules focusing on language and culture. 15.2% of teachers had to change assessment tools in translation modules and 18.2% of teachers had to change assessment tools in interpreting modules.

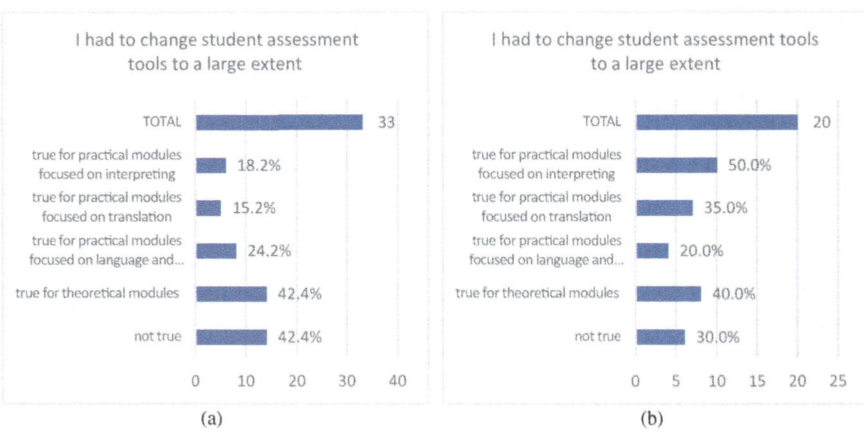

Fig. 14.10 I had to change student assessment tools to a large extent: **a** Year 2021; **b** Year 2022

In 2022, 30.0% of teachers reported that there was no need to fundamentally change the assessment tools in their modules. For theoretical modules, 40.0% of teachers were forced to change assessment tools. For practical language and culture modules, 20.0% of teachers had to modify assessment tools, for practical translation modules it was 35.0% of teachers and for interpreting modules 50.0% of teachers.

In a year-on-year comparison, we see a 12.4% decrease in the proportion of teachers who did not consider it necessary to modify the assessment tools in their modules. There was a slight decrease in the proportion of teachers who had to modify assessment tools in theoretical modules (by 2.4%) and in practical language and culture modules (by 4.2%). On the contrary, there was a substantial increase in the number of teachers who had to modify the assessment tools in translation (by 19.8%) and in interpreting modules (by 31.8%).

14.4.2.4 Teachers' Satisfaction with Knowledge Delivered During Remote Teaching

Analogically to the students' perspective, we were also interested in teachers' satisfaction with the extent and quality of the theoretical knowledge conveyed by them in the remote teaching process (Fig. 14.11). In 2021, 57.6% of teachers were completely satisfied with the knowledge delivered via remote teaching, 33.3% were somewhat satisfied, and 9.1% were somewhat dissatisfied. None of the teachers expressed that they were completely dissatisfied with the knowledge provided by them.

In 2022, 60.0% of teachers expressed complete satisfaction and 35.0% expressed predominant satisfaction with the knowledge provided by them. One teacher (5.0%) was mostly dissatisfied. Again, no teacher expressed complete dissatisfaction with the theoretical knowledge imparted.

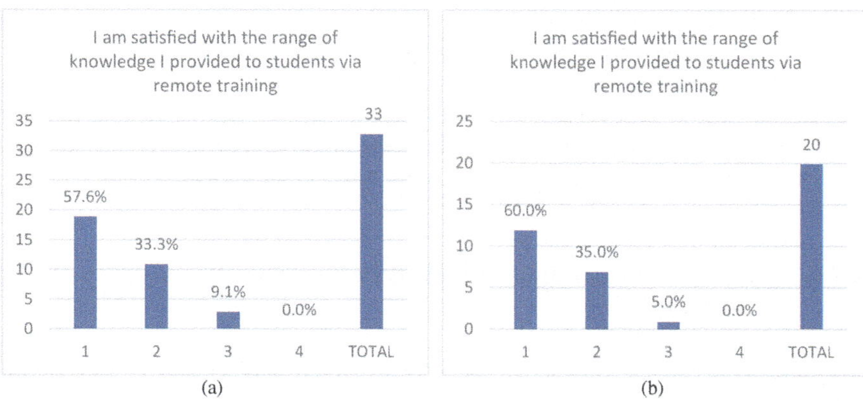

Fig. 14.11 I am satisfied with the range of knowledge I provided to students via remote training: **a** Year 2021; **b** Year 2022

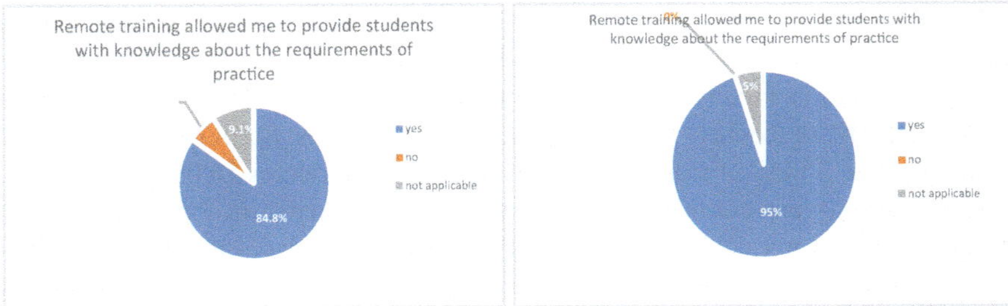

Fig. 14.12 Remote training allowed me to provide students with knowledge about the requirements of practice: **a** Year 2021; **b** Year 2022

Also, from the year-on-year comparison, the predominant satisfaction of the majority of teachers with the theoretical knowledge they had imparted to students via remote teaching is evident. In 2021, 90.9% of teachers were completely or mostly satisfied, and in 2022 the amount increased to 95.0% of teachers.

Similar to the evaluation by students, the research focused also on teacher satisfaction with specific knowledge of practice requirements in both observation periods (2021 and 2022) (Fig. 14.12). In 2021, 84.8% of teachers responded that remote teaching allowed them to convey knowledge about practice requirements to students; in contrast, 6.1% of teachers said that remote conditions did not allow them to convey this type of knowledge to students; for 9.1% of teachers this question was not applicable to the modules they teach.

In 2022, 95% of all teachers reported that remote teaching enabled them to impart knowledge of the requirements of translation and interpreting practice to students, and 5% considered it not applicable to the modules they teach (i.e. one teacher). None of the teachers indicated that it was not possible for them to make students aware of the requirements of the practice under remote teaching form conditions.

The year-on-year comparison reveals an increase in the proportion of teachers (by 10.2%) who positively evaluate the possibilities of remote teaching to familiarise students with the requirements of practice. Compared to the previous year, none of the teachers said that remote form did not allow them to convey this type of knowledge (a decrease of 6.1%). There was also a decrease in the proportion of teachers who felt that this aspect could not be applied to the subjects they teach (4.1%).

14.4.2.5 Teachers' Satisfaction with Skills Delivered via Remote Teaching

In addition to theoretical knowledge, we were also interested in teachers' satisfaction with the extent of practical skills they delivered via remote teaching in both observation periods (2021 and 2022) (Fig. 14.13). In 2021, 42.4% and 39.4% of teachers expressed complete satisfaction and predominant satisfaction respectively with the extent of practical skills they delivered. 18.2% of teachers were rather dissatisfied,

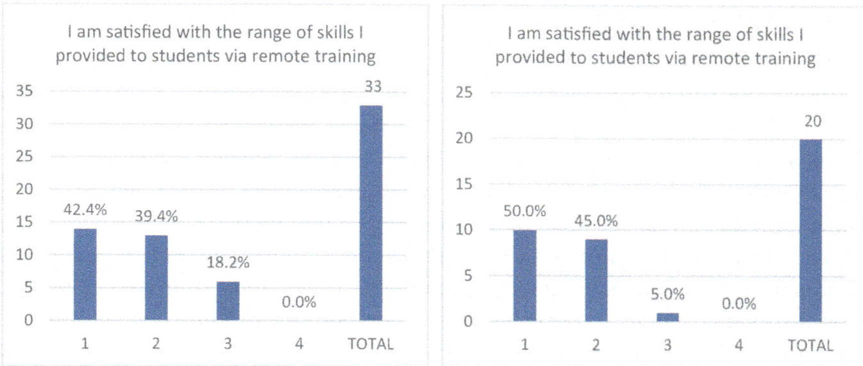

(a) (b)

Fig. 14.13 I am satisfied with the range of skills I provided to students via remote training: **a** Year 2021; **b** Year 2022

and no teacher expressed complete dissatisfaction in this regard. Thus, the majority of teachers (81.8%) were predominately or completely satisfied, however overall satisfaction with the extent of practical skills delivered was slightly lower than for theoretical knowledge.

In 2022, 50% of teachers reported they were completely and 45% were partially satisfied with the extent of practical skills delivered by them during remote teaching. Only one teacher (5%) expressed predominant dissatisfaction. Teachers' level of satisfaction in this respect is comparable to their level of satisfaction with theoretical knowledge imparted.

In a year-on-year comparison, there is a clear increase of 13.2% in teachers' satisfaction with the range of practical skills they delivered. On the contrary, the proportion of teachers who were rather dissatisfied with this aspect decreased.

In total, the proportion of T&I teachers who are satisfied with the extent of theoretical knowledge and practical skills delivered by them has increased in 2022 compared to 2021. It can be assumed that over time, teachers have managed to make more effective use of remote teaching opportunities in the delivery of content in both theoretical and practical modules, both by improving their own technical competence and by modifying the methodological and didactical approaches they have used in their teaching.

14.5 Discussion and Conclusion

The transition to remote teaching and learning has undoubtedly caused changes in many aspects of the academic training of future translators and interpreters in Slovakia. In two follow-up studies, we aimed to map selected aspects of remote education from the perspective of T&I students and teachers in 2021 and 2022. The chapter provides a year-on-year comparisons of perceptions of different stages of the remote teaching and learning process (preparation from the perspective of students and teachers, classroom activities and lessons, assessment tools from the perspective of teachers) and student and teacher satisfaction with the extent of knowledge and skills delivered in the changed training scenario.

In terms of the time taken to prepare for remote training, it can be noted that the number of students who did not have to invest more time in preparation increased in 2022. At the same time, for all types of observed modules (theoretical, practical modules focused on language and culture, practical modules focused on translation, practical modules focused on interpreting), the number of students who had to prepare longer in remote mode than in the in-person one decreased. Based on the results of our research, it can be concluded that over time adaptation to remote training on the part of students has occurred. They have become accustomed to the preparation procedures and acquired effective time management skills. At the same time, however, factors on the part of teachers, their technical skills and their methodological and didactic approach have most probably influenced such development.

From the teachers' point of view, we can also see a slight decrease in the number of teachers who spent more time on preparation for remote teaching compared to in-person form. However, the same number of teachers (12, i.e. 36.4% in 2021 and 60% in 2022) in both observed periods reported that preparing for practical interpreting modules in the remote teaching period was more demanding.

From both perspectives—teachers and students—it is understandable that the preparation process takes more time (and energy). When an activity is new, new skills need to be engaged, requirements need to be modified, ways of working adjusted. After two years of remote teaching, many activities have become more routine and both teachers and students have found technical, organisational and methodological ways to make their work more efficient. All this has certainly contributed to reducing the time invested in preparing for remote teaching and learning.

Another investigated aspect in the case of teachers focused on whether it was necessary to adapt lessons and classroom activities in order to be manageable in remote teaching. In 2022, we observed an overall increase in the proportion of teachers who did not have to modify lessons and classroom activities compared to the previous observed year. At the same time, there was a decrease in the number of teachers who had to substantially modify lessons and classroom activities in all types of observed modules—theoretical, practical language and culture, practical translation and practical interpreting modules. Again, it can be assumed that due to teachers' better knowledge of the technical and methodological possibilities and their greater practical skills in working with the platforms and software used in remote teaching, they have found ways to implement the activities previously used in in-person sessions, thus reducing the need to modify the content of the training. At the same time, teachers also very likely used activities already partially modified from previous semesters conducted in remote form which was also reflected in their response to open questions.

In terms of student performance assessment, in the year-on-year comparison, we see an overall decrease in the proportion of teachers who did not consider it necessary to modify the assessment tools in their modules. There was a slight decrease in the proportion of teachers who had to modify assessment tools on theoretical and practical language modules (by 4.2%). An interesting finding is that the number of teachers who had to modify the assessment tools increased substantially in the case of translation and interpreting modules (up by 31.8%). It can be assumed that with the increasing knowledge of the technical possibilities of teaching and the practical competence of teachers in the use of different platforms for teaching translation and interpreting, as well as their better availability for university departments, not only has the way of teaching changed, but also the possibilities of using different assessment tools have expanded.

We were also interested in the satisfaction of students and teachers with the extent and depth of theoretical knowledge conveyed via remote teaching. The majority of students in both observed periods expressed predominant satisfaction with the knowledge delivered, but in 2022 we can see a decline in student satisfaction with the acquired knowledge to 69%. In contrast, in relation to the more specific question on satisfaction with knowledge of the requirements of the translation and interpreting practice, an increase in the proportion of students who satisfied with this aspect of the learning experience to 78.2% was noted. Overall satisfaction with acquired knowledge has decreased slightly in 2022, which may be related to the fact that students have already completed two years of study almost exclusively remotely and may have more doubts about the extent and depth of knowledge they have acquired. On the contrary, satisfaction with knowledge in relation to practice requirements increased slightly in 2022, which may indicate that lecturers were able to take this aspect of T&I teaching into account and made better use of the opportunities offered by the online form of teaching—e.g. by providing guest lectures by domestic as well foreign experts, inviting practitioners, organising webinars and online workshops.

The students' perspective on knowledge satisfaction was compared with the teachers' perspective. The year-on-year comparison shows the predominant satisfaction of the majority of teachers with the theoretical knowledge they imparted to their students via remote teaching. In 2022, up to 95% of teachers were satisfied with the amount of theoretical knowledge delivered, which is a slight increase in the year-on-year comparison. While students expressed more doubts about the knowledge acquired, teachers felt more satisfied in this respect and probably also more confident in their own competence in implementing desired content into remote teaching. Regarding satisfaction with the transfer of specific knowledge about the requirements of the translation and interpreting practice, 95% of teachers in 2022 reported that the remote form enabled them to transfer this type of knowledge to their students. None of the teachers indicated that implementation of this aspect would be impossible under remote teaching circumstances. In the year-on-year comparison, there is an evident increase in the proportion of teachers who positively evaluate the possibilities to familiarise students with the requirements of practice also remotely. Similar to that of students, teachers' satisfaction with the opportunities to impart knowledge about the requirements of practice has therefore increased, which shows the potential of remote teaching to offer students contact with practitioners as well as market representatives.

In addition to theoretical knowledge, the present research also focused on the satisfaction of students and teachers with the extent of practical skills acquired via remote teaching learning and training. In 2022, the majority of students (61.8%) expressed their predominant satisfaction with the practical skills they acquired. This is a result comparable to the situation in 2021. However, as in the previous year, students were less satisfied with the level of practical skills acquired compared to theoretical knowledge obtained. In response to the open-ended questions in the 2022 questionnaire, students often indicated greater confidence in practical translation skills when compared to interpreting competence. Concerns about a lack of acquired interpreting competence were mainly related to the fact that online interpreting training did not, in their opinion, meet all the parameters of an authentic interpreting situation—they did not have sufficient opportunity to be exposed to pressure, to get to know how to react in stressful situations, deal with specific on-site challenges, etc. The T&I teachers expressed considerably higher satisfaction with the range of skills delivered. In 2022, up to 95% of them were mostly or completely satisfied with the extent of practical skills conveyed. Teachers' level of satisfaction in this respect is comparable to their level of satisfaction with the theoretical knowledge imparted. Teachers' greater satisfaction may be related to their increasing confidence and trust in their own abilities, knowledge and skills applied in remote teaching. However, a natural tendency to not explicitly expressing their own insecurities or shortcomings in the questionnaire could also influence their responses.

The aim of the present chapter was to provide an insight into the attitudes of students and teachers of T&I at Slovak universities towards changes imposed by the changed training scenario and to present the dynamics of their views in a year-to-year comparison. It is evident that the students' and teachers' perspectives on different aspects of remote teaching and training during the COVID-19 pandemic have changed over time. On the one hand, the teachers' sense of competence and satisfaction with the theoretical and practical content of their teaching increased, while on the other hand, the students' satisfaction with the extent of general theoretical knowledge and practical skills decreased slightly. The two groups share similarities in terms of an increasing satisfaction with the opportunity to provide students with T&I practice in a remote manner, and a heightened awareness that this aspect is particularly important in the training of future translators and interpreters. In general, although the changed training scenario has imposed several significant challenges on both T&I teachers and trainers, it has been confirmed that remote learning and training has a potential to enhance students' competence levels and beneficial in the training of future translators and interpreters.

References

Ali, W. 2020. Online and remote learning in higher education institutes: A necessity in light of COVID-19 pandemic. *Higher Education Studies* 10: 16–25. https://doi.org/10.5539/hes.v10n3p16.

Djovčoš, M., and E. Perez. 2021. Training future professionals in Slovakia: Contexts, changes and challenge. In *Translation, interpreting and culture: Old dogmas, new approaches*, ed. E. Perez, M. Djovčoš, and M. Kusá, 221–242. Frakfurt am Main: Peter Lang.

European Master's in Translation. 2017. EMT competence framework. https://ec.europa.eu/info/resources-partners/european-masters-translation-emt/european-masters-translation-emt-explained_en. Accessed 10 May 2022.

Gromová, E., and D. Müglová. 2012. New trends in training would-be translators and interpreters in the light of current market demands. In *Teaching translation and interpreting skills in the 21st century*, ed. J. Zehnalová, O. Molnár, and M. Kubánek, 117–124. Olomouc: Palacky University.

Hodges, C., S. Moore, B. Lockee, T. Trust, and A. Bond. 2020. The difference between emergency remote teaching and online learning. *Educause Review*. https://er.educause.edu/articles/2020/3/the-difference-between-emergency-remote-teaching-and-onlinelearning. Accessed 5 May 2022.

Hubscher-Davidson, S., and J. Devaux. 2021. Teaching translation and interpreting in virtual environments. *Journal of Specialised Translation* 36b: 184–192.

Hurtado Albir, A. 2015. The acquisition of translation competence. Competences, tasks, and assessment in translator training. *Meta* 60 (2): 256–280. https://doi.org/10.7202/1032857ar.

Kiraly, D. 2013. Towards a view of translator competence as an emergent phenomenon: Thinking outside the box(es). In *New prospects and perspectives for educating language mediators*, ed. D. Kiraly, S. Hansen-Schirra, and K. Maksymski, 197–224. Tübingen: Narr Verlag.

Kutz, W. 2010. *Dolmetschkompetenz: Was muss der Dolmetscher wissen und können?* München: European University Press.

Müglová, D. 2018. *Komunikácia, preklad, tlmočenie, alerbo prečo padloa Babylonská veža*. Nitra: Enigma Publishing.

Perez, E., and S. Hodáková. 2021. Translator and interpreter training during the COVID-19 pandemic: Procedural, technical and psychosocial factors in remote training. *Current Trends in Translation Teaching and Learning* E 8: 276–312. https://doi.org/10.51287/cttle20219.

Pym, A. 2011. Training translators. In *The Oxford handbook of translation studies*, ed. K. Malmkjær and K. Windle, 475–489. New York: Oxford University Press.

Soňa Hodáková is Associate Professor at the Department of Translation Studies at the Faculty of Arts of Constantine the Philosopher University in Nitra. She lectures on translation, interpreting and psychosocial aspects of interpreting. She also has a Postgraduate Degree in Psychology. Her research focuses on psychological and cognitive aspects of interpreting, e.g. stress, effort, working memory and motivation. She works as a freelance translator and conference interpreter. She is a member of the examining committee for court interpreters at the Institute of Interpreting in Nitra, Slovakia. She is a member of the editorial board of the scientific journal Bridge: Trends and Traditions in Translation Studies.

Emília Perez is Associate Professor and Head of the Department of Translation Studies, Constantine the Philosopher University in Nitra, Slovakia. She focuses on audiovisual translation and media accessibility, translator competences and business administration in translation. Since 2019, she has been an Executive Board member of the European Master's in Translation network (EMT). In 2020 she set up the EMT working group on AVT and media accessibility training (31 members from 13 countries). She is Editor-in-Chief of the journal Bridge: Trends and Traditions in Translation and Interpreting Studies and a member of the scientific board of the Journal of Audiovisual Translation (JAT). She has also been an invited expert and trainer in AVT, e.g. the One World Film Festival (2020) and the Directorate-General for Education, Youth, Sport and Culture of the European Commission, Brussels (2021).

Chapter 15
Regrouping During COVID: Attitudes Toward In-Person and Remote Instruction in a Graduate Studies Program

David B. Sawyer

Abstract The onset of the COVID-19 pandemic necessitated an abrupt transition to remote instruction in many translation and interpreting programs. For curricula designed for online learning, this change may not have been considerable. For classroom-based models, however, the transition from in-person to remote instruction represented a marked shift. This chapter presents a small-scale case study of the pandemic experience in a graduate-level program designed exclusively for in-person instruction at a university in the United States. Focus groups with students and instructors document the impact of the pandemic on teaching and learning and resulting shifts in attitude to in-person versus remote instruction. The results of the data analysis present options for re-thinking the program's approach to online instruction after the pandemic.

Keywords COVID-19 pandemic · Curriculum · Focus group · Graduate studies · Interpreting · Online instruction · Remote instruction · Translation

15.1 Introduction

The COVID-19 pandemic was a watershed moment for instruction in translation and interpreting, particularly for those programs that had a limited amount of distance or blended learning built into their curriculum models. One such program was Graduate Studies in Interpreting and Translation (GSIT) in the University of Maryland's Department of Communication. Given the proximity of the campus to Washington DC, where there is one of the largest institutional and freelance markets in North America, the program was designed almost exclusively for in-person instruction (Sawyer and Parry-Giles 2013). Aside from field trips and excursions to employer organizations in the greater Washington area, instruction was primarily in-person in College Park, Maryland, roughly 9 miles from downtown Washington

---

D. B. Sawyer (✉)
The University of Maryland, College Park, Washington, Maryland, USA
e-mail: dbsawyer@umd.edu

K. Liu and A. K. F. Cheung (eds.), *Translation and Interpreting in the Age of COVID-19*, Corpora and Intercultural Studies 9,
https://doi.org/10.1007/978-981-19-6680-4_15

DC and accessible via metro. While the role of e-learning had been discussed extensively in the teaching community prior to the pandemic (see Bao 2015; Ko 2015; Moser-Mercer 2015), the discussion has taken on a qualitatively new dimension, given the abrupt transitions necessitated by the pandemic and widely recognized adjustments required in teaching methodology.

The onset of the pandemic in the United States in March 2020 led the GSIT program to shift to synchronous online instruction over a weeklong spring break, resulting in hectic work to try out hitherto unused videoconferencing platforms, set guidelines, and equip instructors and students to finish the remaining weeks of the semester as best they could, including meeting graduation requirements in terms of final testing. One instructor who played a central role in the pivot to online instruction commented as follows on not only the abrupt transition to a virtual classroom but also the role of students who volunteered in their language communities to facilitate communication about the pandemic:

> From a logistics perspective, all language-specific instructors innovated and collaborated across the board in order to deliver those best practices to our students and fulfill GSIT graduation requirements. The challenges of virtual learning only fueled the resolve of GSIT leadership and instructors to carefully curate final exams and meet rapid deadlines and requirements. … This sense of urgency was by no means limited to the classroom. From the very start of the pandemic, our GSIT students turned to the needs of diaspora communities at large in order to inform our publics on pandemic updates and resources available in the community. For example … our students consistently came back to our GSIT professional development classes with updates on how they (our GSIT students) were volunteering as interpreters and translators in order to get the immediate word out on the changing parameters of the pandemic. (Miriam Stanicic, email message to author, March 30, 2022)

While program administrators were left with little choice but to make the transition to online instruction and did so with a remarkable degree of success, they also were faced with tough choices regarding program management. When it became apparent that the pandemic would not subside over the summer of 2020, the program director decided to defer enrolment of incoming first-year students, many of whom would have difficulty traveling to the U.S. from abroad, and concentrate on providing online instruction for students already admitted to the second year. A new cohort of students entered the following year, in fall 2021, and instruction was a mixture of in-person courses, with a mask mandate, and online courses, throughout the academic year 2021/22. As a result of these developments, the program has been able to gain almost two years of experience with remote instruction and two semesters of masked in-person instruction during the pandemic.

As the pandemic subsides and attention turns to the lessons learned from this public health crisis, questions arise about the experience with instruction during this period. The pandemic forced the GSIT program to adapt and build unplanned and unexpected capacity for online instruction in the exigency of the moment. Yet uncertainty remains about the quality of online versus in-person instruction and the future role of remote teaching in the program. An evaluation of this experience during the pandemic supports the program in making long-term decisions on structuring its curriculum. Central is the experience of students and instructors, and whether their views and opinions of in-person and online instruction for translation and interpreting may have changed during the pandemic.

This chapter offers a case study exploring the impact of the transition away from an almost entirely in-person curriculum to remote instruction and the experience with both in-person and online instruction among students and instructors during the pandemic. The case study uses focus group methodology to gather qualitative data on shifts in attitude to in-person versus remote instruction as well as the type and scope of adaptations made to teaching and learning. It is hoped that this analysis will not only serve as an illustrative example but also inform the future direction of the program.

15.2 Study Rationale

Several overarching considerations drove the rationale for and design of a case study employing focus group methodology. The GSIT program enrols on average between 15 and 25 students per year, and the timeframe under consideration was restricted to the pandemic. The limited number of possible study participants meant that a large amount of quantitative data, for example related to learning outcomes, would not be available. However, with a clearly delineated time period under observation and set number of possible interviewees (Merriam 2009: 41), an exploratory case study could generate a rich, 'thick' (Geertz 1973) description of cultural and contextual factors, looking in-depth into the specifics of the GSIT program as a "unique" (Stake 1995: 1–14) and "bounded system" (Merriam 2009; Saldanha and O'Brien 2013: 209).

Given the pre-pandemic curriculum model based upon in-person instruction, the focus of the study is on the impact of abrupt and marked changes in instructional practices in a specific institutional and curricular context. Interest is primarily in the 'how' and 'why' of pandemic-related changes to instruction, in a contemporary 'case' that has the potential to be expanded and eventually include multiple sources of evidence (Yin 2018: 126–129). Thus, the initial goal of this exploratory case study is to capture highly descriptive focus group data that can be grouped into meaningful categories and themes, with the objective of making sense of what is found during the discovery process (Gillham 2000: 6).

The data analysis can (1) inform further steps in gathering evidence and eventually (2) inform decisions on how GSIT's curriculum model might be adjusted based upon lessons learned during the pandemic. These considerations result in the generation of four overarching research questions:

1. What was the impact of the COVID-19 pandemic on teaching and learning in the GSIT program?
2. Did attitudes towards and opinions of in-person and online instruction among students and instructors change as a result of the COVID-19 pandemic?
3. How should the program approach in-person and remote instruction after the pandemic?
4. Did the focus groups generate sufficient data for decision-making, or is additional data collection, through other research methodologies, recommended?

15.3 Methodology

15.3.1 Focus Group Design

Initial steps in designing the focus group methodology included development of the study rationale, interview guide, an e-mail template for recruitment purposes, and consent forms for IRB review and approval. Zoom was chosen as a videoconferencing application for the focus groups given the limited options for in-person sessions on the university campus during COVID, participants' familiarity with Zoom, ease of scheduling, and its technology features including functionality for video-recording, automated transcription, polling, and chat. The focus group design included separate sessions for students versus instructors, given the evident power dynamics that would be in play if the two groups were mingled.

Participants were informed in the consent process that confidentiality of their contributions would be secured to the extent possible but could not be guaranteed in a discussion with multiple participants. The sessions would be recorded and transcribed, and the transcripts coded to remove identifying information. Participants were informed that the data and analysis would be written up in a study to inform curricular planning in the GSIT program, possibly published, and all records would be destroyed. The researcher requested contact information in the event that a need for clarification arose. Providing contact information was optional.

The data collected during the focus group sessions were transcribed using the automated transcription function in Zoom and exported. The transcripts were edited to correct transcription errors and coded for further analysis. Pseudonyms were assigned after the export process. A key was created to link personally identifiable information to pseudonyms. The Zoom polling function was also used to capture participant background data at the start of each focus group. These data were also exported and pseudonyms assigned after the export process.

The following section provides information on the focus group procedures, including the background questions for participants, discussion questions for the sessions, participant recruiting, and the number of participants and sessions.

15.3.2 Focus Group Procedures

The target focus group size was 5–10 participants, and the expected length between 45 and 60 min. Participants were asked to give their consent to be video-recorded at the start of the focus group session. Video recording was mandatory for participation.

Participants were asked to complete a brief multiple choice questionnaire using the Zoom polling function at the start of the focus group session to capture background information. The poll results were not shown to participants during the focus group. Then, participants were asked open-ended questions about their experience with in-person and online instruction before the onset of the COVID-19 pandemic, their experience with in-person and online instruction in the GSIT program during the pandemic, and their conclusions and recommendations for the program based upon this experience. While initial framing questions were included in the participant consent form, the background and discussion questions were developed further and sent to the participants several days before the pertinent session, so that participants had an opportunity to think about them in advance.

15.3.2.1 Focus Group Questions

Participant Background Questions—Demographic baseline questions targeted direct experience in the GSIT program, either as a student or instructor, and captured experience with courses, degree track, and language combination. For students, the Zoom poll included three questions:

1. What is your degree track?
2. What is your semester of study?
3. What is your language combination for studying in the GSIT program?

For instructors, the Zoom poll included four questions:

1. How many years of teaching experience do you have?
2. What is your professional specialization in translation and/or interpreting?
3. What GSIT courses have you taught?
4. What is your language combination for teaching in the GSIT program?

Discussion Questions—The research questions presented under the study rationale above were considered too broad to be asked in the same form in the focus group. They were operationalized as the following discussion questions, which provided a more detailed structure and ensured the flow of the conversation. The discussion questions were worded so that they applied to both students and instructors as interlocutors and addressed three areas: (1) experience with and views of online instruction in general prior to the pandemic, (2) the experience with online instruction in translation and interpreting before and during the pandemic, and (3) considerations and recommendations for the GSIT program post-pandemic. There were 11 questions in total.

There were two general questions about online instruction:

1. What was your experience with online instruction in general before the COVID-19 pandemic?
2. What opinion of or attitude toward online instruction in general did you have before the pandemic?

There were six questions about online instruction in translation and interpreting:

3. What opinion of or attitude toward online instruction in translation and/or interpreting in particular did you have before the pandemic?
4. When the pandemic started, what happened with instruction?

5. What has been your experience overall with online instruction in the GSIT program during pandemic?
6. How have you adapted your learning/teaching strategies to online instruction resulting from the pandemic?
7. For classes offered on campus during the pandemic, what impact has the wearing of masks had on instruction?
8. How did your opinion of or attitude toward online instruction in translation and/or interpreting change as a result of this experience, if at all?

There were two question about considerations for online instruction after the pandemic and one follow-up question at the close of the discussion:

9. What areas of instruction in interpreting and/or translation are suitable or not suitable for online instruction? Why?
10. The GSIT curriculum was designed exclusively for in-person instruction. Should this approach be reconsidered in light of your experience? If yes, what would you recommend?
11. Do you have any other observations that you would like to share?

15.3.2.2 Recruiting

Participants were recruited from students and instructors studying and teaching in the GSIT program from the onset of the pandemic in March 2020 through the spring semester in the academic year 2021/22. Recruitment was conducted via email. The only eligibility criteria were status as a student or instructor in the GSIT program during this time period.

Potential participants were invited via e-mail to a focus group discussion on the video-conferencing platform Zoom and provided information on the consent process. Multiple e-mail messages were required to recruit a sufficient number of participants: five invitations were sent to the student group, and three to the instructor group. Participants received the consent form via e-mail and had the opportunity to discuss it on Zoom or over the telephone. Participants returned the signed form via e-mail attachment.

In total, the focus group candidates included 27 students and 27 instructors. Five students indicated an interest in the focus group sessions, but only three participated due to scheduling constraints. Nine instructors indicated an interest in the focus group sessions, and 6 participated.

15.3.2.3 Focus Group Sessions and Participants

Two focus group sessions were conducted: one with students, and one with instructors.

Student Focus Group—A focus group with three students was held on April 17, 2022, for a duration of 45 min. The participants' provided the following responses to the background questions asked via the Zoom poll:

1. What is your semester of study?

Two participants were in their second semester of study. One participant had graduated.

2. What is your degree track?

One participant was studying in the Master of Professional Studies in Interpreting degree program. One participant was studying in the Master of Professional Studies in Translation degree program. One participant had graduated from the Master of Professional Studies in Translation degree program.

3. What is your language combination for studying in the GSIT program?

Two participants were studying toward the language combination English A, Arabic B. One participant had graduated with the language combination English A, Portuguese B.

Instructor Focus Group—A focus group with 6 instructors was held on April 30, 2022, for a duration of 1 h and 10 min. The participants provided the following responses to the background questions asked via the Zoom poll:

1. How many years of teaching experience do you have?

One instructor had 1–3 years of teaching experience. Three instructors had 4–6 years of teaching experience. Two instructors had 7–10 years of teaching experience.

2. What is your professional specialization in translation and/or interpreting?

Two instructors were specialized in conference/diplomatic interpreting. One instructor was specialized in conference/diplomatic interpreting, court/public service interpreting, and project management. One instructor was specialized in English language enhancement. One instructor was specialized in translation, and one instructor was specialized in translation and project management.

3. What GSIT courses have you taught?

Collectively, the focus group participants had taught introductory and advanced consecutive and simultaneous interpreting courses, introductory and advanced translation courses, intensive writing and fluency enhancement for English, as well as courses in communication management and workplace processes and procedures. They had also prepared students to take their degree examinations and submit and defend their career portfolios, both graduation requirements.

4. What is your language combination for teaching in the GSIT program?

One instructor taught English enhancement courses. Another instructor taught in the language combination English A, Russian A. The third instructor taught in the language combination English A, Spanish B, and French C. The fourth instructor taught in the language combination English and Spanish A, French B, and Portuguese C. Two additional instructors taught in the language combination English A and Spanish B.

15.4 Data Analysis

After export of the transcriptions and assignment of pseudonyms to protect the anonymity of participants, the data were color-coded for basic sentiment analysis: positive and negative attitudes towards in-person and online instruction. A third colour code was used to capture other comments of interest, including recommendations for the period after the pandemic.

After coding, the comments were sorted and grouped and analysed for subthemes within each category. Comments were further grouped into five subcategories:

- Attitudes toward in-person and online instruction pre-pandemic
- Shifts in attitudes during the pandemic
- Advantages of in-person or online instruction
- Disadvantages in-person or online instruction
- Considerations and recommendations for the program post-pandemic.

In each category, themes emerged that were specific to either the students or instructors, or shared.

15.5 Results

15.5.1 Attitudes Toward In-Person and Online Instruction Pre-pandemic

Students—None of the students had fully embraced online learning prior to the pandemic. Some students were comfortable with online instruction, having resorted to virtual platforms with an instructor in a small group class for scheduling and logistical reasons prior to the pandemic, and all clearly preferred in-person instruction. One student was also used to running a business remotely and commented: "*I think my opinions of it were pretty positive. I've been working from home since 2011 anyway, and I was already running the business remotely, so having to do stuff online wasn't that much of a change of pace for me.*"

Some students had primarily negative views of online instruction pre-pandemic and, as students, had little recent experience with remote instruction. Some had not taken any online courses and did not have a specific view of what online instruction might entail: "*I guess my only idea of what online instruction might be … I definitely had a negative view of it. The biggest problem with doing things online would be technical issues. It's very common. In time zones all over the world, it's often very, very difficult to get everyone all together at once.*" Some firmly held the belief that practical skills courses are best held in person: "*So for me interpretation and translation were more about practice than learning [content], which I thought would have been done better if it was hundred percent in person.*"

Instructors—Attitudes of instructors toward online instruction ranged pre-pandemic from neutral—particularly in cases where they were used to or saw the advantages of remote work—to decidedly negative opinions. One comment was echoed several times: "*Before the pandemic … I held a very dim view of it.*" Among those instructors decidedly against the idea, some had little experience with or current conceptualizations of online instruction and how it might work for teaching translation and/or interpreting: "*I … had no previous experience with online teaching and … I had a very dim view of it, I never thought that was a good idea.*" When some instructors accepted their teaching assignments, the trajectory of the pandemic was not yet clear:

> I was pretty adamant that it had to be in person and did not want to teach … online. I was somewhat dismayed that the pandemic was still going on, when I started teaching, because .. at that time we thought we were going to be going back and that you know, things [would be] better.

Chief among their concerns were the difficulties of managing a virtual classroom for the first time, compromised teaching methodology, and inability to build effective relationships with the students in their classrooms, which they felt would suffer from holding class using a videoconferencing platform.

15.5.2 Shifts in Attitudes During the Pandemic

Students—The attitudes of students toward online instruction shifted overall in a positive direction through the experience of the pandemic: "*I do think that my opinion of online communication has changed in that it is a tool that I think is … good … to have around.*" One student remarked that it showed commitment if the instructor was willing to offer online instruction and could make it a positive learning experience. Despite this positive trend, the students identified shortcomings that they continued to associate with online instruction, or that they were able to identify through their pandemic-related experience: "*I think that communication in general is always most effective when it's face to face, and this isn't.*"

Instructors—The attitudes of instructors shifted in a markedly positive direction as a result of their experience during the pandemic, despite initial anxiety about the abrupt transition to online teaching and inexperience with videoconferencing platforms. Several indicated they had been very surprised at how well teaching via videoconference worked in practice and had fundamentally changed their views of remote instruction:

> To my very great surprise, other than the ongoing panic that something terrible will crash or that my own limited understanding of the thing will also crash, it has turned out to be an amazingly satisfying and very pleasant experience and would I continue it, yes, I would.

Some instructors expressed a carefully differentiated view, depending on the course and teaching objectives, with an overall more positive view of remote instruction: "*I have a better, more positive view of online teaching and obviously I think it depends on what you're teaching, of course, but for consecutive and especially beginning consecutive I would say it's definitely preferable to do it in person.*" Of those instructors who expressed concerns about building constructive relationships conducive to teaching and learning with their students, most found that these concerns were alleviated through the online experience:

> The true test was more recently, when I was teaching students who I had never met in person. It wasn't so hard for those I had met in person … and for those I'd never met, it was the same type of relationship-building. I also in the outside world now have actually hired people who work with me who I've never met in person, and so I guess I had the same experience with it.

15.5.3 Advantages of In-Person Instruction

Students—The students found unanimously that in-person instruction continued to be better for practice-oriented classes, such as those dedicated to building translation and interpreting skills: "*If you're trying to practice and hone your skills in something certain, [an instructor] who is present physically can guide better.*" Students found communication in the classroom to be more effective in general and the level of engagement of fellow students to be higher, given the fact that there are fewer distractions in the physical classroom, resulting in classroom dynamics that support their learning better overall. When asked whether in-person instruction is preferable to online instruction, even if everyone has to wear masks, students indicated that it was and pointed to better communication and fewer distractions:

> I still think that it's more effective to teach face-to-face in that you are able to understand what people are asking better. People are more engaged because it's very easy to be distracted by things in your home and around you when … nobody else can see what's outside the frame of your computer screen.

Instructors—The instructors also expressed a general preference for in-person instruction yet found online instruction to be viable under many circumstances. Although this view was not shared among all instructors, some indicated a strong preference for in-person instruction during introductory consecutive interpreting courses, when the foundation for technique and note-taking is being laid: "*Interpreting is a physical profession and for consecutive you want to see how people … sit or stand and how they take their notes … but luckily I had the chance of doing all of this before I started teaching remotely.*" The same concerns were not expressed for teaching simultaneous interpreting: "*the key concept is simultaneous … and the division here is remote … it's not just halfway across the room in a booth, you're halfway across town and in another dimension, but it comes to the same almost.*"

Instructors also found in-person instruction to be essential for professional simulations in large classrooms and conference rooms, where professional dress is expected, and for off-campus excursions to museums and other venues to practice interpreting in real-world environments. Instructors also expressed a preference for in-person instruction allowing for freedom of movement, rather than being bound to a computer screen: "*My teaching style … lends itself to in-person classroom work. I moved around a lot and I can't really do that. I feel a little... stymied when I'm sitting in front of a computer.*"

15.5.4 Advantages of Online Instruction

Students—A clear advantage of remote instruction from the perspective of students is the practical aspect of accommodating changes to the teaching schedule on short notice and flexibility when there is bad weather or unforeseen circumstances that make it problematic to come to campus: "*… some flexibility should be there in terms of rescheduling.*" Students highlighted online instruction as a way to extend the pool of instructors and "*enrich the program with expertise which is not easily available locally.*" Students found virtual platforms to be a strong option for student practice sessions: "*… very useful in group work and projects and things like that between students.*" Meeting online when they would not otherwise come to campus, such as during semester breaks, was a preferred option.

While students had expressed reservations about the utility of videoconferencing platforms for practice-oriented, skill development courses—at least as a preferred solution—they did confirm that online instruction worked well for content or theory courses that did not have the same practice requirements: "*It's okay to be online if it's something which doesn't involve any practical aspect.*" Despite these positive comments, instructor preparation and tech-savviness remain key: "*I feel like I was very lucky in the sense that I was prepared for it and that my instructors were prepared for it.*"

Instructors—Instructors praised remote instruction as an option for bringing a broader selection of guest speakers to their (virtual) classes; in some instances, the same guest speakers would not have been able to attend in-person on campus. Some also remarked that the videoconferencing platform with headphones improved their ability to hear during class discussions. Similar to students, they welcomed the option to be flexible with scheduling under unforeseen circumstances: "*There's a* *huge advantage to … remote teaching for … days when there are snowstorms. There was one day when I had a really bad cold, and so of course I didn't want to go to class, so we had class online, so I think that was great. I think that is a positive.*"

Instructors cited the technology tools available through platforms for recording, text editing, and screen-sharing, particularly for translation, as advantages:

> What's really been helpful is the ability to toggle back and forth between the students screens and my screen … especially for things like subtitles … where you want to go really quickly to the students work and back to the teacher. There might be a way to do that on the university's computer system, but with Zoom it's just seamless.

For language enhancement, instructors mentioned the use of cameras and screens to work on fine details of pronunciation, such as lip and mouth movements. Finally, instructors pointed out that use of online platforms is now a job requirement in the field of interpreting, and conducting at least some classes online supports the students' acquisition of skills that they need in their future careers: "*If we teach them this way, we prepare them for real life and that's another important lesson—using all of the devices for simultaneous interpreting—and I think it works to teach simultaneous online as well.*"

Finally, similar to the ability to access a broader range of guest speakers, instructors thought that an online curriculum component could extend the geographical reach of the program, particularly for translation, and make it truly global.

15.5.5 Disadvantages of In-Person Instruction

Students—The disadvantages of in-person instruction were limited to two factors for students: the commute to campus and (temporary) wearing of masks in the classroom, although they still preferred in-person instruction with masks to online instruction overall. "*The commute is prohibitive,*" given the traffic situation in the Washington DC area, including to College Park, Maryland, during rush hour for an evening class. The students also expressed their awareness of the commute being a factor for their instructors. Students indicated that use of masks in the classroom made it difficult to hear and understand all class participants, particularly with the range of accents spoken in an international program. They even indicated that there can be an emotional impact: "*Masks sometimes create trouble hearing. Not everybody is loud enough, and sometimes it's also detrimental to confidence.*"

Instructors—The chore of commuting in heavy traffic to the College Park campus from downtown Washington DC on business days elicited strong responses from instructors participating in the discussion. They had in some instances moved their classes to the weekend to avoid commuting during the rush hour—"*the only reason I was able to teach those classes [was] because it was on a Saturday*"—and saw the transition to online instruction as an elegant solution to this vexing and stressful problem. In addition, some instructors were finding it challenging to motivate students to form groups for practice sessions outside of regular class and associated these challenges with the students' need to be on campus prior to the pandemic for such sessions. During the pandemic, the students still

> had to engage in group practice, but I pretty quickly realized that there was no way that they're going to be able to do it in person, and that was fine … they didn't need to be physically together to practice together. They could do that over Zoom, and they did, and it worked really well, so I was very appreciative.

Online group practice sessions were a welcome remedy, and instructors found that students engaged and improved.

15.5.6 Disadvantages of Online Instruction

Students—Some concerns of students regarding online instruction were presented as a contrast to the advantages of in-person instruction as described above. In addition to those concerns, students worried about synchronous instruction with people in different time zones, particularly in larger classes, if online instruction were to become the future norm. It was also apparent to students that a few instructors were struggling with the videoconferencing technology and not all instructors welcomed these new developments at the onset of the pandemic, as shown in the above comments about the abrupt, involuntary transition generating anxiety. Students felt that in isolated instances these factors had a negative impact on their learning experience: "*I do remember some cases of other students struggling because their instructors were not the most excited to switch to … online learning and required training … whether it be with working Zoom or other platforms.*"

Specifically regarding classroom dynamics—"*it wasn't necessarily as fun*"—students clearly felt that online breakout rooms do not offer same dynamic as in-person breakout sessions. The interaction in an online breakout room did not have the same degree of spontaneity that facilitates discussions and brainstorming sessions among peers; for example, "*when.. it's just a face with the mute button on most of the time.*" Online classes required more effort—"*the concentration factor is affected a lot if you are doing an online class*"—resulting more quickly in fatigue: "*I had to come up with some coping mechanism like taking notes, too, so that I am fully engaged in the class.*" Students lamented that it was not possible to see all classmates at once on the screen during large online classes. As a result of all these factors, they also felt that their opportunities for relationship-building with other students were negatively impacted. They expressed reservations that peer-to-peer interactions were not possible to the same extent and concerns about building mentoring relationships with their instructors:

> I think the biggest downside to online learning is the relationships that you build in the classroom. I think that … to bond and connect with people [you] really need to be within the same room, seeing how people act … body language is really important.

Hybrid solutions with some students in the classroom and some students online were considered extremely distracting for all parties involved: "... *a hybrid class where one or two students attend on Zoom and the rest of the class is in the classroom [is] the worst just from the perspective of making the class run smoothly.*"

Instructors—The concerns about teaching foundational skills online, which are outlined above, centered on consecutive interpreting. Interestingly, instructors did not express similar methodological concerns with online instruction for translation, simultaneous interpreting, writing, or content and theory courses. However, instructors did note that more students were distracted in their home environment than in the classroom, pointing to the exigencies of the pandemic and the need to resolve them if online instruction is to continue:

> I had a student whose dog was barking in the backyard in the background. I had another student who was ... taking care of his three month old baby son ... during class ... you know that was okay during the pandemic but there comes a point ... where it's not appropriate, so I think those are things that would have to be considered.

Other instructors noted that it is impossible to control completely the online environment and that it is going to be different than in the classroom:

> [If] your standard is that it's the same as in person, in my judgment you're barking up the wrong tree, because it is not the same ... sirens go by outside ... that's one thing, but they shouldn't be running off to do their laundry or go stir something on the stove while they're being taught.

Instructors stressed a strong preference for avoiding a hybrid classroom, with some students in the classroom and some students joining remotely: "... *it was always very frustrating for me to have to manage them on the computer and then my other students in person.*" Instructors noted that some students—even pre-pandemic—asked to join online when classes were scheduled to be in the physical classroom, and were careful to avoid the perception that they were granting exceptions and treating students differently. Issues with technology, such as poor connections and fuzzy images, were mentioned but did not emerge as a central concern.

15.5.7 Considerations and Recommendations for the Program Post-pandemic

Students—While students were perhaps not as optimistic as instructors regarding the utility of online instruction and had a clear preference for in-person classes, they did see online instruction as an important tool to add to the GSIT curriculum model. They expressed the view that it could extend the reach of the program, making it possible to bring in additional instructors who were not willing or able to come to the College Park campus to teach. They thought a balance of in-person and online instruction would serve the program best and be an ideal model for the GSIT program to develop and implement:

> I was already pretty impressed by just the sheer amount of … amazing interpretation and translation professionals … in the DC area alone .... But having potentially access to people from all over the globe … would be really interesting, I think, and like we were saying about scheduling conflicts and adapting to … a pandemic, or a snow storm, … I think it would be really interesting to have that … option.

Despite the drawbacks and challenges of online instruction, students felt that it can work with proper planning, technology support, and effort: "*I think in terms of academics, you can probably get the same thing if you are a disciplined student and apply yourself. I do think it requires a little more discipline.*"

Instructors—While the instructors felt unanimously that an online component would strengthen GSIT's program offerings, instructors needed better tools, guidance, and training to utilize the online capability to the fullest extent—"*making sure that the instructors have what they need to be able to teach and in more creative ways online.*" Instructors signalled a strong interest in clearer parameters and expectations, such as professional standards for online instruction, if it is to be retained for the long term.

Similar to students, they saw a mix of in-person and online instruction generally as the best option for strengthening the program and its reach: "*I certainly wouldn't want it to completely replace the person to person.*" Pointing to different needs for interpreting than translation, some indicated a strong interest in an entirely online translation program:

> One thing the program could consider doing is divorcing itself from geography and creating a worldwide program where we all get together from all corners of the world and get … a very rich experience. I understand that translation is very different from interpreting … It's …hard to say that only part of the program would be completely remote, but that would be my recommendation.

Instructors were surprised at the success of the pandemic experiment with teaching translation and even interpreting online. At the very least, all instructors felt that the program should consider making a combination of in-person and online instruction a core part of the future curriculum model:

> The university really needs to look at, if not making it fully ... remote … if you can't do interpreting fully remote, do it in such a way, where … there's a portion of the time … [when] students have to be on campus … so they have some in-person component … and it sounds to me like you know the courses can be taught that way … why insist that they come to campus … I mean there's just no reason why we should limit ourselves that way.

15.6 Discussion

Focus Group Representation—Of the 27 eligible students and graduates, 5 indicated an interest in participating in a focus group and only 3 attended a session. Three students were considered the minimum number necessary. The 2 remaining students who indicated an interest in participating in a focus group would not have been a sufficient number for a second session. It is difficult to speculate regarding the reasons for low participation, other than the global distribution of graduates across time zones and busy schedules of current students. The participants were both current students and graduates and were studying or had studied in courses across the GSIT curriculum, including translation, interpreting, and content or theory courses. They represented a limited number of languages—Arabic, English, and Portuguese—and historically the highest enrolments have been in Chinese, French, and Spanish. The low number of student participants is a limitation of this study.

Of the 27 instructors eligible to participate in a focus group, 9 indicated interest, and 6 attended a session. They represented all areas of the GSIT curriculum, both first and second-year translation and interpreting courses as well as theory-driven content and language enhancement courses. The range of languages included English, French, Portuguese, Russian, and Spanish. Arabic and Chinese had seen enrolment during the pandemic but were not represented.

Comparison of Student and Instructor Viewpoints—While some instructors expressed initial concern about the very new task of moving their courses online mid-way through the semester and initial anxiety about how well remote instruction would work, students were impressed with how quickly and smoothly the transition was accomplished and thought their instructors, for the large part, were doing a remarkable job: "*I also have to commend GSIT … for turning things around so quickly, especially when things were so uncertain in March 2020, when we didn't know what was going to happen next and vaccines were nowhere.*"

Students and instructors shared similar, positive views of flexible scheduling, technology features of videoconferencing platforms, and students' ability to conduct group practice sessions online as distinct advantages. Their views of remote instruction working well for content courses were similar. It will come as no surprise that, compared to the student group, instructors showed generally greater awareness of the relative advantages and disadvantages of in-person versus remote instruction for teaching methodology and structuring their classroom activities.

The ability to build productive relationships in the classroom was a topic where opinions of some instructors and students diverged. Some instructors saw their concerns about rapport-building during online instruction largely resolved. In contrast, students continued to express concern that the instructor-student and peer-to-peer interaction in the online environment was inherently inferior to the in-person classroom and detrimental to relationship-building, and these views were reinforced by their experience during the pandemic.

Both groups identified limitations of online instruction, particularly for teaching consecutive interpreting, but emphasized different aspects. Students expressed general reservations about teaching practice-oriented, skills-based courses online. In contrast, instructors noted such limitations only with regard to developing foundational interpreting and public speaking skills, including the ability to run real-world simulations on campus and conduct excursions to external institutions. In the end, both instructors and students tended to view online instruction as a highly useful supplementary tool to in-person teaching.

Comparison of Viewpoints with Campus-wide Survey—In fall 2020, the University of Maryland published online the initial results of a campus-wide faculty experience survey. Some of the survey results are interesting to compare with responses from focus group participants, as they place the focus group responses in a broader light. The survey was administered October 29 to November 6, 2020, and was accessed by a link sent out by the Provost. The target population was faculty employed at the university during fall 2020. With 1,651 respondents, the survey achieved a 21% response rate (University of Maryland 2020: 3). Some of the viewpoints expressed in the survey align with the viewpoints expressed during the focus group sessions. For example, faculty were asked "*Thinking about all your courses this semester, have you found that your students have trouble with any of the following course- or learning-related activities? Select all that apply*" (9). The number one response selected was "*Participating in group work,*" with 33% (9). This result dovetails with the concerns expressed in the student focus group about the lack of spontaneous communication in breakout groups during online classes.

Faculty were also asked in the campus-wide faculty survey, "*Thinking about all your courses this semester, have you found that your students have trouble with any of the following related to study habits and their learning environment? Select all that apply*" (University of Maryland 2020: 10). Response options receiving more than 50% were "*Maintaining motivation to keep up with coursework*" with 58% and "*Managing distractions*" with 53% (10). Similar to the above correspondence between the campus-wide survey and student focus groups regarding negative views of online classroom dynamics, students in the focus groups also cited maintaining motivation and engagement, and students and to a lesser degree instructors cited dealing with off-screen distractions as detrimental to learning online in the pandemic.

These two parallels between the students' focus group responses and the campus-wide faculty survey responses are noteworthy, because the instructors participating in the focus groups either did not raise these issues or raised them but had less severe opinions than the students.

Strong Discussion Themes—Several discussion themes emerged as particularly strong, given the emotional reactions of focus group participants. Some instructors were very surprised by how quickly they abandoned their negative views of online instruction and came to fully embrace it. This was a pronounced shift in attitudes towards online instruction. One translation instructor summarized the experience and remarked that students in the virtual classroom shared similar, positive views: "*I did hold a very dim view of remote teaching and that's completely turned around. I love it and, more importantly, I think the students really love it. To the quality of learning, I'm not saying that it's better, but it is at the same level.*"

The option offered through remote instruction to provide greater flexibility with scheduling and, in particular, avoid a rush-hour commute to campus, elicited strong, positive responses from instructors and students alike. Similarly, aspects of relationship-building in the online classroom elicited strong responses during the discussions, with some instructors and some students expressing different opinions on the issue as stated above.

Both students and instructors expressed decidedly negative opinions of hybrid instruction, with some students online and some students in-person in the physical classroom, and were forceful in expressing their views. Negative attitudes toward hybrid instruction stood in stark contrast to positive views of a flexible, mixed curriculum model with some courses offered fully online, separate from in-person courses.

Finally, it emerged in the focus group discussions that in-person instruction and online instruction have different strengths in the minds of students and instructors alike, and in-person instruction is not devoid of challenges either. Identifying these relative strengths and capitalizing on them in a revised, differentiated curriculum model would serve the program well.

15.7 Conclusions

Based upon the analysis and discussion of data collected during two focus group sessions—one with students and one with instructors—the following conclusions can be drawn regarding the four overarching research questions presented at the beginning of this chapter.

1. What was the impact of the COVID-19 pandemic on teaching and learning in the GSIT program?

The abrupt shift to online instruction in response to the COVID-19 pandemic was highly disruptive and forced both students and instructors out of their comfort zones. A number of students and instructors had previous experience with remote instruction and made the transition in stride; however, some students and instructors had negative views of remote instruction that were challenged during the pandemic. While the program as a whole made the transition successfully in a rapid pivot, both instructors and students raised concerns about general preparedness and pointed to the need for additional support and guidance. Instructors expressed a desire for formalized procedures for online instruction if the practice is adopted permanently. While students close to graduation may not have perceived the shifts as detrimental to their overall success in the program, learning was impacted as instructors and students made the necessary ad hoc adjustments to the new instructional environment.

2. Did attitudes towards and opinions of in-person and online instruction among students and instructors change as a result of the COVID-19 pandemic?

Informed by the changes necessitated by the pandemic, students and instructors alike gained direct experience and the ability to identify the relative strengths and weaknesses of in-person and online instruction. This experience led to a twofold shift in views: first, greater appreciation of the affordances offered by classroom instruction and, second, a newfound, unanticipated appreciation of the learning and skill acquisition that can be achieved in an online environment, despite limitations.

Overall, attitudes and opinions of online instruction became more positive through the experience of the pandemic, albeit more strongly among instructors than students. The focus group results indicate a higher level of support for online instruction than previously assumed among GSIT instructors and students.

3. How should the program approach in-person and remote instruction after the pandemic?

Students and instructors both recommended maintaining on online component to ensure flexibility and convenience when scheduling classes and to extend the reach of the program at both the instructor and student levels. In addition, some instructors espoused the view that the technology features of videoconferencing platforms offer options for teaching methodology that had not been present in the in-person classroom prior to the pandemic. However, students and instructors alike noted shortcomings of online instruction that, in their view, are inherent to the online communication environment and, almost unanimously, recommended that online instruction not fully replace in-person teaching. The degree to which an online component can be formalized in the curriculum model will depend on the strategic direction the university pursues with the program.

4. Did the focus groups generate sufficient data for decision-making, or is additional data collection, through other research methodologies, recommended?

The attitudes and opinions expressed during the focus group sessions may not be fully representative of the instructors and, in particular, the students, in view of the low participation in the student focus group. Given the extensive efforts undertaken to recruit participants and limited interest of the target group in participating, it is doubtful whether the dataset could be extended further through additional focus group sessions. An alternative would be to consider administration of a survey generated from the focus group data and results. The comparison of some of the focus group results with initial results of a campus-wide faculty survey show that this could be an informative approach to pursue. Although it would have exceeded the scope of discussion available in this chapter, a follow-up survey could add an additional dimension to this case study, including the triangulation of data that is generally recommended (Yin 2018: 126–129).

As stated in the introduction to this chapter, the curriculum model of the GSIT program was designed with in-person instruction as the sole option in mind. Overall, the results of this initial, exploratory case study show that the GSIT program administrators should extend the analysis, deepen the discussion with faculty and students, and consider options for integrating online instruction into the curriculum in a principled, thoughtful way.

References

Bao, C. 2015. Pedagogy. In *The Routledge handbook of interpreting*, ed. H. Mikkelson and R. Jourdenais, 400–416. London/New York: Routledge.

Geertz, C. 1973. Thick description: Toward an interpreting theory of culture. In *The interpretation of cultures*, 3–30. New York: Basic Books.

Gillham, B. 2000. *Case study research methods*. London/New York: Continuum.

Ko, L. 2015. E-learning. In *Routledge encyclopedia of interpreting studies*, ed. F. Pöchhacker, 139–140. London/New York: Routledge.

Merriam, S.B. 2009. *Qualitative research: A guide to design and implementation*. San Francisco: Jossey-Bass.

Moser-Mercer, B. 2015. Pedagogy. In *Routledge encyclopedia of interpreting studies*, ed. F. Pöchhacker, 303–307. London/New York: Routledge.

Saldanha, G., and S. O'Brien. 2013. *Research methodologies in translation studies*. London/New York: Routledge.

Sawyer, D.B., and S. Parry-Giles. 2013. Launching a new graduate studies program in translation and interpreting: A case study in creative tenacity. *The ATA Chronicle* 42 (3): 11–15. https://www.ata-chronicle.online/wp-content/uploads/4203_11_david_sawyer_shawn_parry_giles.pdf. Accessed 1 June 2022.

Stake, R.E. 1995. *The art of case study research*. Los Angeles: Sage.

University of Maryland. 2020. Fall 2020 faculty experience survey: Initial results. November 20, 2020. https://provost.umd.edu/sites/default/files/inline-files/Fall%202020%20Faculty%20Survey%20-%20initial%20results%20-%20Nov%2020%202020.pdf.

Yin, R.K. 2018. *Case study research: Design and methods*, 6th ed. Los Angeles: Sage.

David B. Sawyer joined the U.S. Department of State in 2003 as the Principal Interpreter for German and supported the most senior levels of the U.S. Government for over a decade. More recently, he served as the founding Director of Graduate Studies in Interpreting and Translation (GSIT) at the University of Maryland, where he continues to teach as a Senior Lecturer. Previously, he was Associate Professor of Interpretation and Translation at the Middlebury Institute of International Studies at Monterey (MIIS). He also taught at the University of Mainz, Germany, and holds graduate degrees and a doctorate from that institution. He is currently Director of Language Testing at the Department's Foreign Service Institute.

Chapter 16
Teaching Interpreting in the Time of COVID: Exploring the Feasibility of Using Gather

Chen-En Ho and Yuan Zou

Abstract Interpreter education has undergone tremendous changes in the past two years due to COVID-19, with training being confined to the virtual environment. Luckily, there are now signs of returning to campus, but the uncertain development of the pandemic renders the arrangement precarious. Many differences exist between distance and on-site learning, and therefore the pedagogy for one cannot be entirely replicated for the other. Interpreting scenarios that rely less on interaction or non-verbal communication are easier to accommodate in both remote and on-site settings, though designing and implementing activities, providing feedback, and maintaining classroom dynamics are still harder in virtual classrooms. By contrast, training for escort and public service interpreting is difficult to be delivered remotely because non-verbal cues, which play a bigger role in these settings, are harder to capture or they disappear entirely, including gesture, facial expressions, posture, and proximity. This study explores how the challenges facing distance interpreter education can be mitigated using Gather, a proximity-based platform. Online synchronous CI and SI teaching setups for two mock events were introduced, and a questionnaire was used to understand students' experience with Gather, Microsoft Teams, and face-to-face training. Preliminary findings show that the majority of the participants are positive about Gather, and it has the potential to bridge the gap between distance and on-site interpreter education in both online and offline scenarios, although its applicability remains to be tested with a larger sample size.

Keywords Interpreter education · Virtual learning environment · Synchronous teaching and learning online · Gather

C.-E. Ho (✉) · Y. Zou
Queen's University Belfast, Belfast, UK
e-mail: c.ho@qub.ac.uk

K. Liu and A. K. F. Cheung (eds.), *Translation and Interpreting in the Age of COVID-19*, Corpora and Intercultural Studies 9,
https://doi.org/10.1007/978-981-19-6680-4_16

16.1 Introduction

The COVID-19 pandemic has wreaked havoc on all levels of education and potentially all disciplines in different ways (Carrillo and Flores 2020), and interpreter education is probably among the most adversely affected, due to its intensely interactive nature, requiring immediate participant feedback in the classroom (Han et al. 2022), and also the need for special facilities and equipment, such as interpreting booths and conference consoles, to familiarize students with real-world scenarios. As courses were forced to move online in early 2020 into the state of "emergency remote teaching" (Bozkurt and Sharma 2020: i) due to sudden lockdowns in many areas of the world, interpreter educators were scrambling to adapt their teaching materials, learning activities, and even teaching mindsets, which had mostly been geared toward on-site teaching, to meet the demands of the unfamiliar, virtual learning environment.

Training interpreters remotely is not an idea that is unheard of (e.g., see Ko and Chen 2011; Mulayim and Lai 2015), as various formats of remote interpreting—defined as "the use of communication technologies to gain access to an interpreter in another room, building, town, city or country" (Braun 2015: 352)—emerged roughly around the last two decades of the twentieth century and have gained some popularity along the way owing to the peculiarity of some contexts and (the limitation of) resources (O'Hagan and Ashworth 2002; Ozolins 1991). Nonetheless, most programs are still "traditional" in that interpreter training is pre-dominantly delivered face-to-face, with some online elements to support learning (Motta 2016; Sandrelli 2015).

It was not until recent years that stakeholders of the interpreting industry, including users of interpreting services, training programs, practitioners, and professional associations, started to pay closer attention to remote interpreting (e.g., see Hickey 2021; Scamman 2020), and COVID-19 has certainly radically reshaped the professional interpreting landscape, to the extent that the International Association of Conference Interpreters (AIIC) has published a document suggesting adequate working conditions and setup for using interpreting service to safeguard both interpreters' and users' health and well-being; the association further acknowledges that "adapting working conditions to the various DI modalities—including remote interpreting from home—is imperative, and may set a precedent for the future" (AIIC 2020: 1). Parallel to the change in the industry, an abrupt shift to distance learning took place in formal interpreter education.

16.2 Distance Learning and Interpreter Education

Distance learning has its fair share of challenges, although bringing with it new possibilities. Poor self-regulation and technical issues (Gao and Li 2021), complexities at home making it an unsuitable learning or teaching environment (Zhang et al. 2020), technological illiteracy—unfamiliarity with the technology used for teaching or learning—of teachers (Ocak 2011) or students (Tshabalala et al. 2014), and many more have been well documented in the literature (see Brown 2016 for a more thorough review).

Interpreter education cannot escape from the above challenges and, in reality, suffers more, as interpreting is both a demanding cognitive task and a complex social activity, and previous studies have sufficiently shown challenges that involve not only the intricate nature of interpreting, but also those who enter the learning environment and the technology used as the medium of instruction. Han et al. (2022) surveyed 106 undergraduate and postgraduate students enrolled in various interpreting modules to understand students' perception of online interpreter education via Zoom. This study looks into student satisfaction in six dimensions, including "(a) instructor, (b) technology, (c) course setup, (d) interaction, (e) outcomes, and (f) overall satisfaction" (Han et al. 2022: 4). The overall findings suggest that students' level of satisfaction did not deteriorate significantly, although motivation was an issue, particularly for beginners, and interaction with others (and for collaborative activities) was problematic, due to the setup of the virtual environment not being conducive to interaction and technical issues the students encountered. Indeed, technology was mentioned by the respondents as a major obstacle. Internet connection aside, Zoom has received criticism regarding its inability to offer users the opportunity to listen to both the source material and interpretation. Combined with other drawbacks experienced by the students, such as not being able to capture non-verbal messages, technical problems contributed to another thorny issue—anxiety. The role played by technology is ever-increasing in both the interpreting industry and education because "online interpreting teaching and learning requires more functions of a platform than other normal language courses, which accordingly makes the learning process more technology-demanding" (Han et al. 2022: 12). However, the endeavour is still ongoing to create a comprehensive platform that meets the requirements of online interpreter education and is easy to use (CIUTI n.d.).

The inflexibility of Zoom is also a pain point felt deeply by Ahrens et al. (2021), whose main finding points out that online interpreting teaching and learning are more strenuous, exhausting, and time-consuming. In this longitudinal study, the authors reflect that the lack of dual-track recording function and the ability to listen to audio signals in both languages lead to heavier workload as complementary software or tools need to be operated in parallel, and "using multiple channels during synchronous lessons has the potential to be a source of additional stress and fatigue" (ibid.: 253; see Lepp et al. 2019: 2 for an overview of the negative relationship between multitasking and primary task performance). In fact, multichannel processing is ranked in the study as the second biggest stressor related to technology, following connection issues (Ahrens et al. 2021: 263). In addition, interaction-related issues stand out. There is consensus that interacting with others is less, particularly with peers (see also Lee et al. 2021), and takes more effort, and the quality of interaction suffers in a remote online environment. Interaction, including detecting and assigning meaning to non-verbal cues in context, lies at the core of interpreter-mediated communication, hence the need for training and practice, but the interface and setup of mainstream video-conferencing platforms, such as Zoom and Microsoft (MS) Teams, are not exactly designed to facilitate interaction and enable perception of non-verbal and paralinguistic messages (see also Ko and Chen 2011).

This study is inspired by the amazing (and perhaps alarming) consensus of difficulties still experienced by teachers and students of interpreting in the context of online interpreter education, especially by the fact that it remains challenging to find a single platform or software that addresses all the needs for synchronous teaching of various interpreting modes. A search for a solution is the overarching goal of this study. Below we introduce the backdrop of our research project, against which we explore the feasibility of using an alternative to mainstream video-conferencing platforms for distance interpreter education.

16.3 Research Context

This study examined how the MA in Interpreting program at Queen's University Belfast (QUB) shifted from on-site education to the remote mode only (and to a hybrid mode afterward) during COVID-19. Although lockdowns were mainly imposed in the early times of COVID in the UK, QUB returned to all online delivery for a short while after the lockdowns were eased, before going back to the classroom again. Therefore, our students in the past two years have experienced some length of both online and offline learning. Echoing previous research, we found that technology, i.e., a lack of a centralised platform suitable for teaching and learning all interpreting modes, was the most significant issue troubling both staff and students, and therefore we were keen to develop an affordable solution, in preparation for the uncertainty of the development of COVID-19 and a future professional world in which remote interpreting will play a more prominent role.

MA Interpreting at QUB is a one-year program consisting of one full-year theoretical module and four practice-based semester modules—consecutive interpreting (CI) and simultaneous interpreting (SI) in the first semester and public service interpreting (PSI) and commercial interpreting (COMI) in the second. Sanako is the software used in the interpreting classroom, which has multiple conference soles and a two-seater mobile interpreting booth. MS Teams was the only distance learning platform for quite a while, and Canvas is the learning management system.

16.3.1 Challenges for Synchronous Interpreter Education Online

When teaching and learning moved online as the lockdown was first imposed, we were scrambling to put together an emergency plan to start with the material that would work for both offline and online settings, which would then give us some time to adapt other teaching materials and activities. We used role-plays, pair practice, and group competitions in class frequently, and all the content, including scripts, scenarios, and background information provided to students, the procedure adopted in class, and the learning activities had all been designed with on-site teaching in mind. Sadly, echoing previously studies, interaction suffered in the online environment, rendering these activities less engaging and ineffective in terms of the use of contact time to some extent (Hubscher-Davidson and Devaux 2021). That said, a bigger issue lied in the technology itself when it intersected different interpreting modalities. The theoretical module could be effectively handled on MS Teams with the functions available to share screens and files, exchange opinions by voice or text, and engage in small group discussions in breakout rooms. On the contrary, practice-based modules encountered great difficulties because MS Teams was—and still is—not equipped to provide a similar learning experience when compared with on-site training, especially when it comes to SI. Sharing the same issue with Zoom (and worse), MS Teams does not take interpretation service into account, so there is no separate channel for the interpreter to work with; therefore, it understandably does not let users listen to both the source material and interpretation. In terms of CI, we could more easily adapt the average conference interpreting setting by moving to the remote interpreting mode, which is becoming more prevalent in professional contexts, although paralinguistic and non-verbal information was often lost or harder to perceive in context (see also Perramon and Ugarte 2020; Ko 2006); dialogue interpreting, on the other hand, was more of an issue as all those cues and the wider context that disappear in the remote mode tend to play a bigger role in constructing (and thus interpreting) meaning. Some features peculiar to on-site interpreter-mediated communication, such as proximity, and how distance is maintained between participants change the dynamics of conversation, and even the nitty–gritty involving which seat to take at a table and who to stay close to during escort interpreting tasks would be impossible to cover in a remote environment using the mainstream video-conferencing platforms. In other words, interaction as a core aspect of interpreter-mediated communication would be difficult to teach and learn.

16.3.2 Interim Measures and the Search for a Comprehensive Solution

In order to teach SI synchronously, we used two platforms at the same time—MS Teams plus Zoom—with one serving as the "conference room", where the source material was either played by using the share function or delivered by the lecturer and teaching assistants directly, and the other as the "interpretation room", where students were divided into groups of 2–3 to provide interpretation to make the best of the contact time. Teaching staff would rotate between breakout rooms to observe student performance, guide group discussion, and provide feedback. Technical issues were numerous. Primarily, the 40-min limitation of Zoom means we had to create multiple sessions, making the progression of activities in class difficult to plan, and there was little room for errors or unexpected needs to arise. A related issue was that the stability of the internet connection depended on where each student was and even the weather conditions in the area. At times we faced the awkwardness of being cut off in the middle of a practice session when exceeding the 40-min limit because students had trouble logging in, seeing the shared screen, or failing to receive audio/video signals, thus requiring time for troubleshooting. Students would also drop in and out occasionally due to unstable connection, seriously disrupting the dynamics of interaction and learning activities.

Having two platforms running in parallel requires a meticulous and timely control of the mute button, so no one accidently interrupts when others are speaking or cuts across the source speech, not to mention the unlucky situations when some laptops cannot cope with two platforms fighting for microphone access, leading to a temporary "forced silence" for some users. On the other hand, teaching CI using MS Teams is straightforward, as concurrent incoming audio (and/or video) streams are not required. Nonetheless, teaching was limited to the remote conference mode, in which each participant occupied a grid on the screen filled with headshot images. Cues other than linguistic information and facial expressions were minimal, if any, and issues revolving around proximity and the management of interpreter-mediated communication could not be sufficiently covered and experienced by students but only discussed in abstract ways (see also 3.1).

It was under these circumstances that Sanako Connect,[1] a remote module to extend the functions of the Sanako language learning software, was subscribed to facilitate remote SI training. In fairness, Sanako Connect is a good platform which allows teachers to create classes and exams in an orderly fashion. Dual-tack recording is supported, and both video and audio files are accepted. Individual and group activities are easy to create and manage, as the lecturer can move in and out of breakout rooms easily and engage in two-way communication, although the "group discussion" button has to be switched on before everyone in the group can hear each other. Listening to both the source material and interpretation is not a standard function but still possible, albeit not straightforward and requiring some coordination among group members. However, the downside is that only the creator of each virtual class can take up the role of the lecturer and assign participants to groups, meaning it will be more cumbersome to use teaching assistants as they cannot move freely among groups. In truth, Sanako Connect is designed with a focus on self-paced learning, and therefore when everyone is in the "common room" for plenary activities, such as role-plays or overall feedback sessions, only the lecturer can speak to the whole class, and all other participants can only use the chat box or personal messages to interact with others. Another major drawback is the upper limit for uploading video or audio materials, capped at a meagre 100 Mb per file. Another blow to the usefulness of the platform is that only the lecturer can turn on her webcam or share her screen, which is not conducive to learning the interactional aspect of interpreting.

[1] https://sanako.com/connect/.

Sanako Connect successfully addressed some issues of MS Teams and Zoom while others remained unsolved, and how synchronous SI and CI teaching could be effectively delivered was not intuitive. Consequently, we were again on the quest for a more suitable solution. CIUTI (n.d.) announced an open call for developing an online platform for teaching SI, for which Green Terp[2] won the prize with its GT EDU. As mentioned on CIUTI's website, the main advantage of this platform is the possibility it offers for students to work alongside a partner in a virtual booth, engaging in real peer observation and conversation without being confined to text messages, while the lecturer can enter each booth to observe students and provide feedback. Attractive as it sounds, the platform was still in development in the initial stages of the lockdowns and later was not pursued due to budget concern. MA Interpreting had two small cohorts, when compared with other subject areas, during the time of this study, with a total of 17 students, so more expenses on top of the funding already allocated to support the transition seemed disproportionate.

Accordingly, this study emerged out of the necessity to find an affordable alternative. We aim at testing the viability of Gather, the platform we later located, and reflecting on our and students' experience with it. Admittedly, a plethora of issues remain to be tackled in distance learning, which include but are not limited to how we can—similar to face-to-face learning—create an "ecosystem…to support learners with formal, informal, and social resources" (Hodges et al. 2020: para. 11). That said, we choose to concentrate on synchronous CI and SI teaching for this study and hope to help address some of the difficulties of teaching interpreting synchronously online experienced by fellow educators.

16.4 Methodology

This study was an action research project carried out by us, as both lecturers and researchers. To allow time to familiarize ourselves with Gather and avoid causing too much disruption, we decided to first test the feasibility of the new platform in two mock events on two consecutive days, during which both SI and CI were required. We announced in advance the use of a new platform, and students were divided into teams to provide interpreting service. We met on Gather days before the mock events to explain the ins and outs of the platform and the procedures on both days, followed by a rehearsal to troubleshoot potential issues. On the first day, the mock event was attended by the teaching team and students. The students were asked to log in, test their microphone and camera, and prepare for the event one hour earlier. On the second day, the event was open to a wider audience, and the students logged in 1.5 h earlier. A questionnaire was administered immediately following the second event. The results were analyzed, coupled with our observations and informal

[2] https://www.gtmeeting.com/.

conversations, to understand students' experience with Gather. The sections below introduce the platform and how the interpreting environment was set up to teach SI and CI.

16.4.1 Gather

Gather is a proximity-sensitive online chat and video-conferencing platform that simulates participant interactions in real life (Gather n.d.). Its main functions are similar to mainstream platforms, such as Zoom and MS Teams, but it stands out from the crowd by offering a 2D map where you can use an avatar to navigate the space and explore different functions and objects in various settings, including conferences, classes, and social events, and it is possible to design a comprehensive experience to accommodate different needs. For example, multiple rooms can be created on the map for a single class, so students can convene in the conference room for a lecture and then walk to their own workstations for individual study or use "private areas", enclosed spaces where conversations will not be heard by passers-by outside, for group discussion or one-to-one feedback sessions. There are also miscellaneous objects and functions to facilitate teaching and learning, including whiteboards for brainstorming, bulletin boards for announcements, audio/video and document/photo-sharing mechanisms, loudspeakers for broadcasting messages and sharing screens to everyone in the event, regardless of their location on the map, and even emojis for immediate interactions, among other tools. Instructions can be written anywhere on the map to help users navigate the space.

Most relevant to interpreter education is the function to create an interpreter area for SI service (Gather 2022), which interestingly gives a quasi-authentic on-site vibe. A really clever design of Gather is that proximity is a factor that affects the video and audio signals received when having a conversation with others. If your avatar is more than about four steps away from another person, you will neither see nor hear her. When the distance between you narrows, the signals become stronger. That is, the closer you are, the clearer you can see and hear each other. This design, along with the avatar system, could be helpful when we teach how interpreters can manage interpersonal distance and how personal space affects (the dynamics of) conversation, and even discuss the nuances of choosing where to sit when interpreting for clients on-site—which the average remote interpreting mode completely deprives students of the chance to experience first-hand.

16.4.2 Virtual Space for Interpreter Education

In our study, the environment, or the map, encompassed different rooms, including a conference room, dozens of individual workstations in the central area of the map, three offices in different corners, which were then used for a work placement offered

Fig. 16.1 Gather's interface and the conference room for mock events

by our Centre for Translation and Interpreting, and also a few other amenities, such as kitchens and dining areas, to simulate a real-life work environment.

Figure 16.1 demonstrates the conference room designed for our mock events. Aside from rows of chairs, two podiums, a whiteboard, and two loudspeakers were arranged for the speaker and the interpreter for CI. When stepping on a loudspeaker, both people would be seen and heard from every corner of the whole map.

The private area circled by a red rectangle in Fig. 16.1 is the interpreter area for SI. Those who need interpreting service can stay in the area and mute the speaker, thereby only hearing the interpretation. The teaching team can enter the area without muting the speaker and listen to both the source speech and interpretation.

16.4.2.1 Setup for SI

Figure 16.2 shows a close-up of the actual setup on the days of the mock events. The interpreter area is clearly labelled as the booth, while there are instructions to tell where the speaker and the interpreter should be to use the broadcasting function properly.

Although only one private area is demonstrated here, one can actually create numerous smaller private areas to accommodate multiple teams of interpreters. A convenient function is that each private area can be assigned a number and does not have to be adjacent blocks to classify as the same private area. Using the current layout in Fig. 16.2 as an example, it is possible to create several small private interpreter areas in the bottom-left corner, number them, and then set up a row of one-block private areas in the upper-left corner, again numbered. In this way, when stepping on each block, the teaching team can see and hear what is happening in the interpreter area labelled with the same number.

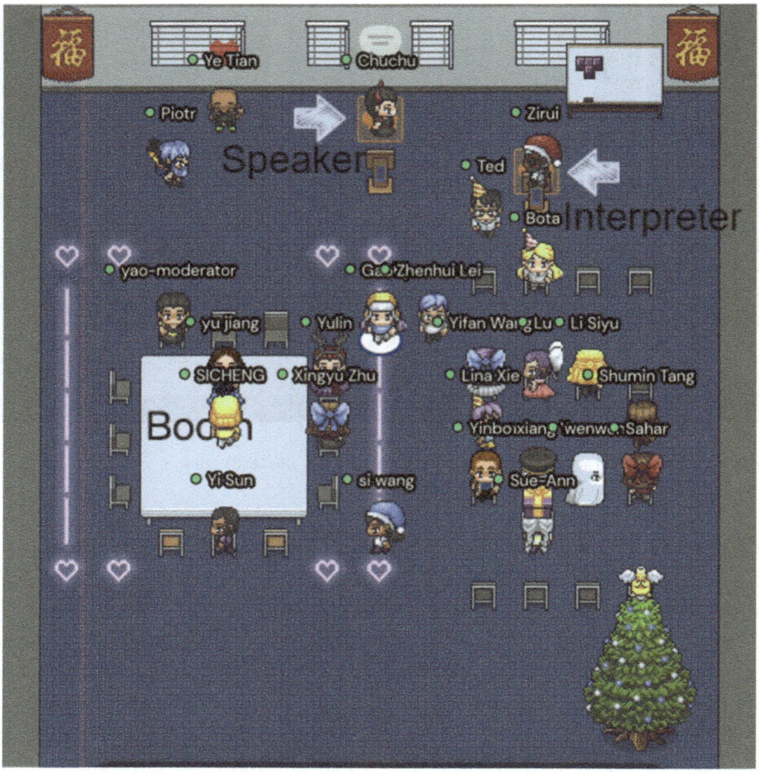

Fig. 16.2 Setup of the mock events

16.4.2.2 Task Arrangement for CI

As CI only requires a functioning microphone and camera and hence no need for a particular setup, we organized a tour of the map on the second day for the attendees of the mock events to learn about how different offices on the map were used and what work placement projects different teams of students were working on. Each team of interpreters was tasked with accompanying one visitor as they walked around the whole map, taking turns among themselves to provide interpreting service.

16.5 Survey Results and Discussion

The section below presents the results of the survey and is divided into three subsections: background information, experience with on-site and distance (interpreter) education in general, and experience with Gather. Our observations and conversations with students provide additional insight to the discussion of the results.

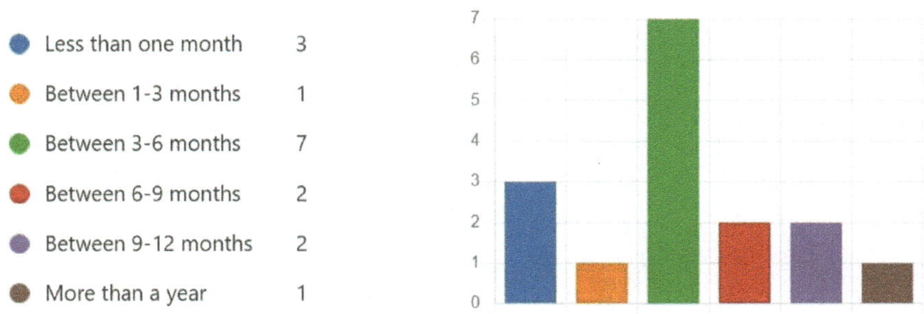

Fig. 16.3 Participants' experience with distance learning

16.5.1 Backgrounds of the Participants

Sixteen students participated in this study: Three are male and 13 are female, and a total of 13 people are between 22 and 25 years of age, with a mean of 24.8. Figure 16.3 shows how familiar the participants are with distance learning in general. The majority (68.8%) of the students have little experience, which means less than six months, whereas only one indicates having spent more than a year engaging in online synchronous learning.

When asked about experience of learning interpreting, 12 participants had received less than one year of interpreter education prior to joining QUB—among which four with none—while four students had exposure to relevant training for more than one year.

Following on from the question on how much interpreter training they had received, Fig. 16.4 demonstrates how much of their training had been done remotely. Out of the 13 participants who answered this question, six (46.2%) indicated almost no experience with distance learning (i.e., below 10%). Only two are in the range of 61–80% and can count as being somewhat familiar to distance interpreter education.

16.5.2 Previous Experience with Distance and On-Site Interpreter Education

Looking into how participants feel about distance and on-site training for interpreters in general, we divide questions into three categories: personal feelings, interaction, and learning support. Participants were asked to rate each statement on a scale of one (absolutely disagree) to five (absolutely agree).

Table 16.1 presents results on users' feelings about taking interpreting modules online and on-site, respectively. The scores for all questions for the online mode sit consistently between three and four, and many are in the lower region of this band, showing that the respondents feel slightly unsure and less confident about distance

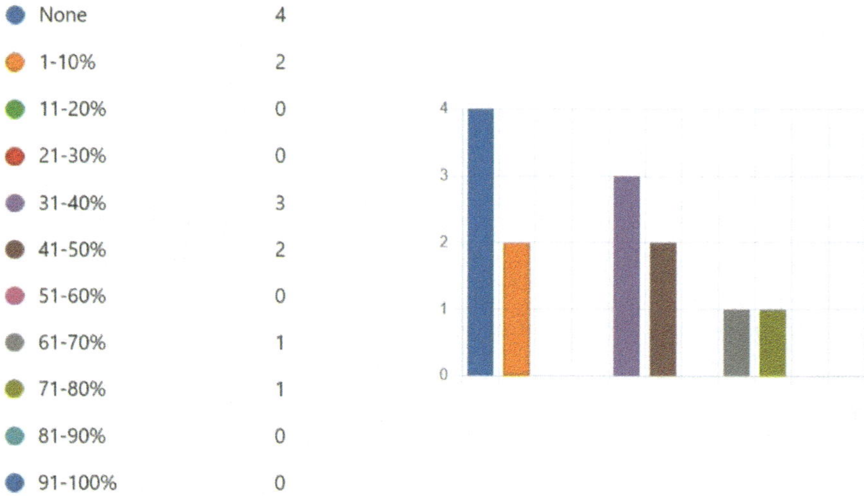

Fig. 16.4 Experience with distance interpreter education

interpreter education. The question in this category that receives the highest score is the one asking whether they are comfortable with taking interpreting modules online ($M = 3.6$, with only 53.4% either agreeing or absolutely agreeing with the statement), while the lowest score goes to engagement ($M = 3.07$, with overall positive responses dropping to 33.3%, and 46.7% actively disagree with the statement). As engagement is about whether students can stay focused on the task at hand and engage with class activities and others, this low score could potentially come from the fact that the interface of the distance learning platform may not be conducive to focused attention. As mentioned in previous studies, a lack of "proximity" among the students could lead to the feeling of isolation and alienation, hence difficulty in continuing to engage the task (Ahrens et al. 2021: 257). Being alone in a space could also weaken one's focus on the task remotely as no one else is observing or seemingly "in it together", lacking the sense of the task being collective. The participants also do not consider online interpreter training stimulating (only 33.3% in agreement) or motivating (only 40% in agreement), neither do the majority think the online learning atmosphere is sufficiently good.

A glance at the scores for on-site interpreter training in Table 16.1 immediately tells the difference. All scores cluster around the middle of the region between four and five, as engagement comes out on top at 4.5 (93.8% positive) and atmosphere in the last position ($M = 4.25$; 87.5% positive). Aside from the familiarity with how interpreters have always been trained, the result highlights the importance of a sense of community, which is easier to cultivate when you are physically in and as a group, exerting a collective effort toward achieving the goal of the class.

In terms of the interactional aspect of the participants' experience with both teaching modes, Table 16.2 points out that the mean score for each statement again

Table 16.1 Personal feelings about distance interpreter education

Teaching mode	Online		On-site	
Descriptive statistics	Mean	SD	Mean	SD
I'm comfortable with interpreter training online	3.6	1.12	4.38	1.02
It's easy to study/practice interpreting online	3.2	1.15	4.44	0.63
Distance learning stimulates my interest in interpreting	3.13	1.25	4.38	0.89
Distance learning motivates me to learn interpreting	3.2	1.08	4.31	0.87
It is easy to stay engaged online	3.07	1.22	4.5	0.82
It is easy to fully participate in class online	3.2	1.15	4.31	0.87
Classroom atmosphere is good online	3.53	1.06	4.25	1.06

falls in the region of three to four for distance learning. Having interactions with others is not particularly easy, scoring a mean of 3.47, with 53.3% agreeing or absolutely agreeing to its easiness. Collaboration is perceived to be even more cumbersome, with a mean of 3.27 and the percentage of participants being positive standing only at 40%. The score for the easiness of giving feedback is slightly higher, standing at 3.53 (53.3% positive). One of the reasons could be that when giving or receiving feedback, each person is given an uninterrupted chunk of time, without having to pay close attention to how the situation develops, as required during interpreting; in other words, the pace is slower, and students can delve into their thoughts more. Still, the overall impression is not optimistic, which is further corroborated by the score given to classroom dynamics ($M = 3.47$; 46.7% positive). On the contrary, scores for on-site education sit comfortably in the region between four and five, again convening in the middle of the band.

The above two tables both show the importance of creating an environment that facilitates exchanges, as interaction and the community of practice are crucial in both the interpreting profession and the learning environment that nurtures future interpreters (e.g., Braun et al. 2020; D'Hayer 2012).

Interestingly, when it comes to the learning support available, the respondents seem to be slightly more optimistic than in other aspects of distance education, as all mean scores tilt toward the relatively higher end of the 3–4 region, with their perception of technology being the exception that moves into a higher band. Table 16.3

Table 16.2 Participants' experience with interactions in distance and on-site interpreter education

Teaching mode	Online		On-site	
Descriptive statistics	Mean	SD	Mean	SD
It is easy to interact with others online	3.47	1.13	4.63	0.81
It is easy to collaborate with others online	3.27	1.16	4.44	0.63
It is easy to receive and give feedback on interpreting performance online	3.53	0.92	4.44	0.63
Classroom dynamics are good online	3.47	1.06	4.56	1.03

Table 16.3 Perception of learning support available in distance and on-site interpreter education

Teaching mode	Online		On-site	
Descriptive statistics	Mean	SD	Mean	SD
Instructors can easily notice my needs online	3.53	1.06	4.56	0.63
Instructors can easily address my needs online	3.67	1.11	4.63	0.62
New teaching methods are very available online	3.87	0.83	4.13	0.72
Technology can be used to promote learning online	4.07	0.89	4.38	0.72

shows that the participants are generally more satisfied with the support that comes from the instructor, compared with other elements of the online environment, scoring a mean of 3.53 for the possibility to notice individual needs and 3.67 for addressing the needs. The majority are even more positive about the range of technologies that can play a role in facilitating online training, with the mean score reaching 4.07 (73.3% either agree or absolutely agree).

On-site training again surpasses the online mode in every statement posed, with the swiftness to address individual needs scoring the highest ($M = 4.63$; 93.8% in agreement) and the availability of new teaching methods the lowest ($M = 4.13$; 81.3% in agreement).

Participants were then asked to directly compare face-to-face and distance education in a few aspects and rate each on a continuum from face-to-face being much better to the opposite. For simplicity, the continuum is converted to a five-point Likert scale, with "face-to-face being much better" representing the highest score.

Table 16.4 demonstrates the participants' overall preference for on-site interpreter training. The possibility of moving around and presence in class, meaning students being more visible to others, both score the highest at 4.44, with 93.8% and 87.6% much preferring face-to-face to online training, respectively. Interestingly, the awareness of proximity, i.e., the awareness of the distance between people and how this awareness could affect the interpreter, comes in last at a mean of 3.94, and only 56.3% of the participants lean obviously toward on-site learning, while an amazing 37.5% consider the two teaching modes similar in this regard. One possible reason is that seven of the participants are from the second cohort, who have not yet received training in dialogue and escort interpreting, which rely heavily on the awareness of proximity. As still in the first semester at the time of the study, they mostly sit in their own seats practicing interpreting to avoid too much burden on their limited cognitive resources at an early stage of their training. Accordingly, it is possible that sitting in a classroom is not enormously different from sitting in front of a laptop, hence the lack of awareness of proximity.

Table 16.4 On-site versus distance interpreter education

Descriptive statistics	Mean	SD
Ability to move around	4.44	0.63
Motivation to participate	4.19	1.17
Presence in class	4.44	0.73
Engagement or interaction with others and learning activities	4.31	1.14
Awareness of proximity	3.94	1.06
Giving and receiving feedback	4.19	0.91
Possibility to practice various types of interpreting (including escort interpreting)	4.31	0.79
Possibility of having backup plans if issues arise	4.00	1.10

16.5.3 User Experience with Gather

When asked what they feel about Gather, most participants have a good impression of the platform ($M = 4.25$ out of five; 88% positive); the majority also consider it a convenient and interesting tool for interpreter training, scoring a mean of 6.88 out of ten.

Prompted to directly compare MS Teams, Gather, and on-site learning, the participants' preference is presented in Fig. 16.5, which clearly shows that face-to-face instruction is still seen as the best format, although one participant specifically mentioned that "Gather…in the future may become a trend" (Participant 13) as the professional landscape is gradually leaning more toward remote interpreting. Among all participants, 81.3% put Gather behind on-site learning, but surprisingly 6.3% think Gather is much better and 12.5% place the two on equal terms. This is where we believe some features of Gather could potentially supplement on-site training and even be better suited to some scenarios, such as remote interpreting, which was indeed mentioned by four students as Gather's advantage, while being more interesting and less awkward to use than learning interpreting on MS Teams. When faring against MS Teams, Gather is considered to be much better (25%) or better (25%) by half of the respondents; however, 25% are in favour of MS Teams (reasons see below) (see McClure and Williams 2021 for similar student responses, although for self-paced learning and a different discipline).

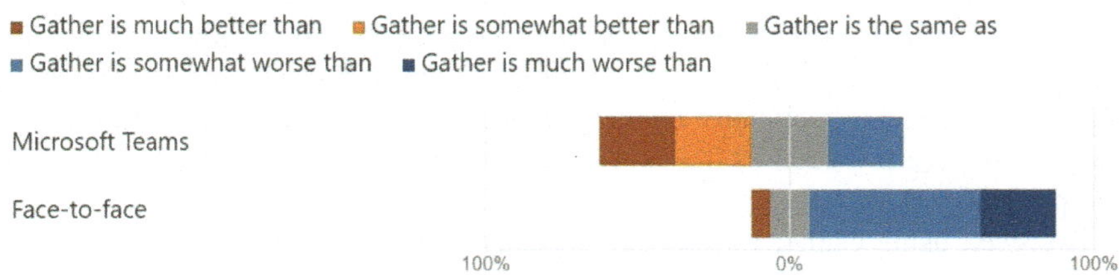

Fig. 16.5 Comparison of platforms and formats for interpreter education

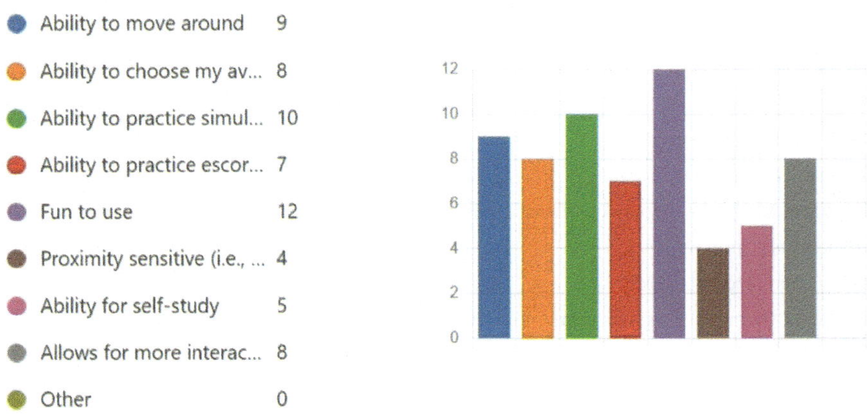

Fig. 16.6 Perception of important features of Gather for interpreter education

Another question asks the respondents to select all the features of Gather they deem important for interpreter education (see Fig. 16.6). Scoring highest is "fun to use" (75%), followed by "ability to practice SI" (62.5%) and then "ability to move around" (56.3%). Meanwhile, "ability to choose my avatar (for online visibility)" and "allows for more interactions than other online platforms" both sit at 50%, while the "ability to practice escort interpreting" is still appreciated by some participants (43.8%).

From previous sections we can see that all aspects of interpreter education seem to fare worse for mainstream video-conferencing platforms, among which activities involving interaction seem to be especially challenging. The limitations of teaching SI on these platforms, which seep into some participants' comments (e.g., Participant 12 and 14), further plague educators and students in our field. In comparison, Gather seems to fill some of the gap between distance and on-site interpreter education by providing the flexibility to accommodate synchronous CI and SI teaching in various contexts, covering both on-site and remote interpreting modes, while offering a more interesting and interactive virtual world than its counterparts (Participant 4, 9, and 12) (see Kapp 2012 about how using the avatar and tapping into learner's interest can improve motivation and learning). Furthermore, Gather has some additional features that are well suited to addressing individual needs. For example, Participant 7 mentioned that "the function of muting someone [from] our end is…interesting because we can choose to practice on our own or check how the other one is performing or just simply listen to the speaker". Participants 15 and 16 also praise Gather's design that specifically enables students to develop "communication skills" and see "service provided in front [of one's own eyes]", particularly during escort interpreting.

However, using Gather for our mock events was not without a hitch. Technical issues did appear. Some students experienced dropouts or delays at times due to bad internet connection, whereas some others were struggling with operating their avatars and using the correct functions timely. This may partly explain why the overall impression of Gather is quite positive but not exceptionally well. In addition, 25% of the participants still prefer MS Teams to Gather. Reasons could be numerous. First of all, MS Teams is the standard platform used by QUB, so students are much more familiar with its functions than with Gather, which they used for the first time during the mock events, despite having had three rehearsals totalling 3–4 h to try out the platform in advance. Gather offers better functionality but also requires more conscious control to stay attuned to the camera and microphone (to position oneself in clear view and mute/unmute oneself when appropriate) while paying some attention to what is happening in the environment, as the proximity-sensitive feature demands the interpreter to control her avatar to follow service users around closely so they can continue to see and hear each other. Secondly, MS Teams is developed and maintained by Microsoft, one of the largest world-leading companies. MS Teams is optimized for remote video conferences and can accommodate users with different bandwidths; by contrast, our experience with Gather is that the number of users has a proportionate impact on the stability of connection, but of course individual technical conditions, including campus versus home Wi-Fi, could have skewed our findings. Several other attempts at using Gather were made after we started writing this article, and we found a general rule of thumb: connection was smooth for a normal interpreting class (with up to 15 people), whereas an event of a larger scale—our mock events hosted almost 30 people—should keep the setup relatively simple by using fewer complex interactive objects, including sound and visual effects, animations, or teleportation portals to different areas of the map (or even different maps).

Our last observation pertains to the element of proximity in interpreting activities. As mentioned previously, some students found it taking more time to get used to devoting their attention to multiple aspects of the environment, including controlling their avatars. However, some other students chose to use an inherent "follow" function to automatically follow a user of their choice, saving them the time and effort to monitor where their avatars were. Yet unfortunately, the decision made them revert to the remote conference interpreting mode and simply focused on the visual and audio information from the interlocutors. Even so, using the avatars is a more intuitive and flexible way (than putting every possible scenario on slides) to demonstrate and discuss how distance between participants affects communication, or even how interlocutors perceive our role as an interpreter or team member simply because of our seat choice in a meeting or business negotiation. Nonetheless, the two mock events in our study were our first attempt, instead of a normal interpreting class, so only a small portion of the time was allocated for in-depth discussion on various issues, including proximity. This is perhaps why fewer students have actively mentioned the potential of Gather on this point.

16.6 Conclusion

This is an exploratory study investigating the feasibility of using Gather for distance interpreter education. Our findings corroborate previous studies and show the limitations of mainstream video-conferencing platforms, such as Zoom and MS Teams, and how they affect students' experience and the development of interpreting competence—with drawbacks in the interactional dimension and impracticality for learning SI being particularly challenging. Gather does provide some advantages in this regard, as demonstrated in Sects. 4.1 and 4.2, and can offer an expandable, immersive virtual experience, with the ability to accommodate both CI and SI in on-site and remote modes; added to the ranks of benefits is its proximity-sensitive feature, which gives better hands-on experience than the average video-conferencing platforms. This additional feature could better feed into the discussion of proximity in interpreting in various contexts.

Due to limited space, we have decided to focus on testing the viability of Gather as an interpreter education platform, instead of diving into the challenges encountered and good practices when using Gather. The small sample size also makes it impossible to claim, at this stage, that Gather is definitely better than other video-conferencing platforms, although the preliminary results show a glimpse of hope. As this is the first cycle of an iterative teaching design, the logical next step is to give students longer time to familiarize themselves with the platform and recruit more participants to understand what it can really offer to complement other formats of interpreter education. In addition, this study zones in on synchronous CI and SI teaching, but as previously mentioned, a good distance education design should be an ecosystem, covering both synchronous and asynchronous aspects of education. Therefore, Gather as a self-paced learning platform (e.g., see McClure and Williams 2021) to supplement in-class activities is another avenue worthy of pursuit for further research.

References

Ahrens, B., M. Beaton-Thome, and A. Rütten. 2021. The pivot to remote online teaching on the MA in Conference Interpreting in Cologne: Lessons learned from an unexpected experience. *The Journal of Specialised Translation* 36b: 251–284.

AIIC. 2020. AIIC interpreter checklist: Performing remote interpreting assignments from home in extremis during the Covid-19 pandemic. https://aiic2.in1touch.org/document/4845/AIIC-Interpreter-Checklist.pdf. Accessed 20 Apr 2022.

Bozkurt, A., and R.C. Sharma. 2020. Emergency remote teaching in a time of global crisis due to coronavirus pandemic. *Asian Journal of Distance Education* 15 (1): i–vi. https://doi.org/10.5281/zenodo.377808.

Braun, S. 2015. The remote interpreting. In *The Routledge handbook of interpreting*, ed. H. Mikkelson and R. Jourdenais, 352–367. New York: Routledge.

Braun, S., E. Davitti, and C. Slater. 2020. 'It's like being in bubbles': Affordances and challenges of virtual learning environments for collaborative learning in interpreter education. *The Interpreter and Translator Trainer* 14 (3): 259–278. https://doi.org/10.1080/1750399X.2020.1800362.

Brown, M.G. 2016. Blended instructional practice: A review of the empirical literature on instructors' adoption and use of online tools in face-to-face teaching. *The Internet and Higher Education* 31: 1–10. https://doi.org/10.1016/j.iheduc.2016.05.001.

Carrillo, C., and M.A. Flores. 2020. COVID-19 and teacher education: A literature review of online teaching and learning practices. *European Journal of Teacher Education* 43 (4): 466–487. https://doi.org/10.1080/02619768.2020.1821184.

CIUTI. n.d. Online platform conference interpreting. https://www.ciuti.org/education-training/online-platform-conference-interpreting/. Accessed 18 Mar 2022.

D'Hayer, D. 2012. Public service interpreting and translation: Moving towards a (virtual) community of practice. *Meta* 57 (1): 235–247. https://doi.org/10.7202/1012751ar.

Gao, J., and C. Li. 2021. A case study of multi-platform collaborative ICT integrated online language teaching during the pandemic: Advantages and challenges. *Applied Linguistics Research Journal* 5 (5): 221–232. https://doi.org/10.14744/alrj.2021.89410.

Gather. 2022. Design a more accessible space. Last modified 4 April 2022. https://support.gather.town/help/accessibility-best-practices. Accessed 18 Apr 2022.

Gather. n.d. Building a better way to meet online. https://www.gather.town/about. Accessed 22 Apr 2022.

Han, L., Y. Wang, and Y. Li. 2022. Student perceptions of online interpreting teaching and learning via the Zoom platform. *The Electronic Journal for English as a Second Language* 26 (1): 1–19. https://doi.org/10.55593/ej.25101int.

Hickey, S. 2021. Innovation and investment in remote interpreting. https://www.nimdzi.com/innovation-remote-interpreting/. Accessed 9 Mar 2022.

Hodges, C., S. Moore, B. Lockee, T. Trust, and A. Bond. 2020. The difference between emergency remote teaching and online learning. *EDUCAUSE Review* (blog). https://er.educause.edu/articles/2020/3/the-difference-between-emergency-remote-teaching-and-online-learning. Accessed 6 Feb 2022.

Hubscher-Davidson, S., and J. Devaux. 2021. Teaching translation and interpreting in virtual environments. *The Journal of Specialised Translation* 36b: 184–192.

Kapp, K.M. 2012. *The gamification of learning and instruction: Game-based methods and strategies for training and education.* San Francisco: Pfeiffer.

Ko, L. 2006. Teaching interpreting by distance mode: Possibilities and constraints. *Interpreting* 8 (1): 67–96. https://doi.org/10.1075/intp.8.1.05ko.

Ko, L., and N.-S. Chen. 2011. Online-interpreting in synchronous cyber classrooms. *Babel* 57 (2): 123–143. https://doi.org/10.1075/babel.57.2.01ko.

Lee, K., M. Fanguy, X.S. Lu, and B. Bligh. 2021. Student learning during COVID-19: It was not as bad as we feared. *Distance Education* 42 (1): 164–172. https://doi.org/10.1080/01587919.2020.1869529.

Lepp, A., J.E. Barkley, A.C. Karpinski, and S. Singh. 2019. College students' multitasking behavior in online versus face-to-face courses. *SAGE Open* 9 (1): 1–9. https://doi.org/10.1177/2158244018824505.

McClure, C. D., and P. N. Williams. 2021. Gather. town: An opportunity for self-paced learning in a synchronous, distance-learning environment. *Compass: Journal of Learning and Teaching* 14 (2): 1–19. https://doi.org/10.21100/compass.v14i2.1232.

Motta, M. 2016. A blended learning environment based on the principles of deliberate practice for the acquisition of interpreting skills. *The Interpreter and Translator Trainer* 10 (1): 133–149. https://doi.org/10.1080/1750399X.2016.1154347.

Mulayim, S., and M. Lai. 2015. The community-of-inquiry framework in online interpreter training. In *Interpreter education in the digital age: Innovation, access, and change*, ed. S. Ehrlich and J. Napier, 95–124. Washington, DC: Gallaudet University Press.

O'Hagan, M., and D. Ashworth. 2002. *Translation-mediated communication in a digital world: Facing the challenges of globalization and localization.* Clevedon: Multilingual Matters.

Ocak, M.A. 2011. Why are faculty members not teaching blended courses? Insights from faculty members. *Computers & Education* 56 (3): 689–699. https://doi.org/10.1016/j.compedu.2010.10.011.

Ozolins, U. 1991. *Interpreting translating and language policy: Report to the Language and Society Centre, National Languages Institute of Australia*. Melbourne: National Languages Institute of Australia.

Perramon, M., and X. Ugarte. 2020. Teaching interpreting online for the Translation and Interpreting Degree at the University of Vic: A nonstop challenge since 2001. *Translation and Translanguaging in Multilingual Contexts* 6 (2): 172–182. https://doi.org/10.1075/ttmc.00052.per.

Sandrelli, A. 2015. Becoming an interpreter: The role of computer technology. *MonTI* (Special Issue 2): 111–138. https://doi.org/10.6035/MonTI.2015.ne2.4.

Scamman, K. 2020. Changing trends in language interpretation services. https://telelanguage.com/blog/changing-trends-language-interpretation-services/. Accessed 9 Mar 2022.

Tshabalala, M., C. Ndeya-Ndereya, and T. van der Merwe. 2014. Implementing blended learning at a developing university: Obstacles in the way. *Electronic Journal of E-Learning* 12 (1): 101–110.

Zhang, W., Y. Wang, L. Yang, and C. Wang. 2020. Suspending classes without stopping learning: China's education emergency management policy in the COVID-19 outbreak. *Journal of Risk and Financial Management* 13 (3): 55. https://www.mdpi.com/1911-8074/13/3/55.

Chen-En (Ted) Ho is Senior Lecturer (Education) in the School of Arts, English and Languages of Queen's University Belfast in Northern Ireland, the United Kingdom. His research interests span from cognitive translation and interpreting studies, through T&I education and industry, to public service interpreting, with foci currently landing on the cognitive aspect of T&I and students' learning motivation and employability.

Yuan Zou is a Ph.D. student in the School of Arts, English and Languages of Queen's University Belfast in Northern Ireland, the United Kingdom.

Chapter 17
Use of Computer-Assisted Interpreting Tools in Conference Interpreting Training and Practice During COVID-19

Nan Zhao

Abstract In the age of COVID-19, a major change has been seen in the conferencein-terpreting industry and the teaching of interpreting, i.e., the online mode has become the new normal. Interpreting practitioners are facing an increasing demand for interpreting services online while interpreting trainers and trainees are balancing on-campus, online and mixed-mode teaching. This challenging change has been induced by the pandemic but potentiated by the development of information and communication technologies (ICTs). Due to COVID-19, computer-assisted interpreting (CAI) has begun to receive considerable attention. In a broad sense, CAI is defined as all interpreting activities conducted with the help of ICTs. In this article, CAI technologies are categorized into four groups: remote interpreting (RI), computer-assisted interpreting training (CAIT), pre-task tools, and in-task tools, especially automatic speech recognition (ASR). The article reviews the development of CAI technologies in the past two decades and briefly evaluates the state-of-the-art CAI technologies and presents their practical use in real-life scenarios.

Keywords Computer-assisted interpreting (CAI) · Information and communication technologies (ICTs) · Remote interpreting (RI) · Computer-assisted interpreting training (CAIT) · Pre-task tools · In-task tools · Automatic speech recognition (ASR)

17.1 Development of Computer-Assisted Interpreting Technologies

Computer-assisted interpreting (CAI) has been around for several decades, but up till 2010, only a small number of studies had been dedicated to it (Braun 2006; Fantinuoli 2006; Berber-Irabien 2010; Winteringham 2010). Fantinuoli (2018a) defined CAI as "as a form of oral translation, wherein a human interpreter makes use of

N. Zhao (✉)
Department of Translation, Interpreting and Intercultural Studies, Tong Hong Kong Baptist University, 224 Waterloo Rd., Hong Kong, China
e-mail: nanzhao@hkbu.edu.hk

K. Liu and A. K. F. Cheung (eds.), *Translation and Interpreting in the Age of COVID-19*, Corpora and Intercultural Studies 9,
https://doi.org/10.1007/978-981-19-6680-4_17

computer software developed to support and facilitate some aspects of the interpreting task with the overall goal to increase quality and productivity." He also proposed two ways of distinguishing CAI technologies/tools: (a) process-oriented ("computer programs … assist interpreters in at least one sub-processes of interpreting") versus setting-oriented technologies ("booth consoles, remote interpreting devices, training platforms, etc."); (b) first (mere terminology management) and second generation ("holistic approach to terminology and knowledge"). Corpas Pastor and Fern (2016) put forwards a rather large coverage of CAI tools, including five types: terminology management tools, note-taking tools, speech-to-text converters, computer-assisted interpreter training (CAIT) tools and other assisted applications. Braun (2019) distinguished three modes of interpreting with the help of technology, i.e., technology-mediated interpreting, technology-supported interpreting, and technology-generated interpreting. Prandi (2020) summarized that CAI tools are software solutions for terminology and knowledge management, and workstations to support each phase of interpreting tasks. This article adopts these previous definitions of CAI and categorization of CAI tools. CAI refers to interpreting practice and training that utilizes information and communication technologies (ICTs) and CAI tools fall into four groups: remote interpreting (RI), computer-assisted interpreting training (CAIT), pre-task and in-task tools. By defining CAI and categorizing CAI tools, this section provides a chronological review of the previous research in CAI technologies.

17.1.1 Remote Interpreting

Fantinuoli (2019) and Ziegler and Gigliobianco (2018) defined remote interpreting (RI) as a form of interpreting where the interpreter and the speaker are located in different sites and the interpreting service is delivered with the help of ICTs. The definition fits the purpose of this article appropriately and thus is borrowed here. According to a report by the Interpretation Directorate of the European Parliament (Bouchard et al. 2001), the first major RI experiment can be traced back to 1976 and more were performed in the 1990s, but all generated unsatisfactory results due to technical limitations. Noticing the potential of RI, the International Association of Conference Interpreters (AIIC), together with other interpreters' associations and international organizations, standardized the requirements for RI settings (2000). However, up till the beginning of the twenty-first century, RI was still deemed an unacceptable option for providing interpreting services at the European Parliament (Bouchard et al. 2001, 2002). Nevertheless, the exploration of RI did not stop because of two motivations (Mouzourakis 2006). First, RI improves the availability and reduces the cost of interpreting services as interpreters do not have to be present in the meeting room. Second, RI is an alternative when on-site interpreting is not feasible because of some constraints, e.g., insufficient booths for all languages, booths cannot be installed in the meeting room, or interpreters must be separated from the meeting participants out of security considerations. Mouzourakis (2006) then suggested to "define a prototype remote booth configuration ... within which future RI experimentation might be conducted under standardized and controlled conditions" and expected a more reliable and cohesive delivery of video and audio information from meeting rooms to interpreters and regular use of RI. Despite the fact that there were problems to be solved, researchers still believed in the rise of RI (Braun 2006; Winteringham 2010). As ICTs advanced, larger bandwidth, lower Internet latency and more efficient coding of video and audio were achieved, which made RI more reliable and accessible (Causo 2011). Coming to the end of the 2010s, RI received much more attention and was believed to have the potential to become mainstream in the market and deemed necessary in the interpreting training courses.

Later on, systematic teaching methods of RI were studied and introduced (Amato et al. 2018; Fantinuoli and Prandi 2018; Fantinuoli 2019). Ziegler and Gigliobianco (2018) designed an experiment of three RI modalities focusing on how the meeting room was presented to interpreters, i.e., switching between two pictures from two fixed cameras facing two speakers, remotely controlling one camera in the meeting room, and using virtual reality glasses. From the experiment, they proposed further utilization of ICTs in RI, such as augmented reality and home interpreting hub, but these two solutions both required a dedicated Internet connection, specific devices, and even technical support. Approaching the 2020s, researchers continued to study and develop the practice of RI. Davitti and Braun (2020) performed "a qualitative analysis of how interaction unfolds in ... VRI [video remote interpreting] dialogue settings" which "provides fruitful ground" for systematically integrating RI in interpreting training courses. And through surveys and experiments, it was found that RI, adopted as a pedagogical tool in virtual classes of interpreting training courses, provides interpreting trainees chances not only to learn about the use of RI, but also to get in touch with the real market where there is a variety of scenarios (Riccardi et al. 2020; Eraslan et al. 2020).

17.1.2 Computer-Assisted Interpreting Training

"In simple terms, CAIT is the idea that computer technology can be used to enhance interpreter training" (Pochhacker 2015). As early as the 1990s, some interpreting trainers studied the use of multimedia technologies and integrated computer programs in their interpreting training courses (Cervato and de Ferra 1995; Merlini 1996; Carabelli 1999). This was when the idea of computer-assisted interpreting training (CAIT) started to take shape. CAIT can be divided into three categories, i.e., repository approach (creating speech banks), courseware approach (trainers prearranging the pedagogical materials) and virtual learning environment (VLE) (Pochhacker 2015; Sandrelli and Jerez 2007; Şahin 2013). IRIS and Marius are two databases of interpreting training materials created in the early twenty-first century. The former contains both oral and written texts while the latter features speeches from real-live events (Gran et al. 2002). Black Box is a tool of courseware approach, with which trainers can create interpreting training exercises and materials easily (Sandrelli

2007). The interpreting trainers in the University Jaume I in Spain introduced a virtual classroom in which their trainees could attend training sessions from home, and this virtual learning environment was "conceived as a complement to the usual space–time interaction" (Mayor and Ivars 2007). Lim designed a computer-assisted platform (CAP) with lecture notes, glossaries, online dictionaries and pedagogical video and audio files. After the comparation between the CAP and traditional interpreting training methods, it was revealed that CAP is "a valuable and alternative means of interpreter training." (Lim 2007). Kajzer-Wietrzny and Tymczyńska (2014) reviewed different CAIT tools ranging from "websites, speech repositories, video corpora, interpreter training software, course management systems (CMS), video conferencing tools to a self-contained 3D virtual learning environment with bespoke pedagogical materials" and presented the use of these tools for various interpreting training purposes. Ciordia (2017) offered "a sociocognitive perspective on how online interactive pedagogical environments can make interpreter training collaboration more efficient" by examining the motivating effect of CAIT and overviewing the potential impact of some virtual tools in interpreting training. In 2020, researchers continued to show great interest in the study of CAIT. Braun et al. (2020) conducted an experiment on VLE, and the subjects expressed an overall positive attitude towards VLE, but there were three points to be considered: comprehensive preparation and technical support are needed for successful use of VLE, collaborative effort is necessary to utilize VLE in interpreting training, and inter-institutional collaboration is required to integrate VLE technologies. Other studies similarly found that VLE has the potential to improve interpreting training, but some challenges need to be overcome (Eraslan et al. 2020; Riccardi et al. 2020; Rodríguez Melchor 2020).

17.1.3 Pre-task Tools

The preparation of an interpreting task includes the acquisition of linguistic and extra-linguistic information (Gile 2009). As known to all interpreters, such preparation prior to the actual interpreting task, e.g., collection, management and memorization of terminology, comparation of parallel text, and familiarization of topic-specific knowledge, can be time-consuming. Thanks to the emergence of the World Wide Web (the Web) and search engines in the Information Age, interpreters are relieved from extensive reading and excessive paperwork when preparing for their interpreting tasks. And it has become easier than ever to get their hands on information by just few clicks. Therefore, the Web can be conceived as the very first pre-task tool. Since the Web was not designed specifically for interpreters, it is still not efficient enough when interpreters try to search and collect terms online. Therefore, attempts were made to create an automated procedure to search and extract terms of a certain topic from the Web and generate a term list that was directly usable to interpreters (Fantinuoli 2006; Baroni et al. 2006; Lim 2007). Terminology management tools for interpreters began to sprout in the twenty-first century, e.g., LookUp,[1] Interplex,[2] Interpreters'Help,[3] AnyLexic[4] and Intragloss[5] and InterpretBank,[6] just to name a few. Most of these terminology management tools are flexible and user-friendly, but none is able to fulfil all the needs of interpreters (Berber-Irabien 2010; Costa et al. 2014a, b). Xu (2015, 2018; Xu and Sharoff 2014) emphasized the study of corpus-based terminology preparation for interpreting and conducted several experiments on various term extraction tools and concordance tools to find out the effects and drawbacks of these tools. Fantinuoli (2018c) also saw the usefulness of corpus-based preparation of terminology and suggested the integration of the use of comparable corpora into interpreters' workflow. Approaching the end of the 2010s, researchers, through surveys, reviews or comparisons, revealed the common lack of awareness among interpreters of the existence of new CAI tools and the lack of empirical study on the use, effect, and trend of CAI tools (Corpas Pastor and Fern 2016; Fantinuoli 2018a, b; Costa et al. 2018).

As more and more attention and studies are devoted to terminology management tools, those tools keep updating to meet the evolving needs of interpreters. With the acquisition of linguistic and extra-linguistic information being re-emphasized, a new generation of terminology management tool, InterpretBank, has come to the market with features including text management, automated term extraction, term memorization, etc. (Fantinuoli 2016, 2017a).

17.1.4 In-Task Tools

In the late 2000s, some researchers worried that using ICTs during interpreting tasks, whether consecutive or simultaneous, might be impractical, as such behaviour could be time-consuming and distracting for interpreters (Donovan 2006; Winteringham 2010). Still, the prospering ICTs encouraged researchers to continue their exploration of using ICTs in interpreting, and many visionary ideas sprouted up. Digital pens were used to take notes in consecutive interpreting, and they could record the process of notetaking and the source speech synchronically (Orlando 2010). Some automatic oral translation devices were put to the market, indicating the emergence of machine interpreting (Kelly 2008; Dillinger and Gerber 2009; Winteringham 2010). The mid-2010s saw the turning point of the study of CAI, as growing attention and interest were placed in the field and scholars started to put more effort into it. Prandi (2015) initiated a pilot study on student interpreters' use of InterpretBank, more specifically using InterpretBank to look up terminology in the booth, and it was found that,

[1] https://www.lookup-online.de (not accessible as of May 14th, 2022).

[2] https://www.fourwillows.com/interplex.html (last access date: May 14th, 2022).

[3] https://www.interpretershelp.com (last access date: May 14th, 2022).

[4] https://www.anylexic.com (last access date: May 14th, 2022).

[5] https://intragloss.com (not accessible as of May 14th, 2022).

[6] https://interpretbank.com/site/ (last access date: May 14th, 2022).

after proper practice, student interpreters were able to work with the CAI tool in the booth. Diving further into the field, Prandi (2017, 2018) then proposed a methodology which applies Seeber's Cognitive Load Model (Seeber 2011, 2013) to study the cognitive effect of CAI in simultaneous interpreting. Fantinuoli (2016, 2017b) proposed to integrate automatic speech recognition (ASR) with CAI to reduce interpreters' cognitive burden when using CAI during interpreting. Such integration of the two aroused the interest of more scholars, and more research, empirical and bibliographical, was performed (Ortiz and Cavallo 2018; Desmet et la. 2018; Defrancq and Fantinuoli 2021). Among them, two empirical studies explored how CAI with ASR affects interpreters' rendition of numbers, and the experiment results were quite promising (Desmet et al. 2018; Pisani and Fantinuoli 2021). Orlando (2014) and Chen (2017) updated the study on the use of digital pens in consecutive interpreting and found it a powerful method of studying the balance between notetaking and interpreting. Goldsmith (2018) ran a pilot study on tablet interpreting and discovered that, to some extent, tablets are an alternative to pen and paper. To further fill in the gap of scarce studies on CAI with up-to-date technology, a research and development project, named VIP, was introduced, and one of its project modules is dedicated to developing tools used during interpreting tasks (Corpas Pastor 2017). The use of ICTs in interpreting also garnered attention from interpreters working in emergency situations with refugees, and it was revealed that ICTs are important to their interpreting services (Atabekova et al. 2018). Wang and Wang (2019) conducted an experimental study on the influence of CAI tools on consecutive interpreting.

17.2 Current Use of Computer-Assisted Interpreting Technologies

This section briefly reviews the selected state-of-the-art CAI tools and technologies and then presents the use of them.

17.2.1 Remote Interpreting

17.2.1.1 Zoom[7]

Ever since the outbreak of COVID-19 and the lockdown, travel restriction and social distancing policies that came along with it, a great portion of people's daily activities have shifted from the physical world to the virtual world. Workplaces, classrooms, meeting venues and clinics are now moved to online platforms, e.g., Zoom, Google Meet, Skype, Microsoft Teams, etc. This dramatic change profoundly affects the conference interpreting market. As an increasing amount of conferences are held

[7] https://zoom.us/ (last access date: May 14th, 2022).

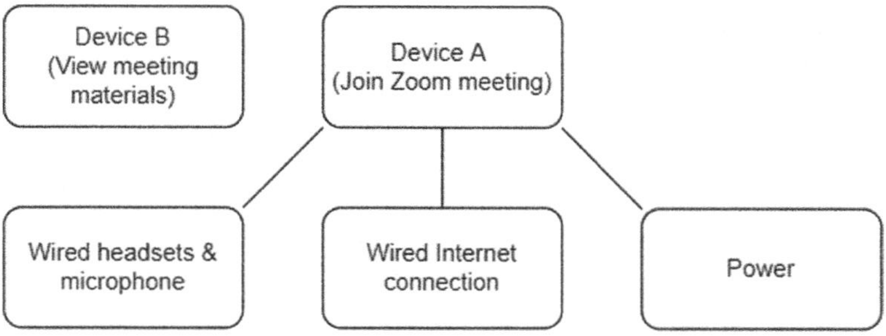

Fig. 17.1 Settings for CI mode and single-interpreter mode

online, the demand for RI services has also seen a sharp rise. And among all those videoconference platforms in the market, Zoom distinguishes itself, not only because of its large volume, but also its unique feature of Language Interpretation (Zoom 2022). It is easy to use the interpretation feature as an audience member, but for the interpreter, some basic setting requirements must be met. First of all, the working environment of the interpreter must be quiet enough and even insulated in order to ensure the sound quality of the interpreter's output. The Internet connection should have a speed of at least 100 Mbps and a latency below 200 ms so as to stay stably connected. The devices, gadgets, Internet connection, audio signal and video signal should be checked prior to the meeting. There are also some additional requirements varying for the three interpreting modes, i.e., consecutive interpreting (CI) mode, single-interpreter simultaneous (SI) mode and paired SI mode.

(1) For consecutive interpreting and single-interpreter SI mode, the setting should be as shown in Fig. 17.1.

In CI mode, the feature of Language Interpretation is disabled, and the interpreter joins the meeting as a normal meeting participant. In single-interpreter SI mode, regardless of its non-reasonability, the feature of Language Interpretation is enabled, and the interpreter is assigned as interpreter when joining the meeting. Device A is used to join the Zoom meeting and must be charged and plugged in during the whole meeting to avoid power shortages. Device B is used for presenting meeting materials, e.g., slides and vocabulary. It would be safer not to saddle Device A with tasks other than joining the online meeting. A wired Internet connection is preferred over a wireless connection, and fibre over broadband, for a more stable and reliable Internet connection. Wired headsets and microphones ensure stable and reliable transmission of audio signal and avoid echoing.

(2) For paired simultaneous interpreting mode, the setting should be as shown in Fig. 17.2.

In paired SI mode, the feature of Language Interpretation is enabled, and the interpreter is assigned as interpreter to join the meeting. On top of the setting in CI mode, a third device is needed. Device C is used to communicate with the partner for handover. Zoom (version 5.9.6 or higher) also supports interpretation relay, so it is

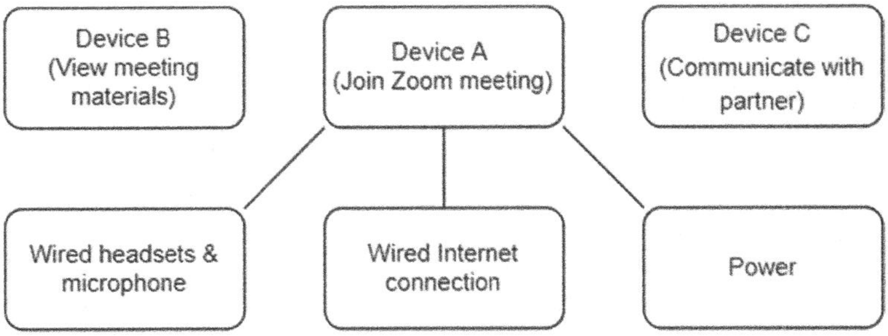

Fig. 17.2 Settings for paired SI mode

feasible to listen to the partner's output by selecting their output language channel, i.e., interpreters can work in pairs.

To sum up, Zoom is designed more for videoconference than for remote simultaneous interpreting (RSI). But because of the feature of Language Interpretation, it is possible to set up a simple and functional RSI platform with Zoom. However, a third device is still needed in paired SI mode to make up for the missing function of handover. And such a makeshift solution does not work seamlessly and might distract the interpreter from the already attention-demanding RSI task. Furthermore, this makeshift RSI platform can easily go wrong as there are three devices involved.

17.2.1.2 RSI Platforms

As shown above, establishing a simple RSI platform by oneself is possible, but it is not necessary since there already are several ready-to-use RSI platforms available on the market, including Interactio,[8] Interprefy,[9] VoiceBoxer,[10] Ablio Conference,[11] KUDO,[12] QuaQua[13] and Green Terp.[14] These RSI platforms work in various ways. Some can work as stand-alone videoconference platforms. Some offer an add-on option which can work with common videoconference platforms. And some are installation-free and can be simply used with a web browser. Although they all look different in terms of button layout and some minor features, to the core, they share a common point: imitating the logic of a real SI booth, which differentiates them from those common videoconference platforms.

Interactio is taken as an example of how these RSI platforms work. Firstly, to work with Interactio, the interpreter needs to fulfil some requirements. Beyond relevant

[8] https://www.interactio.io/ (last access date: May 14th, 2022).

[9] https://www.interprefy.com/ (last access date: May 14th, 2022).

[10] https://voiceboxer.com/ (last access date: May 14th, 2022).

[11] https://ablioconference.com/home (last access date: May 14th, 2022).

[12] https://kudoway.com/ (last access date: May 14th, 2022).

[13] https://quaquameeting.com/ (last access date: May 14th, 2022).

[14] https://www.gtmeeting.com/ (last access date: May 14th, 2022).

experience of working as an interpreter, the interpreter also needs to have a stable ethernet cable connection with backup, a headset with an attached microphone and noise cancellation feature and a personal computer that can run videoconferences without any problem (Interactio 2022). And training will be given before the interpreter starts to provide interpreting services on the platform. The interpreter's console on the platform is a replication of an in-booth console. It allows the interpreter to switch between the speaker and their slides, and it provides buttons for choosing channels, changing the volume of each source channel, muting the microphone temporarily, and more importantly, performing handover. The other RSI platforms are more or less similar to Interactio, but the mechanisms of handover may vary from one another.

These RSI platforms are getting more and more popular among event organizers for several reasons. Firstly, as already mentioned above, the pandemic forces them to hold their event online. Secondly, RSI is more flexible and convenient than the traditional on-site SI. Thirdly, compared with normal SI, RSI is much more cost-effective and affordable as it incurs no cost from renting fancy booth and SI devices or covering interpreters' travel expenses. Therefore, it is reasonable to assume that RSI will continue to exist and grow even after the pandemic.

17.2.2 Computer-Assisted Interpreting Training

In the age of COVID-19, CAIT has moved a step forward as training activities are moved to the virtual world, which brings many challenges to interpreting trainers and trainees alike. The two biggest challenges are RSI practice and online mock-conference. As said above, Zoom is one of the most popular videoconference platforms and is used by many universities and institutions for online classes, which means that there is no extra cost to buy one RSI platform. Furthermore, the feasibility of using Zoom for RSI has been proven. Therefore, Zoom is an appropriate example of a CAIT tool.

In SI classrooms or laboratories, trainees use a built-in console to practice interpreting while trainers use a master console to monitor trainees' output and record them for later assessment. To conduct RSI practice on Zoom, the settings are similar to Figs. 17.1 and 17.2, but with some modifications (see Fig. 17.3).

As shown in Fig. 17.3, for RSI practice, the trainer, also meeting host, enables the feature of Language Interpretation and assigns trainees as interpreters of different language pairs (nominally). Device A is used to host the Zoom meeting and play practice materials. To transmit the practice materials, be it video or audio, to the trainees, the trainer needs to share their screen together with Device A's audio. Device B is a must for monitoring trainees' output, as monitoring via Device A would also transmit the monitored trainee's output to all the other trainees. By switching among language channels, the trainer is able to monitor up to 20 trainees in one meeting (limit set by Zoom). On the trainees' side, Device B is used to record themselves, and the recording files need to be sent to the trainer afterwards. The dotted lines between

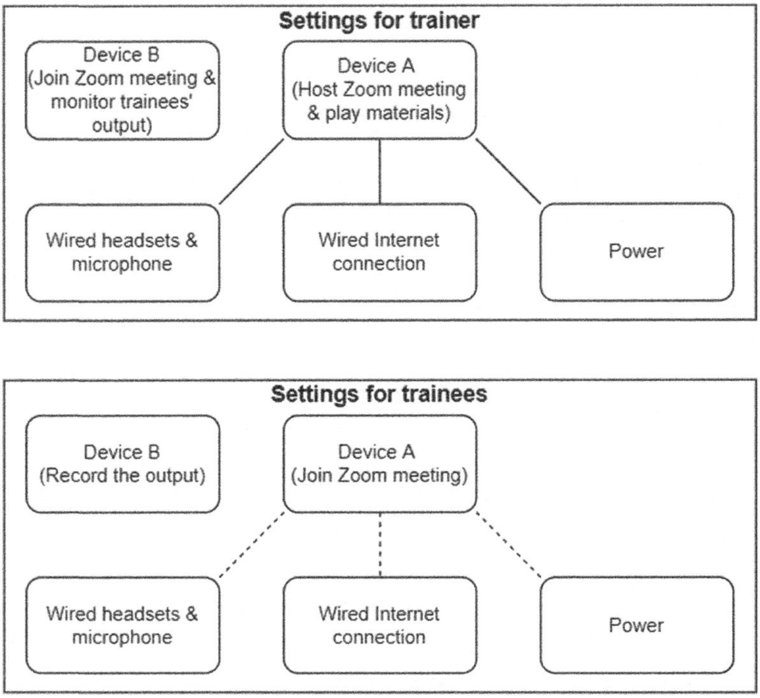

Fig. 17.3 Settings for practicing RSI on Zoom

Device A and three setting requirements indicate that these settings are preferable, but not compulsory, because it is difficult to unify dozens of trainees. However, it is necessary to inform the trainees that these settings are the accepted standard in the market. As for slides and vocabularies, the trainees can either view them on Device B or print them out.

Mock-conference is a comprehensive method to test the result of interpreting training. Holding a mock-conference on Zoom allows trainers and trainees to realistically simulate RSI. The settings are basically same as in RSI practice, but a third device (Device C) is needed for the trainees to communicate with their partners (see Fig. 17.4).

Obviously, CAIT can also be brought to those RSI platforms, and it would be easier to do RSI practice and hold mock-conferences although universities and institutions do need to purchase an RSI platform. Among all the RSI platforms mentioned above, it is worth noting that Green Terp designs a solution dedicated to CAIT: True Virtual Booths (TVB) (Green Terp 2022). Apart from the simulation of SI booths, TVB also offers interpreting trainers a virtual master console, with which trainers can monitor and record each virtual booth. The recording is dual-tracked, so the source and target can be played synchronically, which is important for reviewing the interpreting performance.

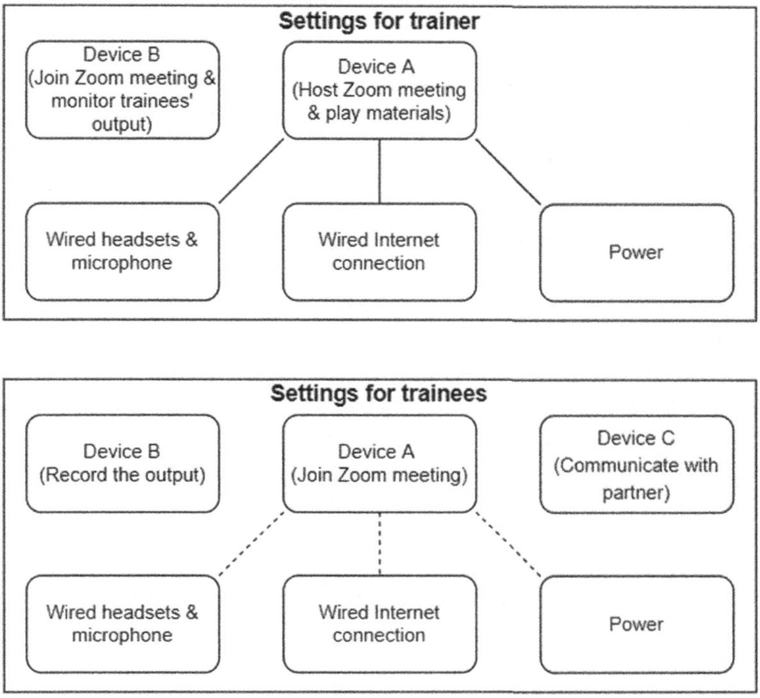

Fig. 17.4 Settings for conducting SI mock-conference on Zoom

17.2.3 Pre-task Tools

As reviewed in Sect. 17.1.3, there are several pre-task tools available on the market. Among them, InterpretBank stands out, as its features go far beyond terminology management, and it is categorized as one of the second-generation CAI tools (Fantinuoli 2016; Ortiz and Cavallo 2018).

The basic terminology management features of InterpretBank are just like those of its counterparts. It allows users to manually input terms one by one or to batch import them from existing glossaries; to categorize glossaries according to topics, domains or events; to look up terms; to export glossaries for printing or sharing, etc. It is worth mentioning that when looking up a term, users (interpreters) do not have to type from the beginning of the term, but can type any continuous string of the term, so as to ease the process of searching for interpreters during their interpreting tasks. Apart from basic features mentioned above, InterpretBank also offers the following useful features:

Machine translation: The tool comes with built-in term bases from Interactive Terminology for Europe (IATE)[15] and InterpretBank's resources. And it allows users to add additional term bases. Therefore, when building a glossary, users can get

[15] https://iate.europa.eu/about (last access date: May 14th, 2022).

machine translation suggestions. If there is a long list of terms to translate, users can have them all translated by machine with just a few clicks. Although the quality of machine translation is sometimes in doubt, the idea itself is exciting, especially for interpreters who have a tight timeline.

Automatic term generation: This is another time-saving feature. The tool can automatically generate a list of terms about a topic or from a webpage or a Word file. Users just need to input a few keywords about the topic or a link to the webpage or upload the file and leave the rest of the work to the program. From the author's subjective user experience, broad and vague keywords, e.g., economy, politics, technology, would lead to a massive list of unwanted terms. And this feature can be used together with machine translation, which means that the tool can create a complete glossary by itself. Again, human review is needed as the quality of it is not assured.

Manual and automatic term extraction: Users can upload documents to InterpretBank and then manually extract terms from the documents by highlighting them. Furthermore, parallel texts can be opened side by side in one window, which is more efficient for finding the equivalents of terms. Alternatively, users can give the work to the program which extracts and lists out terms for selection. Since this feature is based on algorithms, the quality of terms is decided by the volume of text input into the program, i.e., the more documents are uploaded, the better the result will be.

17.2.4 In-Task Tools

Since interpreting itself is a task with heavy cognitive load, the in-task tools must not require much cognition from interpreters (Fantinuoli 2018a, 2019). Some pre-task tools, such as InterpretBank and Interpreters'Help, offer the feature of looking up terms by entering any continuous string of the terms, so as to ease and quicken the process. However, when interpreters are working, especially in SI, they cannot afford even one second of distraction. Among those CAI tools currently available in the market, ASR presents a promising future as an in-task tool.

ASR is nothing new, and there have already been many mature products being used for a long time, e.g., Google's voice typing,[16] IBM Watson Speech to Text service,[17] iFlytek's Jarvisen Translator,[18] Tencent's SI solution,[19] etc. However, these products are not designed for interpreters, and some are even designed to replace human interpreters. Now the question is "how to integrate ASR into interpreting". InterpretBank gives an answer, although it's an experimental one.

To use the ASR feature of InterpretBank, users need to select a glossary first (only terms in the glossary will be captured by the program), then get a link to the ASR interface and open the link on a web browser. Once the ASR session is started,

---

[16] https://support.google.com/docs/answer/4492226?hl=en (last access date: May 14th, 2022).

[17] https://speech-to-text-demo.ng.bluemix.net/ (last access date: May 14th, 2022).

[18] https://www.iflytek.com/en/products/#/translat (last access date: May 14th, 2022).

[19] https://cloud.tencent.com/product/tsi (in Chinese only, last access date: May 14th, 2022).

instead of showing a complete transcription of the source speeches, the program will prompt the terms and numbers it captures only. InterpretBank's ASR can be applied to on-site interpreting or RI. However, to input source speech to the program, users must have some technical skills (InterpretBank 2022). This is one of the downsides of the feature among others, e.g., the quality of ASR result can be easily affected by the input quality of source speech, few languages are supported, one ASR session only lasts for five minutes (Build 8.12) and it needs to be manually restarted for a second session. However, this experimental feature is exciting enough to attract more attention, thus more study on ASR in CAI can be expected which, in turn, will accelerate the advancement of ASR in CAI.

17.3 Conclusion

This article provides a brief review of the historical development of CAI before introducing the state-of-the-art CAI tools of four categories, i.e., RI, CAIT, pre-task tools, and in-task tools. The study of CAI and the development of CAI tools have seen much improvement since the 2010s, and many exciting ideas have sprouted up since then, such as ASR in CAI. Although results of surveys and experiments show a generally positive attitude towards CAI tools and their use, current interpreting training courses do not put enough emphasis on the teaching of CAI tools (Wang and Wang 2019; Davitti and Braun 2020; Rodríguez Melchor, Horváth, and Ferguson 2020; Yuan 2021; Defrancq and Fantinuoli 2021; Pisani and Fantinuoli 2021). Therefore, while the study on CAI continues, the training of CAI also deserves improvement.

References

Amato, A., N. Spinolo, and M. J. González Rodríguez, eds. 2018. *Handbook of remote interpreting - SHIFT in orality.* Bologna: University of Bologna, Department of Interpretation and Translation. https://doi.org/10.6092/unibo/amsacta/5955.

Atabekova, A., R. Gorbatenko, T. Shoustikova, and C. Valero-Garcés. 2018. Cross-cultural mediation with refugees in emergency settings: ICT use by language service providers. *Journal of Social Studies Education Research* 9 (3): 351–369. https://doi.org/10.17499/jsser.71392.

Baroni, M., A. Kilgarriff, J. Pomikálek, and P. Rychlý. 2006. WebBootCaT: Instant domain-specific corpora to support human translators. In *Proceedings of EAMT 2006-11th annual conference of the European association for machine translation*, 247–252. Oslo: The Norwegian National LOGON Consortium and The Deparments of Computer Science and Linguistics and Nordic Studies at Oslo University (Norway). https://www.muni.cz/en/research/publications/638048.

Berber-Irabien, D. 2010. Information and communication technologies in conference interpreting. PhD thesis, Universitat Rovira i Virgili.

Bouchard, M., S. Carriles, F. Denis, B. Gevaert, M. Gomes, T. Gram, P. Mouzourakis, et al. 2001. *Report on the remote interpretation test.* Brussels: Interpretation Directorate, European Parliament.

Bouchard, M., S. Carriles, F. Denis, B. Gevaert, M. Gomes, T. Gram, P. Piels, et al. 2002. *Report on the 2nd remote interpretation test.* Brussels: Interpretation Directorate, European Parliament.

Braun, S. 2006. Multimedia communication technologies and their impact on interpreting. In *Proceedings of the marie curie euroconferences MuTra: Audiovisual translation scenario–copenhagen 1–5 May 2006*, ed. M. Carroll, H. Gerzymisch-Arbogast, and S. Nauert.

Braun, S. 2019. Technology and interpreting. In *The Routledge handbook of translation and technology*, ed. M. O'Hagan, 271–288. London: Routledge. https://doi.org/10.4324/9781315311258.

Braun, S., E. Davitti, and C. Slater. 2020. 'It's like being in bubbles': Affordances and challenges of virtual learning environments for collaborative learning in interpreter education. *The Interpreter and Translator Trainer* 14 (3): 259–278. https://doi.org/10.1080/1750399X.2020.1800362.

Carabelli, A. 1999. Multimedia technologies for the use of interpreters and translators. *The Interpreters' Newsletter* 9: 149–155. http://hdl.handle.net/10077/2217.

Causo, J.E. 2011. Conference interpreting with information and communication technologies-experiences from the European commission DG interpretation. In *Videoconference and remote interpreting in criminal proceedings*, ed. S. Braun and J.L. Taylr, 199–203. Guilford: University of Surrey.

Cervato, E., and D. de Ferra. 1995. 'Interprit': A computerised self-access course for beginners in interpreting. *Perspectives: Studies in Translation Theory and Practice* 3 (2): 191–204. https://doi.org/10.1080/0907676X.1995.9961260.

Chen, S. 2017. Note-taking in consecutive interpreting: New data from pen recording. *Translation and Interpreting* 9 (1): 4–23. https://doi.org/10.12807/ti.109201.2017.a02.

Ciordia, L. S. 2017. Implementing safe and effective collaborative environments in technology-enhanced interpreter training. *CLINA Revista Interdisciplinaria De Traducción Interpretación Y Comunicación Intercultural* 3 (1): 35–55. https://doi.org/10.14201/clina2017313555.

Corpas Pastor, G. 2017. VIP: Voice-text integrated system for interpreters. In *Proceedings of the 39th conference: Translating and the computer*, ed. J. Esteves-Ferreira, J. Macan, R. Mitkov, and O.-M. Stefanov, 7–10. London: AsLing. http://hdl.handle.net/2436/621167.

Corpas Pastor, G., and L. M. Fern. 2016. *A survey of interpreters' needs and practices related to language technology.* Technical report, Universidad de Malaga.

Costa, H., G. Corpas Pastor, and I. D. Muñoz. 2014a. A comparative user evaluation of terminology management tools for interpreters. In *Proceedings of the 4th international workshop on computational terminology (Computerm)*, 68–76. Dublin, Ireland: Association for Computational Linguistics and Dublin City University. https://doi.org/10.13140/2.1.1799.3602.

Costa, H., G. Corpas Pastor, and I. D. Muñoz. 2014b. *Technology-assisted interpreting.* https://multilingual.com/articles/technology-assisted-interpreting/. Accessed 12 May 2022.

Costa, H., G. Corpas Pastor, and I. D. Muñoz. 2018. Assessing terminology management systems for interpreters. In *Trends in e-tools and resources for translators and interpreters*, ed. H. Costa, G. Corpas Pastor, and I. D. Muñoz, 57–84. Leiden, The Netherlands: Brill. https://doi.org/10.1163/9789004351790_005.

Davitti, E., and S. Braun. 2020. Analysing interactional phenomena in video remote interpreting in collaborative settings: Implications for interpreter education. *The Interpreter and Translator Trainer* 14 (3): 279–302. https://doi.org/10.1080/1750399X.2020.1800364.

Defrancq, B., and C. Fantinuoli. 2021. Automatic speech recognition in the booth: Assessment of system performance, interpreters' performances and interactions in the context of numbers. *Target* 33 (1): 73–102. https://doi.org/10.1075/target.19166.def.

Desmet, B., M. Vandierendonck, and B. Defrancq. 2018. Simultaneous interpretation of numbers and the impact of technological support. In *Interpreting and technology*, ed. C. Fantinuoli, 13–27. Berlin: Language Science Press. https://doi.org/10.5281/zenodo.1493291.

Dillinger, M., and L. Gerber. 2009. *Machine translation used by the US Government.* https://www.translationdirectory.com/articles/article1967.php. Accessed 12 May 2022.

Donovan, C. 2006. Where is interpreting heading and how can training courses keep up? *EMCI conference: The future of conference interpreting: Training, technology and research.* https://silo.tips/download/where-is-interpreting-heading-and-how-can-training-courses-keep-up.

Eraslan, Ş., M. Şahin, G. Alankuş, Ö. Altıntaş, and D. Kaleş. 2020. Virtual worlds as a contribution to content and variety in interpreter training: The case of Turkey. In *The role of technology in conference interpreter training*, ed. M. D. Rodriguez Melchor, I. Horvath, and K. Ferguson, 101–128. Oxford: Peter Lang. https://www.peterlang.com/document/1057013.

Fantinuoli, C. 2006. Specialized corpora from the Web and term extraction for simultaneous interpreters. In *Wacky! Working papers on the Web as corpus*, ed. M. Baroni and S. Bernardini, 173–190. http://wackybook.sslmit.unibo.it/pdfs/fantinuoli.pdf.

Fantinuoli, C. 2016. InterpretBank. Redefining computer-assisted interpreting tools. In *Proceedings of the 38th conference: Translating and the computer*, ed. J. Esteves-Ferreira, J. Macan, R. Mitkov, and O.-M. Stefanov, 42–52. London: AsLing.

Fantinuoli, C. 2017a. Computer-assisted preparation in conference interpreting. *Translation and Interpreting* 9 (2): 24–37. https://doi.org/10.12807/ti.109202.2017.a02.

Fantinuoli, C. 2017b. Speech recognition in the interpreter workstation. In *Proceedings of the 39th conference: Translating and the computer*, ed. J. Esteves-Ferreira, J. Macan, R. Mitkov, and O.-M. Stefanov, 25–34. London: AsLing.

Fantinuoli, C. 2018a. Computer-assisted interpreting: Challenges and future perspectives. In *Trends in e-tools and resources for translators and interpreters*, ed. G. Corpas Pastor and I. D. Muñoz, 153–174. Leiden, The Netherlands: Brill. https://doi.org/10.1163/9789004351790_009.

Fantinuoli, C. 2018b. Interpreting and technology: The upcoming technological turn. In *Interpreting and technology*, ed. C. Fantinuoli, 1–12. Berlin: Language Science Press. https://doi.org/10.5281/zenodo.1493289.

Fantinuoli, C. 2018c. The use of comparable corpora in interpreting practice and training. *The Interpreters' Newsletter* 23: 133–149. https://doi.org/10.13137/2421-714X/22402.

Fantinuoli, C. 2019. The technological turn in interpreting: The challenges that lie ahead. In *Proceedings of the conference übersetzen und dolmetschen 4.0: Neue Wege im digitalen Zeitalter*, 334–354.

Fantinuoli, C., and B. Prandi. 2018. Teaching information and communication technologies: A proposal for the interpreting classroom. *Journal of Translation and Technical Communication Research* 11 (2): 162–182. https://www.trans-kom.eu/bd11nr02/trans-kom_11_02_02_Fantinouli_Prandi_Teaching.20181220.pdf.

Gile, D. 2009. *Basic concepts and models for interpreter and translator training*. Amsterdam: John Benjamins Publishing Company. https://doi.org/10.1075/btl.8.

Goldsmith, J. 2018. Tablet interpreting. *Translation and Interpreting Studies. The Journal of the American Translation and Interpreting Studies Association* 13 (3): 342–365. https://doi.org/10.1075/tis.00020.gol.

Gran, L., A. Carabelli, and R. Merlini. 2002. Computer-assisted interpreter training. In *Interpreting in the 21st century: Challenges and opportunities*, ed. G. Garzone and M. Viezzi, 277–294. John Benjamins Publishing Company. https://doi.org/10.1075/btl.43.27gra.

Green Terp. 2022. GT EDU-Green Terp simultaneous interpreting training platform. https://www.gtmeeting.com/solutions/edu. Accessed 14 May 2022.

Interactio. 2022. Requirements to be an Interactio interpreter. https://www.interactio.io/interpreters-community. Accessed 14 May 2022.

International Association of Conference Interpreters (AIIC). 2000. Code for the use of new technologies in conference interpretation. https://www.staff.uni-mainz.de/fantinuo/class/files/cai/aiic_code_interpreting%20technologies.pdf.

InterpretBank. 2022. InterpretBank ASR: Artificial boothmate for interpreters. https://www.interpretbank.com/ASR#hardware. Accessed 14 May 2022.

Kajzer-Wietrzny, M., and M. Tymczyńska. 2014. Integrating technology into interpreter training courses: A blended learning approach. *inTRAlinea Special Issue: Challenges in Translation Pedagogy*. https://www.intralinea.org/specials/article/2101.

Kelly, N. 2008. *Telephone interpreting: A comprehensive guide to the profession*. Victoria: Trafford Publishing.

Lim, L. 2007. Computer assisted training for interpreters' vocabulary preparation. In *Language and languages: Global and local tensions*, ed. C. Gitsaki, 171–291. Newcastle: Cambridge Scholars Publishing. https://www.researchgate.net/publication/289525261_Computer_assisted_training_for_interpreters'_vocabulary_preparation.

Mayor, M.J.B., and A.J. Ivars. 2007. E-learning for interpreting. *Babel* 53 (4): 292–302. https://doi.org/10.1075/babel.53.4.01may.

Merlini, R. 1996. Interprit - Consecutive interpretation module. *The Interpreters' Newsletter* 7: 31–41. http://hdl.handle.net/10077/8989.

Mouzourakis, P. 2006. Remote interpreting. *Interpreting. International Journal of Research and Practice in Interpreting* 8 (1): 45–66. https://doi.org/10.1075/intp.8.1.04mou.

Orlando, M. 2010. Digital pen technology and consecutive interpreting: Another dimension in note-taking training and assessment. *The Interpreters' Newsletter* 15: 71–86.

Orlando, M. 2014. A study on the amenability of digital pen technology in a hybrid mode of interpreting: Consec-simul with notes. *Translation and Interpreting* 6 (2): 39–54. https://doi.org/10.12807/ti.106202.2014.a03.

Ortiz, L. E., and P. Cavallo. 2018. Computer-Assisted Interpreting Tools (CAI) and options for automation with automatic speech recognition. *Tradterm* 32: 9–31. https://doi.org/10.11606/issn.2317-9511.v32i0p9-31.

Pisani, E., and C. Fantinuoli. 2021. Measuring the impact of automatic speech recognition on number rendition in simultaneous interpreting. In *Empirical studies of translation and interpreting*, ed. C. Wang and B. Zheng, 181–197. New York: Routledge. https://doi.org/10.4324/9781003017400-14.

Pochhacker, F., ed. 2015. Computer assisted interpreter training. In *Routledge encyclopedia of interpreting studies*, ed. F. Pochhacker, 75–77. London: Routledge. https://doi.org/10.4324/9781315678467.

Prandi, B. 2015. The use of CAI tools in interpreters' training: A pilot study. In *Proceedings of the 37th conference: Translating and the computer*, ed. J. Esteves-Ferreira, J. Macan, R. Mitkov, and O.-M. Stefanov, 48–57. London: AsLing.

Prandi, B. 2017. Designing a multimethod study on the use of CAI tools during simultaneous interpreting. In *Proceedings of the 39th conference: Translating and the computer*, ed. J. Esteves-Ferreira, J. Macan, R. Mitkov, and O.-M. Stefanov, 76–88. London: AsLing.

Prandi, B. 2018. An exploratory study on CAI tools in simultaneous interpreting: Theoretical framework and stimulus validation. In *Interpreting and technology*, ed. C. Fantinuoli, 29–59. Berlin: Language Science Press. https://doi.org/10.5281/zenodo.1493293.

Prandi, B. 2020. The use of CAI tools in interpreter training: Where are we now and where do we go from here? *inTRAlinea Special Issue: Technology in Interpreter Education and Practice*. http://www.intralinea.org/specials/article/2512.

Riccardi, A., I. Čeňková, M. Tryuk, A. Maček, and A. Pelea. 2020. Survey of the use of new technologies in conference interpreting courses. In *The role of technology in conference interpreter training*, ed. M. D. Rodriguez Melchor, I. Horvath, and K. Ferguson, 7–42. Oxford: Peter Lang. https://www.peterlang.com/document/1057013.

Rodríguez Melchor, M. D. 2020. Meeting the challenge of adapting interpreter training and assessment to blended learning environements. In *The role of technology in conference interpreter training*, ed. M. D. Rodriguez Melchor, I. Horvath, and K. Ferguson, 59–76. Oxford: Peter Lang. https://www.peterlang.com/document/1057013.

Rodríguez Melchor, M. D., I. Horváth, and K. Ferguson, ed. 2020. *The role of technology in conference interpreter training*. Oxford: Peter Lang. https://www.peterlang.com/document/1057013.

Şahin, M. 2013. Virtual worlds in interpreter training. *The Interpreter and Translator Trainer* 7 (1): 91–106. https://doi.org/10.1080/13556509.2013.10798845.

Sandrelli, A. 2007. Designing CAIT (Computer-Assisted Interpreter Training) tools: Black box. In *Proceedings of the marie curie euroconferences MuTra: Challenges of multidimensional translation–saarbrücken 2–6 May 2005*, ed. H. Gerzymisch-Arbogast and S. Nauert.

Sandrelli, A., and J.D.M. Jerez. 2007. The impact of information and communication technology on interpreter training. *The Interpreter and Translator Trainer* 1 (2): 269-303.https://doi.org/10.1080/1750399X.2007.10798761.

Seeber, K.G. 2011. Cognitive load in simultaneous interpreting: Existing theories—new models. *Interpreting* 13 (2): 176–204. https://doi.org/10.1075/intp.13.2.02see.

Seeber, K.G. 2013. Cognitive load in simultaneous interpreting: Measures and methods. *Target* 25 (1): 18–32. https://doi.org/10.1075/target.25.1.03see.

Wang, X., and C. Wang. 2019. Can computer-assisted interpreting tools assist interpreting? *Transletters. International Journal of Translation and Interpreting* 3: 109–139.

Winteringham, S.T. 2010. The usefulness of ICTs in interpreting practice. *The Interpreters' Newsletter* 15: 87–99. http://hdl.handle.net/10077/4751.

Xu, R. 2015. Terminology preparation for simultaneous interpreters. PhD thesis, The University of Leeds. https://etheses.whiterose.ac.uk/10164/.

Xu, R. 2018. Corpus-based terminological preparation for simultaneous interpreting. *Interpreting. International Journal of Research and Practice in Interpreting* 20 (1): 33–62. https://doi.org/10.1075/intp.00002.xu.

Xu, R., and S. Sharoff. 2014. Evaluating term extraction methods for interpreters. In *Proceedings of the 4th international workshop on computational terminology (Computerm)*, 86–93. Dublin, Ireland: Association for Computational Linguistics and Dublin City University. https://doi.org/10.3115/v1/W14-4811.

Yuan, R. 2021. Interpreters vs machines: Can interpreters survive in an AI-dominated world? *The Interpreter and Translator Trainer* 15 (2): 282–285. https://doi.org/10.1080/1750399X.2021.1915575.

Ziegler, K., and S. Gigliobianco. 2018. Present? Remote? Remotely present! New technological approaches to remote simultaneous conference interpreting. In *Interpreing and technology*, ed. C. Fantinuoli, 119–139. Berlin: Language Science Press. https://doi.org/10.5281/zenodo.1493299.

Zoom. 2022. Using language interpretation in your meeting or webinar. https://support.zoom.us/hc/en-us/articles/360034919791-Using-Language-Interpretation-in-your-meeting-or-webinar. Accessed 14 May 2022.

Nan Zhao is an Assistant Professor in Department of Translation, Interpreting and Intercultural Studies (TIIS), Baptist University of Hong Kong. She received her Ph.D. in psycholinguistics and MA in interpreting studies. Her main areas of research are psycholinguistics of interpreting and translation, and interpreting training and competence test.

The manufacturer's authorised representative in the EU is Springer Nature Customer Service Centre GmbH, Europaplatz 3, 69115 Heidelberg, Germany. If you have any concerns regarding our products, please contact ProductSafety@springernature.com

Printed and bound by CPI Group (UK) Ltd, Croydon, CR0 4YY
30/09/2026
02225245-0011